Sargent Bush
May 1993

This book explores the power and influence of emigration as reflected in the British passage to America and the establishment of a new country and society. From this migration sprang a separate and unique "American character" and the creation of literature which returns repeatedly to narratives of the emigration experience. What was, and remains, the American difference? Can it be found in the self-reliance of its citizens, their hunger for an independent livelihood and readiness to change and break with the past? Every one of these supposed qualities can be traced to the psychology of emigration. In a fascinating analysis, Stephen Fender examines this ideology: how it unlocked creative potential in the accounts of ordinary people through diaries, letters and contemporary documents and in the literature of writers such as Cooper, Jefferson, Thoreau, Hawthorne, James, Dreiser and Willa Cather, among others.

Cambridge Studies in American Literature and Culture
Editor: Eric Sundquist, *University of California, Los Angeles*

Recent books in the series

54. Peter Stoneley, *Mark Twain and the Feminine Aesthetic*
53. Joel Porte, *In Respect to Egotism: Studies in American Romantic Writing*
52. Charles Swann, *Nathaniel Hawthorne: Tradition and Revolution*
51. Ronald Bush (ed.), *T. S. Eliot: The Modernist in History*
50. Russell Goodman, *American Philosophy and the Romantic Tradition*
49. Eric Sundquist (ed.), *Frederick Douglass: New Literary and Historical Essays*
48. Susan Friedman, *Penelope's Web: Gender, Modernity, H.D.'s Fiction*
47. Timothy Redman, *Ezra Pound and Italian Fascism*
46. Ezra Greenspan, *Walt Whitman and the American Reader*

Cambridge Studies in American Literature and Culture 55

Sea changes

Emigrants in Alfred Stieglitz's "The Steerage" (73–87–50: the Philadelphia Museum of Art; given by Carl Zigrosser). Which way were they traveling?

Sea changes

British emigration & American literature

Stephen Fender

Published by the Press Syndicate of the University of Cambridge
The Pitt Building, Trumpington Street, Cambridge CB2 1RP
40 West 20th Street, New York, NY 10011-4211, USA
10 Stamford Road, Oakleigh, Victoria 3166, Australia

First published 1992

Printed in Great Britain at the University Press, Cambridge

A catalogue record for this book is available from the British Library

Library of Congress cataloguing in publication data

Fender, Stephen.
Sea Changes; British emigration and American literature/
Stephen Fender.
p. cm.–(Cambridge studies in American literature and culture)
Includes bibliographical references and index.
ISBN 0 521 41175 0
1. American literature–English influences. 2. Great Britain–Emigration and immigration. 3. American literature–History and criticism. 4. Emigration and immigration in literature.
5. Immigrants in literature. 6. British–United States. I. Title.
II. Series.
PS169.EBF46 1992
810.9′355–dc20 91-21347 CIP

ISBN 0 521 41175 0

TAG

Contents

Acknowledgments

It is a pleasure to recall the friends, colleagues, librarians and historians of emigration (not all of them exclusive categories, I am happy to say) who have so generously helped this book on its way. The historians' encouragement was welcome particularly since they knew from the outset that I was planning a different kind of study from the one in which they have been so productively at work in recent years. Frank Thistlethwaite provided important early guidance, as did Bernard Bailyn on a visit to Sussex. Timothy Breen gave me an invaluable two hours of his time when we coincided for an afternoon in Oxford – a pure-gold tutorial that left me envying his students. Charlotte Erickson has encouraged me throughout, always adding new tips on where to find the next batch of emigrants' letters. Roger Haydon, of the Cornell University Press, shared his expertise in anglophone emigration through long letters detailing locations of documents and suggesting lines of analytical approach. Over many lunches (whether *sur l'herbe* in the Boston Public Garden or in Charles's Kebab House in London) Roger Thompson has shared his immense knowledge of East Anglian emigration, while encouraging, prompting and correcting my own work.

The Public Records Offices of East and West Sussex have been an important source of emigrants' letters, and I am grateful to Christopher Whittick, of the ESRO, not only for his help there, but for leading me to Leonard Maguire and Don Burgess, local historians of the Sussex General Baptist Assembly, a number of whose members emigrated to an area now encompassed by Ossining, NY, in 1794. Maguire presented me with a rare copy of his private edition of *The "Browne" American Letters, 1794–1831*, and Burgess took the trouble to print off a special copy of the disk holding his transcription of the letters of John Burgess, later supplementing the gift with a copy of his edition of the Burgess papers, *No Continuing City: The Diary and Letters of John Burgess, a Sussex Craftsman, between 1785 and 1819*. John Burgess's letters constitute one of the most complete, informative and moving records of the anglophone emigration that I have seen, and readers of this book will soon understand how greatly I am indebted to his descendant for introducing me to them, and for his permission to reproduce parts of them.

The librarians of Friends House, London, of the British Library, of the Institute of Historical Research and Senate House in the University of London all guided me through their substantial collections of manuscripts and out-of-the-way periodicals containing hundreds of valuable transcriptions of early letters, settlers' tracts and related material. Angela Raspin helped me to interpret the varied collection of letters from emigrants to North America which she supervises at the British Library of Political and Economic Science in the London School of Economics. Robert Stevens, Director of the Lewis Historical Library at Vincennes University, Indiana, generously provided free xeroxes of fascinating letters from back-migrants in the Rawlinson Papers. In Boston I luxuriated in the manuscript holdings and kind attention of the Boston Public Library, and the Boston Athenaeum, and appreciated particularly the help of Jerome Anderson and David Dearborn at the New England Historic Genealogical Society. Peter Drummey and Kathy Griffin, at the Massachusetts Historical Association, were especially friendly and helpful, taking time away from other duties to guide me through their perplexingly rich collection of manuscript and printed materials relating to early emigration to New England.

Apart from its other sources, this book grows out of many discussions with students and colleagues, past and present. I have pinched ideas shamelessly from David Trotter, Danny Karlin and Neil Rennie at University College London, and from John Barrell and Andrew Crozier at Sussex. My colleague Peter Way has guided me through the historical literature on working-class immigration to Canada and the US, and shared with me his original and convincing perspective on the subject. Janet Floyd, working under my supervision on a Sussex D.Phil. on British women migrants to the American and Canadian West, has helped me to a better understanding of how the variables of gender, class and nationality affect the emigrants' discourse. My fellow professor of American Studies at Sussex, Rupert Wilkinson, has never tired of finding out new books for me to read on aspects of the American character, and has taken a friendly and informed interest in this book, parts of which he read, annotated and discussed in an early version. Colin Brooks has been of the greatest help throughout this project: through his friendship, his immense knowledge of English and American history in the colonial period, and (as Dean of the School of English and American Studies at Sussex), his grants of money for research travel, and to help cover the cost of going to conferences to give interim papers on the subject. Above all, I am indebted and grateful to Janet Pressley, who read most of the manuscript in draft, pinpointing fractures in logic, dud notes in tone, and some (at least) of the more boring bits. Finally, my thanks go to my son Matthew for helping with a dozen minor (and at least one major) aspects of the computer.

A note on sources

My business here is the Anglo-American thesis of the American exception, and my method the close analysis of the rhetoric for and against American emigration by which that discourse was produced, promulgated and challenged. So for two reasons, I have stuck to documents in English.

In the case of manuscript sources, I have transcribed without modernizing either spelling or punctuation, since the history of usage is part of the history of rhetoric (to take just one significant example, "travail" once meant both travel and laborious effort); and since spelling, particularly in the seventeenth century but in vernacular communications well into the nineteenth, sometimes gives a clue to national or regional pronunciation.

Still, the corpus studied here is a dominant discourse, which means a palimpsest of texts, most of which have been selected, transcribed and usually published by people who thought them important. These mediators have worked on various principles of editing. From as early as 1632 the English Puritan divine Nehemiah Wallington was collecting letters from his co-religionists in Massachusetts, copying them from secretary hand into his neat italic, and no doubt regularizing the spelling in the process. The indefatigable antiquarians of nineteenth-century New England ransacked local archives, and made numerous trips over to the Old Country to search for materials relating to the settlement of their region. These they published, almost always regularized, in journals like the *Collections of the Massachusetts Historical Society*, *Archaeologica Americana: Transactions and Collections of the American Antiquarian Society*, *Proceedings of the Essex Institute* and *The New England Historical and Genealogical Register*. These are invaluable resources for the study of American emigration.

More recently important collections, like the Winthrop papers, have been re-edited according to the best modern practice, with the result that in some of the most recent texts, the spelling has reverted to its original form.

Faced with the choice either of modernizing everything in the interests of consistency, or of taking the best available text and transcribing it as I found it, I chose the latter course, leaving ample evidence as to provenance in the endnotes. This seems more true to the overriding thesis of the book: that the raw material subject to analysis here is not really "raw" at all, but the product of a collaboration, a communal discourse of American foundation.

Introduction

Certain pictures of American immigration stick in the mind, perhaps because they have been used repeatedly in books on the subject, or in museum exhibits, or as illustrations accompanying a magazine article. There's that engraving in which white-bearded patriarchs and their wives and daughters in shawls and kerchiefs look left over the ship's rail towards the Statue of Liberty. Or maybe they are just expressive in themselves, "tell a story," as newspapermen used to say. Alfred Stieglitz's photograph "The Steerage" is always included in exhibitions and folio volumes as one of his characteristic images of American life, alongside his stark skyscapes of New York City, the chuffing steam engine laboring a commuter train through bleak industrial outskirts, called "The Hand of Man" (1902) and that picture of the horse-drawn omnibus lumbering up through the sleety mist of "Winter, Fifth Avenue, New York" (1893).

In "The Steerage" people gaze over a ship's rail down into the cargo deck of a transatlantic steamer, where women hold fractious children on their hips to comfort them. A catwalk crosses over the lower deck, dividing the composition into the two groups. Most of those above appear to be single men. One of them wears a jaunty straw boater. Are they looking down on those below in more than the literal sense? What attitude do we read on their faces: disdain? idle curiosity? boredom?

And those on the lower level? What mood, what feelings do their faces, postures and gestures convey? The bemused reaction to unfamiliar surroundings following the shock at having been uprooted from their native cultural soil? Fatigue after a long voyage in cramped conditions? Grim determination to see it through to the landing place, and to make good in the New World against all the odds? Hope for the future?

In fact, these people were not arriving in America but leaving it. They were back-migrants whom Stieglitz photographed on his first trip to Europe in the summer of 1907. And all the people in the picture, not just those on the lower level, were sailing in steerage. Stieglitz recalled "how distasteful [he] found the atmosphere of first class on that ship, especially since it was impossible to escape the *nouveaux riches*," and how he finally broke away, to be captivated by the scene in steerage, a "picture of shapes, and underlying it, a new vision that held me: simple people, the feeling of ship, ocean, sky; a sense of release that I was away from the mob called 'rich.'"[1]

Why were these "simple people" going home? Perhaps some had been turned back after failing one or another of those physical, occupational or moral tests imposed on would-be immigrants by close questioning at Ellis Island. But on average, only two percent of those seeking entry were disqualified in this way. Others must have gained entry to the United States, only to fail at whatever venture they undertook, or simply to make the adjustment to another way of life.[2]

Knowing where they were heading, what do we now read on those faces in Stieglitz's photograph? The shock, not of uprooting, but of defeat; a grimness, not of a determination to succeed against adversity, but of despair. Glazed with apathy, those eyes seem to look into the bleak future of a past they failed to escape.

But why are we so ready to read "The Steerage" that way? Why, first, should we assume that it is about going to America? Why should we feel such vicarious disappointment – mixed, perhaps, with suppressed contempt – on learning that the people were returning to Europe? Why, above all, are we so ready to interpret that voyage back as a form of failure? For it is equally likely that these people were returning through no fault of their own. Illness in America or back home might have necessitated their return; possibly they had been defrauded of their savings, or had them stolen.

It is even possible, much as this might disconfirm our expectations, that some of Stieglitz's back-migrants were returning *because they wanted to.* Maybe they were happily settled in America and going home only for a visit. Or their emigration might have been planned as temporary from its outset: perhaps they had wanted to see something of the world, or to accumulate a specified sum of money. Granted, the wealthy world traveler, or the adventurer who had made it very big, would not be likely to travel in steerage. But not all travelers are rich. Some work their way as they go; others just drift, husbanding their capital to prolong the voyage. And not all successful, speculative, temporary migrants return with fortunes; some come back with modest nest-eggs – enough for a house or farm or improvements at home, or to get married on – which a more expensive ticket would begin to waste. Some of the passengers on the upper level of "The Steerage" may well belong to this category of youngish and single travelers, adventurers or nest-egg accumulators we know were included among the back-migrants. Certainly the man sporting the boater as a trophy of his American sojourn doesn't appear especially demoralized or downtrodden. No doubt that's one reason why we might have mistaken him at first for an ordinary passenger.

In other words, take away the parameters of "success" and "failure" as measured materially; deconstruct the fiction that though an emigrant goes out with a well-disciplined, heroically proportioned capacity for free will, the same person returns as a back-migrant with no free will at all: remove these intellectual barriers, and whole new lines of interpretation open up.

Historians of American immigration have, of course, been following them for over a century. Though not immune to the mythology of the American dream, historians have been interested in harder facts like the demography of emigration (the flow forwards and backwards across the Atlantic and the patterns of settlement within the North American continent), the reasons prompting emigrants to leave their native countries and the social and economic structures through which they assimilated to their new environment. Historians of the "old" immigration from northern Europe until the end of the nineteenth century have argued over whether emigrants were forced out of their home countries by economic distress, natural calamity, religious or political marginalization; or whether they were attracted by the greater opportunities for an independent livelihood and the promise of a better future offered by the American economic, religious and political dispensation: whether, in other words, they saved, planned and excercised the freedom to "invest" in their emigration. Arguments on the "push" side of the debate include William Forbes Adams's study of *Irish Immigration to the New World from 1815 to the Famine* and Oscar Handlin's later, more general survey of European immigrants, *The Uprooted*, whose title declares his model of the phenomenon. For historians on the other side of the argument, immigrants to the United States were not so much "the uprooted" as "the transplanted," the title of John Bodnar's recent, forceful contribution to the "pull" thesis.

Then there is the dispute over what sort of identity the immigrants established for themselves once they got there. Was it the melting pot of un-hyphenated American nationality both celebrated and prescribed by notables from Benjamin Franklin through Theodore Roosevelt down to Ronald Reagan? Was it tied to affiliations of race or class? Or, as the prevailing fashion now has it, on the street as in the academy, was it an "ethnic" identity gounded on the original immigrants' place of birth?

And if the ethnic variable overrides all the other possible models for assimilation, how do ethnic conventions and values come to be transmitted from native to adopted home, and what is left of them once they have been transplanted? Recent historians of immigration have turned their attention to cultural questions, and to do so have returned to English-speaking emigrants in the colonial period, with David Cressy exploring the complex feelings and reciprocal movements of the New England Puritans; Bernard

Bailyn the lives of migrants, both free and indentured, on the eve of the Revolution; and David Hackett Fisher the transfer of eighteenth-century British "folkways" to the New World. Finally, the very process itself of becoming American has been theorized in a new kind of ethnic studies, most notably by Thomas Archdeacon and Werner Sollors.[3]

This book does not address the statistics of migrant flow back and forth across the Atlantic, except as a datum from which the more popular view of American immigration has departed, nor the hard social and economic reasons for those movements. If the following pages had been allocated in proportion to who went, and when, even the earliest of them would have been taken up largely by Germans and Irish, who outnumbered English emigrants by over four to one even in the period of old immigration. It has nothing to say about theories of ethnic studies. Instead it deals with the mentality that has led (as perhaps the least of its consequences) to that misreading of "The Steerage": it is about a *discourse* of anglophone emigration that, because it belongs to that formative period of American cultural evolution, underpins the very self-definition of the United States of America.

Discourses may disagree, perhaps never more so than when disputing national identity. For instance, a modern historian may want to argue that nineteenth-century processes of commercialization and industrialization left many European immigrants worse off – less free to deploy their increasingly devalued skills, more subject to impersonal market forces – than they were before they left home. But the perception, whether or not illusory, which (as we shall see) was so central to the psychology of emigration – that they had made the choice to go of their own free will – left a large majority of those whose opinions are still on record feeling both more free and more prosperous. So which is more "true": the perception or the underlying condition?

Or, as the example of Stieglitz's "The Steerage" suggests, there have always been more back-migrants leaving America (for whatever reason) than the normative discourse has been willing to admit. Even when (as we are told) the huddled masses of southern and eastern Europe were flooding into the United States in their greatest numbers, a sizeable minority were ebbing out again. Oscar Handlin estimates that around a quarter of the sixteen million European emigrants to the United States in the first three decades of the twentieth century returned home in the same period.[4] Yet we need to believe, or like to think, that the traffic was all one way. Why? America was built of emigrants, and was (and is) sustained by their continued arrival. Though like other countries the United States has needed to restrict immigration, it has always proclaimed its value. Benjamin Franklin fretted that English immigrant workers got lazier in Philadelphia the better they got paid, and worried that the Germans, with their alien language and authoritarian temperament, would undermine American political institutions. But there was no more wittily vehement proponent of European emigration to America than Benjamin Franklin. The Puritans of Massachusetts became uneasy when immigrants began (as they did from as early as the beginning of the eighteenth century) to include a growing number of Irish Catholics, but the journals and histories of their early leaders show just how desperate they were to increase their numbers. This apparent contradiction can be partly explained by the different ways the ideas of emigration and immigration work on the American imagination. It may have something to do with the psychology of the sect – the religious sub-group defining itself through difference. Sects need to make converts to increase their strength, but they have also to be on their guard lest further recruitment dilute their pristine purpose.

America has sometimes behaved as a sect, even in the twentieth century, and it continues to define itself through difference. In the constitution of this difference, too, the discourse of immigration has played an important role. Certain traits widely agreed by Americans to distinguish the national character may well have been derived from the expression of that common experience. Individual enterprise, the readiness to experiment in both private lives and public institutions, the willingness to forgo immediate gratification as an investment in future possibilities – indeed the whole mosaic of middle-class values that have virtually precluded the development of American communism, socialism or other collectivist social structures – all these qualities can be put down to the purifying trials of emigration itself: the need to save or scrape money for the venture, to leave behind family, friends, a familiar daily culture; to remake one's fortunes from scratch in a foreign environment.

Or at least that's the story. But why are we Americans so ready to inquire into our country's "character" in the first place? The Spanish and French seldom talk about the Spanish or French character. If subjects of the United Kingdom wished to refer to themselves in this way, they would have first to decide which adjective to use. I have heard people talk of being "typically" English, Scottish or Welsh (the association with a "character" is rare), but "British" is a nationality, not a trait, and "Britishness" is virtually unknown to contemporary usage. And why do Americans insist that America is an exceptional dispensation? Could these propositions too be an effect of the emigrant experience?

Maybe, but a moment's reflection will call that connection into question. Other countries have also been formed of emigrants, yet we hear much less of the unique Canadian or Australian "character" than we do of the American. Nothing daunted, American historians have done their best to explain how the United States could have been settled in a way similar to other "new" nations, yet still remain as different from them as from its parent country. Louis Hartz thought that the character of the colonial offspring depends on that moment in history when it branches off (or in Hartz's more extreme imagery, "fragments") from the metropolitan center: when history ceases to work on it. When the colony "leaves its first antagonist [the metropolitan authority], it leaves all of the future antagonists that the first inspires," and "cuts short the process of European contagion at the point of leaving." Thus South American countries replicate feudal structures because Spain and Portugal were still feudal when they shed their colonies. Australia has developed a culture of "mateship" because it broke away during the "proletarian turmoil of the Industrial Revolution," when solidarity was the worker's only effective weapon. The United States has enshrined the principles of Lockean free-enterprise, property-valuing liberalism because it became independent when these values were in the ascendant in Great Britain. And so on.

According to a more recent analysis by John McElroy, America has always been exceptional in the freedom and equality it offers its citizens, and remains optimistic about its future – because of the kind of people who went there, and because of its geography. Immigration to Canada and South America was tightly controlled by the relevant European governments, he argues; hence colonial populations tended to replicate metropolitan values for far longer than in the American case, where immigrants selected themselves and came from all over the world. Expansion was easier along the existing waterways into the American Great Plains than into the chilly arctic and subarctic terrain of Canada, or the dense jungles of Brazil. As a result, the United States became more populous and prosperous than other ex-colonies in the Americas, and also developed a culture of the possibility and legitimacy of constant self-improvement. Unlike Hartz, McElroy does not deal with South Africa, Australia or New Zealand.[5]

There is something self-constructed about both these hypotheses. Hartz's thesis needs deconstructing into its Hegelian dialectic of opposing forces – his assumption that history is progress and that both depend on "antagonism" – and his double anxiety about European "contagion" and the American "fragment." Part of McElroy's argument is really that the communities that became the United States differed from other British colonies in asserting their independence from the metropolitan center – or simply, that America was different because it was different. The circularity of that proposition may make us suitably wary of looking for a cause "out there" for the American difference.

I am not confident that a diachronic analysis of cause and effect can ever deal with the question of whether or why America is exceptional. What is needed is close attention to an idea, or set of ideas, that constitute a dominant thesis of the American ideology of identity. It is quite true that the experience of emigration is closely related to the sense of being American, but not because the one *caused* the other; rather, because the experience and the sense are both constituted by the same discourse, which itself has a history. The narrative by which the country has come to define itself – even the assumption of American exceptionalism and the recurrent image of American "character" – is part of that discourse which moved people to go there in the first place.

That, in brief, is what I am arguing, and that dominant discourse is what this book explores. It is a discourse in both the main senses of the word. Sometimes it was a kind of lecture or sermon promoting the American dispensation, or attacking it. It may have been spoken or heard in either Britain or America, for both countries collaborated in its production. At other times it was a dialogue between the colonial and metropolitan voices, sometimes going on in the same head. It is dominant because it is a chief constituent in the American nation's founding narrative, overriding other discourses of emigration, like that of the middle-class English sisters Susanna Moodie and Catharine Parr Traill in Canada, or the perception of the Irish that their move to North America was a kind of exile, so massively and movingly documented in Kerby Miller's *Emigrants and Exiles*. What Miller demonstrates is that coming from a Catholic and predominantly peasant culture, the Irish felt their emigration – not as an invigorating test of their self sufficiency strengthening their individuality and increasing their personal responsibility, nor as a life-changing, irreversible transformation to a higher state of awareness – but as exile from a metropolitan center from which all their cultural strength radiated, or at best as the attenuation of familial, social and other cultural ties they had no wish to break.[6] The mentality of the dominant discourse, by contrast, was predominantly English (and, to an extent, Scottish) and above all, Protestant. Chapter 3 will attempt to show how closely the theology of Protestantism, particularly that concentrated and articulate form of Protestantism expressed by the English Puritan migrants to New England, fitted the dominant psychology of anglophone emigration to the New World.

This ideology of American emigration and settlement was first articulated in European ideas about the New World, and from the beginning these ideas were organized around the classical dichotomy of culture and nature. America represented nature and Europe culture. Upon their first encounters with the New World, the Europeans imagined it as a sort of paradise, from which the cultural accretions of the Fall working itself out through history were providentially absent. In time, particularly in British imperial theory, the paradisal model gave way to a model of settlement. Now American nature was promoted for its positive and material values, for the resources that could sustain an emigrant population and be exploited for metropolitan manufactures.

Even before the American Revolution, the American colonies (and especially Massachusetts) began to construct themselves, and to be constructed, in a posture adversarial to the Mother Country. After American independence, during the unrest that followed the Napoleonic Wars, British progressives and conservatives began to inscribe the domestic debate for and against reform within an argument about the viability of the new republic across the Atlantic, and particularly about the wisdom of emigrating there. Though almost twice as many British subjects left their native shores for Canada, Australia and New Zealand during the same period, it was emigration to the United States that was the lively political issue.

What did the British migrants to the United States think themselves? Though skeptical of the more visionary promotional tracts written by boosters and radicals alike (especially when the propagandists had invested in American property on which they hoped to persuade their readers to settle), the emigrants were not immune to the general promise of the New World: its liberal institutions, its relative freedom from inherited class distinctions, the opportunity afforded by its cheap land to convert the one commodity they possessed in abundance – their labor – into an agrarian self-sufficiency.

From the beginning of American settlement British emigrants to North America had expressed these feelings in the rhetoric of both the paradisal and colonial models: of stripping away Old World culture and embracing the nature of the New. The Puritans who migrated to Massachusetts found in their theology of the portable faith a ready-made ideology in which to accept, propose and justify their departure from the worldly comforts of England, but they were as ready as were later emigrants to celebrate the material profusion of nature they encountered in their new home.

There were moral issues implied in both the paradisal and the colonial branches of emigration rhetoric. The paradisal model cast a cold eye on cultural institutions – in some hands it was really a satire on the Old World – and raised questions about the proper use of the leisure that life in the New held forth as a promise. The colonial model put nature to the scientific test. Its catalogs of natural profusion awaiting exploitation were also a way of authenticating the fabulous traveler's report in the material reality of the verifiable. Furthermore even the apparently neutral economic technicalities of mercantilist circulation – a guaranteed supply of raw materials for metropolitan manufacture and in turn a captive market for the finished goods in the colonies – increased value at every stage of its process, and put the unemployed to productive work. Crèvecoeur's *Letters from an American Farmer* explored both these models of emigration rhetoric, and thus gave America its first moral geography – and when that scheme was overtaken by the violence of the Revolutionary War, its first narrative to end with the protagonist lighting out for the wilderness.

So the rhetoric of emigration gave words and figures to a distinctively republican American voice. If the influential metropolitan culture caricatured American speech and institutions as degenerate, and if even some Americans began to suspect that a lack of imaginative "association" and paucity of local social stratification would render American poetry and fiction impossible, others like Tom Paine and Thomas Jefferson drew on the discourse of emigration to fashion a national project out of the conflict between culture and nature. In Paine's *Common Sense* Old World hierarchies and prerogatives were satirized as they had been by emigrants casting off the culture they had to leave behind, and American rebellion naturalized through the imagery of irresistible growth. Jefferson borrowed from the emigrant's natural catalog to authenticate the American environment on the level of physical climate and nurture, disproving Count Buffon's theory that species degenerated when transplanted to the New World with scientific-looking inventories of American animals to demonstrate the superiority of their dimensions and variety over their European equivalents.

As with the physical environment, so with the cultural. Repeatedly the proponents of a distinctly American literature, from Emerson and Whitman to William Carlos Williams, sought to establish their national cultural projects in words and arguments drawn from the rhetoric of emigration. The settlers' material nature became the poets' native materials. Like the settler, the poet answered the felt lack of American quality with an endless profusion of American quantity, thus valorizing the ideas of process and the material. The self-interrogating narrative that never comes to rest on a final, determinate interpretation, and the long poem that never ends, and also remains open to chance material encounters along its way, fashioned the emigrants' rhetoric of process into the two distinctive American literary inventions.

Characteristically the settlers described their migration as an irrevocable transformation in their personal and physical condition, the "travail" initiating them into a new dispensation of better health, reformed manners, and sometimes even a higher spiritual state. Consequently the decision to migrate was momentous, personal and irreversible. Any reluctance to accept the new home, or inability to adapt to its demands and conventions, seemed to constitute a failure, for which the unhappy emigrant had to accept individual responsibility. In seeking to reverse the irreversible – that is, in failing to conform to the paradigm of initiation – back-migrants were thought to have disgraced the families to whom they returned, and aroused the contempt of the emigrants who stuck it out. So their stories had to be discounted in advance, and written out of the record. Conversely, the "successful" emigrant's letter home was treasured and preserved, as the badge of the initiate.

This special drama of the rite of passage in which the experience of emigration was inscribed also contributed to the formation of the national consciousness and the literature which reflected and conditioned it. The sense of reformation is both communal (in that the process is simultaneously happening to others in the sect or sodality) and individual (in that it is motivated by personal election and conviction). This paradox is reflected in the American legal fiction of the collective singular: in the principle of the sovereignty of "We the People" and in the very idea of an "American character." Novels based on the immigrant experience express the crisis of uprooting and resettlement in the imagery of adolescence, distributing the opposing values of Old World and New between the generations of immigrant parents and children. More generally the characteristic focus on adolescence in American fiction – the country's fondness for stories of good–bad boys like

Huckleberry Finn and Alexander Portnoy – reflects and reinforces the national culture of the emigrant's rite of passage.

In another popular American form, the western, an individual is initiated into a higher condition of knowledge through the act of transcending the frontiers of his communal and individual culture. In the first western, and arguably the American foundation narrative, Captain John Smith is captured and his life threatened by the Indians, then saved by Pocahontas, the Chief's daughter, after which he returns to the settlers' camp to stiffen their resolve and prevent their back-migrating to England. As the frontier moved westwards, so did the drama of initiation. Francis Parkman's *The Oregon Trail* extends the narrative of the emigrant's rite of passage into a definition of American identity: as an American explores the furthest reaches of his continent, so he learns what makes up the American character, and his own.

Not everyone reacted favorably to the experience of emigration, however, or could turn its exhilarations into new forms of expression. Some emigrants – though how many is not clear, since their written remains are few and fragmentary – were disappointed with the New World as they found it. Of those who returned, some converted themselves into "travelers," thus saving face and exploiting a ready market for hostile comments on the audacious republic. Back-migrants and literary travelers alike – and sometimes, as in the case of Mrs. Trollope, the categories overlapped – addressed themselves as much to the British political debate (and much more so to a British audience) than to anything American, but their books also disconcerted and annoyed the Americans, who took their criticisms at face value.

So for the most part the disappointed migrants either fell silent or recast themselves as conservatives on re-entry. The exceptions to this rule were the Puritans, whose general standard of literacy and respect for the word, and whose habit of semi-public self examination, ensured that they set down and preserved a fuller record than most other settlers of their motives for emigrating and their feelings on arrival. The Puritans' evidence provides fascinating insights on the choices to be made before leaving home, but also suggests a sense of personal anticlimax, a sort of spiritual backsliding, shortly after arrival. On the more public level of experience, Puritan leaders sometimes complained of the community having fallen away from its "first love" in charity.

What the Puritans reveal, and less articulate witnesses fail to convey, is the difference between a *rite* of passage and just a passage. The rite is a ritualized journey out to the borders of the culture and back again, whereas the passage – which is what "successful" emigration actually is – goes one way only. This expectation that the experience of emigration would be more ritualized and symmetrical – more susceptible to narrative shaping – than it turned out to be in the event, may account for the frustration and anticlimax experienced on arrival in the new setting. Significantly the characteristically American narratives of initiation, like Mary Rowlandson's story of her captivity or Parkman's *Oregon Trail*, not only send the protagonist out beyond the frontier, but ritualize the passage by bringing him or her back as well.

So emigration could be disabling as well as enabling, could trouble the American imagination as well as stimulate and liberate it. Some of these doubts and discontents became internalized in American thought and writing. One recurrent theme is the nostalgic longing to return to a culture more settled, more architecturally and institutionally substantial, than the commonplace American reality: a reverie that always collapses of its own improbability. Another, related motif is the paradox of death in life, or old age in youth. Yet another is the mirror that gives back no image, or the window presenting no perspective. This last stands as a figure for a recurrent feature of the American literature of initiation: that it tends to elide, or even efface, the middle distance between the individual and the horizon, so that the social and political context of the immediate community goes virtually unimagined. As late as World War II and Vietnam, American authors were still registering these most "immediate" and "real" experiences in terms of captivity and individual development, displacing the historical enemy with a threat closer to home, in their own ranks.

Sometimes, as with Hawthorne and Henry James, these anxieties were openly thematized, even joked about. Sometimes they were suppressed, so that they appear only obliquely, as fault lines cutting across the more orderly layers of narrative. Or again, some of these discontents, like the cultural nostalgia, were the inescapable regret for what the emigrant had to give up, while others, like the elided middle distance, represented an inevitable weakness in what was otherwise a powerful imaginative recourse for the emigrant: the narrative of initiation. The organic model of an individual's adolescent growth – the irresistible, irreversible process by which Paine naturalized the Revolution and countless emigrants proclaimed their assimilation to their adoptive country – was and remains a powerful enabler of both individuals and societies.

But the organic development of the individual must not be mistaken for human history. Thanks to the rhetoric of emigration, American identity has often been modeled as a form of personal evolution. This is as true of much canonical "American literature" as it is of Frederick Jackson Turner's influential thesis that the ever-receding (and now vanishing) frontier has always conditioned the American character. However invigorating, the analogy is also dangerous. Unlike countries, individual organisms grow old and die. Except through a distorting haze of nostalgia, their past is always as irretrievable as any lost childhood, and their future limited to their natural lifespan. A country, on the other hand, can review and analyze its past, and renew itself in social and political interaction. The threat in the emigrant's impulse to move "westward the course of empire" lies in its hidden apocalyptic agenda: when the land runs out, so does time itself.

So much for the outline. What still needs explaining is my choice of material and my method of treating it. The letters, diaries, promotional tracts and other primary documents on which this book draws have not been selected, as they might have been by a historian of anglophone emigration, so as somehow to represent all the classes and conditions of men and women who emigrated from the United Kingdom, the various countries to which they went, and the British regions they left behind them. What is studied here, just as in any critical survey of a literature (including the canonical texts of English and American literature) is what has been published, or preserved in archives, by the process of the dominant discourse seeking to represent a particular view of American identity.

This may come as a surprise. We have grown accustomed to think of – and now often to question – the canon of American literature. But is it accurate to represent the tracts, letters and other documents advertizing and recording the experience of American settlement as themselves constituting a canon? Yes it is. Because they are no more a neutral record than is the body of literature affirmed in countless courses conducted in the United States and abroad as representing "American studies." Even in the matter of library holdings there is a strange corollary to the construction of the dominant discourse. Although in the first half of the nineteenth century nearly twice as many people left British ports for destinations in the Empire as did for the United States, the greater proportion of materials available for study concerns emigration to the United States alone. Even more striking, although about one-third of those emigrating to the United States are known to have returned to (more or less) their point of departure, all but a tiny fragment of the extant letters and other personal records show considerable satisfaction at their decision to emigrate in the first place.

This might be expected of the printed materials. The most powerful country might well produce the greatest number of books about itself. But manuscripts? And in British County

Records Offices as well as American libraries? The preponderance of American-related materials may be explained by one or more practical causes in the process of writing and preservation. Perhaps fewer emigrants to the rest of the Empire were literate. Someone transported to Australia would hardly have been in a mood to write about the experience, even if she or he could write at all. Maybe for one reason or another the emigrants to the United States were better off and more articulate than were those to the British Empire, and their families at home more prosperous too – hence more settled, and both able and willing to preserve their correspondents' letters down to the 1940s, when most of the County Records Offices were established. But it is also possible that deciding to live in the United States, that "other place" that stood so famously outside the Imperial dispensation, was construed as the product of more deliberate thought than emigration to Canada, Australia and New Zealand. To follow this line of reasoning, emigrants to the United States would be more likely to go to the expense and trouble to write home – and their relatives at home to save their letters – than was the case of emigrants to other English-speaking areas. Life in the United States, then as now, was news.

In any case, the process by which such documents came to be written, saved by whoever found or was sent them, given to a library and preserved for the scholar's disinterested gaze, produces a sample not much more random than does the process of publication and subsequent selection of a canon of literature. In fact, it might be called a sort of vernacular publication. Both sequences involve a communal sense of the importance of an event struggling against a series of barriers to the final "published" result. The author of the book has to interest a publisher's reader, then convince the editor and publisher that the topic is worth backing, and finally persuade enough readers to buy the thing.

Similarly, the emigrant must feel that his or her experiences are important enough to write up in the first place (often against the disincentives of inconvenience, fatigue and – early on, anyway – the cost of postage); his or her "posterity" has to share that sense of the event's importance enough to keep the communication, to live long enough in the same place or at least the same household to bequeath it to the local County Records Office or historical asociation; the library (and in turn, the scholar) must be sufficiently intrigued to preserve and study the document, and so on. Not really a process likely to preserve a representative selection; and a warning to all historians who feel inclined to reify their "primary documents," as though they represented nuggets of neutral historical truth.

So something influenced the selection of the extant documents. What it was, and why it operated as it did, is what this book now sets out to examine: the psychology of anglophone emigration to the United States. For the time being let us restrict what we think we know to one or more of the following three propositions. One: more British emigrants wrote home from the United States than from the rest of the countries of the Empire, and all but a tiny minority of them expressed their satisfaction with their decision to emigrate. Two: their parents and other relatives tended to preserve communications relating to successful American settlement in preference to accounts of settlement elsewhere, and to privilege accounts of success over those expressing disappointment and failure. Three: later generations thought that as historical documents, narratives of happy transplantation to the United States were somehow more significant than those to the Empire – or than those documents recording an unhappy migration to anywhere.

This rather simple paradigm leaves out the possibility that the libraries themselves were biassed in their choice of what to accept, preserve, catalog and present. It might flatter us to assume greater neutrality the closer we come to the "scholarly" end of the process of vernacular publication, but libraries are made up of people too, custodians of learning – like the emigrants and their relatives –

possibly susceptible to the dominant idea, voiced but not invented by Bishop Berkeley, that the course of empire, the successful transmission of culture through settlement, moves ever westwards.

~~~~~~~~~~~~~~~~

If the letters, diaries and other testimonies to the psychology of American emigration have been produced by a process not unlike the publication of more conventional literature – including the writing we select and study as the subject "American literature" – there seems no justification in logic for not reading these documents in the same way as we would the canonical texts. But before I get accused of confusing an emigrant's letter with *Moby Dick* or *The Golden Bowl*, let me say now that I do acknowledge the difference in value, which has much to do with the disparity in sophistication and self-consciousness, between the two ends of the spectrum. But this book is about the rhetoric of American emigration and its relationship to the rhetoric of American national identity. Rhetoric is studied in the same way, whatever the value of the sample under examination. Furthermore, as I hope to demonstrate, much of "American literature," like much of the rest of American culture, is also a construction of the psychology of emigration. What the discourse of emigration defined was not just the identity of a self-invented country, but the literature which that country identified as distinctively its own. So I am trying to read the discourse of American emigration through American literary and cultural history, and vice versa.

It follows, then, that even the emigrants' letters are part of American literature. In fact a highly typical part, for they conform to that specifically American genre of which the best known instance is Benjamin Franklin's, the exemplary autobiography, or personal narrative set out as a how-to-do-it guide for the rest of the community (in their case, the family left at home and the friends and neighbors to whom they might be expected to show the letters). But as with Franklin's autobiography, the element of "how-to-do-it" is not of an immediately practical nature, and the
~~~~~~~~~~~~~~~~

advice could not have been followed to the letter. Some settlement tracts and emigrants' letters did contain particular instructions about how much money to bring, what kinds of clothing, food, pots and pans to take along on the sea voyage, and so forth, but that is not what I mean by "how-to-do-it." More commonly the "it" in question was the much more general achievement of becoming American, and the "how" a matter of attitudes and expectations – habits of frugality, deferred gratification, adaptability, enterprise, courage and persistence – as illustrated by their own stories of how they made it.

Sacvan Bercovitch has named this kind of exemplary personal narrative "auto-American-biography,"[7] and suggests that the New England Puritans invented it. They certainly practiced it, and later adapted it for various urgent appeals to their immediate community, but in this respect, as in many others that have been attributed to them, their psychology and its rhetoric were not different in kind from that of other emigrants generally, but only more closely observed and more articulate.

In fact, the Puritans are crucial to any study of the psychology of emigration for at least three reasons, only one of which marks them as distinct from other emigrants. Firstly, as an exception to the dominant discourse – or indeed even an alternative voice to it. Unlike most of the other emigrants, the Puritans – in ridding themselves of priests to intercede for them – had developed the discipline of examining their own motives. When they got to Massachusetts the newly arrived emigrants were required to seek admission to the local congregations by giving a "relation" of their spiritual state, a discourse in which the form was not to express too much confidence in one's election. So whereas typically the non-Puritan emigrants left no record of their reasons for leaving home (because their literary deposits tended to be letters, which they did not begin to write until the decision was already taken and they were on their way), the Puritans often analyzed their spiritual careers in journals that afford insights into their choice of whether or not to emigrate to the "Citty on a Hill" in

Massachusetts. Similarly, though few ordinary emigrants would admit to disppointment with the New World as they found it (and would often remain silent until they had good news to report home), the Puritans had ready to hand a convention – a forerunner of the modern encounter group – that positively invited expressions of doubt on arrival in America.

That way the Puritans were different from other emigrants, but in another, they simply expressed more articulately what others were trying to say. This was because their theology, that the only mediator between man and God was Jesus Christ, rendered their faith eminently portable. Those aspects of the church that the emigrant could not take with him – its physical and institutional architecture in cathedrals and unwieldly hierarchies – were precisely what the Puritans taught should be cast off anyway. So the Puritan theology provided terms for that satire on the Old World which many emigrants expressed from time to time, by way of compensating themselves for having to leave it behind.

But the Puritans' rhetoric of emigration makes contact with that of other emigrants in a third way, and in this respect there is no difference between them whatsoever. This may come as the biggest surprise, because we are accustomed to thinking of the American Puritans as so apocalyptically motivated, so engaged in endless attempts to match the types of Biblical events with the antitypes in their own history, that they paid scant attention to the actual world around them. In fact, as early letters home show, even from clergymen like Francis Higginson and Thomas Welde, they could be just as excited about the material potential of the New World, the seemingly endless prosperity of American nature, as any booster's tract, settlement narrative or letter from an ordinary, secular emigrant. Governor Bradford's history of Plymouth Plantation strips the New World in which the Puritans land of its physical properties, abstracting it into a "hideous and desolate wilderness," so that it can be deployed the more easily as the antitype of the wilderness in which the people of Israel wandered.

But ten years earlier the same landscape and the same first encounter was described as

> a deep valley, full of brush, wood-gaile, and long grass, through which we found little paths or tracks, and there we saw a deer, and found springs of fresh water, of which we were heartily glad, and sat us down and drunk our first New England water with as much delight as ever we drunk drink in all our lives.

This comes from *Mourt's Relation*, the first account of the Plymouth Puritans' exploration of Cape Cod and their settlement of Plymouth. Its air of physical contentment is so different from the usual Puritan discourse that it is often ignored in courses and books about the Puritans, and usually omitted from anthologies of their writing. Yet it may have been written by the very man – Bradford himself – who wrote the later, retrospective, typologically plotted "history" of Plymouth Plantation. *Mourt's Relation*, like so many of the emigrants' letters, is a narrative of settlement, directed at potential emigrants and investors in the "western planting." The enormous difference is just one small example to show how important it is to understand the nature of a particular discourse: the purpose of a text, the audience for which it is intended, and the psychological, social and ideological conditions of its production.

Part I

Culture and nature

I

The British idea of America: how it became politicized

America started off as a European idea, so the history of the dominant discourse begins with the first texts of New World discovery. At first Europeans saw the New World as the site of nature, and their earliest conception of that nature was essentially negative. American nature was the absence of (European) culture, like Paradise before the Fall. So in a letter of 1502 the explorer Amerigo Vespucci described the American Indians in terms of what they blessedly lacked. "Among these people we did not learn that they had any law... [nor] offered any sacrifice: nor even had a house of prayer... they use no trade, they neither buy nor sell... The wealth that we enjoy in this our Europe... they hold as nothing."

Montaigne expanded on the theme in his essay "Des Cannibales" (1580). The natives of the New World, Montaigne wrote (in John Florio's translation of 1603), have

> no knowledge of Letters, no intelligence of numbers, no name of magistrate, nor of politike superioritie; no use of service, of riches or of povertie; no contracts, no seccessions, no partitions, no occupation but idle; no respect of kindred, but common, no apparell but naturall, no manuring of lands, no use of wine, corne, or mettle. The very words that import lying, falshood, treason, dissimulations, covetousnes, envie, detraction, and pardon, were never heard of amongst them.

And Shakespeare, in turn, would crib from Florio's Montaigne for the ideal commonwealth he has Gonzalo propose in *The*

Tempest (1611). It didn't matter whether any of these writers had actually gone to Virginia or the Caribbean to see the people they were describing. Even Vespucci might just as well have stayed home and read his Hesiod and his Ovid, both of whom used the same beneficent negative catalog to describe life in the Golden Age, before time and history began to wear it down: when (in Hesiod's formulation) men lived "apart from sorrow and from painful work, / Free from disease," while "ungrudgingly the fertile land / Gave up her fruits unasked." The inhabitants of the Golden Age lived justly without the need of laws or fear of punishment, said Ovid, and "knew only their own shores." Cities had no need of moats or walls; "they had no straight brass trumpets, nor coiling brass horns, no helmets and no swords... The earth itself, without compulsion, untouched by the hoe, unfurrowed by any share, produced all things spontaneously."[1]

Parallel to the line traced by Hesiod, Ovid, Montaigne and Shakespeare is a related tradition deriving from Virgil's *Eclogues* and Horace's *Epodes*, in which the pastoral ideal of a country villa with an enclosed garden is established – again, in terms of negatives. Horace's second *Epode*, whose first words, "Beatus ille..." ("happy is he...") have given a name to a whole subgenre of poetry praising the virtues of the rural retreat, defines the happiness of the country farmer in terms of the socially more organized pursuits he has given up: money-lending, serving in the army, trade, travel, the demands of party and pressure group. English poems celebrating country houses also defined their topics at the outset of the discourse through the negation of excessive culture. "Within this sober frame expect / Work of no foreign architect," as Andrew Marvell's "Upon Appleton House" (ca. 1652) begins. The start of Ben Jonson's earlier (ca. 1612) encomium on Sir Philip Sidney's country retreat in Kent extends the negatives into a catalog:

Thou art not, Penshurst, built to envious show
Of touch or marble, nor canst boast a row
Of polished pillars, or a roof of gold;
Thou hast no lantern whereof tales are told,
Or stair, or courts...

And the process of negation, of stripping culture away, continues until the imagination is led to contemplate the innocent candor of the first condition of mankind. In the New World, as in the Golden Age or Eden before the Fall, nature gives of its bounty unforced; no tillage is needed, no planting, no toil, no eating bread in the sweat of one's brow. With no private property, there is no need to guard one's right or wish to covet that of others. Without travail there is no cause for travel. Since nature provides everything at home, there is no need to trade, or to sail overseas to war. It was not so much an account of the New World as a satire on the Old, in the vein of Utopian romance.

The second, or colonial, stage in Europe's inscription of America was also an exploration of the theme of nature, but this time the propositions were all positive. Now the Indians disappeared, because their benign culture had become irrelevant – or even a barrier – to the abundant raw materials the Europeans wanted to exploit, and it was nature in its non-human profusion that interested the European writers. Now their subject was not the discovery of America, but its exploration and settlement.

For this topic too they drew on traditional materials. A classical and medieval literary convention for describing the realm of Nature is a catalog of trees enclosing the *locus amoenus*, or place of sexual delight, where the goddess holds court when she functions as Venus. Chaucer's "Parlement of Foules," in which the birds approach Nature seeking her guidance in their choice of mates, provides an early instance in English:

The byldere ok, and ek the hardy asshe;
The piler elm, the cofre unto carayne...

The saylynge fyr; the cipresse, deth to playne...
The olyve of pes, and eke the dronke vyne;
The victor palm, the laurer to devyne.

It is possible to track these lines through Edmund Spenser's variant on them in Book I of *The Faerie Queene* (1590) ("The sayling Pine, the Cedar proud and tall... / The builder Oake, sole king of forests tall") at least to William Wood's version in *New Englands Prospect* (1634):

The long-lived oak and mournful cypress tree,
Sky-towering pines, and chestnuts coated rough,
The lasting cedar, with the walnut tough;
The rosin-dripping fir for masts in use...

Wood's catalog of New World trees, though more formal than others, was hardly unique. No early account of American exploration and settlement was without its natural catalogs. There are several in Thomas Hariot's *Brief and True Report of the New-Found Land of Virginia* (1588), and in Walter Ralegh's *Discovery of the... Empire of Giana* (1596), in John Smith's *Description of New England* (1616) (where they are arranged elaborately under headings suggesting the Book of Genesis, like mountains, waters, fruits, trees, animals that fly, swim and walk upon the earth), and in many, many more.

This time, though, the authors altered the convention to suit conditions encountered in the New World. Chaucer's catalog is an ideal setting, containing a sampling of trees from various climates and regions. Hariot's, Smith's and even Wood's poetic version contain only those trees and other species of animal and plant life actually found in New England. The reasons for this new concern for accuracy were partly scientific and partly commercial. Now the implied questions about America were, what can we know about it? how do we know we know it? and (above all) what can we use?

And so English descriptions of the New World were recruited

into the ideology of Empire. From the late sixteenth century Richard Hakluyt the elder and younger (the lawyer and the compiler of travel accounts) and others of similar vision began to argue vehemently for the "western planting," as they called the project of North American settlement. The reasons for the western planting were both pressing and manifold. Great Britain needed to extend the reformed religion to the Americas to counterbalance the influence of the Catholic Spanish and Portugese settlements in the South. She had to open new trade routes to replace those made "beggarly or dangerous" by the Spanish, and to establish new bases to check Spanish sea power outside European waters. Above all, Britain needed a guaranteed supply of cheap raw materials from her own dominions, which would then become captive markets for her manufactures.

But first those nether regions had to be settled. As it happened, the population of England had been increasing, and the enclosure of common lands, a process begun in the sixteenth century, had recently thrown an unsettled (and to the authorities, unsettling) band of "vagabonds" on the road. This "ranckness and multitude of increase in our people" and these "vagrant people that swarme up and downe at present" were perfect candidates for emigration. Transplanting them to America would give work to "a great number of men which do now live idly at home, and are burthenous, chargeable, & unprofitable to this realme," and stop them "pilferinge and thevinge" in their native country.[2]

The numerous accounts of British exploration and settlement in the New World were really tracts promoting the western planting. That was the immediate purpose of all those natural catalogs: to set out nature's bounty as raw materials awaiting exploitation; to entice investment and emigration. So alluring were the prospects of American colonization that for a time even the British government became worried that emigration to North America was reaching too high a proportion of contemporary population values. Between the end of the Seven Years' War and the American Revolution over 125,000 English, Scots and Ulster "Scotch Irish" left for the colonies. Though prevented from banning American emigration by a lively debate on the rights of subjects and the limits of governmental power, Parliament ordered the customs officers in England and Scotland to record the name, age and other details of all emigrants, together with their reasons for leaving.

From the early nineteenth century, though, the attitude of the metropolitan government reverted to form. Now, with the population again on the rise, with thousands of tenant farmers already uprooted by a new wave of enclosures, and handloom workers and other craftsmen beginning to lose their jobs to the new factory system, the unruly "superflux" seemed more threatening than ever. Furthermore, from the 1820s Australia and New Zealand joined the ranks of colonies inviting British settlement.

Now various authorities were not only anxious to encourage emigration, but even to find ways of paying for it. In 1831 the Treasury approved a scheme for subsidizing emigration to Australia financed from revenue raised in the colonies themselves. The Poor Law Amendment Act of 1834 allowed the Poor Law Guardians to use the rates to assist the emigration of paupers, and Scottish and Irish landlords contributed to their tenants' emigration costs during the 1840s and 1850s.[3]

By this time money had begun to be raised by public subscription too. Mrs. Caroline Chisholm's Family Colonisation Loan Society financed emigration to Australia in the 1850s. Charles Dickens devoted part of the first issue of his family magazine *Household Words* to an approving survey of Mrs. Chisholm's plan, illustrated by a selection of letters sent home from her happy clients. (Significantly, Dickens's opinion of emigration to the United States had been much less encouraging.) And *Punch* approved heartily of her efforts, which it celebrated with "A Carol on Caroline Chisholm," printed under an engraving showing her holding a spade and gesturing towards the horizon, pointing the way to a pauper's family prostrate at her knees:

Come all you British females of wealth and high degree
Bestowing all your charity on lands beyond the sea,
I'll point you out a pattern which a better plan will teach
Than that of sending Missioners to Tombuctoo to preach...

Beyond the roaring ocean; beneath the soil we tread,
You've English men and women, well housed and clothed and fed,
Who but for help and guidance to leave our crowded shores,
Would now be stealing, begging, or lie starving at our doors.

Who taught them self-reliance, and stirred them to combine,
And club their means together to get across the brine,
Instead of strikes, and mischief, and breaking of the law,
And wasting time in hearing incendiaries jaw?[4]

Emigration would augment the military and commercial strength of the Empire. It might even assist the downtrodden at home to fulfill themselves abroad. But as those references to incendiaries, their strikes and general mischief make clear, emigration could also convey political benefits to the more comfortable propertied classes remaining behind.

But by this time the United States had ceased to be part of British North America. And the Americans had done more than merely separate from Great Britain. They had also struck out in a new constitutional direction. Now a democratic republic, in which sovereignty was vested in the people, opposed an oligarchic monarchy taking its authority from the sovereignty of the King in Parliament.

This confrontation started long before 1776. Over a century earlier a delegation of Royal Commissioners visited New England to hear various grievances and settle territorial disputes between the colonies. Most of the settlements protested their loyalty to the King – indeed all, with one notorious exception:

They of this Colony [Massachusetts Bay] say that King Charles the first, gave them power to make laws and to execute them, and graunted them a Charter as a warrant against himselfe, and his Successors, and so long as they pay the fifth part of all Gold and Silver Oar which they shall gett, they are free to use their Priviledges graunted them, and that they are not obliged to the King, but by civility.

"A Charter as a warrant against" the King's personal fiat – authority grounded in the law rather than in the individual: this idea (whether or not Charles I intended it for Boston) was and remains the core principle of constitutional government. The Commissioners may not fully have understood the theory, but they knew that Massachusetts Bay was heading for rebellion when it began to call itself a "state" and a "commonwealth." There were other signs too:

Their houses are generally wooden, their Streets crooked, with little decency, and no uniformity. There neither Days, Months, Seasons of the year, Churches nor Innes are knowne by their English names. At Cambridge they have a Wooden Colledge...It may be feared that this Colledge may affoard as many Schismaticks to the Church, and the Corporation as many Rebels to the King, as formerly they have done, if not timely prevented.[5]

It hardly needs pointing out that the other colonies and provinces visited by the Commissioners – Plymouth, New Hampshire, Connecticut and Rhode Island – also had houses made of wood and streets as crooked as those in Boston. But in Massachusetts Bay these details assumed extra dimensions of meaning not present elsewhere in New England; they were redolent of decay, disorder, dissention, separation. It may have been the first time – though, as we shall see, it was certainly not the last – that a British commentator would evoke the dilapidation of an American rural or urban landscape to express an opinion on its republican institutions.

The final defeat of Napoleon after twenty-three years of war with the French brought England little peace at home. In the year of

Waterloo the Corn Law pushed the price of a loaf of bread to one shilling, at a time when wages ranged from eight shillings per week for farm laborers, to thirty-six for the best skilled workers in London. To relieve the supposed plight of the farmers and landed gentry, the Government repealed the already-much-evaded income tax. This left tradesmen, mechanics, tenant farmers and other low-income groups to pay the interest on the war debt, now amounting to one-third of the capital wealth of the country, through anti-redistributive duties and indirect taxes on tea, sugar, tobacco, beer – even candles, soap and paper. A sudden slump in exports produced wage cuts and widespread unemployment. The factory system was rapidly displacing home-based craftsmen like handloom workers, whose wages within three years of the war's ending had declined to the level of the poorest unskilled farm laborers.

With the franchise concentrated in counties and boroughs (some of latter now virtually uninhabited) in which the nobility and gentry could supervise open elections, and with large towns like Birmingham, Leeds and Manchester completely unrepresented in Parliament, opposition was bound to take the form of agitation, protest, organized resistance. Radical propaganda, as a leading historian of the British working-class movement has written, was directed in favor of parliamentary reform to sweep away "the 'borough-mongering' or 'fund-holding' system – taxes, fiscal abuses, corruption, sinecures, clerical pluralism... stemming from a venal, self-interested clique of landowners, courtiers, and placemen."[6]

The rhetoric of reform was carried in the pages of T.J. Wooler's *Black Dwarf* and William Cobbett's *Weekly Register*, and later his much cheaper *Weekly Political Pamphlet* (or "Twopenny Trash" to his political enemies). It was proclaimed by "Orator" Henry Hunt at public meetings like the three great demonstrations in Spa Fields, London, in 1816, and at Manchester's St Peter's Fields in 1819, the infamous "Battle of Peterloo." But like all good educational enterprises, the movement needed more than lectures and required reading. Even before the war had ended local associations had been formed to disseminate ideas for the reform program. By 1817 nearly every provincial town had these Hampden Clubs, as they were called, meeting regularly in coffee houses and the upper rooms of pubs to discuss the need, ways and means of universal manhood suffrage and a radical reform of the tax system.

Fearing a domestic outbreak of the jacobinism they had defeated abroad, the Government fought back with ad hoc legislation and even espionage. Habeas Corpus was suspended in 1817 and 1818. In 1817 Lord Sidmouth's Gagging Acts subjected all public meetings, all taverns, reading rooms and other meeting places, to a system of advance licensing. Three years later the Six Acts enabled magistrates to search any private house they suspected of harboring radical people or papers, and to shut down public meetings summarily.

Spies were sent to public meetings and to infiltrate the Hampden Clubs – so comprehensively that to this day a major source for the historian of radical agitation remains the collection of Treasury Solicitor's papers in the Public Record Office, in which the informers' reports were deposited. Even nastier was the spy who functioned as *agent provocateur*. In the spring of 1817 one Oliver went the rounds of the radical groups in the North and the East Midlands pretending to be a delegate from the London "Physical Force Party," which, he claimed, had fifty thousand men ready to seize the Tower of London. Most of those he contacted were suspicious of or indifferent to the supposed campaign, but in Pentridge, Derbyshire, Jeremiah Bandreth agreed to lead an armed band of stocking weavers, quarrymen and laborers (among the most depressed and desperate of trades at the time) against Nottingham, convinced that his was only one of a number of similar rough battalions converging on the town. They were intercepted by a party of soldiers with advance knowledge of their intentions, captured and tried for high treason. Eleven of them were transported – another political use for the colonies – and four, including Bandreth, hanged. When even the pretext of legal process did not serve, the authorities resorted to brute force. At the St. Peter's Fields meeting, Hunt offered to be taken into custody if it would quiet things down. His concession was refused. Set loose among the crowd, the sabres and horses' hooves of the soldiers and Manchester yeomanry killed eleven people, including two women and a child, and injured hundreds more.

By this time the War of 1812 had renewed the hostilities between Great Britain and the United States begun with the Revolution. As the one modern democratic republic not to have blown itself up in civil strife or to have been conquered by British military endeavor, the United States remained an inconvenient disconfirmation of Tory jeremiads against jacobinism. From the moment the early republic began to flourish – or at least refused to wither – British travelers of various political persuasions wrote fascinated or horrified accounts of their adventures there, and their many books served as pegs on which reviewers for journals like the Whig *Edinburgh Review*, the Tory *Quarterly* and the radical *Westminster Review* could hang substantial essays about the viability of American political and social culture.

But how did the United States appear to the unenfranchised British laborer, tenant farmer, artisan and merchant? As a republic offering the vote to the common man and cheap land to those who would work it, would it attract the attention and stir the imagination of the prospective emigrant? Would America be a magnet to the many British subjects who felt locked outside the dominant political and economic structure? Or would its hostile posture to Great Britain repel all such feelings? Which would prevail: class interest or national sentiment?

The answer to that question depends on which discourse you are engaged in. The statistics of emigration suggest one alternative, and the dominant discourse of emigration its exact opposite. In the seventeen years between the end of the Napoleonic Wars and the passing of the Great Reform Bill in 1832 plenty of people emigrated from United Kingdom ports to the United States,

Canada and (from 1821) New Zealand and Australia: well over half a million in all. But while around 206.5 thousand went to the United States, over 334 thousand emigrated to Canada, and another 14.2 thousand to Australia and New Zealand. In other words, total emigrations to the United States were only just over sixty percent of those to Canada alone. National feeling appeared to be winning over class affiliation.[7]

But not according to the flurry of books and pamphlets urgently arguing the case for emigration – or, equally vehemently, against it – that flooded the market during the same period. Here the dominant question was, almost without exception, the desirability of emigration to the United States. Why? Because by now the whole issue of emigration had become inscribed within the discourse for and against the extension of the franchise and a reform of the tax system. Loathe it or love it, the United States was now the "other" – the alternative, radical dispensation. Its suitability as an environment for emigration was also its viability as an independent, sovereign state. Hardly a British book of travels in America published in the first half of the nineteenth century (and there were many, almost invariably reviewed at great length in the quarterly magazines) failed to include the question of emigration among its observations on the new country. By the same token, scarcely a tract promoting American emigration or a guidebook showing how to go about it omitted its satire on the depressed condition of the voteless British poor paying their tythes and taxes to a hard-hearted parish, a distant Church authority and an unrepresentative government. If the disadvantaged could not vote in a ballot, they could at least vote with their feet.

At first glance the proponents of emigration to the United States might seem to have been motivated purely by commercial self-interest. Some of them had bought large tracts of American land, on which they wished to settle their countrymen at a profit to themselves. Among these speculators were Morris Birkbeck, the Hertford brewer Richard Flower and George Courtauld, the silk manufacturer. Birkbeck, son of a prominent Quaker minister in

Guildford, Surrey, who had himself visited America and bought an estate in North Carolina, had raised enough capital to buy a large tract in Edwards County, Illinois, on which he hoped to settle a substantial "English Colony." His *Notes on a Journey in America...to the Territory of Illinois*, first published in 1817, ran to five editions in two years. Courtauld published a guidebook in 1819. Flower's *Letters from Illinois* came out in 1822. An associate of Courtauld's, James Knight, wrote bogus letters to the papers supposedly from emigrants who had settled happily in Athens County, Ohio.

Like the advocates of colonial settlement from Hakluyt to Mrs. Chisholm, these speculators were engaged, if only implicitly, in a political statement about the condition of England. But they took the other side of the argument. Whereas the proponents of emigration to the colonies wanted to secure property at home and to enlarge opportunity abroad – to enable settlers to be more British, as it were – the speculators wanted the emigrants to stop being British altogether.

Nor was the political point left implicit. Birkbeck's *Notes on a Journey* bases its promotional case on a deft summary of the conditions of the British tenant farmer before the Reform Acts:

> An English farmer, to which class I had the honour to belong, is in possession of the same rights and privileges with the *Villeins* of old time, and exhibits for the most part, a suitable political character. He has no voice in the appointment of the legislature unless he happen to possess a freehold of forty shillings a year, and he is then expected to vote in the interest of his landlord: he has no concern with public affairs excepting as a tax-payer, a parish officer, or a militia man. He has no right to appear at a county meeting, unless the word *inhabitant* should find its way into the sheriff's invitation: in this case he may shew his face among the nobility, clergy, and freeholders: – a felicity which once occurred to myself, when the inhabitants of Surrey were invited to assist the gentry in crying down the Income Tax.

The immediate impact of Birkbeck's book was enormous, and it was felt at least as strongly on the domestic political debate as on discussions about the advantages of emigration. in 1819 Henry Bradshaw Fearon tried to refute it in his *Sketches of America: a Narrative of a Journey*... An anonymous pamphlet appearing in the same year, *A Clear and Concise Statement of New York and the Surrounding Country*..., attacked the "spurious writings of Morris Birkbeck" and promised a refutation of "the base impositions which are so constantly and uniformly practised upon British emigrants by crafty, designing and unprincipled adventurers." Again in 1819, William Savage's *Observations on Emigration to the United States*... attacked British authors "who had purchased large tracts of land, at the extremity of a country that could hardly be said to be settled," and who now "for the purpose of selling this land at a great profit, represent [it]...as a terrestrial paradise."

Even William Cobbett, the radical agitator for reform (now best known as the author of *Rural Rides*), had been skeptical of what he called the "transalleganian romance" of English schemes to settle emigrants in Illinois Territory. By 1829 he had changed his mind. Now he felt pressed to issue his own guide to emigration, illustrated by letters from happy settlers in the States. And now his strongest advice concerned the "worthlessness" of the "English colonies," and the need for the emigrant to go to the United States if at all possible. Otherwise, it was a case of frying pan and fire: "We read the other day...of the execution of *nine culprits at once* in the happy colony of New South Wales...and that the governor had, by *proclamation*, just increased the *duties* on tobacco and spirits." One of the settlers whose letters he reproduces emigrated first "to our sweet colony of New Brunswick; but he soon found he could not live there." Moving south to the States, "the English pauper became a good solid landowner" and prospered.[8]

So between 1815 and 1832, while nearly twice as many emigrants left British ports for Canada and Australia as for the United States, the political debate in Britain for and against the reform of the franchise was displaced by the argument over the reformed politics of the United States, and more particularly over its suitability as a site for emigration. And whereas the British political establishment had favored and would continue to support emigration to the colonies, now they took exactly the opposite view with respect to the United States. Far from advocating the "western planting" to that part of the New World, they now deprecated it as an insulting, even treacherous, defection to a jacobinical foreign republic and (late in the day and a trifle disingenuously) a haemorrhage of labor from the British body politic.

But what about the human objects of all this concern – the voteless, landless, disadvantaged and downtrodden poeple of England, Scotland and Wales? What did they think about transplanting themselves to the United States? What went through their minds as they prepared to leave and after they arrived in the new country? Was emigration to America a political issue for them too?

Charlotte Erickson, a leading historian of anglophone emigration to the United States, offers at least some negative answers to these questions. She argues that prospective emigrants quickly learned to distrust the emigrant's guides and collections of letters from satisfied customers produced by the land speculators, and came to believe only such information as was conveyed in private, personal letters from close friends or members of the family. She says too that ordinary British emigrants were largely indifferent to contemporary politics – or at least "had no clearly formulated views about reform" – and did not yearn to live under a democracy. What they wanted were economic and social mobility, leisure (surprisingly, given the likely conditions of a frontier farm), and above all, independence. If they could be said to have had any political cast of mind, it was conservative rather than radical. Many emigrants were fleeing the British present and future: taxes and tythes, the increasing power of the factory system, perhaps even a violent revolution.[9]

The question of whether emigration was prompted by radical or conservative feelings is important (historians have long asked the same of the American Revolution itself), and will be discussed in Chapters 2 and 3 below. Meanwhile, it is certainly true that emigrants were loath to settle where the speculators had bought land – places like Birkbeck's Wanborough, Illinois, and George Courtauld's Englishtown, Ohio. They seem to have been quick to detect the possible bias in advice based on the advisor's self-interest. The bigger question is, how persuasive did they find their arguments in favor of emigration generally? It is not easy to answer, because of course there is no hard evidence for what went on in their minds – only the "literary" remains of their letters on the topic, the style and even content of which will always be open to the subjective interpretations of various readers.

First of all, though the prospective emigrant may have distrusted the letters published by the propagandists for emigration, there is little direct evidence that many of the letters, apart from Knight's, were invented by the speculators themselves. The specimens published by Cobbett in 1829 were as carefully dated and placed as were the letters from Australia that Dickens published in *Household Words*. Cobbett got his collection of letters, written home to Sussex from parts of Indiana and New York State, from Benjamin Smith of Mountfield, who published them in an edition of his own. "I have found Mr. Smith's publication to be perfectly correct," Cobbett wrote in his preface, "the orthography only being mended, and a little pointing supplied." He then placed the originals in Fleet Street for anyone to inspect them who wished.[10]

More to the point – though admittedly this "evidence" is of a subjective literary judgment – the emigrants' letters reproduced in promotional tracts resemble very closely those from the "purer" archives that have sat, free from exploitation by contemporary politicians or speculators, awaiting the attention of disinterested scholars. They have the same kind of news, the same family concerns, the same fluctuations of mood about the new experience in a new country. Even more surprising, perhaps, the emigrants' letters home now being discovered and edited employ much the same language of attraction and distaste – the same rhetoric of the drama of emigration – as do the promotional tracts. Either the "real" emigrants didn't distrust the speculators and politicians as fundamentally as historians now think they did, or they were moved to imitate the general outlines of their arguments while declining their biassed particular advice on where to settle.

It is also possible that speculators, politicians and emigrants alike shared a common rhetoric that came from a source deeper than their recent reading or conversation; or rather that when they thought about or performed the act of emigration, they found themselves expressing the experience in similar figures of speech, almost (though never entirely) irrespective of what they had been reading or hearing. If this were true, it would suggest that the experience of emigration was – or rather, was constructed as – a fundamental human experience, like birth, adolescence, perhaps even death, and therefore most appropriately dramatized in symbols and figures that transcend (though never completely elide) immediate influences.

This is not to say that the concerns of the genuine emigrant somehow floated beyond contemporary politics. Here is John Fisher, a young farmer who emigrated from Suffolk to Michigan, writing to his brothers in 1832:

> I have left England and its gloomy climes for one of brilliant sunshine and inspiring purity. I have left the country cowering with doubt and danger, where the rich man trembels and the poor man frowns, where all repine at the present and dread the future. I have left this country and am in a country where all is life and animation...Is not this a community in which one may rejoice to live? is not this a land in which one may be proud to be received as a citizen? Is not this a land in which one may be happy to fix his destany and ambition? I answer for one, it is.

This passage, with its pattern of rhetorical questions arranged in threes, reads as something remembered from a public political meeting or field-preacher's sermon. In fact, it is taken almost verbatim from a speech that Washington Irving gave at a dinner in New York celebrating his return to the United States after seventeen years of living and working in Europe: an address widely reported in the American newspapers just two days before John Fisher wrote to his brothers.

But when he wants to tell his family what he has been doing, Fisher shifts to a different register:

> I bought one farm [of] 80 acres and went to work on it, but finding it had too much timber on it and I could not chop very well I bought 80 acres more clear openings, something similar to a pasture. I still own both of them and have but a small morgage on one, about the amount of 22. The first I bought is worth nearly double the money I gave for it.[11]

Because John Fisher's "political" statement comes over as stylistically so distinct from the rest of his letter, is so manifestly larded on to it, it could plausibly be argued that its politics are not central to his "real" concerns. Yet the borrowed oratory of his Anglo-American comparison is not what I mean by the politics and rhetoric of the emigrant letter. Those are more properly represented by the second passage. For what does it document, if not the economic and social mobility – above all, the independence – for which the emigrant so fervently yearned? And what is the independence earned by economic and social mobility, if not a political aspiration – indeed, one central to the politics of reform? And finally, what is that quiet confidence in which he documents his achievements, if not a rhetoric appropriate to its subject?

In other words, it all depends on what you mean by politics. We may want to say that English radical discourse appropriated the issue of emigration for its own purposes, but it remains a verifiable fact that the year of Peterloo was a peak year for English and Scottish emigration. It is also a fact that at least two popular emigrant guides – actual handbooks, not land-speculators' propaganda pretending to be travel narratives – nevertheless quoted in full Birkbeck's satire of the English farmer's political predicament. You could not desire the New World without rehearsing your distaste for the Old.[12]

The rhetoric of emigration transcends class and period – and yet never ceases to be political. There are certain ideas, or concepts – or perhaps the old word "conceits" is more appropriate – that most emigrants found themselves using, both before and after the experience, whatever their condition, whenever they were born. But the act of emigration itself, both objectively and subjectively, was always a political act when it concerned the British going to the United States. Or at least that is how the emigrants themselves told their stories.

2

Nature affirmed and culture denied: positive catalogs of material bounty; negative catalogs of corrupt institutions, prerogatives and titles to be cast off; the vision of American leisure; whether emigration was a radical or conservative movement

Rhetoric is defined in the *OED* as the art of using language so as to persuade or influence others. Emigrants needed to be persuaded, or had to persuade themselves, to undertake the hazardous, expensive and alienating enterprise of removing to a foreign country. Very few had to go. Rhetoric may have had nothing to do with getting the African slave or the transported criminal to Virginia, but most of the anglophone emigrants to the United States up to the end of the nineteenth century – even, to an extent, the famished Irish and fugitives from the Highland Clearances – had the choice whether to go or stay, or go somewhere else. They may have been poor, powerless, despised in their own communities, but they had to have money "up front" to emigrate, even if the finance was collected from friends, family or a parish glad to see the back of them. Sustained by their faith in future possibilities, they had to be capable – or to make themselves capable – of advance planning, of deferring their gratifications, of steeling themselves against a radical break with a relatively settled past. No wonder the United States is said to be composed of one vast middle class: the very attitudes typically attributed to the middle classes were exactly those enjoined or reinforced by the experience of emigration.

So what arguments did the prospective emigrant need in order to make this crucial choice? Can we imagine what went on in the minds of British subjects contemplating, then experiencing, the act of emigrating to America? What did they hope to gain? A freehold, or self-employment; independence from feudal constraints to physical, social, and financial mobility; the chance (as John Smith wrote in his *A Description of New England* of 1616) to build "a foundation for his posterity, got from the rude earth by God's blessing and his own industry"; perhaps the right to participate in the politics of their new region and country.

What would they need to give up? Their comfort, perhaps their lives, on a risky sea voyage against the prevailing winds; a settled life (however humdrum); the protection and convenience of city walls (in the seventeenth century anyway), solid houses, public meeting places; the parish church with its social networks and spiritual comforts; schools, banks, post offices – on the frontier possibly even shops, mills, transport and a good water supply; friends, gossips, the emotional, moral and material support of the extended family (for typically it was the individual or nuclear family only that made the trip at first, perhaps financed by the larger kinship group); the transmission of a whole culture of cooking and household management, childbirth and child-rearing (most of which lore is handed down even today in more traditional societies through the network of the extended family). Not all these benefits were equally shared, and it is important not to convert the picture into a child's fantasy of tiny town. Above all, as Charlotte Erickson has warned,[13] it is essential to realize that the British were no longer a peasant society by the early nineteenth century (the enclosures and the beginning of the Industrial Revolution had seen to that). Yet traditionary communities answering roughly to the description above were around and in place. Even if not equally accessible or always regarded as advantages, they were certainly missed after they were left behind.

◇◇◇◇◇◇◇◇◇◇◇◇◇◇◇◇

Faced with the sobering choice of whether to go or not, the prospective emigrant would look first for authentic good news from the New World. For example, the poorer people needed to know the price of food and other basic commodities. Common to most of their letters home are shopping lists of the vital statistics.

"I will tell you the price of goods," John Harden wrote to his parents from New York State in 1828: "wheat 8*s*. per bushel; all other grain 4*s*. per bushel; beef and mutton 2 or 3 cents per pound; veal 3 cents; pork 8 cents; sugar 10 to 12 cents; tea 75 cents per pound; spirits 3*s*. 6*d*. per gallon." "I are not spaking how it is all over aMerica but what I see & know," John Burgess wrote to his son in Cuckfield, Sussex, shortly after he arrived in Westchester County, New York, in 1794. "Good Beef to be had up with us at about 2 1/2d per pound Mutten about the Same But in the City of york it is Nearly as dear as in England apples up with us are about 8d pr Bushel Good juice Cider at 2d per gallon or under Wine & Rum much Cheeper than in England."[14]

Good news for the shopper was bad for the farmer, of course. As John Fisher wrote to his mother and brother from his farm in Michigan in 1835, "Wheat is selling for 18s. per comb; oats 9s. 6d. per comb and other things in the same proportion." In case that didn't sound a very grand return for his labor (a comb was four bushels), he added quickly, underlining as he went, "*Recollect* no *Tythes* nor *Taxes*. I cannot say that I make much money, for I lay it all out in improveing my farm which will eventually repay me."

This increase in value, by which the settler documented his annual progress, was also susceptible to the itemized list, as an earlier letter of John Fisher's has already shown. If for various reasons – bad transport, backward technology, a shortage of labor – the farmer could not count on high prices at the mill or market, at least he could catalog the land, crops and animals he was accumulating for immediate subsistence and future investment. "We are still farming," John and Mary Watson wrote to his father and mother from Dearborn County, Indiana, in 1825. "Have got this season about 10 acres of very promising wheat, 7 acres of oats, 13 acres of corn, 1 acre for flax, between 1 and 2 acres for potatoes and other garden stuff. We have got a horse, a yoke of oxen, a pair of young steers, a milch cow, and plenty of pigs and fowls." "We live in our own house on our own land," Thomas and Jane Morris wrote to his father from Washington County, Ohio, early in 1832:

> We have cleared a little land. We raised about 100 bushels of corn and about 40 bushels of potatoes and about 8 bushels of cucumbers and about 10 bushels of pumkins besides beans, peas, turnips &c. last year and I erned 21 bushels of wheat with mowing & reaping, &c. at 10 bushels per day. We have 2 cows, 2 bull calves, which I intend to have for a yoak of oxen if the[y] have luck, 2 sheep and 14 hogs and 3 we have killed for our winter and spring meat and 13 head of poltrey and a dog and cat.[15]

It is easy to see how such bare lists might encourage the prospective settler as well as, more practically, inform him or her about what material conditions to expect in the New World, and also how the verifiable inventory could underpin the settler's sense of success. Even the Puritans took such pleasure in their material achievements, and expressed it in the same way. Joshua Scottow, quoting the austere Revd John Norton, reminded his New England contemporaries "*that they are a* PLANTATION *Religious*, *not a* PLANTATION *of Trade*," but this was in 1694, in the context of a jeremiad recalling New England to the imagined purity of its origins. Three years before his death in 1657 Governor Bradford tallied up the accumulated cultivars of Plymouth Plantation. Were it not in verse, it would look little different from equivalent passages in letters from John Fisher and the Morrises:

> How greatly all things here began to grow...
> As wheat and rye, barley, oats, beans and pease.
> Here all thrive, and they profit from them raise;
> All sorts of roots and herbs in gardens grow,
> Parsnips, carrots, turnips, or what you'll sow,
> Onions, melons, cucumbers, radishes,
> Skirrets, beets, coleworts, and fair cabbages...
> Pears, apples, cherries, plums, quince, and peach,
> Are now no dainties; you may have of each.

The question is, in what sense can such communications be called rhetorical, let alone political? As far as the cheap food is concerned, the subtext running through all the shopping lists is of material plenty available to every man, whatever his condition: news that even an other-worldly Puritan minister could not forbear from making explicit when he wrote home from Massachusetts as early as 1632: "Blessed be God, here is plenty of corne that the poorest have enough. Corne is here at 5/6d a bushel. In truth you can not imagine what comfortable diet the Indian corn doth make and what pleasand and wholesome food it makes."[16] As for the tallies of land and animals, the message is even clearer. This is what the ambitious can accomplish, given health and a fair share of luck, whose only wealth is their work. Taken as a whole, the itemized lists imply a whole political economy – and a morality as well: the material richness of ordinary commodities as against vain expectations of luxury; trade as against hoarded wealth; the potential for improvement as against instant gratification.

But rhetoric? The bare lists hardly conform to the conventional idea of that word. Yet there is something persuasive in the very poverty of their construction – their lack of adjectives or other qualifiers, their simple, paratactic compounding of one substantive after another, their minute quantification down to the last halfpenny. How better, after all, to convey an authentic sense of what was relatively unfamiliar to the writer, and absolutely unknown to the reader? What better style to deflect the suspicion of fanciful exaggeration so often attaching to travel accounts of faraway places – to ground the settler's discourse in the solid materiality of actual experience?

There is more to it even than that. The catalogs also convey a sense of endless process. A long compound sentence like Thomas and Jane Morris's ("2 sheep *and* 14 hogs...*and* a dog *and* cat") could go on forever; only the bathos of the last two items – and the fact that they belong to another category of animal called pets – gives any sense of closure. It's as though the process –

which is to say, within the world of material accumulation, their progress – was only a matter of time. Every year would bring new increase to their worldly store.

So the catalog of prices and posessions may be read as an authenticating device: one of several guarantees in the private letter that what the prospective emigrant was reading had really happened to a relative or close friend. Was it also a sort of cipher to which the journalist, or political traveler or speculator in American land had no key? No. As Bradford's poem shows, the more official accounts of American settlement were just as full of the specifics of agrigultural increase as were the personal letters. This is also true of the nineteenth-century promotions, which added price lists, wage rates and other such statistics to their summaries of material conditions. Cobbett's *A Year's Residence in America* has whole pages of them, stuffed with portly paragraphs on clothing, furniture, fish, fruit and groceries – and not missing out the politics either: "Tea, sugar, coffee, spices, chocolate, cocoa, salt, sweet oil; all free of the Borough-mongers' *taxes*... so cheap as to be within the reach of every one. Chocolate, which is a *treat* to the *rich*, in England, is here used even by *the negroes*." Birkbeck's *Notes of a Journey* has them. *Noble's Instructions to Emigrants* and Robert Holditch's *Observations of Emigration to British America and the United States*, the guidebooks that excerpted Birkbeck's summary of the English farmer's condition in 1818, list the prices of meat, poultry, game, fish and vegetables in elaborate tables. So did John Knight in *The Emigrant's Best Instructor*, published in the same year, alongside lists of rivers, land areas of American states and territories, and even a summary of the constitution of Ohio.[17] The public projection needed the authenticating device just as sorely as did the private letter – if not more so.

Yet the emigrants' catalogs were not confined to the prices of commodities and services, and the value of agricultural capital. Many of the letters home also speak of a natural bounty outside the cash nexus. In 1842 Edward Phillips, a handloom weaver turned farmer, wrote from Greenville, Illinois to his father back in Shropshire, wondering at the

great many Deer and turkeys in the country. Any man may shoot if he pleases, and plenty of smaller game, such as rabits, squirrals, partriges, prairie chickens, a fowl something less than the common dunghill fowl, and equally as good.

"We live close by a large river," wrote J. and E. Thorpe to her parents in Sussex from the banks of the Hudson. "A very fruitful place; for apples, cherries, raspberries, grapes, plums, growing anywhere, *any one may get them without money*, what they please. Dear Mother...my paper is not half big enough to say all that I want to say."

Sometimes the naivety of these documents – Mrs Thorpe's breathless emphasis and the literalism of the paper too small for its expansive subject – is both more touching and more revealing than fine writing. This is especially true of a puzzling inconsistency in a letter from James Roberts, a widower of fifty-nine when he left the cutlery trade in Sheffield in 1849 to work in a more modern factory in Waterville, Connecticut. This comes from his first letter home, to his children:

Now I will give you a description of the country. It is a country of hill & vale. It produces wood in abundance and also fruit in abundance, particularly aples, grapes, raspberrys, bilberrys, blackberrys, strawberrys and nuts & all descriptions. I will just tel you what we did one day. We went out one day. We was from home about 1 1/2 hours and we got 1 1/2 pecks of grapes, 1 peck of nuts, and a half peck of aples. The grapes we preserved. Their was three of us to get them. John Loxley stated that he would send me some rubarb seed. If he can I will be verry much obliged to him. I will be verry glad if he could send me some berry tree seed as there is no good berrys in the country.[18]

A more sophisticated writer might have covered his tracks better, and thus hidden an important feature of the rhetoric here.

For what Mr. Roberts's contradiction between an abundance and dearth of berries reveals is that there are two distinct levels of discourse here that, logically speaking, can neither refute nor confirm each other – or to put it another way: that properly read, his letter does not contradict itself at all. On one of these levels is a personal narrative, that might, without stretching the term, be called "realistic," of the walk he took with his two friends, and of what John Loxley said; and on the other a *blazon*, or conventional description felt to be appropriate to the topic under discussion. The "realistic" narrative says nothing about their having found berries. They belong to the general description of the country, the new abundant land of plenty.

It would be impossible to identify a single "source," let alone to imagine him having steeped himself in a two-hundred-year-old tradition of writing, from which James Roberts might have picked up the convention that the New World be most fittingly described in terms of a profuse inventory of natural bounty. Yet from their first appearance, narratives of exploration and settlement tracts promoting emigration to America included these natural catalogs alongside the more common price lists and wage tables.

The practical reasons for such reports are clear enough. The nascent British empire needed raw materials for its workshops at home, and in time would want captive markets overseas for the finished goods they would produce. What better inducement to investment and settlement than a fulsome list of natural bounty awaiting exploitation? Even the Puritans had to advance such promises – and not just to the unregenerate planters and merchants who accompanied the saints to Massachusetts. Scottow's jeremiad notwithstanding, the actual settlement of Massachusetts invited plenty of interest in its material promise, expressed even by its most saintly founders. In 1629 John Winthrop, soon to be chosen the first Governor of Massachusetts Bay, sent papers in favor of the New England planting to supporters of the enterprise, like Sir John Eliot and John White of Dorchester, for their additions, subtractions and other alterations. In the most complete copy of a promotional tract included in the circulation an important reason for emigrating to Massachusetts is "Charitie to our neighbors impoverished by decay of Trade," and the commodities to assist that end are listed as "Fishes[:] Sturgion, Salmon, Mullett, Bas, Codd, Lobsters, Eeles; Fowle, as Turkie, Feasant, Partridg, Goose, Duck, Teal[;] and Dear." The pious early emigrants appear to have found just such a rich natural profusion in New England as did James Roberts. Writing from Massachusetts to his friends in Leicester in 1629, the Revd Francis Higginson set out a catalogue of over a hundred items, grouped under the medieval elements of earth, air, fire and water.

Yet like those in the nineteenth-century emigrants' letters, the catalogs of the early explorers and settlers express more than the practical inducements and material achievements of early colonization. They share the same unsubordinated, compound construction, and the same implied inability to close each series. In his *A Description of New England* John Smith keeps his endings open with concluding phrases like, "and many other sorts," "and divers others, &c." and "and many other sorts whose names I know not." John Josselyn's *An Account of Two Voyages to New England* (1675) ranks his lists in columns – thus, by escaping conventional syntax, defeating expectations of closure altogether.[19] Insofar as the lists relate to material things, they document the traveler's experience. Insofar as they are simply constructed, they escape the imputation of fine style, of fanciful invention, of travel lying. Insofar as they could go on forever, they convey the sense of endless progress, and infinite bounty – as though outrunning, as one critic has noted acutely, even the most learned vocabularies. So plentiful is New World nature that Old World language, like Mrs. Thorpe's stationery, is too small to contain it.[20]

And that indeed is the central force of the catalog: not just to authenticate the inevitable process of material accumulation and exploitation, but more generally, to celebrate the power of nature itself. This is how the catalog of the idealized, mixed forest had been used in Chaucer's *Parlement of Foules*. But the usual trace of literary influence doesn't explain how the device came to appear almost universally in prose accounts of American exploration, let alone in the letters home of James Roberts and Mrs. Thorpe. The writer's reading will not explain his or her impulse to celebrate nature in a material catalog. Perhaps it is nothing more than the common assumption that nature should be unplanned, innocent of complex structures, candid, grounded on a material base – above all, fecund and infinitely extendable. But understood in this sense ("nature" has conveyed other meanings, after all, including that of a highly complex structure and another of a principle of savage competitiveness) nature cannot be articulated without another idea conceived as its antithesis. That opposing concept, of course, is culture: the influence that must be stripped away in order to produce the beneficent attributes given above.

The old antinomies of nature and culture, so troublesome in turn to philosophers, Romantic poets, literary historians and deconstructionists, also engaged the attention of prospective emigrants to the New World, however unfamiliar they may have been with the terms themselves. To accomplish the tremendous break with their settled past, even unsophisticated emigrants had to develop an ideology of the relative attractions of nature over culture. In the new dispensation they knew they would be deprived of the traditional deposits laid down over time in their home setting – their familiar physical and social architecture: everything from the cathedral to the market days and harvest homes – so the compensations of nature had to be made the more manifest. The catalogs of raw materials, the bare lists of prices and wages, were consolations of a sort: the lowest common denominator of material expectations and a sly hint of unlimited, almost paradisal natural bounty buttressed by the documentary plainness of the inventory.

But equally emigrants had to disabuse themselves of whatever fond attractions the old way of life still held. The rhetoric appropriate to this imaginative exercise was yet another catalog – only this time one borrowed from the old paradisal vision of the New World, the negative list of (not things, but) institutions, conventions and other abstract artifacts that the radical act of emigration had blessedly stripped away. In many of the emigrants' letters the negative catalog takes a rudimentary form, like John Fisher's "*Recollect* no *Tythes* nor *Taxes*," inserted exactly where he needed additional support to his argument. Sometimes, as in this letter from John Burgess to his son in Sussex in 1794, the catalog was more inclusive:

> But [the American farmers'] rents are Low Rates Next to Nothing & No tythes at all in the State of New york...I would not advise you to Marry in England if ever intended to Come hear for there is no Such a set out of Marrying here No Liceance nor asking at Church or anywhere else...No Expenc of a ring very little to say over but what you Chuse your Self & But little Expence only pay the person for his troble Coming to your house.

Others again fleshed out the list of missing forms with the advantages bestowed by their absence. "*Those animals called* in your *country Excisemen*, are not known in this country," wrote John and Mary Watson to his father in 1823, "so that we boil soap, make candles, gather hops, and many other things without fear, which *you must not do*. We are under no fear *about our children not having food*." In 1632 Thomas Welde, who fled to Massachusetts in 1632 to escape the Church Pursuivants sent from Bishop (then of London) Laud to arrest him, remembered a different set of Old World adversaries:

> Here are none of the men of Gibea, the Sonnes of Belial, knocking at our doors, disturbing our sweet peace, or threatening violence. Here, blessed be the Lord God forever, our eares are not beaten nor the air filled with oaths, swearers, nor railers, nor our eyes and eares vexed with the vnclen conuersation of the wicked.[21]

The beneficent negative catalog had its counterparts in the published literature, of course, though tracts aimed at the prospective emigrant stuck to more prosaic concerns. In 1819 John Noble warned the prospective emigrant not to expect the Americans to be especially generous, friendly or honest in their business dealings. On the other hand they were "a people reaping the full reward of their labors, not paying tythes and not subjected to heavy taxation without representation...without spies and informers...without an enormous standing army." George Scrope's *Extracts from Poor Persons who Emigrated...to Canada and the United States* (1832) puts the case tersely: "no rent, tythes or taxes." Cobbett is graphically and sarcastically excessive:

In short there is no *excise* here; no *property tax*: no *assessed taxes*...No window peepers. No spies to keep a look out as to our carriages, horses and dogs...We may wear hair powder if we like without paying for it, and a boy in our houses may whet our knives without our paying two pounds a year for it.

But, then, we have not the honour of being covered over with the dust, kicked up by the horses and raised by the carriage-wheels of such men as Old George Rose and Old Garnier, each of whom has pocketted more than *three hundred thousand pounds* of the public, that is to say, the people's money. There are no such men here.[22]

But the beneficent negative catalog of culture stripped away had been used of the New World from almost the moment it was discovered, and long before that as a classical trope for the Golden Age and the happy country gentleman's enclosed garden, and a utopian satire on the complexity, cupidity and violence of contemporary life. At first sight it is hard to see how the myth of the Golden Age can have appealed to the imagination of the actual American settler. What use could he or she have made of the traditional projection of an ideal society in which no one envied another country because no one had traveled abroad, in which no one worked? How could prospective planters have believed – why should they have needed to believe – in a magical land where no one bothered to plant, where nature poured forth her riches without "tilth" or harvest, without the private ownership of land and the legal apparatus to enforce it? Yet strange to report, the myth of the blessed state before the fall – whether classical or Biblical – infiltrated their New World descriptions. The old commonplace of America as Eden unfallen, by which the continent was described even before it was discovered and which survives, for example, in the phrase "Garden of the World and the Terrestrial Paradise" in a tract promoting emigration sold in Glasgow in the late seventeenth century,[23] was established not least by the negative attribute that the New World lacked culture – that is, not only the institutions and conventions of organized society (as in the Second Epode) but culture in its original association with cultivation: plowing, "manuring," working the soil, governing and programming the production of plants and animals. In Golden Age, New World and ideal commonwealth alike, the earth gives up its bounty "without compulsion," producing "all things spontaneously."

It is this rhetorical tradition, then, that explains – or at least provides a context for – the occasional, rather surprising, references in the emigrants' letters to America as an idealized, pastoral setting. Alexander Cumine was sufficiently educated consciously to allude to the convention, citing Virgil's third *Eclogue* to describe spring in Charleston, South Carolina in 1763: "I like this place very well as yet, its very pleasant just now everything is green and beautifull & as Virgil says, nunc formosissimus annus" ("now the year is at its fairest" – the passage, at line 57, occurs in a dialogue between shepherds). "People Hear are naterly kind one to another," James Metcalf wrote his fiancée in Yorkshire from Nova Scotia in 1772. Even the Indians will share their food "if they have aney meat at all." "It is not to be imagined, the general curse of mankind does not prevail here, of reaping the fruits of the Earth by the Sweat of their Brow," James Campbell wrote from Maryland to his cousin, then a student in the University of Edinburgh in 1771, "tho it may in a less degree, than in many other parts – a man of slender fortune can live here much more easy and to his Satisfaction, than he can in Britain." In 1831 John Fisher thought the land in Lenawee County, Michigan looked "like a gentlemans park." "I admire the providence of God," he added to his mother, "in providing such a country for the rescue of the distressed of all nations." John and Mary Watson writing home in 1828 described Dearborn County, Indiana, as "this Palestine land."[24]

And the letters also deploy the myth of the Golden Age in their (even more surprising) references to the fruits of nature being "[brought] forth" out of the American soil "without industry," as one early traveler put it. At this date, 1602, "industry" is at least as likely to have meant meant skill or craft as systematic work or hard labor, and the skill being negatived here is agricultural. As in the Golden Age, the New World, "unforrowed by any share, produced all things spontaneously."

An early variant of this convention was the supposed ease and lack of skill with which one could catch fish – more than anyone could use – off the coast and in the bays of North America. "While we were at shore, our men aboard, with a few hooks got above thirty great cods and haddocks, which gave us a taste of the great plenty of fish, which we found afterward wheresoever we went upon the coast," wrote James Rosier of George Waymouth's voyage to Virginia in 1605. So powerfully is the idea working on his imagination, that he "tastes" the abstract "plenty" rather than the fish themselves. To intensify the impression that multitudes of fish could be taken "without industry," the proposition was often embodied in the figure of a boy fisherman. "And in the harbors we frequented, a little boye might take of Cunners, and Pinacks [blue perch and mussels], and such delicate fish, at the ships sterne, more than six or tenne can eat in a daie," John Smith claimed in his *Description of New England*. "In the same bay, lobsters are in season during the four months – so large, so full of meat, and so plentiful in number as no man will believe that hath not seen...And the least boy in the ship, with an hour's labour, was able to feed the whole ship's company with them for two days,"

John Pory wrote to the Earl of Southampton early in 1623.[25] Of course the figure had – and still has – real grounding in actuality. Still, it is interesting to recall that perhaps the most striking images of the idealized relationship between country house and garden in Jonson's "To Penshurst" are the fish and wild animals happy to die for their lord's dinner: the "painted partridge...willing to be killed"; the "pikes, now weary their own kind to eat...[which] "officiously, at first, themselves betray" and the "bright eels... [which] leap on land / Before the fisher, or into his hand."

The emigrants' letters home speaking of fruit, wild birds and animals ready for the taking, or so plentiful in season that they are given away, are part of this trope of nature unforced. However detached from their physical experience or their actual needs, the rhetoric of the Golden Age served a purpose in the emigrants' imagination. So urgent was their need to turn their cultural loss to advantage that they fell upon, as if inventing it anew, a whole, traditional rhetorical complex. Their customs they would have to leave behind; very well, make the loss into a ceremony: count culture but as a suffocating heap of dead institutions. Unpeel them one by one, and embrace in their place the delicious materialism of unmediated nature perpertuating itself forever. Before long the emotional need and its inevitable imaginative response had recreated a traditional rhetoric of positive and negative catalogs: a vision of a life of idleness in a prelapsarian natural paradise not actually suited to their earnest, hardworking enterprise – actually separate from its articulation, even within their letters home – but no less necessary to their sense of themselves.

◇◇◇◇◇◇◇◇◇◇◇◇◇◇

Of all the motives for emigration expressed or implied in the emigrant letters, the most surprising is their hope to find greater leisure in the United States. "It seems incredible that people with a high preference for leisure should have contemplated clearing farms in America," writes Charlotte Erickson, "but this was another of their less realistic aims. Immigrants hoped that they would find the leisure on American farms they believed their forefathers had enjoyed in Britain." There was a strong preference for farming over other occupations, even for craftsmen, handloom weavers and others with no experience of agricultural labor at home. Many of the the British who went to American farms in the period of social unrest following the Napoleonic wars, Erickson adds, "were social conservatives who clung to a partly idealized view of the past which was their agrarian myth."[26]

"Myth" is certainly the right word here, even if "agrarian," in its associations with French physiocrats and American anti-federalists of the late eighteenth and early nineteenth centuries, is too specialized. The myth goes back further than that. A more accurate taxonomy would probably place it alongside agrarianism as a parallel derivation from that older tradition of the Golden Age and ideal garden. What the rhetorical history suggests is that the exploration of the New World owes something to the exploration of the human place in the world in general.

"Conservative," though, gives more trouble. On the level of contemporary politics, it may be that the apparent concerns of the English-speaking emigrants, even when barely distinguishable from those of radical journalists like Cobbett, were somewhat removed from the contemporary political debate. It may also be true that emigrants were fleeing from the British present and future more than from its past. Yet the question to be asked is this: do not all revolutions of thought, faith and political system build on a powerful sense of nostalgia for a lost purity of one kind or another?

The Reformation itself was an attempt, not to move to an untried form of ecclesiastical organization, but to return the Church to what was believed to be the simple polity of its first days and months when people met, without the benefit of liturgy or surpliced clergy, to worship their God in the upstairs rooms of ordinary houses. The sermons and public speeches promoting the English Commonwealth, not to mention even more radical movements like Gerrard Winstanley's Diggers, harked back to an "ancient of days" (in Winstanley's tracts, an age, not an old man) before the "Norman yoke" had imposed the alien sovereignty of kingship upon the self-governing communities of old England. In turn, tracts, speeches and sermons promoting the American revolution partook of both these earlier movements in rhetoric and feeling. The Americans were pursuing their claim against Parliament as citizens of the British Commonwealth trying to restore rights they thought were being rapidly eroded under the administration of George III. At the final break with London, the Declaration of Independence arraigned the King under a numerologically organized set of accusations that he had undermined this traditional polity. There the King is presented, not as an inflexible authority against which the jacobinical Americans are struggling to invent a new system of government, but as an agent of anarchy, a destroyer of order like the goddess Dulness in Pope's *The Dunciad*.[27]

Yet no one would claim that these enormous shifts in public attitude and political structure were anything less than radical. Overthrowing the hegemony of the Roman episcopacy and Catholic forms of worship, beheading a king and recasting thirteen colonies into an independent, federal republic can hardly be described as conservative behavior. Whatever nostalgia they may have felt for a presumed ancient purity, the people leading and joining these movements sought to restore that blessed state by extirpating, root and branch, the contemporary order of things. And the same qualification must be entered on behalf of the emigrants to the United States after it had declared itself a sovereign people. However defensive their move, it was not to a colony of the British empire, but to a country that had established itself in an adversarial posture vis-à-vis Great Britain, and had continued to be seen that way as in the mother country. And the act – even the contemplation of the act – of uprooting must be taken as radical by definition.

By the same test, in the rhetoric of culture and nature the ideal visions of past and future are, literally, interchangeable. Virgil's fourth *Eclogue* prophesies the coming of a future Golden Age, when the Virgin Astrea will return under a restored age of Saturn's sovereignty, and when a child just born will grow up to see "the earth untilled, pour forth, as her first pretty gifts, straggling ivy with foxglove everywhere, and the Egyptian bean blended with the smiling acanthus." In time:

> uncalled, the goats shall bring home their udders swollen with milk, and the herds shall fear not huge lions; unasked, the cradle shall pour forth flowers for thy delight...the trader shall quit the sea, nor shall the ship of pine exchange wares; every land shall bear all fruits. The earth shall not feel the harrow, nor the vine the pruning hook; the sturdy ploughman, too, shall now loose his oxen from the yoke.[28]

Of course the discourses of prophecy and praxis are very different. On one level Virgil was just flattering a patron's baby, just as the promoters of New World planting were "really" advertizing real estate, the Declaration of Independence was only announcing a new country open for business, and the emigrants were writing home to cheer up their families – or, more probably, themselves. But not only could prophecies of the future look very like idylls of the past; both could themselves be uprooted for other purposes. Virgil's vision of a Golden Age to come, with its child and virgin, was widely interpreted in the Middle Ages as a prophecy of the birth of Christ, a sort of pagan equivalent to the great typological passage of Isaiah 9:6 ("For unto us a child is born... "). More to the point here, though, is that prophecy and praxis could, and sometimes did, meet most powerfully – in the radicalism of mass progressive movements. The Reformation, the English and American revolutions were all three articulated and motivated by millennial prophecies of a Golden Age restored. And so, in its quieter way, was the movement of English-speaking emigrants to the New World.

3

The rhetoric of renunciation; the Puritans' portable theology; the emigrants' satire on the Old World

The prospect of emigration required strong inducements. Most immediate and powerful of these was the colonial model of settlement propaganda, offering a seemingly endless process of material accumulation. But as we have seen, the old paradisal image, of the New World as the revival of a lost Golden Age, continued to attract the emigrants' imagination, even to the point of leading them to the apparently inappropriate expectation that life in America would afford them greater leisure.

But if the psychology of emigration required a set of powerful arguments in favor of the New World, it also needed a rhetoric for renouncing the Old. Here again the old paradisal model was useful, since it offered a structure for casting off the accretions of culture that could be developed into a generalized satire on what Europe had and America didn't. As will become clear later in this chapter, emigrants of all sorts could deploy this Old World satire as part of their own mental preparation for leaving, and of their argument to persuade others to do the same.

If the Puritans were no less sensitive than other emigrants to the nostalgia of the lost Golden Age, they had their own radical rhetoric of renunciation, derived from their special faith. No American movement looked more ambiguously both forwards and backwards than the English Puritan migration to Massachusetts and Connecticut. Social, political and literary historians have argued over whether the Puritans were radical or conservative in temperament. Their millennarianism looked to the future; they were willing to uproot old traditions, to forge new social, political and economic structures. On the other hand, they were also traditional in outlook, fighting to restore a purity of dogma and practice they thought had been obscured in the Anglican Church after the Elizabethan Settlement.[29]

The obvious answer is that the Puritans were both radical and conservative: that their imagined past was also their imagined future, and that to escape their present they had, in one sense or another, to overturn it. A recent good book in the debate comes to just this conclusion. Theodore Dwight Bozeman uses the word "primitivism" to account for the Puritans' values of simplicity and purity, their concern to restore a lost innocence of belief and candour in worship.[30] This word is exactly right, for it links the Puritans' nostalgia for what ecclesiatical historians have called the "Primitive Church" with more secular conceits of a lost Golden Age and nature idealized, to which literary historians have given the name "primitivism."

Why have the New England Puritans assumed such prominence in the historiography of American political and literary culture? After all, the Pilgrim Fathers were a tiny band of separatists who settled a humdrum stretch of the mainland just inside Cape Cod Bay. Their confederates in Boston just to the north, though better connected to English Church and State, more prosperous and much more numerous, still formed only one of a large variety of plantations and colonies established on the North American continent by the Dutch, Spanish, and French by the end of the eighteenth century. Even the other British settlements included people of all varieties of faith – Anglicans in Virginia, Catholics in Maryland, Quakers in New Jersey and Rhode Island – and many of no particular religion at all.

The quick answer is that it was Massachusetts that first struck (and was first so perceived by the Royal Commissioners) that adversarial posture the rest of the colonies were eventually to assume against the mother country: that of the radical, republican commonwealth. The longer answer, already implied, is that much of American Puritan culture can be understood within the broader category of the emigration experience and how it was articulated. Certainly there is no evidence that the early Puritan settlers were any less interested in the material promise of the New World than were later emigrants. An early letter from Massachusetts, apart from its assurance that "the word of God [is] sincerely taught us every Sabbath," is virtually indistinguishable in rhetoric from countless nineteenth-century equivalents. William Hilton came over in the *Fortune*, arriving in Plymouth in November, 1621. Almost immediately he wrote to a relative in England to report the usual catalogs of American nuts, berries, flowers, fruits and wildfowl. As for beneficent negatives, his political focus was as sharp as any in Cobbett: "we are all freeholders; the rent-day doth not trouble us."[31]

Yet by virtue of their belief, the Puritans were better prepared than other emigrants for that necessary mental discipline preliminary to uprooting and resettlement: the imaginary stripping away of Old World cultural accretions that had to be left behind. Perhaps, indeed, it is this relative advantage over others who came to America that accounts for the Puritans' primacy in the American foundation discourse.

Take their soteriology, or doctrine of salvation, as an instance. A Roman Catholic might have found it difficult to imagine moving to a wilderness where no parish priest existed to hear confession, grant absolution or extend the sacrament of extreme unction. Even an Anglican might have wondered how the guidance of the Church, as offered by bishop and local incumbent, would reach him or her on the frontier. But the American Puritans believed in a modified form of predestination; they had been chosen (or not) for salvation before the Fall, and had no need of priestly mediation to help them to heaven. Because they were chosen, what works for good or evil they performed in this life had no bearing on their expectations of salvation. They had no need of confession, absolution or extreme unction, or even of admonitions and moral support from the local vicar. What guided the devout

Puritans were the Bible, understood in the simplicity of its primitive sense, and their sense of direct access to God through Jesus Christ. And these they could carry with them.

But soteriology aside, the Puritans' austere version of Protestantism itself prepared them emotionally for the inevitable loss of removing to a wilderness. What had they to leave behind, if not the very physical and institutional edifices that Protestants had come to distrust: cathedrals, the parish church rooted in local religious and social custom; the mediating power of iconography (whether in statues or stained glass), set forms of worship in word, music and gesture; the whole apparatus of canon law, the episcopal hierarchy, learned interpretations of Scripture and other accumulated traditions that got between Christ and the individual worshiper? Puritanism fits America's idea of itself because it was the most articulate expression, just as its followers were the most deliberate and self-conscious exponents, of that essential precondition of emigration, the thesis of portability:

> But now we are all in all places strangers and pilgrims, travellers and sojourners, most properly, having no dwelling but in this earthen tabernacle; our dwelling is but a wandering, and our abiding but as a fleeting, and in a word our home is nowhere but in the heavens, in that house not made with hands, whose maker and builder is God, and to which all ascend that love the coming of our Lord Jesus.

Thus Robert Cushman in 1621, trying to persuade the English Puritans of the "Lawfulness of Removing...into the Parts of America."[32] In all the swollen body of writing by and about the Puritans it would be hard to find a more powerfully concise expression, either of what set them off within the Christian community, or of why they should have been especially attracted to American settlement. His language comes from II Corinthians 5:1 ("we have a building from God, a house not made with hands, eternal in the heavens") and Hebrews 11:14 ("they were strangers and pilgrims on the earth"). But the Biblical "they" refers to the Old Testament prophets, priests and kings like Abel, Enoch,

Noah, Abraham and Moses, who "died in faith, not having received the promises, but having seen them and greeted them from afar." St. Paul (or whoever wrote Hebrews) was distinguishing between those courageous men and the inhabitants of his own time, whose hopes in God had been perfected in the body of Christ, and who had all the more reason for the belief that the Old Testament figures had to take on faith.

But Cushman demotes his contemporary Puritans to the status of Old Testament faithful travelers – in order to express their provisional condition, their existence in a permanent state of process, and the uncertainty of their imminent voyage across the Atlantic. In other words, this is not yet another instance of Puritan typology, the interpretative (or, more often, rhetorical) practice of seeing the present as the ultimate fulfillment of the past. It is important to be clear about this. Typology is useful if you are writing retrospectively, trying to convince your contemporaries of their specialness, of the divine plot that led them to where they were – trying, that is, to get them to stay. So Bradford's history of Plymouth is hesitantly typological; Cotton Mather's *Magnalia Christi Americana* (1702) strenuously so. But when you are trying to get the faithful to uproot themselves, the last idea you want to propagate is that there is something chosen about where they live, or fulfilled about their present lives. Don't linger in England awaiting the millennium, Cushman writes, for "now there is no land of that sanctimony, no land so appropriated, none typical, much less any that can be said to be given of God to any nation."

New England was for the Puritan nothing more or less than the world properly understood: with its "worldly" trappings stripped away; fallen from that primacy of place and status to which God had assigned Eden before the Original Sin, and to which idolaters still exalted the vain metropolises of King and Pope; yet redeemable under republican principles – and above all, as Milton says after the Fall in *Paradise Lost*, lying "all before them, where to choose, and Providence their guide."

So though the Puritans may have written much as other

emigrants when it came to surveying their material prospects and accumulations, their treatment of both the renunciatory stage and also the feeling of having settled in an ideal environment brought a special conviction and language to the discourse. "It hath been no small inducement to us to choose rather to remove hither than to stay there," wrote John Cotton, the leading minister of the Massachusetts Bay Colony during its first decade, to a clergyman in England, "so that we might enjoy the liberty not of some ordinance of God but of all, and all in purity." "As for our condition," wrote Edward Browne from Ipswich, Massachusetts, to his old friend and fellow Puritan Nehemiah Wallington in London, "I blesse God it is much more comfortable then I could expect, for we haue that which I could not expect in a wildernesse in respect of the outward man, [and]...peace, and the gospell of peace." Or, as *New England's First Fruits*, a tract published in London in 1643, put it: "Our endeavour is to have all [God's] own institutions, and no more than his own, and all those in their native simplicity, without having any humane dressings." God was most with them when the world was least, as Governor Bradford's poem of 1654 remembered:

...God in th'wilderness with them did dwell,
And led them long in that dangerous place,
Through fears and trials for so long a space;
And yet they never saw more of his glory,
Than in this time where he advanced them high.[33]

Nothing shows more movingly how Puritan belief and mental discipline conditioned the debate whether or not to emigrate than the correspondence within his family around the time John Winthrop sailed for Massachusetts – and incidentally nothing belies more convincingly the old canard that their faith made the Puritans mean and cold-hearted. Would his son accompany him to New England? "As for my selfe," John Winthrop, Jr. wrote from London in 1629 to his father on his manor farm at Groton in Suffolk:

I have seene so much of the vanity of the world that I esteeme noe more of the diversities of Countries than as so many Innes, whereof the travailer, that hath lodged in the best, or in the worst, findeth noe difference when he commeth to his Journies end, and I shall call that my Countrie where I may most glorifie God and enioy the presence of my dearest freindes.

And so he went, strengthened (though perhaps a little prematurely, for one of his youth) by a version of the same idea Cushman borrowed from St. Paul. "My good Husband cheare up thy hart in the expectacion of Gods goodnesse to us," Margaret Winthrop wrote to the Governor preparing his journey in London three months later. "If the Lord be with us who can be against us?" Their God they had with them everywhere. "If he did not watch ouer vs," Winthrop wrote to her in February, 1630, still from London, "we need not goe ouer sea to seeke death or miserye, we should meet it at euery steppe, in euery iournye: and is not he a God abroad as well as at home? Is not his power and prouidence the same in N[ew] E[ngland] that it hath been in old E[ngland]?" "Thou must be my valentine," he added, for none hath challenged me."

Nor did his tone change when, after such lengthy preparations and what he described as "a longe and troublesome passage" across the Atlantic, John Winthrop finally reached Massachusetts. In July, 1630 he wrote home to Margaret assuring her that "howsoeuer our fare be but coarse in respect of what we formerly had (pease, puddinges, and fish, beinge our ordinary diet) yet he makes it sweet and wholesome to vs, that I may truely say I desire no better." Two months later, though the settlers had seen "much mortalitye sickness and trouble, yet...we here enioye God and Jesus Christ; is not this enough?...I neuer fared better in my life, neuer slept better, neuer had more content of minde...for we haue not the like meanes of these comforts heer which we had in England, but the Lord is allsufficient."[34]

As in the myths of the garden and the Golden Age, this stripping away of culture may be seen as a form of satire. In the discourse of emigration this satire is directed against the Old World, sometimes offering the New in exemplary contrast. Like the promotional literature of Birkbeck and Cobbett, a few of the private letters tapped into the public language of contemporary religious or political debate. In 1794 John Burgess wrote a long letter to Thomas Hallett, one of his friends and political affiliates in Ditchling, Sussex, explaining what caused him to leave his English home:

> While I lived at Ditchling... I know & God knows that I did all that lay in my Power to live, & to live decent but it was all in vain... it was Necessity that generated a will in one to take so great a flight, & most happy flight it has been, for hear I am landed safe in a Land of Liberty & Plenty, where a Man by industry, may provide for himself & family, without any fear of having his dear Children taken away from him, & put into a Workhouse to be made Slaves to the Averice of parish Office Fatgut Farmers, Butchers & Publicans.[35]

Sometimes, in other words, the satire was specific and topical. But when (as in the myth of the Golden Age) it holds the whole world up to ridicule, satire exaggerates and generalizes, extending its attack to a wide survey of a fallen condition, no more "realistic" than Swift's Lilliput. When it offers an ideal alternative, that paradisal condition bears the same relationship to actuality as does a pastoral setting to life on a working farm. Satire works by altering the accustomed perspective of its audience, prompting people to look at the world around them in a new way. The ideal social economy of the Golden Age – no agriculture, no trade, no defenses, no laws, no taxes – was never possible in an orderly community. Even the United States required its people to pay taxes, then as now.

Satire as fiction: that is how Thomas More read Amerigo Vespucci's letter on the blessed state of the Indians. Their environment became *Utopia* – literally, no-place – so there was no question of More trying to pass the vision off as true except in the most important sense of the true ideal to which humankind ought to aspire. And this too is how other works of the English renaissance – *The Tempest*, or Francis Bacon's *New Atlantis* (1627) – used the news from the New World: as a statement of one or another ideal position, admittedly unachievable in a fallen world.

So when addressing the oldest version of the world it knew, the discourse of emigration frequently attacked on a much wider front than might be expected from an extrapolation of the writer's interests. In a letter back to his brother in 1635 Edward Trelawny thanked New England that the Lord's mercy had allowed him "to tread on thy grounds and to enjoy and partake of these many sweet examples and holy practices as thou hast afforded." Then turning the example homewards, he added:

> Oh that Old England could but speak in thy language; then...would not thy streets be everywhere so garnished (nay, rather disfigured) with so many beastly, barbarous, belching drunkards as now they are; then would not there be so many abominations and wickedness committed in the hearth and houses of thy people, as to this day is seen, but thou shouldst then be blessed and beloved of the Lord as New England is.

Yet one would search in vain for a contemporary abuse mentioned here; when has London, or any large city, not exhibited its share of "barbarous, belching drunkards"?

Similarly, John Winthrop's argument for the planting of Massachusetts anatomizes the collapse of England under various headings like its overpopulation ("The land groneth vnder her inhabitants"); its greedy competitiveness ("We are growen to that hight of intemperancy as noe mans estate will suffice him to keepe sayle with his equall"); its shady commercial relations ("Trades are carried...deceiptfully and vnrightusly"); and the corruption of schools, universities and seminaries, "The fountaynes of learning and religion." Though later the document asks and answers whether they would support or undermine the reformed cause by transplanting themselves to New England, this general preamble might as well be aimed at any man or woman of good public conscience, whether Puritan, Arminian or agnostic. As for the state of England presented here, it has nothing to do with Star Chamber, the unsleeping interference of Bishop Laud, or the dissolution of Parliament by Charles I on March 10, 1629 (according to the editors of the Winthrop papers, the event that triggered his decision to write this document and prepare to go over).

Thirteen years before that, John Smith had grounded his fervent plea for American planting in *The Description of New England* on an even wider survey of England's condition, a highly wrought (and very funny) social anatomy of a whole metropolitan culture:

> Then, who would live at home idly...only to eate, drink, and sleepe, and so die? Or by consuming that carelesly, his friends got worthily? Or by using that miserably that maintained vertue honestly? Or, for being descended nobly, pine with the vaine vaunt of great kind in penurie? Or (to maintaine a silly shewe of bravery) toyle out thy heart, soule, and time basely, by shifts, tricks, cards, and dice? Or by relating newes of others actions, sharke here or there for a dinner or supper; deceive thy friends by fair promises, and dissimulation, in borrowing where thou never intendest to pay; offend the lawes, surfeit with excesse, burthen thy Country, abuse thy selfe, despaire in want, and then couzen thy kindred, yea even thine owne brother, and wish thy parents death...to have their estates.[36]

Here the English language is deployed across its whole range of diction. Latinisms like "dissimulations" and "surfeit," chosen carefully for their general application, make the moral force explicit, punctuated with suddenly abasing anglo-saxon words like "shifts" and "tricks" and slang like "shark." It is an Old World already grown decadent with excess, idleness, lassitude, but it is not England as such that is being assaulted here – or rather not England governed by this or that king and Parliament, under whatever threat of fire, plague, or foreign invasion. Nothing but its wonderfully deployed language (like Shakespeare's, by the Geneva Bible out of a good grammar school) fixes the furious paragraph in the early seventeenth century. For this is what Londoners have been getting up to throughout most of English *literature*. This is the Court in *Piers Plowman*, or the city of Ben Jonson's *The Alchemist* and *Bartholemew Fair*, the world of Restoration comedy, the sink of manifold sins and wicked gossip from which Fielding and Jane Austen snatch their more favored protagonists just in the nick of time.

To this extent, then, satire of the Old World seems to have been a necessary component of the psychology of emigration, and hence a recurrent feature of its rhetoric, down to the nineteenth century. However closely they may have attended to contemporary abuses in pre-reform British politics, the emigration tracts of the early nineteenth century also generalized the decline of England. Robert Holditch's is virtually an anthology of contemporary satire, incorporating not only Birkbeck's paragraph on the plight of the tenant farmer, but also part of "A Prospect of Society," Oliver Goldsmith's more sweeping lament for a lost English social cohesion:

Behold the duteous son, the sire decay'd,
The ancient matron, and the blushing maid,
Forc'd from their homes, a melancholy train,
To traverse climes beyond the western main,
Where wild Oswego spreads her swamps around.
And Niagra stuns with thund'ring sound!
E'en now, perhaps, as there some pilgrim strays
Through tangled forests, and through dangerous ways.
Where beasts with man divided empire claim,
And the brown Indian marks with murd'rous aim.

In this mood the rhetoric of emigration derives much of its force from the sweeping reference and despairing tone of the millennial sermon. Though closely attentive to contemporary abuses, even Cobbett sometimes treats the Old World as though it had come to the end of time on earth. "Not only has there been . . . no change for the better," begins *The Emigrant's Guide*, "but things have gradually become worse and worse." Now the problem goes way beyond taxes, tythes and the greed of the boroughmongers. Now that the Government, "by causing the small notes to be drawn in," has restricted the currency, the very medium of trade itself has been destroyed. Now the talents, industry and frugality of the laborer, artisan and tradesman are so generally wasted that they "must labour all [their lives] long without even the hope of adding to the ease and comfort of [their families]." And all the Poor Law commissioners can think of doing is to "*pay* for getting rid of such people!" So distorted has the state of England become that the poor are now worth more dead than alive:

> during this last session of parliament, a bill passed the House of Commons, authorizing the keepers of poor-houses, of hospitals, and of debtor-prisons to *dispose* of the dead bodies of the most unfortunate part of the poor, for the purposes of dissection...though this bill did not pass the House of Lords, the Prime Minister said that he approved the principle of it.

And, he added, notice had been given that it would be revived next year.[37]

4

America as "reality"; the scientific test of nature; circulation: the moral economy of mercantilism; the fabulous verified: Crèvecoeur's Letters from an American Farmer

In the discourse of emigration, then, both the Old World and the New were turned into fictions: the one of a benevolent, procreant nature and the other of a decadent culture. So quickly had the rhetorical pattern become fixed (and so thoroughly had even the Puritans adopted it) that by the middle of the seventeenth century it was being parodied by satirists of the Puritan plantations in Massachusetts. "A Proper Ballad, called the 'Sommons to New England'" attacks the "counterfeit elect" of the "Purisidian sect" for enticing settlers to New England with promises like:

There milke from springs like rivers flows,
And honey upon haythorne grows;
Hempe, wooles, & flax there growes on trees
Their mould is fatt, & cutte like cheese...
There's venison, of all sorts, great store;
Both stagg & buck, wilde goat & boare...

Nor is the negative catalog of blessed absences forgotten:

Noe feasts, or festivall sett-dayes,
Are here observed. The Lord we praise,
Though not in churches rich & strong,
Yet where noe masse was ever sunge.
The bulls of Bason war not here;
Surplis & capp dare not appeare.

Let it all happen, the poem continues. "Let Amsterdam send forth her bratts... Let Bedlam, Newgate, & the Clinke / Disgorge themselves into the sinke," so long as "*our* church, cleans'd & made pure, / Keepe both itself & State secure."

Such attacks from the conservative forces of Church and State might be expected. What is more surprising is that fervent advocates of New World planting could also turn on the more unrealistic expectations of prospective emigrants and investors. People who "look after great riches, ease, pleasures, dainties, and jollity in this world," said Robert Cushman in a sermon he gave during his short stay in Plymouth, then published in London in 1622, "I would not advise... to come there, for as yet the country will afford no such matters." "And whereas it hath been formally reported that boys of ten or twelve years of age might do much more than get their living," William Wood wrote in *New Englands Prospect* (1634), "that cannot be, for he must have more than a boy's head and no less than a man's strength that intends to live comfortably." "If any men be so improvident as to set men about building castles of air," he added, "they may grow poor." Occasionally these warnings took the form of parody, just like that deployed by the "ballad" for another reason. "As to say something of the country," Christopher Levett wrote in his *A Voyage into New England... in 1623 and... 1624* (1628):

> I will not do therein as some have done to my knowledge, speak more than is true; I will not tell you that... corn doth grow naturally, (or on trees,) nor will the deer come when they are called, or stand still and look on a man until he shoot him... nor the fish leap into the kettle... neither are they so plentiful, that you may dip them up in baskets... which is no truer than that the fowls will present themselves to you with spits through them.

Benjamin Franklin would use the same joke in his own emigration tract, *Information to Those Who Would Remove to America* (1784):

In short, America is the land of Labor, and by no means what the English call *Lubberland*, and the French Pays de Cocagne, where the streets are said to be pav'd with half-peck loaves, the Houses til'd with pancakes, and where the fowls fly about ready-roasted, crying *come eat me*![38]

So the figure of unforced nature had become such a commonplace that it could be ridiculed by both sides of the emigration debate. Yet all four promoters cited here agree with the consensus that given luck and hard work in the new setting, the poor may prosper as the undeserving rich at home. Levett even continues with a conventional natural catalog that does much to underpin the vision of natural plenty he has just ridiculed: "But certainly there is fowl, deer, and fish enough for the taking, if men be diligent; there be also vines, plum trees, strawberries, gooseberries..."

One obvious explanation for this apparent disparity of tone is the immediate intertextual environment. Cushman, Levett, Wood and later Franklin were defending not only the prospective settler from disappointment, but also their own texts from ridicule of the sort meted out by the "Proper Ballad." They were, in other words, acting rhetorically as well as practically. Yet their rhetoric was more than a matter of immediate forensic tactics. It was a way of saying that some news from the New World could be taken literally, and other only figuratively; or that in one mood it may be necessary to imagine America in terms of conventions borrowed from the European classics, but in another – say, in the vein of Old World satire – these figurative traditions become as preposterous as the other elaborate hierarchies, ceremonies and customs of a decadent age. After all, was not the artifice of fiction itself one aspect of that general decline – especially the fanciful visions that the Old World entertained of the New?

It must be emphasized (even if by now it should have become obvious) that the rhetoric of emigration worked in several tones and on several levels of meaning. The positive catalog of procreant nature will serve as paradigm: it both authenticates the narrative through the illusion of the plain, material list, and also extends the sly promise of unlimited bounty. The promotional tract and emigrant's letter may evoke traditional expressions of unfallen paradise, but they "make them new" as befits their subject matter, by investing them with the materials of the new world.

Above all, they insist on the value of truth: not just implicitly in the documentary force of the catalogs, but explicitly too. The titles themselves of the early reports – "A True Relation..."; "A Brief and True Relation..."; "A Brief and True Report..." – proclaim something different from the usual sweepings of notorious travelers' lies about people who go about on one foot, which they raise over their heads when it begins to rain. These accounts will be different because they are true, and true because based on physical evidence, not on the imagination, or hearsay or something in a book. Like Levett, they all spoke no "more than is true." "As the idle proverb is, 'Travellers may lie by authoritie,'" wrote Francis Higginson to his friends in Leicester, "Yet I may say of myself as once Nehemiah did in another case, 'Shall such a man lie?' No, verily. It becometh not a preacher of truth to be a writer of falsehood..."

So they put great stress on the proper media of their information – their own eyes and ears, and so forth – the basis of their claim to speak from first-hand knowledge, and (most interesting, given that the early reports came out before what is supposed to have been the "scientific revolution") the limits to their knowledge. Holditch asserts the authority of having sailed the Atlantic twice. Cobbett "actually saw the colony of New Brunswick begun to be settled...almost saw the axe laid to the stem of the first tree that was felled." Higginson was "careful to report nothing of New England but what I have partly seen with my own eyes and partly heard and inquired from the mouths of very honest and religious persons." William Morell, an Episcopal clergyman who lived in Plymouth for about a year from 1623, was even willing to interrupt the decasyllabics of his poem on New England in order to draw the boundaries of his first-hand experience:

Foxes both gray and black (though black I never
Beheld) with muscats, lynces, otter, bever,
With many other which I here omit,
Fit for to warme us, and to feed us fit.

What makes the gesture even more remarkable is that he was translating from a Latin version he had already composed, and which runs smoothly on without the qualification. Unlike the classical tongue, English could not compromise with the truth in the interests of symmetry.

In *A Brief and True Report of... Virginia* (1588) Thomas Hariot, a mathematician accompanying the expedition financed by Walter Ralegh, shows just how early had developed the habit of reasoning inductively from empirical evidence – the method we call "scientific." Of a plant given the Indian name *Metaquesunnauk*, he writes that it resembles the valuable cochineal, "but whether it be the true cochineal or a bastard or wild kind, it cannot yet be certified." They took sugar canes to plant, "which being not so well preserved as was requisite, and besides, the time of the year being past for their setting when we arrived, we could not make that proof of them as we desired." "Proof" is used here in its old sense of "test" or "experiment."[39]

Private letters had less need to proclaim their veracity, of course, since they would be invested with whatever conviction the individual character was known to carry. For the most part the claim to authority was left implicit in the rhetoric of the personal communication – in the catalogs and other authenticating devices already discussed. John Burgess comes right out with it ("I hope I shall not give any flattering account of [this New World] I would not wish to say any more than what I see & believe"), but this is in a somewhat hesitant letter to Thomas Hallett, a respected political ally, not to a member of his own family.

Yet at least one transatlantic exchange of letters within an extended family shows how persistent was this convention that while the Europeans might dream of the United States as an exotic Utopia beyond the western horizon, it was the Americans' role – almost a function of their national identity – to present the unromantic truth of the situation. Following the Revolutionary War, John Cranch, of Axminster, Devon, a lawyer, "hacking writer," antiquarian and painter of historical subjects, resumed his correspondence with his American relations. Cranch was an enthusiast for America, and for the revolutionary cause. Two uncles had settled in Germantown (later Quincey), Massachusetts, and a cousin had married the sister of Abigail Adams. "The cause of *America* [is the cause] of *mankind* in general," he wrote his uncle Joseph Palmer from Axminster in 1783. "In this country it is certain that America is generally looked to as the grand asylum of persecuted liberty and property."

But his political idealism moved into the romantic cult of the primitive when he turned his attentions to his female cousins. "My curiosity in regard to America . . . is *unbounded*," he wrote Elizabeth Palmer Cranch in 1784:

> Elizabeth, did you ever see a rattle snake, or a wild indian? Have you any vineyards or orangeries, or orchards of apples about you? How far back in the wild parts of your country have you ventured? Are yr horses and cows ab origines or were they brought from Europe? Have you slaves? . . . Did you see any battle or skirmish in the course of the war, and how many did *you* kill or wound? . . . *Finally* . . . did you ever read such a parcell of stuff as your loving cousin has wrote here?

As he says, Cranch knows he is being silly (and the letter also had its practical purpose: he wondered if she had any money to buy a first shipment of a strong Devonshire ale he wanted to start exporting), but still, his curiosity about America is conditioned by the European mental set of the exotic – reflected not only in his fascination with wildness and violence (safely to be savored at a great distance) but also in his odd question about the farmyard animals, as though the ordinary succession of animal generation could not occur in such a remote setting.

But Elizabeth's answer, and that of her sister Mary (who though not addressed originally, took it upon herself to write on her own), are even more diagnostic. The two come over as self-proclaimed plain folks – the former with a good deal more wit than the latter. "What a thing of interrogations!" Elizabeth answered, though clearly enjoying answering his questions at great length. "No Sir – I never saw a wild Indian but during our Army's stay at Cambridge in 75...fine looking fellows they were – yet there was a ferociousness in their visages that made me tremble." And no, she had "not been far into the heart of the country. Perhaps 70 miles or therabouts." As for money, "Yes – some of us have – and some have not – those that have spend it for frippery – & those who have none – sigh for Galloon Hats, Caps & fringed waistcoats." And then, as though catching herself out in a mismatch of national characteristics, she remembers where the "frippery" comes from: "Tis a Pitty we can't consent to do without so much of your European finery till Our Pine-trees, codfish Pot-ash &ct coud be Exchanged for them." About her role in the War she is delightfully – well, disarming: "I saw no battles, nor did I do any kind of mischief except tareing my gown to Peces clambering the rocks to see the cannonade when Charlestown was Burnt."

If the Cranches and Palmers might almost have been the prototype for one of Henry James's Anglo-American families, the spirited Elizabeth could stand in for Daisy Miller. Her sister is more like Mrs. Pocock. Mary's realism is not a matter of self-irony, but a dogged cancellation of all John's romantic fantasies, one by one. She asserts their plain values and the ordinariness of their daily life – until a provincial defensiveness moves her to claim for Boston a fashionable finery the equal of any in London. "Rattle snakes thank fortune are not to be seen at Germantown...Wild Indians are a sight seldom to be met with...We know nothing of the wild parts of the country." Of course they have orchards, but "Orangeries we leave to those who can support the charge of them... We have few slaves, rather none... We never saw any battle." Above all, they are not the exotic "other," but

> Our Dress, Manners & behaviour are quite english – our language in general very pure... You think of us who live near Boston... as if we were a sort of savages – Boston is a large town & a very handsome one [of] near 30,000 inhabitants. The inhabitants dress very much indeed, more than they do in London, we have fashions, trinkets & finery from thence in a few weeks, & there are many very handsome & genteel ladies.[40]

But the idea of America as reality, the experimental experience of which banishes European illusions, has a very long history. It can be seen even in borrowings from European rhetorical conventions, like those natural catalogs in which explorers and settlers accounted for the landscape of the New World. Chaucer's list of trees is a mixed catalog. It contains varieties unlikely to have co-existed in any one place in the real world: ash and elm, but also olive, palm and laurel. The attributes of each tree are just that – attributes, not uses – assigned so as to give a sense of the whole range of experience and course of human life in its natural context: architecture, (the "piler elm" is so called because it makes pillars), war, peace, victory, defeat, death and mourning. The species are mixed precisely because this is no realistic setting but an ideal vision in which the goddess Nature reconciles struggling opposites – the birds themselves who forswear competition to have their mates chosen for them within a feudal hierarchy; lust and charity; even the various meanings (order, savagery) of "nature" itself – all in the overriding purpose of perpetuating life in the face of the fallen world's mutability.

By the time this trope gets into Spenser's hands, as a description of the grove into which Una and the Redcross Knight wander to escape a storm, its symbolic force has changed and weakened. The grove only "seemes" a "fair harbour"; actually it is the "wood" (a pun involving the sense of madness) where the monster Errour has her lair, and the place where the protagonists' misadventures begin. It may be that Spenser's allusion to Chaucer carries some sort of meaning like: in the realm of the epic, and certainly before the heroic enterprise has been accomplished, paradisal bowers of love in nature have no place, or are at best an evasion of duty. It is equally likely, given his manner of citation elsewhere in *The Faerie Queene*, that he is using the Chaucer as a bit of ready-made poetic wallpaper, providing more decoration than meaning.

When the explorers and settlers of North America pick up the natural catalog, they change it again. Now the test of the actual unmixes the lists of trees, fish, quadrupeds and birds. Even in the formal verse of William Wood only such varieties and species are cited as could really survive in one particular climate – which is to say, only those listed as might actually have been encountered there. More to the point, although an echo remains of Chaucer's and Spenser's attributes (in Wood's "the mournful cypress tree," for instance), now the emphasis is on the use to which the trees can be put – "fir for masts in use," "The boatmen seek for oars light, neat-grown spruce" – or not: "The water-spungy alder good for naught." In Chaucer's natural bower nothing would be "good for naught."

One way to account for this development in the trope of the natural catalog would be to judge it as yet another "dissociation of sensibility" occurring when (and because) people began to think of nature as a morally neutral commodity to be exploited for trade rather than a fundamental value governing the order of all creation. Yet it might be more productive of understanding to examine this new way of regarding nature in more detail. It was not simply the erosion of the old moral complexity, but a distinctive political, economic and indeed moral ideology in its own right.

British reasons for exploring and colonizing North America had been set out and largely agreed by the end of the sixteenth century. They included the impulse to propagate the Protestant cause, the search for a northwest passage to the Orient, the securing of a cheap and reliable source of raw materials, the establishing of American and Caribbean ports for the British navy, and an outlet for Britain's supposed surplus of destitute and restless population.

Implicit in much of this policy was an adversarial stance vis-à-vis Spanish and Portuguese settlement in South America. The American Indians were "idolaters" (the word is Richard Hakluyt's).[41] Their conversion to Christianity would be much more safely effected by Protestant English than by Iberian papists – idolaters of another sort. American naval ports, and the uninterrupted trade with the Far East guaranteed by a northwest passage, would increase British military and civil strength against Spain. Above all the stress on humble commodities for the exploitation of British manufactures was an attempt to strike out on a commercial trail quite distinct from that of the Spanish.

The Spanish had found gold, and lots of it, in that part of the New World they explored and colonized. They found it in the ground, and extracted it. They found it in the form of fabulous Indian artifacts, which they melted down for their metropolitan treasuries. The English had found next to no gold or silver in the part of America left for them to exploit. So they had a choice of alternative policies. Either they could count on hijacking enough Spanish ships on the high seas to redress the balance of wealth between the two countries – not very practical, really – or they could develop another kind of economy altogether, based on the humble materials afforded by Virginia and New England: the vegetables, fruits and wild animals to sustain a *permanent* colony in its early months of settlement; the timber, medicinal herbs, furs and (above all at first) fish to enable the colonies to trade for manufactured goods with the rest of Europe.

"The principal thing that hath been the destruction of most plantations," wrote Francis Bacon in his essay, "Of Plantations" (1625), "hath been the base and hasty drawing of profit in the first years." When considering where to plant, he continued, "first look about, what kind of victual the country yields of itself to hand; as chestnuts, walnuts, pine-apples, olives, dates, plums, cherries, wild honey, and the like; and make use of them." Then work out what crops will grow soonest, "as parsnips, carrots, turnips, onions, radish...and the like." After that, search the land for commodities to export: "Iron is a brave commodity where wood aboundeth...bay-salt...pitch and tar...drugs and sweet woods...soap-ashes likewise, and other things that may be thought of" – but above all do not fantasize about getting rich quick through the discovery of precious metals. "Moil not too much under ground; for the hope of mines is very uncertain, and useth to make the planters lazy in other things."

In order to argue so fervently for an American colony of energetic yeoman planters in *The Description of New England*, Captain John Smith had to draw the same contrast between the quick fix of gold and the long-term growth potential of the more ordinary commodities afforded by northerly settlements. We have found few deposits of precious metals, he wrote, but a lot of fish. Was this a disappointing result? Was he joking? Consider the alternative examples set by the Spanish and the Dutch, Smith continued. The latter "labour in all weathers in the open Sea" to catch fish, and so become "hardy, and industrious." Then they trade "this poore commodity" for "Wood, Flax, Pitch, Tarre, Rosin, Cordage, and such like" to service the ships, not only that catch the fish but that carry their trade and float their navy. What is left over they sell to the French, Spanish, Portugese and English, and so

> are made so mighty, strong and rich, as no State but Venice, of twice their magnitude, is so well furnished with so many faire cities, goodly Townes, strong Fortresses...as well of Golde, Silver, Pearles, Diamonds, Pretious stones, Silkes, Velvets, and Cloth of gold...What Voyages and Discoveries, East and West, North and South, yea about the world make they? What an army by Sea and Land, have they long maintained in despite of one of the greatest Princes of the world? And never could the Spaniard with all his Mynes of golde and Silver pay

his debts, his friends, and army, halfe so truly, as the Hollanders stil have done by this contemptible trade of fish.[42]

So what started out as an ideological dialogue with a competing colonial power, before any permanent British colony had been established on the American continent, developed into the engine of the British imperial economy until well into the twentieth century: the mercantilist system of trade by which a safe supply of cheap raw materials supplied home manufactures that in turn would find a guaranteed market in the very dependencies that supplied the raw materials. But as Smith's satire on the Spaniard's failure to pay his debts and Bacon's warning about laziness make clear, it was a moral system too – or at least it was when it was first articulated as an argument against the Spanish procedure of royal land grants that allowed grandees to strip the new country of its wealth without putting anything back into it. The Spanish enslaved whole peoples, literally melting their culture down, in order to extract their wealth and then bury it unproductively in vaults at home. The English, by contrast, would strengthen their merchant and naval shipping, develop the capital base and put people to work both home and abroad, increasing the value of the product at every stage of its manufacture. The Spanish hoarded wealth; the British would set it free.

So although there would be a certain symmetry in the claim that fictions of the Old World were needed to imagine the New, the epigram would be too simple. Emigrants and propagandists of American settlement alike did indeed draw on European rhetorical conventions to express what was attractive in nature and repulsive in culture, but they also reinvented them in the process. The overriding theme of emigration discourse is of the fabulous verified. Now, as though for the first time, Paradise is regained; Nature's bower, the pastoral retreat, the moral economy of the Golden Age are all given authenticity, grounded in the material evidence of documented experience.

The dialectic between the fabulous and its material authentication, between the vision of a leisured paradise and the bourgeois ethic of hard work and capital accumulation that underpins it – indeed the whole discourse of American settlement, including the economic morality of the mercantilist "western planting" – are exhibited plainly in Hector St. Jean de Crèvecoeur's *Letters from an American Farmer* (1782). Conversely, the *Letters*, with its odd conflations of heterogeneous moods, methods and even materials, becomes less perplexing by being placed (where it assuredly belongs) in the context of New World transplantation and settlement.

At first the structure of *Letters*, though complex, looks comprehensible enough. It is plotted upon a grid of what might be called moral geography, and the morality is grounded on the material base of economics. Crèvecoeur believed in two French ideas that turned his analysis of American settlement into a dramatic struggle between opposing natural forces. One was the thesis, promulgated by Count Buffon in his *Histoire Naturelle* (44 volumes, from 1745, Englished in 1775) and the Abbé Raynal's *Histoire...des Européens dans les deux Indes* (6 volumes, 1770, part Englished in 1779), that animals and vegetables would degenerate in size, number and vigor as they were transplanted to the cooler, less drained, more "miasmic" environment of North America.[43] *Letters* is dedicated to Raynal, and the passage on the hummingbird tearing flowers to pieces comes from the English translation of his *Histoire*. Crèvecoeur's other idea was the thesis of the Physiocrats, who argued that the soundest economy was agricultural, because farming alone guaranteed a gain of return over investment, grounded on the natural increase of growth and proliferation.

According to Crèvecoeur, then, the American farmer's life was a continuous struggle between progress and regress; as his crops and livestock grew, so they would also wither away by the process of New World degeneration. In the middle-Atlantic colonies on the East Coast – New York, Pennsylvania, New Jersey – the settlers were more than holding their own, with good farm management and by steadily improving their stock and land. (As more land was made available by good drainage, so also the "miasma" was slowly dried out, lessening the effects of degeneration.) But in the West, on the frontier, men were forced to live by hunting, fishing and trapping. "Once hunters, farewell to the plough. The chase renders them ferocious, gloomy, and unsocial... Their success in the woods makes them neglect their tillage." Because "Hunting is but a licentious idle life," they soon degenerate into "a mongrel breed, half civilized, half savage."

The North–South axis affords a different contrast. In New England, especially on the sandy island of Nantucket, "tillage" becomes possible only after the soil has been manured with seaweed. So the Nantucketers have turned to exploiting their raw materials for trade, an exchange made to sound very like John Smith's encomium on fish:

> they are well acquainted with the cheapest method of procuring lumber from Kennebec River, Penobscot, etc.; pitch and tar from North Carolina; flour and biscuit from Philadelphia; beef and pork from Connecticut [, for which] they know how to exchange their cod-fish and West Indian produce... By means of all these commercial negotiations, they have greatly cheapened the fitting out of their whaling fleets and therefore much improved their fisheries. They are indebted for all these advantages not only to their national genius but to the poverty of their soil.

What it suffers in uncertainty of return by comparison to farming, the New Englanders' trade makes up in energy and ingenuity. Not so the economy at the other end of the North–South axis, the slave-worked plantations of South Carolina. Here wealth and work, effort and reward, are totally divided. On the one side, the gentlemen planters lounge about in Charleston, "enjoying all that life affords most bewitching and pleasurable, without labour, without fatigue, hardly subjected to the trouble of wishing." On the other, the "unfortunate race" of black slaves "grubs up the ground, raises indigo, or husks the rice, exposed to a sun full as scorching as their native one, without the support of good food, without the cordials of any cheering liquor."

So the North of America works hard, the South tyrannizes and dissipates, the East plants and improves, and the West barbarizes. Except that it is not as simple as that. Yet another grid, the rhetorical formula of emigration and settlement, has been placed over the work. The evidence is not far to seek. It appears, for instance, in Crèvecoeur's utterly conventional use of positive and negative catalogs. America's fundamental advantage over Europe consists of having "no aristocratical families, no courts, no kings, no bishops...no great manufactures employing thousands, no great refinements of luxury." And when he wanted to underpin the reader's conviction that Andrew the Hebridean, his exemplar of the American dream, had transplanted himself successfully to the New World, how does Crèvecoeur end his story?

	Dollars
The value of his improvements and lease.........	225
Six cows, at 13 dollars..............................	78
Two breeding mares................................	50
The rest of the stock	100
Seventy-three bushels of wheat	66
Money due to him on notes........................	43
Pork and beef in his cellar	28
Wool and flax...	19
Ploughs and other utensils of husbandry	31
£240 Pennsylvania currency – dollars...........	640

But these features merely identify the discourse. What is it about the convention that contributes to a better understanding of *Letters from an American Farmer*? If nothing else, it helps to explain what are otherwise very puzzling excursions from, or even contradictions to, the pattern of moral geography on which the book seems to be cut. For example, the short "Letter" about Charleston follows five others on Nantucket and its neighboring island of Martha's Vineyard. Since the islanders' disadvantage of poor soil turned out to be their strongest inducement to hard work, what would one expect the South's counterbalancing "advantage" to be at the other pole of the axis, if not a soil so rich and climate so favorable that the inhabitants did no work at all, developed no trade, made no improvements? Yet the engine of their depravity turns out to be something quite different from rich soil and a favorable growing climate:

> With gold dug from Peruvian mountains, they order vessels to the coasts of Guinea; by virtue of that gold, wars, murders, and devastations are committed in some harmless peacable African neighbourhood where...the daughter [is] torn from her weeping mother, the child from the wretched parents, the wife from the loving husband; whole families swept away and brought through storms and tempests to this rich metropolis!

This is very strange. It doesn't fit the perceived logic of the book's apparent organization. It doesn't fit the facts. The slave trade was actually financed by an exchange of English trinkets for African slaves, the slaves in turn for sugar and rum, which returned to Liverpool and Bristol to pay for more gewgaws. This was the notorious triangular trade, in which (by the way) the good burgers of Boston and ships of Nantucket played a willing part. Yet Crèvecoeur seems determined to drag South America into the issue, and not just in that odd detail of "gold dug from Peruvian mountains." "Charles Town is, in the north," he says, "what Lima is in the south." The North Carolina law of property and inheritance means that "in another century, the law will possess in the north what now the church possesses in Peru and Mexico."

So the emphasis has very little to do with the economics of slavery or the South, and everything to do with the value assigned to gold by the English discourse of American planting. The most anthologized of the "Letters," "What is an American?", puts the opposite case:

It is here...that the idle may be employed, the useless become useful, and the poor become rich; but by riches I do not mean gold and silver – we have but little of those metals; I mean a better sort of wealth – cleared lands, cattle, good houses, good clothes, and an increase of people to enjoy them.

Instead of creating wealth in this way, the economy of the south exploits the existing riches of nature: ripping gold out of its natural setting and using it to do the same with the African daughter and husband. The process is predatory and extractive, destructive and vicious. What is wrong with the south is that it has adopted a foreign politics and economics – and not just foreign in general or specifically Iberian, but feudal, European, reactionary. The south has reversed the progress achieved by travel and colonial planting. It has established a hereditary monarch of an economy, where people take whatever nature offers them as though by right, without effort and without putting anything back, and in doing so, it has turned itself back into a "metropolis."

But perhaps the most puzzling apparent inconsistency in *Letters from an American Farmer* is the question of what kind and degree of leisure the American emigrant can expect. Clearly on one level (or on certain parts of the continent) leisure is a sign of weakness, degeneration, moral decline. Leisure is the distinguishing feature of the southern planters' depravity. On the western frontier people barbarize because "hunting is but a licentious, idle life." The New Englanders redeem themselves from the poverty of their soil by their hard work.

Yet the small freeholders of the middle-Atlantic colonies seem able to develop the advantages of leisure without its debilitating effects. In order to bring about this happy conjunction Crèvecoeur had to invent a representative of their number whose circumstances are quite different from his own when he settled a farm in New York. Farmer James has not cleared his own land. That labor, he says, his father did before him, leaving him, "an artless countryman tracing himself through the modifications of his life," free for "useful reflections" on himself, on his family and its orderly succession of generations; to "contemplate" his bees and the "myriads of insects...dancing in the beams of the setting sun [and]...carefully improving this short evening space." From his father's laborious, physical improvements of the land to his contemplation of the insects "improving" their time is a giant step; a step measured by the distance between the actuality and the fantasy of the colonial settler's life.

Similarly the "Letter" detailing the visit to the Botanist John Bartram portrays a man already well advanced in the process of settlement. Bartram has almost completed the heavy clearing, diking and ditching of his farm to remove the cause of the degenerationists' miasma, so that now an "amazing number of cattle and horses" feed "on solid bottoms, which but a few years before had been covered with water." Bartram is encountered actually at work on a ditch alongside his hired men – a most republican posture – but he is able to leave his labor immediately to take his visitor on a tour of his property. They "ramble" through his fields, while his cows, in imagery reminiscent of Virgil's fourth *Eclogue*, return "home, deep-bellied, short-legged, having udders ready to burst." Over "several days" spent "in ease, improvement, and pleasure" (a significant triad), the visitor dines with Bartram, listens to his Eolian harp, discusses the present and future destinies of Russia and America, and hears how the botanist came to "cultivate" the science by which he is now known throughout the world. "What a shame," Bartram remembers having said to himself, "that thee shouldest have employed so many years in tilling the earth and destroying so many flowers and plants without being acquainted with their structures and their uses!" So the simple farmer became the philosopher of his own occupation.

John Bartram was a Quaker, and his modest simplicity here owes something to the cult of *le bon Quaker*, a French expression of the republican middle way since Voltaire's *Lettres Philosophiques* (1734), where William Penn's colony is presented as a return to the Golden Age. Even the Eolian harp might be said to symbolize the Quaker meeting, since it is neither played upon by human hands nor plays itself like a mechanical music box, but is silent until stirred fortuitously by a "spirit" wind. Yet the problematic value of leisure in the context of the *Letters* must owe something to the same overlay of opposing virtues in the discourse of exploration and settlement, since the double tone is so exactly similar. Like other emigrants, Crèvecoeur wanted, on the one hand, to valorize hard work and republican virtue, to disabuse the prospective settler of any fancies about the land of Cockaigne, and to ground his claims for the new land in the verifiable material accumulation of ordinary commodity. On the other hand, he could not escape the gravitational field of the classical Golden Age and the Renaissance enclosed garden in which no one worked because someone had arranged things so that nature gave of her bounty unbidden. Nature sheds culture only to be re-constituted by it in a happy synthesis of alternatives.

5

The degeneration and regeneration of the English language; the impossibility of American literature; Paine, Franklin, Jefferson and republican discourse

If Crèvecoeur's *Letters from an American Farmer* can best be understood as a settlement tract, it was also the first general survey to argue for the distinctiveness of the American physical and social landscape, as against the European model. Other assertions and defenses of the American difference, though not necessarily intended or read as arguments in favor of settlement, derived inspiration, ideas and procedures from the rhetoric through which it was promoted.

So the dispute between culture and nature within the discourse of emigration was not just a symptom within a rhetorical syndrome; it also became a means of establishing America's distinctive voice within a debate the very medium of which – the English language itself – originated in the metropolis from which the young country had fought to be free. If the British assault on the viability of American republicanism, the "paper war" that began, roughly speaking, with the War of 1812, soon focused on the undesirability of emigration to the United States, then the Americans defined and authenticated their dispensation by means of the figures and arguments that had drawn them, or their ancestors, to the New World in the first place. This chapter and the next explore the way in which proponents of a distinctively American character – in social and physical climate, in politics, life patterns and even imaginative range – used the settler's dialog between culture and nature to affirm the national project.

The chief vehicle for hostile accounts of American life were travel reports, of the sort that were then extensively noticed in the Tory *Quarterly Review* and (though it was usually more even-handed under Francis Jeffrey's editorship) the Whig *Edinburgh*. The thesis common to most of the attacks was a cultural version of Buffon's that species degenerated when moved to an environment less settled than their native one. British conservatives turned this idea to apply to men too, and their manners, their architecture, politics and religion. Cut off from its native stem, even the English language had deteriorated under the influence of republican institutions. Above all, America had no native "literature," which then meant book-learning of any sort – scientific and humanistic alike – as well as poetry, drama and fiction.

Not all contemporary Americans were equally robust in refuting the thesis of their own degeneration. Though William Tudor, E.T. Channing and the elder Richard Henry Dana had founded the *North American Review* in 1815 to counter slurs against American culture in the British quarterlies, their fellow Bostonian, Harvard Professor of Hebrew and Oriental Languages Sidney Willard, took up some of its early pages to worry about the state of the American language. "Violations of the genuine idiom, in a country separated from the parent stock, but professing to speak and write the same language, often escape with impunity," he wrote. These depredations were "commonly the result of negligence; sometimes however, of pardonable ignorance. Even where the language is most cultivated, all the vigilance of criticism is requisite to preserve its idiom pure."[44]

For Washington Irving the American separation from Europe meant a dissociation of the imagination. David Hartley's *Observations on Man* (1739) and Archibald Alison's *The Nature and Principles of Taste* (1790) had developed the theory that our immediate perceptions take their emotional life from what we associate with them. The more remote the association in time, the greater the imaginative stimulus to link it with the present perception. But without a history, Irving asked, how could Americans even begin to enter imaginatively into that most "philosophical" association of all, the judging of the present against the standard of the past? "Never need an American look beyond his own country for the sublime and beautiful of natural scenery," he wrote in the preface to *The Sketch Book* (1820), trying to explain why so many of the essays to follow were set in England, "but Europe held forth the charms of storied and poetical association. There were to be seen the masterpieces of art, the refinements of highly cultivated society, the quaint peculiarities of ancient and local custom." A hundred years later T.S. Eliot, though immune to the more naive features of this famous lament, and applying the sense of loss to the condition of being modern rather than American, would express something of Irving's anxiety in his essay, "Tradition and the Individual Talent."

For Hawthorne the task of the American writer was rendered problematic by a decay of his countrymen's belief in the peculiar truth of fiction. "In the old countries, with which Fiction has long been conversant," he wrote in his Preface to *The Marble Faun* (1860), "a certain conventional privilege seems to be awarded to the romancer; his work is not put exactly side by side with nature; and he is allowed a license with regard to every-day Probability." The cult of the commonplace, of plainness and direct expression free of the traditional hierarchies of linguistic register and degrees of literalness, had led the American reader to suspect the contract offered him by the romancer. "No author, without a trial," Hawthorne continued, "can conceive of the difficulty of writing a romance about a country where there is no shadow, no antiquity, no mystery, no picturesque and gloomy wrong, nor anything but a commonplace prosperity, in broad and simple daylight, as is happily the case with my dear native land."

So for some American writers the absence of culture was nothing to celebrate. But to express even this feeling so antithetical to the settlers' consensus, they could not escape the gravitational field of their promotional rhetoric. They merely inverted its tone, turning the exhilaration of the the emigrants' negative catalogs into a recitation of debilitating vacancies. Hawthorne's was neither the first nor the last of such laments. "There is nothing to awaken fancy in that land of dull realities," a young Bostonian traveling in Europe wrote in *Blackwood's Edinburgh Magazine* in 1819. "It contains no objects that carry back the mind to the contemplation of early antiquity; no mouldering ruins to excite curiosity in the history of past ages; no memorials commemorative of glorious deeds...no traditions and legends and fables to afford materials for romance and poetry."[45]

But the young republic was missing more than historical relics and complex levels of reference. The American novelist of manners felt the lack of something too: the gradations of social status conferred by title, wealth, occupation – and the physical signs, like uniforms or other dress, which made these distinctions manifest – hierarchies of land use and town planning, like the landscape around a country house or parish church: all were ideologically (if not always actually) absent from the American scene. Without these particulars, how was the novelist to articulate the irony of social distance, the vocabulary of social ambition? Hence Fenimore Cooper's *Notions of the Americans* (1828) complains that American society is signposted by "no costume for the peasant (there is scarcely a peasant at all), no wig for the judge, no baton for the general, no diadem for the chief magistrate." And ten years later, in his Preface to *Home as Found*, he summarized the same condition more abstractly: "Without a social capital...her people...possess no standard for opinion, manners, social maxims, or even language." So by the time Henry James wrote his book on *Hawthorne* (1879) this little sub genre of American metafiction already had a long history. Indeed, James seems to have been aware of that, since his catalog of what he thought Hawthorne had found missing from the American scene gathered and synthesized not only Hawthorne's own complaint about the materials missing for the romancer, but also Cooper's about the thin environment for the satirist and novelist of manners:

No state, in the European sense of the word . . . no sovereign, no court, no personal loyalty, no aristocracy, no church . . . no army, no diplomatic service, no country gentle men, no palaces, no castles, nor manors, nor old country-houses, nor parsonages, nor thatched cottages nor ivied ruins; no cathedrals . . . no great Universities nor public schools . . . no literature, no novels, no museums, no pictures, no political society, no sporting classes – no Epsom nor Ascot!

Unlike its precursers, however, James's catalog edges slowly towards parody – of the form (it's just too complete), and of itself, as those last two instances and the exclamation point make clear. And unlike them it ends with a joke – or at least a mysterious reference to one: "The natural remark, in the almost lurid light of such an indictment, would be that if these things are left out, everything is left out. The American knows that a good deal remains; what it is that remains – that is his secret, his joke, as one might say."

What was this joke? It is possible to think of several. One is that Cooper and Hawthorne managed to develop their own forms of native romance, the former exploiting the (in fact) already plentiful materials of American history alongside the essentially European nostalgia for the disappearing tribe; and the latter turning Massachusetts Puritan self-analysis into a wholly new kind of narrative text that interrogated itself over precisely that distance between "romance" and "reality" which Hawthorne thought America had rendered so problematic.

But novels of manners are something else. Realistic tragedy and comedy in a social setting requires the ironic distance set by class distinctions. A culture that denies class based on hereditary advantage has neither the ideological terminology in which to articulate, nor the emotional conditioning to respond to, the tragedy and comedy of such a predicament. For their novels of manners, Cooper and James had to go to Europe, or bring Europeans to America, or Americans to Europe. Where they understood European class distinctions, they used them; where not, they substituted the next best thing: the ironic distance of hereditary national difference.

The real joke took two forms, both derived from the more tough-minded psychology of emigration. One confronted European criticism directly, often deflecting it with ridicule. The second sought to maximize the advantage inherent in the very absences confronted by the settler's imagination, and subsequently listed by writers like Cooper and James: to celebrate a new dispensation free of distinctions (and, admittedly the discrimination of them) – of status, of points of focus in the physical or social landscape.

As with the rhetoric of emigration, these responses stripped away old culture and piled up new nature to take its place. European social and political conventions were not savored for their ironies; they were ruthlessly satirized for their artificiality. "Male and female are the distinctions of nature, good and bad the distinctions of heaven," wrote Tom Paine in *Common Sense* (1776), but the "distinction for which no truly natural or religious reason can be assigned...is the distinction of men into KINGS and SUBJECTS." Apply the satirical change of perspective to the institution of hereditary monarchy – redescribe the hallowed tradition in the words of plain men, then take another look at it; how does it appear now? If the people of a country grant a man sovereignty over them, can they bind their successors to obey his descendants? "Such an unwise, unjust, unnatural compact might (perhaps) in the next succession put them under the government of a rogue or fool," Paine continued. Besides, that initial claim to sovereignty may have been as dubious as its hereditary transmission. Look at what happened to England, which

> since the conquest, hath known some few good monarchs, but groaned beneath a much larger number of bad ones, yet no man can say that their claim under William the Conqueror is a very honorable one. A French bastard landing with an armed banditti, and establishing himself king of England against the consent of the natives, is in plain terms a very paltry rascally original. – It certainly hath no divinity in it. However, it is needless to spend much time in exposing the folly of hereditary right, if

there are any so weak as to believe it, let them promiscuously worship the ass and lion, and welcome. I shall neither copy their humility, nor disturb their emotion.

Generally English satire (except for the old radical attack on the Norman Yoke, which Paine deploys here) has been the weapon of conservative interests and sympathies. Here it is put to revolutionary use. Though enlisted on the other side, Paine's "plain terms" are the equivalent of Swift's sudden alterations in the size of his characters. William "the Conqueror" is demoted to a bastard leading a raiding party; the royal insignia becomes "the ass and lion," and dutiful subjects turned into idolaters. It was Dr. Benjamin Rush, educated at Edinburgh University, who gave Paine's book its title, wishing perhaps to insinuate some consanguinity with the contemporary (and fashionable) Scottish Common Sense philosophy. Paine wanted to call it "Plain Truth."

Plainness is also inherent in the positive response to America's predicament, its supposed lack of culture, tradition, distinctions and focus. An essential part of the ideology of emigration is the determination to consider culture first in its material (and root) sense of plowing, and the physical operations for which that stands: clearing, draining, planting – all the operations by which settlers turned the raw topography of the continent into a landscape. Did European men and institutions degenerate when transplanted to America? Hard to say, since there were so many possible criteria of "culture" in this more sociological sense, and so many other kinds of variables too. But return the question to the physical terms of its original hypothesis, and then we are on more solid, verifiable, scientific ground. Did the cool, miasmic atmosphere of an uncleared wilderness constitute an inferior environment for wild and domestic animals? And what about human beings, transplanted by the process of emigration and settlement? Those questions, at least, they could deal with.

One of the first American counterblasts to Buffon's thesis was

Benjamin Franklin's essay published in 1755, "Observations Concerning the Increase of Mankind." Extrapolating from Pennsylvania census statistics, Franklin predicted a doubling of the American colonial population every generation. So convincing was his demonstration that Buffon himself subsequently published a supplement to the *Histoire Naturelle* retracting that part of his theory that applied to human animals, and attributing his correction to "the respectable testimony of the famous Dr. Franklin."[46]

But now the best known of these responses was Thomas Jefferson's *Notes on the State of Virginia* (1784). Ostensibly a "philosophical" response to questions posed by the Marquis de Barbé-Marbois on the topography, natural history, population and institutions of Virginia, *Notes* was really a general defense of the cultural viability (in all senses of both words) of his native country. In tone and content – in its "disinterested" deployment of experimental data – it resembles both an emigration tract and a "philosophical" presentation to a learned society (not surprisingly, since, as we have seen, the two forms are related). Its very beginning places the region "scientifically," in terms of latitude and land area, with the same kind of precision with which John Smith locates his landfall at the outset of *A Description of New England* as "at the Ile of Monahiggan, in 43 1/2 of Northerly latitude." Like the promotional tracts and emigrants' letters, *Notes* also flourishes abundant topographical detail, comments on legal, religious and governmental institutions, and catalogs of prices, commodities and animal life, both wild and cultivated.

It may have been the Marquis de Barbé-Marbois who asked the questions, but it was Buffon who set the agenda. Jefferson knew that before he attempted to justify America's political culture, he had to establish its physical culture: to refute the thesis (as he put it himself) "1. that the animals common both to the old and new world, are smaller in the latter. 2. That those peculiar to the new, are on a smaller scale. 3. That those which have been domesticated in both, have degenerated in America: and 4. That on the whole it exhibits fewer species." His argument attacked on two fronts. The first was theoretical. How could American species be smaller and fewer, he asked, when

> Every race of animals seems to have received from their Maker certain laws of extension at the time of their formation. Their elaborative organs were formed to produce this, while proper obstacles were opposed to its further progress. Below these limits they cannot fall, nor rise above them. What intermediate station they shall take may depend on soil, on climate, on food, on a careful choice of breeders. But all the manna of heaven would never raise the Mouse to the bulk of the Mammouth.
>
> ("Query VI")

I do not know whether this idea comes from a contemporary zoological authority (Jefferson's tentative "seems" suggests that it is his own), but it goes back at least to St. Augustine's Commentary on the Book of Genesis. Concerned to make the case that all of mankind fell along with nature, St. Augustine proposed that all plants, animals and men that would ever live on the earth had been created at once, each (except for the original inhabitants of paradise) as *rationes seminales*: the "seminal causes" that program the plant or animal to be born at a particular time and develop in a certain way. So when Adam fell, everyone fell, and was in need of God's redemption through Christ. It was from this idea that Calvin developed his doctrine of predestination. Even before the Fall, the election or damnation of all human beings had been determined by the nature of the seed from which they would develop. In other words, under pressure of the need to defend American nature against Buffon's immensely prestigious theory, Jefferson came up with his own thesis of portability, a sort of zoological version of predestination. If animals, like Puritans, were programmed at birth with certain innate qualities, transplanting would not affect their growth or reproduction.

But theory would carry Jefferson only so far. True to the spirit of the promotional tract, he preferred to ground his case on material evidence. Ultimately, as he writes, "Our only appeal to such question is to experience; and I think that experience is against the supposition." There was his evidence of the mammoth, for instance. The only living pachyderm in the New World was the South American tapir, so Buffon thought that the elephant had degenerated into something about the size and shape of a pig. But Jefferson had been fascinated by tusks, bones and teeth "of unparalleled magnitude" found in the Ohio Valley, and had begun to collect some. Specimens were placed in the vestibule of Monticello (and are there to this day) so that the sceptical European visitor had to walk between them to enter the house. Whether mammoths still lived in North America or not Jefferson wasn't certain, but what he was sure of was that "it has been the largest of all terrestrial beings," and that "it should have sufficed to have...stifled, in its birth, the opinion of a writer, the most learned too in all others in the science of animal history, that in the new world, 'La nature vivante est beaucoup moins agissante, beaucoup moins forte:' that nature is less active, less energetic on one side of the globe than she is on the other."

He continues the argument at some length, but chief among his rhetorical specimens is a development of the settler's natural catalog, lists of animals running over four pages, each attributed with the weight of the largest known individual. Jefferson's catalogs owe even less to conventional syntax than usual, since they are arranged in tabular form, European species on the left and American to the right. They are set out as the objective facts of nature in its raw state, unencumbered by the judgment – let alone the prejudice – that stylistic conventions both hide and promote. In one table the wild "quadrupeds" common to both Europe and America show all the American samples outweighing the European: the bear by 273 pounds to 153.7. The same is true of the domestic and farm beasts, where an American cow tops the scales at 2,500 pounds, as against the European 763. A comparison between wild "aboriginals of one [continent] only" has the European column giving out (with the mouse at .6 of a pound) after only eighteen entries, while the American runs on through oppossum, ground squirrel and unheard of things like "Tapeti" and "Agouti," for a page and a half alongside the white exhaustion of Europe's empty space. It's a very good joke.

6

The American cultural project; quality and quantity; status and process: the possibility of American literature; Hawthorne, James, Whitman and the open-field poem

Franklin and Jefferson were concerned to confront the degenerationist theory at the level on which it was originally advanced: the physical vitality and increase of plants and animals (though *Notes* goes on to address wider cultural issues too). Yet though they could not have anticipated the exact terms in which conservative essayists would later extend the thesis to attack the moral, social and political degeneration of the Republic newly fallen away from its mother country, they certainly exhibited the rhetorical means by which later commentators could take up a vigorous defense of the American self-identity. And those means were derived, ultimately, from the rhetoric of settlement. What, finally, did this rhetoric express? The answer can be summarized in two words: material and process.

In the settler's discourse of culture and nature, "material" is set against its opposite, "immaterial." Under this antinomy can be grouped other binary sets: the concrete as against the abstract; Bacon's and Smith's raw materials to live on and to be exploited for trade, as against the morally undermining fantasies of instant wealth through the extraction of gold; the useful as against the useless; the material evidence of actual experience (sometimes presented as "scientific" experiment) as against disembodied hypotheses.

Within this rhetorical structure "process" had its opposite too. At every juncture the amassing of things to set against ideas confronted static institutions: customary arrangements like hereditary power, social and political status; the traditional gradations established in Old World hierarchies of rank, occupation, landscape, even linguistic usage and stylistic levels of register. The implicit – sometimes the explicit – American argument was: you may have the quality, but we have the quantity. That, finally, is what the positive catalog "says" – why it was such an essential rhetorical tool of emigrant and promoter alike. And that is also why Jefferson and Franklin took so much trouble to refute Buffon. The hypothesis of the degeneration of transplants undercut America's only viable response to its supposed deficiency in quality, focus, tradition and "association": quantity and size. Everything comes together in the catalog – materials, evidence, experience – but its effect is to scramble traditional stylistic categories even as it breaks down traditional syntax. The catalog is always open to chance occurrence, always willing to enfold what is actually encountered, almost as the writer experiences it. Above all, it is open-ended, because nature properly understood is not culture: its fecundity admits of no limits, no classical "finish" drawn from the abstract formulae of custom.

It is an old (and true) maxim that Americans found it easier to assert their independence in politics than in literature. Even more problematic was the aspiration to secede in language. English originated in England, after all, and the metropolitan power still set the standards of its usage, not to mention its literary canons and conventions. A simple-minded assumption about the relationship between language and literature – that the former is a vehicle to carry the burden of the latter – might just make it possible to fill old forms with new materials: so Joel Barlow's massive epic poem of American foundation was finally born in 1807 as *The Columbiad*. But more vigorous American responses attacked the forms themselves, even the conventions by which the language was presumed to be regulated.

So not everyone agreed with Sidney Willard that "all the vigilence of criticism" had to be exercised against "violations of the genuine idiom" in the "language of the parent stock." His colleague, the Professor of Greek and editor of the *North American*, Edward Everett – later Governor of Massachusetts, United States Minister to the Court of St. James and finally President of Harvard – recognized that language "is a fluctuating thing, never stable, but constantly on the improvement and decline, or at any rate changing." A "good and useful word brought to America by its first settlers," he continued, might "have survived on this side of the water, while it was lost on the English side." And if American English preserved the "useful," it also found room for the new. Critics of American innovations in usage, wrote Everett, might pause to consider

> whether a few such words as *congressional*, of, or belonging to a body of representatives equally chosen by the people, a sort of body, we believe, unknown in England; or *presidential*, of, or belonging to a chief magistrate ruling by the consent of the people, an idea also not familiar to the old world, – whether a few such terms, forced upon us by the peculiarity of our institutions, really furnish any ground for the charge of corrupting the language.

Everett understood that the language of politics and the politics of language were bound up with one another. American English, like the American political system and the settler's idea of American nature itself, was a process; like the positive catalog, it was open to accident, responsive to innovation, infinitely extendable, growing as a natural organism.

No one should emigrate "who has no other Quality to recommend him but his Birth," wrote Benjamin Franklin in his *Information to Those Who Would Remove to America*. "In Europe it has indeed its Value; but it is a Commodity that cannot be carried to a worse Market than that of America, where people do not inquire concerning a Stranger, *What is he?* but *What can he do?*"[47] This is the politics of material process, the point reinforced by the ironic application of "commodity" and "market" to hereditary status. It permeates the Americans' sense of themselves. "What has he ever done?" Caspar Goodwood asks Isabel Archer of Gilbert Osmond in *The Portrait of a Lady* (1881). In Franklin's sense, nothing. "He has no profession," says Isabel, who later tells Ralph Touchett, "Mr Osmond has never scrambled nor struggled – he has cared for no worldly prize." Osmond and Madame Merle have dis-Americanized themselves – not just by back-migrating to Europe but by denying accident and process, by seeking to bring themselves to classical perfection.

The narrative insists on this. When Isabel first meets Madame Merle, two things go through her mind: that she can't make out Merle's nationality, and that "her features were thick, but in perfect proportion and harmony...[her] hair, arranged somehow "classically"...[her] hands, of a perfect shape." "She does everything beautifully," says Ralph. "She's complete." Ralph's assessment comes as a coded message to his compatriot. "Isabel looked at her cousin a moment. 'You don't like her.'" Isabel's first sight of Osmond prompts the same reactions. He has an "extremely modelled and composed face" and "a foreign, traditionary look." One "would have been much at a loss to determine his original clime and country." Of course he surrounds himself with "old cabinets, pictures, tapestries" chosen with "perfect" taste. That is Madame Merle's tribute to him. They are two of the vilest characters in American fiction.

A third is Roger Chillingworth in Hawthorne's *The Scarlet Letter* (1850). It is not just that he fails to pardon Hester Prynne when she asks his forgiveness, nor even that he dodges responsibility for his cold refusal, saying, "It is not granted me to pardon. I have no such power as thou tellest me of." Chillingworth's evil lies in the way he explains his emotional impotence:

> My old faith, long forgotten, comes back to me, and explains all that we do, and all we suffer. By thy first step awry, thou didst plant the germ of evil; but since that moment, it has all been a dark necessity. Ye that have wronged me are not sinful, save in a kind of typical illusion; neither am I fiend-like, who have snatched a fiend's office from his hands. It is our fate. Let the black flower blossom as it may!

Chillingworth returns from the Old World using his old faith to reassert his old authority over his wife, fixing her hard-earned fluidity of spirit within the old hierarchy of gender-based possession. In order to accomplish this, he has to revert to the interpretative custom in which Biblical types are read as anticipating and being brought to completion by contemporary events – the very expectation of fulfillment in this world which Cushman said the Saints had to abandon if they were to contemplate the radical dislocation and endless process of emigration. Yet his evil goes deeper than that. It is not that his personality is distorted by a spasm of jealous wrath at Hester; he gives no more evidence of hating than of having ever loved her. Nor does he really feel his faith renewed, except as a system to impose shape on his chaotic life, and authority over his wife. Both faith and wife are being reassumed by a passionless act of willful "illusion," an exertion of blind power over the unruly processes of human emotion and its interpretation.

Properly read, this passage should arouse the same kind of frustration as has the prolonged business in *Huckleberry Finn* when the boys plan to free Jim from his "captivity" at the Phelps's farm. After his experience on the river – after the fluidity of process has dissolved his fixed ideas about the relative status of white and black, it is profoundly wrong that Huck should respond once again to the racial conventions of the old South and to the second-hand boy's-own romance in which Tom articulates them. In *The Scarlet Letter* Hawthorne has been working on his readers so as to break down traditional priorities of tenor over vehicle, of interpretation over story. So it is all the more intolerable that Chillingworth should assert his authority over his wife by seeking to freeze her behavior and its explanation into a "typical illusion" in which he no longer believes.

Unlike Chillingworth, the narrative of *The Scarlet Letter* interrogates itself, almost to the point of self parody. Restlessly, again and again, alternative interpretations are held up to people and events. Is little Pearl an elf, a badge of sin, a precocious, unsocialized child, her mother's "Pearl of great price"? Is Mistress Hibbins a witch or an embittered old woman, and was her encounter with Hester "authentic" or "a parable" or a modern "illustration" of the psychology of motherhood? While Dimmesdale keeps his vigil on the scaffold in the dead of night, a meteorite streaks across the sky, perhaps (or perhaps not) making the shape of a giant "A"; but what does it stand for: adultery? "Angel," say the townspeople next morning, "for as our good Governor Winthrop was made an angel this past night, it was doubtless held fit that there should be some notice thereof!"

Clearly this device was developed from the European gothic novel, which plays the supernatural off against the rational interpretation of the same event, and makes much use of partly indecipherable manuscripts given a "modern" reading. But Hawthorne's restlessness of narrative is no mere mannerism, not even a nervous tic in an environment hostile to fiction. It is his answer to that felt lack of a traditional relationship between fiction and commonplace reality in American culture: to play upon the deficiency, exaggerate it, turn it to advantage. And the beginning of the story itself prepares the reader quite deliberately for this process. As Hester leaves the jail, she passes a rose bush whose flowers "might be imagined" to offer their "fragrance and fragile beauty" to the prisoner going in or out. The rose bush "has been kept alive in history" (itself an ambiguous phrase), and its origins are mysterious: either it "merely survived out of the stern old wilderness" or "had sprung up under the footsteps of the sainted Anne Hutchinson." The narrative "will not take it upon [itself] to determine" which of these alternatives to invest with its authority, but:

> Finding it directly on the threshold of our narrative ... we could hardly do otherwise than pluck one of its flowers and present it to the reader. It may serve, let us hope, to symbolize some sweet moral blossom, that may be found along the track, or relieve the darkening close of a tale of human frailty and sorrow.

So at the beginning of his story Hawthorne deconstructs the various conventions by which traditional poetry and fiction have assigned meaning. With successive swipes of the eraser – through layers of allegory, symbol and ornament – Hawthorne renders each interpretation less explicit. At the same time he thickens the narrative from a transparency through which the reader sees and composes the action, into an opaque stratum containing its own circuits of self-reference: the "threshold" which belongs to the jail as well as to the narrative itself; the flower that "symbolizes"...another flower. Like Chillingworth – like America, according to Hawthorne – the narrative has also ceased to believe in "typical illusion"; but instead of reacting to this vacancy in a fit of defensive authoritarianism, the narrative empties into the void, allowing itself to flow in an endless (or at least endlessly indeterminate) process of interpretation.

And thus the narrative of *The Scarlet Letter* prepares for, and earns, that astonishing, apocalyptic ending, in which Hester is said to become "the angel and apostle of the coming revelation [who] must be a woman indeed, but lofty, pure, and beautiful: and wise moreover, not through dusky grief, but the ethereal medium of joy." Hester's "joy" in these circumstances is an American invention. Long after *The Scarlet Letter* European heroines – even the most independent of them in the most intelligent of narratives – would continue to subside smugly into the traditionary hierarchy of marriage and the classical ending of settled family life in the country – "Reader, I married him!" – or if they "fell" from sexual propriety (and male posession) they would have to fall under a train in due course. But Hester Prynne, like Dreiser's Carrie Meeber, would go restlessly on: unpunished, aspiring, doubting, learning.

Hawthorne may be said to have invented the modern novel in English. His narratives are what Roland Barthes would call *scriptible*; they invite the reader's collaboration in their writing. Sometime after reviewing *Mosses from an Old Manse* in 1846, Herman Melville picked up the idea from Hawthorne and applied it in his later fiction – most famously in the "Spouter-Inn" and "Doubloon" chapters in *Moby Dick*, in *The Confidence Man* and *Pierre*. So this too may be called an American invention. Its furious resistance to static hierarchies, its valorizing of process, come from somewhere deep in America's narrative rhetoric of its own foundation.

The Scarlet Letter was written at mid-century, the moment (most literary historians agree) when American writers first succeeded in establishing a vigorous program for a distinctive national literature. From as early as 1815 William Tudor, Edward Everett and others had addressed the Phi Beta Kappa society with spirited defenses of American culture,[48] but it was Ralph Waldo Emerson's talk on "The American Scholar" (1837) that Oliver Wendell Holmes called "our intellectual Declaration of Independence."

How did the idea of American literature succeed in authenticating itself for other Americans? First (as Holmes's remark makes clear) by striking the same adversarial posture against the Old World literary culture as the Declaration had against its politics. The phrase from "The American Scholar" that still rings out from a dozen American literary textbooks is, "We have listened too long to the courtly muses of Europe." But how would this posture outline itself as different? In exactly the same way as emigrants and propagandists for American settlement had authenticated their project: by recourse to process and native materials.

It is no coincidence, then, that America's other great literary invention, the open-field long poem, first took shape (if "shape" is the right word) in the middle of the nineteenth century. "We have had yet no genius in America, with tyrannous eye," wrote Emerson in "The Poet" (1844), "which knew the value of our incomparable materials, and saw, in the barbarism and materialism of the times, another carnival of the same gods whose picture he so much admires in Homer; then in the Middle Ages, then in

Calvinism." The first step would be to stop fretting about the lack of American association, the absence of historical tradition or an established hierarchy of references, some of which were suitable for "poetry" and others not. "America is a poem in our eyes," and its "Negroes and Indians," its "log-rolling...stumps...politics...fisheries...boasts and repudiations...northern trade, southern planting...[and] western clearing" "rest on the same foundations of wonder as the town of Troy and the temple of Delphi."

But not only would American materials upset the traditional prerogatives of "poetic" reference; the American poet himself would lose the special status conferred on the bards of Europe. If "America is a poem in our eyes," or if, as Walt Whitman put it in his preface to the 1855 edition of *Leaves of Grass* (since unlike Emerson he realized that it was its institutions that made the country an aesthetic invention), "The United States themselves are essentially the greatest poem," then in a sense the power of the country's material presences would break through to express themselves, as though without the poet's intervention. However "tyrannous" the poet's eye, it would also have to be transparent, like the eyeball in Emerson's "Nature" (1836). Too "gigantic and generous" to "trot back generation after generation to the eastern records," as Whitman wrote in his Preface, the poet nevertheless responds "to his country's spirit...incarnates its geography and natural life and rivers and lakes."

What Whitman made of this project is too well known to require citation here, let alone lengthy description. But something should be said about the American modernist genre that *Leaves of Grass* spawned. What do long poems like *Leaves*, Pound's *Cantos*, William Carlos Williams's *Paterson* and Charles Olson's *Maximus* have in common? They are all material catalogs, expressing (as Williams would have it) "no ideas but in things." Like the catalogs, they are open to chance occurence, however "unpoetic." Almost anything the author happens to encounter can "go in": something found or seen along the road, on a train or ferry boat or in an out-of-the-way book or private letter. Like the settlers' catalogs they eschew complex syntax – both immediate and long-term. That is, they refuse to subordinate one event – or kind of event – to another, and they have no plots: no stories or arguments. They fix their attention on quantity, not quality; their method on process, not perfection. So like the catalogs they too are open-ended. *Leaves*, *Paterson*, *The Cantos* came to an end only with their authors' lives. Without a plot, after all, how could they be finished?

So Americans turned to the rhetoric of emigration and settlement whenever they needed to authenticate their culture in contradistinction to Europe's. Never mind that even from the start both "culture" and "Europe" had so many meanings as to render this project intellectually inconsequential; it was consistency of rhetoric that galvanized attention and forged literary alliances. "No ideas but in things" would not stand up in a first-year philosophy class, but it worked as a figure of speech when the tide of American cultural innovation seemed to be ebbing back to Europe: when even American writers like Eliot, Pound, Hemingway and Gertude Stein were moving to London and Paris to be modern.

To the writers who stayed at home this counterflow seemed profoundly wrong, almost against nature. Modernism ought to be synonymous with America, the first modern new nation. There must be something unmodern (not to mention un-American) about any American who would need to back-migrate to Europe in order to find his or her style. So once again the old rhetoric of settlement was cranked up. First, the renegades were satirized as old-fashioned, dependent on borrowed forms, passing second-hand off as new. "Eliot's more exquisite work is rehash, repetition," wrote Williams in the "Prologue" to *Kora in Hell* (1918). "Eliot is a subtle conformist." Four years later *The Waste Land* would consolidate Eliot's credentials as an American modernist, even as it would increase Williams's dismay. As late as 1948 he was still in the war, using the same weapons. "When Mr.

Eliot came along he had a choice," he wrote in "The Poem as a Field of Action." He could join the crowd of American poets at home, "adding his blackbird's voice to the flock," or he could "go where there was already a mass of more ready distinction...an already established place in world literature – a short cut, in short." Compare this with "our" position, he continued:

> It is *not* that of Mr. Eliot. We are making a modern bolus...profusion, as, we must add in all fairness, against his distinction...We are in a different phase – a new language – we are making the mass in which some other later Eliot will dig. We must *see* our opportunity and increase the hoard others will find to use. We must find our *pride* in *that*. We must have the pride, the humility and the thrill in the making. (Tell the story of Bramante and the building of the dome of the Duomo in Florence.)

Material "profusion" as against "distinction"; "making," "building" (the gerunds convey the sense of process) for a later perfection for which we have not (and never will have) the leisure: these are the values of settlement, exploited once again to authenticate the American project. It is no accident that the American modernists who stayed at home in the 1920s and 1930s feasted so joyously on the imagery and actual texts of New World exploration and settlement; that deepest in the American grain (to use Williams's title of 1925) should be the words and works of Columbus, Cortez, de Soto, Walter Ralegh, Daniel Boone and Benjamin Franklin; or that Hart Crane, when he looked for an American nativist tradition to counterbalance the prestigious gravitas of *The Waste Land*, came up with Columbus, John Smith and Pocahontas, linked by his symbols of process and continuum, the river and the railroad in *The Bridge* (1930). Even Wallace Stevens's more measured verse forms retain that exciting sense of anticipation, material richness and provisionality conveyed by the planter's prospectus – not to mention the imaginary occasion of planting itself:

Upon these premises propounding, he
Projected a colony that should extend
To the dusk of a whistling south below the south,
A comprehensive island hemisphere.
The man in Georgia waking among pines
Should be pine-spokesman. The responsive man,
Planting his pristine cores in Florida,
Should prick thereof, not on the psaltery,
But on the banjo's categorical gut,
Tuck, tuck, while the flamingoes flapped his bays...
The melon should have apposite ritual,
Perfumed in verd apparel, and the peach,
When its black branches came to bud, belle day,
Should have an incantation... Hence it was,
Preferring text to gloss, he humbly served
Grotesque apprenticeship to chance event,
A clown, perhaps, but an aspiring clown.

This comes from "The Comedian as the Letter C" (1923). It is another project for an indigenous American poetry (by now it should be more than clear why), but it is also a distinguished example of that category. This odd conflation should give us pause. The way they usually tell the literary history, Emerson outlined the program that Whitman later performed. In fact the logic of the literary invention, and the rhetoric of settlement on which it draws, forbids any such distinction between type and fulfillment. Over a hundred years after Emerson published "The Poet" William Carlos Williams was still writing as though he were at work laying out the territory for an American poetry yet to come. "The Poet" and *In the American Grain* have the same energy, the same richness of material image – indeed, "The Poet" has the same catalog form – as *Leaves of Grass* and *Paterson*. In the formal terms that they both establish (or dis-establish) they *are* the same. Who can tell the programmatic "prose" from the illustrative "poetry" of *Spring and All* (1922), Williams's own response to *The Waste Land*, since both forms are both programs and illustrations? Wallace Stevens's *Notes toward a Supreme Fiction* (1942) is both the notes and the supreme fiction, though the supremacy of the fiction consists in its remaining tentative, provisional, note-like. The project *is* the poem. That is, finally, the American's best cultural joke.

Part II

Rites of passage

7

The passage over: how the journal disrupted the author's usual prose; how "history" converted the experience into the declaration of a personal and communal transformation

Rites of passage are rituals that represent and mark irreversible human changes of state within the community. The changes may be physical, like birth, adolescence or death; or social, like leaving home to find a job, reaching one's majority, getting married or divorced, retiring from work; or spiritual – say, a religious conversion. The rituals celebrate these changes. The ethnologist Arnold Van Gennep divided the characteristic rite of passage into three phases: separation (from the subject's initial state), *limen* (the condition of transition on the margin) and aggregation (the process by which the initiate is established within the new state). The more recent work of Victor Turner has focused particularly on the liminal period of the ritual. The liminal condition celebrates the element of passage itself; as such, writes Turner, it is always transitional, in flux. The appropriate imagery is St. Paul's of travel and pilgrimage – on process rather than status.

In the passage to, and conditions on the border, markers of status left behind at the separation phase and to be re-assumed in altered form at aggregation are dissolved, scrambled or even inverted. The neophyte has to leave even his or her clothing behind; so class status and the social construction of gender are confused. Sex is either forbidden or shared in common; as Turner writes, "both continence and sexual community liquidate marriage and the family, which legitimate structural status." In the liminal phase, "the underling comes uppermost...[and] the supreme political authority is portrayed 'as a slave.'" Stripped even of clothing, the initiate possesses nothing, so property is banished as well as social position. Everything is shared, as in Gonzalo's ideal commonwealth, which Turner cites as a statement of the liminal "seamless and structureless whole." In the process of the initiation the neophytes develop "an intense comradeship and egalitarianism," and subject themselves to the authority of the whole community. Thus, according to Turner, *communitas* is inherent in the liminality of the passage.[1]

If emigrants to America and the tracts promoting the enterprise expressed the experience as a rite of passage, one would expect to see the emigrant's change in social and physical circumstances expressed as a transformation of attitude, perhaps even of physical and spiritual condition. One would expect the passage itself – the transitional period between uprooting and resettlement, including the actual journey across the Atlantic – to be imaged as an initiation. Above all, the experience would have to be thought of as fundamental and irreversible, as are all changes in state celebrated by such rituals. Looking backwards on his or her life in the Old Country, the subject would see it simply as the past. The old life would no longer belong to the emigrant's personal or communal history, forming a continuum with the present, but would be cut off, irretrievable, relegated to a more primitive stage of existence.

Enough has been said already of the sense of stripping away, and of the Old World satire, to make it a plausible candidate for Van Gennep's "separation" phase. The emigrants' valorization of process over status, their desire to demote social and political elites, even the hierarchies of diction and syntax, in favor of an egalitarian sharing of nature's bounty, may all be expressions of the liminal phase.

The transatlantic passage itself forced a radical break with settled habits – including conventions of writing. For some it was simply and frankly a disorientating experience, dissolving the established hierarchy of art over nature. On his first voyage in

1638 John Josselyn committed this feeling to poetry (the rest of his narrative is in prose), perhaps seeking the reassurance of formal expression as a buttress against uncertainty:

The sad clouds sink in showers; you would have thought,
That high-swoln-seas even unto Heaven had wrought;
And Heaven to Seas descended: no star shown;
Blind night in darkness, tempests, and her own
Dread terrours lost; yet this dire lightning turns
To more fear'd light; the Sea with lightning Burns.
The Pilot knew not what to chuse or fly,
  Art stood amaz'd in Ambiguity.

Josselyn did not consider himself a poet, and has not been remembered as one, yet his versifying skill was sufficient to match manner to matter: the rush of his run-on lines and the punch of his spondees mimic the feel and sound of a thunderstorm at sea.

Yet Edward Taylor, who certainly was a poet, not to mention a Puritan minister – and whose sermons and Preparatory Meditations display a lifetime's fascination with interpretation – committed the experience of his crossing in 1668 to a lively prose record of surface phenomena: his emotions (homesickness, elation) as they occurred; the sights, sounds – even the taste – of the unfamiliar experience. Though his poetry would later pay no less attention to physical reality, it would always build the concrete detail on which it dwelt into an abstract meditation on the work of God's grace; Taylor's poetic particulars were, so to speak, his local incarnation.

Yet the physical accidents of his voyage are noted without any search, either restless or pious, after deeper meanings. Taylor's transatlantic diary is full of acute observations and wondering reactions, innocent of interpretation. While still riding at anchor to wait out a storm, he marvels that he could hear "a trumpet play most curiously in one of the king's men-of-war." The obvious comment – that the beleaguered refugee from the Restoration Act of Uniformity (for such Taylor was) was finding it very hard to escape the King's gravity – goes unrecorded. At sea three weeks later:

> We had a strange dish at dinner; a leg of mutton boiled and cut in gobbits, and powdered with salt and pepper, then some of the broth put into a dish with some claret wine, and the gobbits put into it; then they broke some eggs and [added some?] vinegar, and boiled them on a chafing dish of coals...

So it continues, in detail sufficient for a recipe. He hears a whale blowing in the fog, "a rough, hoarse noise, blothering in the water." He sees "an old tree swimming on the sea." Another they fetch for firewood, scraping off the barnacles to eat – "things like dew-worms skins about two inches long hanging to the wood, and the other end that did not stick to the wood had little shells on them, and that which is in the shell is the meat of them." They see "a pair of sunfish lie flapping on the water," and later, in sight of Massachusetts, "I saw a flying creature like a spark of red fire (about the bigness of an humble-bee) fly by the side of the ship; and presently after there flew another by. The men said they were fire flies."

For Taylor the voyage was full of minute particulars, accurately rendered with an unembarrassed naivety hiding sophisticated skill in descriptive prose. Only when he came ashore and lodged with the President of Harvard, were the accidents of nature subjected once again to Puritan interpretation. Having retired for the night, Taylor and the President's son heard a pigeon outside their casement window:

> we took him in, and when he was in, we would have caught him, and he ran from us, and cooed and bristled at us. In the morning he was let out again. The President, when he heard it, said he would not (of any good) he should be hurt, for one should not hear of the like; it was ominous surely.

...and even then the "meaning" is imposed by someone else.[2]

A similar divergence between landside and seaborn prose exhibits itself in the journal of George Fox, the founder of

Quakerism. In 1672 Fox sailed to the West Indies, Virginia, Maryland, New Jersey, New York and Rhode Island to visit the young colonial Quaker meetings. The Atlantic crossing was recorded by his companion John Hull, but from Jamaica onwards, Fox took over the narrative, dictating lively details of the remaining sea journey: nautical terminology of ship management, the weather encountered, the state of the sea bottom when they got near land. Unlike Taylor, Fox does incorporate the minor reverses of weather and the other accidents of sea travel within providence of God's word, but his references to the wider meaning of his experience are brief, notational, unforced. In a storm in April, 1672, "our boltsprit broke and blew the jibsail into the sea to the great hazard of the ship, but all was well, praises be unto the Lord." A week later, "we had a great storm so that they tied up the rudder bands and let the ship go as she would and whither she would, and towards night it ceased, praised be the Lord who hath power over the wind." He never omits to acknowledge God's "dominion" over their "travails" by sea, but the energy of his prose is devoted mainly to the physical means – broaching and heaving to – by which the danger was transmitted and alleviated. And so it continues whenever they traveled by water – even inshore, along the coast and up creeks.

On dry land, though, Fox reverts to what might be called a characteristically Quaker style. In Rhode Island:

> I was at a marriage...for example's sake. It was such a one as was never in New England and many of the world were there, and three justices of the peace. And the people and Friends never saw such a solemn assembly and so weighty and such order, so it was beyond words and the Truth was set over all...Then I had a great travail concerning the Ranters for they had been rude at a meeting where I was not at. I appointed a meeting among them and I knew that the Lord would give me power over them and he did, to his praise and glory, blessed be his name for ever.

Whereas at sea all was concrete and active, here both the nature of the "travail" and the means of its resolution are left unspecified.

Though we know exactly how the ship was threatened and saved – can see, feel and hear it – here the Ranters' opposition and Fox's response (soothing compromise? unanswerable counter-proposition?) are effaced. All blessings are received passively: "the Truth was set over all"; noise subsides into quiet; ultimately (the phrase is much repeated in Fox's landside prose) the experience is "beyond words for me to utter."

It seems that however the traveler was accustomed to write on land, the transatlantic voyage would interrupt the settled conventions of his or her usual prose style. The sharp break with tradition, or at least with everyday habits, the contrary excitements of physical danger and its sudden abatement, the first sight of odd life forms in a vast seascape, the stresses and consolations of a ship's company crammed together in confined quarters – all this and much else might be expected to have stimulated even the most metaphysical writer into a concrete record of vivid sense impressions, savored for themselves alone.

And so it happened – with journals or diaries kept at or near the time of the experience. But as soon as the crossing was turned into a story – not to mention "history" – it began to take on the rhetorical color of a foundation discourse. There is no better way to demonstrate this important difference than by comparing George Fox's account with a "relation" of his Quaker contemporary, Robert Fowler, who crossed the Atlantic to New York and Rhode Island in his own ship in 1657.

Even his title announces the typological frame of Fowler's narrative: "A true relation of the voyage undertaken by me, Robert Fowler, with my small vessel called the 'Woodhouse'; but performed by the Lord, like as he did Noah's Ark, wherein he shut up a few righteous persons and landed them safe, even at the hill Ararat." After that, which sets the journey within the larger plot of God's providence, the reader can hardly escape thoughts of the spiritual significance of every occurrence at sea, however physically compelling in itself. Fowler does record some adventures – an initially frightening encounter with a mysterious frigate, the dangerous passage through Hellgate, where the East River meets Long Island Sound – but most of what he mentions stands for something else. Just after getting through Hellgate, he notices a shoal of fish "close by our rudder; and in our meeting it was shewn me, these fish are to thee a figure. Thus doth the prayers of the churches proceed to the Lord for thee." The very sea itself "was my figure, for if anything got up within, the sea without rose up against me." Not surprisingly, then, his prose is not clearly demarcated between events on land and sea. While still on board, his thoughts occur in the passive, quietist manner of the Quaker contemplative: "The power of the Lord fell much upon us, and an irresistible word came unto us, That the seed in America shall be as the seed of the sea; it was published in the ears of the brethren..."[3]

"In our meeting it was shewn to me..." The significance occurred not with the event, but as a post-facto construction. And the same imaginative process worked again and again in the minds of travelers trying to argue the general case for American emigration from the particulars of their own transatlantic passages. The journey may have destabilized their expectations, but when they got back on dry land, they quickly recuperated any disconfirmations within a characteristic rhetorical pattern. And that rhetoric modeled the transatlantic voyage as an initiation: an episode of travel as travail through which one moved to a higher state of existence.

Often that improvement was registered simply as physical. Emmanuel Altham, an investor in the Plymouth Company, first crossed over on an extended visit to the young colony in 1623, during which "I praise the Lord for his goodness that I never had my health better." Less convincingly, at a time (Bradford would later recall), when some of the Plymouth people had "dyed of could & hunger" and others been reduced to scavenging for clams and groundnuts, Altham found "all our plantation in good health, and neither man, woman or child sick." Far from decreasing in numbers, Plymouth was actually adding to its population – not just by continued immigration, but through the emigrants' natural increase during the passage. "One good wife Jennings was brought abed of a son aboard our ship and was very well." But when it came to death, nature seemed to suspend her iron laws: "We had an old woman in our ship about four score years of age, which was in good health – and this I speak of not as needful to write of, but to show that God did give us our health when we looked not for it, and to those, likewise, that had not been well a year before on the shore."

"Whereas I have for divers years past been very sickly and ready to cast up whatsoever I have eaten," Francis Higginson wrote to his friends in Leicestershire in the summer of 1629, "yet from the time I came on shipboard to this day I have been strangely healthful." The improvement was sustained in New England, as he wrote in his settlement tract, *New England's Plantation*, in the same year: "I have had perfect health, and freed from paine and vomiting, having a stomacke to digest the hardest and coarsest fare, who before could not eat finest meat." The plot is clear: his health is transformed, not despite, but because of the testing rigors of coarse fare and plain, cold water. Cut off from the "strong and stale" food and drink of the Old World, he has been initiated into a higher physical state. Within a year of writing this he was dead.

Thomas Welde told the same story to his former parishioners at Tarling, Essex, in 1632. "I and all mine are passed the deepes and are alive and well." His wife and children "went ill into the ship but well there and came forth well as euer." Again, as in Altham's account, the "travail" is both travel and childbirth: the voyage brings forth babes, staves off death, delivers a new dispensation. Among the safe arrivals were "some women big with childe, and one deliuered of a lusty child within forty houres after she landed...Another woman in our ship of sixty yeers old who had labored of a consumption...VII yeares...came forth of the shipe fully cured of the cough, as fresh as egle that hath cast her bill and renewed her strength."[4]

So powerful was the model of the transatlantic passage as a purifying ordeal that it could be stretched to encompass even the most devastating personal grief. It comes as a surprise, after all his emphasis on his own health restored, to read that Francis Higginson's children Samuel and Mary contracted smallpox during the voyage, and that his little daughter died, "being the first in our ship that was buried in the bowels of the great Atlanticke Sea." However, Higginson was anxious to recall God's mercy even in this judgment, "For being about four years old...[she] swayed in the back, so that it was broken and grew crooked...so that in respect of her we had cause to take her death as a blessing from the Lord to shorten her misery." Yet only seven pages (in the modern text) later, he can still write that "our passage was...healthful to our passengers" and "we had none that died of the pox." Well, up to a point. Of course there was "that wicked fellow that scorned at fasting and prayer" and "indeed two little children, one of my own, and another besides, but I do not impute it merely to the passage, for they were both very sickly children and not likely to have lived long if they had not gone to sea."

The "wicked fellow" is a reminder that the passage could work God's punishment as well as His grace. "Given to swearing and boasting of his former wickedness...that he had got a wench with child before he came this voyage and mocked at our days of fast, railing and jesting against puritans, this fellow fell sick of the pox and died." Bradford's *Of Plymouth Plantation* was to turn the voyage across into an even more schematic opposition of justice and mercy. By the time he began to set Plymouth's affairs to "history," around ten years after the colony was planted, Bradford had (with two significant exceptions) effaced all the concrete details of the Atlantic passage – perhaps from his memory but certainly from his idea of what was necessary to tell the story. Now the good weather is reduced to general summaries like "fair winds and weather for a season," and the contrary to "crosse winds, and...many fierce stormes." What is left in this stripped down account of the voyage (only two pages in the modern edition) are two episodes arranged like a verbal diptych, so as to set each other off. In the first:

a proud & very profane younge man, one of the sea-men, of a lustie, able body, which made him the more hauty; he would alway be contemning the poore people in their sicknes, & cursing them dayly with grievous execrations, and did not let to tell them, that he hoped to help to cast halfe of them over board before they came to their jurneys end... But it pleased God before they came halfe seas over, to smite this yong man with a greeveous disease, of which he dyed in a desperate maner, and so was himself the first that was throwne overbord.

In the second:

as they thus lay at hull, in a mighty storme, a lustie yonge man (called John Howland) coming upon some occasion above the grattings, was, with a seele of the shipe throwne into [the] sea; but it pleased God that he caught hould of the top-saile halliards, which hunge over board... till he was hauld up by the same rope to the brime of the water, and then with a boat hooke & other means got into the shipe againe & his life saved; and though he was something ill with it, yet he lived many years after, and became a profitable member both in church & commone wealthe.

Here (where the technical means of threat and resolution are rendered as vividly as anywhere in Fox's voyage) God's Old Testament justice is set against the mercy of His new dispensation. Each has its own characteristic plot type. Justice balances eye against eye, tooth against tooth, turning the victim's own wickedness back on him as a weapon. Mercy grants the grace of unexpected salvation in the happy chaos of a ship's unmade running rigging.

If you are going to narrate the foundation of a new, reformed society, it is as well to be clear about who's in and who's out. Yet on the surface, at least, the distinction between Howland and the profane sailor is not that clear: both are described as "lustie," for example. Also, (and unexpectedly, perhaps, unless you know your Gospels), mercy is much less neat and tidy than justice. If the captain had enforced "justice" aboard ship, the tails of the halyards would have been coiled up on belaying pins, and Howland would have been lost. Through slack discipline a young man is preserved to play his orderly role in the reformed commonwealth.[5]

8

The liminal phase: how it reformed manners, class distinctions, health and spiritual condition; emigration as initiation; personal responsibility for failure; migrants to and from early Massachusetts; how back-migrants were written out of history

The values of initiation were powerfully inscribed within the discourse of emigration. Emigration was a test of manly fortitude, a stage in one's natural development, almost a part of growing up. Of course that test could be failed. But within the rhetorical complex of the rite of passage, emigrants always failed through their own fault: not because of illness, or because they had been defrauded of their life savings in a phoney land deal, or for any of a thousand other reasons why they may have found the American physical or social environment uncongenial, but because they were lazy, or stuffed with fantasies of instant wealth, or too "chicken-hearted" to sustain the adventure in political and economic enterprise. More generally, they failed because they had never made the crucial rupture with the customs, comforts and expectations of their old lives, remained rooted in the past, refused their inherent potential for human development.

A typical rite of passage removes the initiates from their accustomed patterns of life to the *limen*, or border state, where old prerogatives and status are stripped away, to be replaced by a new fellowship bonded by love and mutual respect rather than authority and obedience. The Puritans wanted to escape the Arminian structures of the established Church government, though they were interested in other kinds of political reform as well. For others the new order was frankly secular, though still grounded (as was much of the English radical impulse) on the idealistic fervor of religious non-conformism. "We had a tollerable good passage as is Common though much Crouded there being 103 passengers on boord the Ship," John Burgess wrote his son in 1794, "but we was remarkabley happy in having a good Captain he behaved like a true republican & gentleman." In the new dispensation of "true" value, a man (even in authority) could be both a "gentleman" and a "republican." No wonder, then, that Burgess had "not been Sick nor Sorry since I left England"; he had been carried to "a glorious land of liberty."

The apparent classlessness of America – especially in phenomena like dress and manners – has been a common theme in British accounts of travel to the United States from the nineteenth century onwards, and the topic was certainly part of the contemporary political debate in which the quarterly reviews engaged. But the observation goes back much further than the establishment of the independent republic – further even than the polarization of politics into parties like Whigs, Tories, Radicals, Federalists and Democrats. As early as 1619 John Pory, the Secretary of Virginia, took much the same tone as would later travelers, when he wrote to Sir Dudley Carleton to report that "Our cowkeeper here of James citty on Sundays goes accowtered all in freshe flaming silke; and a wife of one that in England had professed the black arte, not of a scholler, but of a collier of Croyden, weares her rough bever hatt with a faire perle hattband, and a silken suite thereto correspondent."

Pory writes as an amused observer, making no attempt to understand why New World society should have attempted to shake off the marks of rank appropriate to the Old. But for the more committed proponent of the western planting the transformation of manners in America had grown directly out of the shared "travail" of the Atlantic passage. And the "manners" thus reformed went deeper than dress and etiquette – down through behavior into the economic infrastructure that motivated it. No one makes this connection between ordeal and reformation clearer than Robert Cushman, preaching to the Plymouth settlers in December, 1621:

What then must you do? May you live as retired hermits, and look after nobody? Nay, you must seek still the wealth of one another, and inquire, as David, How liveth such a man? How is he clad? How is he fed? He is my brother, my associate; *we ventured our lives together here, and had a hard brunt of it; and we are in league together*. Is his labor harder than mine? Surely I will ease him. Hath he no bed to lie on? Why, I have two; I'll lend him one... It is now therefore no time for men to look to get riches, brave clothes, dainty fare; but to look to present necessities. It is now no time to pamper the flesh, live at ease, snatch, catch, scrape, and pill, and hoard up; but rather to open the doors, the chests, and vessels, and say, Brother, neighbor, friend, what want ye?... Let there be no prodigal person to come forth and say, Give me the portion of lands and goods that appertaineth to me, and let me shift for myself. It is yet too soon to put men to their shifts.[6]

Cushman's sermon is worth citing at such length not only because (as usual) his diction enlivens general principle with pithy specific instance, but also because it serves to modify the popular view that the Pilgrim Fathers taught us Americans how to be self-reliant. In fact, soon enough the Plymouth settlers would have to abandon their agreement to hold all the property and profits of the plantation jointly with the London-based investors; judging from Cushman's sermon, some of his congregation had already begun to express their impatience with this arrangement. The point is that the travail of transplantation and resettlement had first to be projected as promoting a communitarian social order: in the sharing of property, wealth and political power, as in the dissolution of class markers like clothing.

However motivated they may have been by the promise of an independent freehold and economic self-sufficiency generally, later emigrants also represented the New World in the imagery of liminal community values. For Alexander Cumine, writing from

South Carolina to his old neighbor and fellow Jacobite Alexander Ogilvie in 1763, America dissolved European constraints of property and wealth, and hence scrambled the old social codes:

I like the Countray very well, its a Countray very good for a poor man for any person who will be industrious & carefull will get his Bread here. The people who are reckond poor here are not in the condition they are wt you difficulted to get a Subsistance; but eat and drink well...have houses and small pieces of Land where they bring up Horses & Cattle & Fowls like wt Rice & Corn by which means they live very happily.

"America is...the Country for Me," wrote the cleric Jonathan Boucher to his friend and advisor the Reverend Mr. John James in Cumberland, from Caroline County, Maryland, in 1767. For Boucher the specific liberations from custom were ecclesiastical: "We are much less under the Controll of dogmatic'l Superiors here than you are, & amongst other acceptable Effects of such Inatten'n in our Government, let me whisper in your Ear...that I have not above two or three times in the 5 Years I have been an official Min[iste]r here, read the Athanasian Creed." But his taste for the productive disorder of liminal process did not stop with Church government; more generally, "I do not think my Pride would suffer me to act in a subordinate Capacity to any Man whatever."

"There is nothing so hateful in my sight [as] to see one Man try to oppress another," John Burgess wrote to his old Ditchling friend and political ally Thomas Hallett in 1794. "For what are we, we are all alike, all Mortal Creature, all dependent...one upon another." "Since I saw you last," he added:

I suppose I have not Travelled less than Six thousand miles, to some this would have been a most desport undertaking, but to me it was not so...[for] I have been obligd to make many Shifts while I lived at Ditchling...I did all that lay in my Power to live, & to live decent but it was all in vain, and those who should have been my best friends was my greatest enemies.[7]

Like Alexander Cumine, Cobbett was struck by the reformed status of the poor in America. "A pauper in England is fed upon bones, garbage, refuse meat, and *substitutes for bread*," he wrote in *A Year's Residence*. "A pauper here expects, and has, as much flesh, fish and bread and cake as he can devour." In America even the beggars are "dressed very much like other people." In fact, there is "*no begging*, properly so called," because the request for money is made without servility. "An American beggar...walks up to you as boldly as if his pockets were crammed with money, and...very civilly asks you, *if you can* HELP *him to a quarter of a dollar*. He mostly states the precise sum; and never sinks below *silver*."

The actual emigrants felt the same freedom from class strictures. Unlike Pory and other travelers, they greeted the new condition as a personal blessing. "I look forward with a confident and well-founded hope, to the time, as not far distant, when *I shall be a freeholder, and call no man by the degrading name of master*," John Watson wrote to his father from Seneca, New York, in 1820. His niece Mary Jane, who emigrated with her parents to Albany, New York, when she was in her early teens, elaborated on the theme. "I have got good clothes, and *I can dress as well as any lady in Sedlescomb* [Sussex]," she wrote to her grandparents in 1825. "I can *enjoy a silk and white frock, and crape frock and crape veil, and Morocco shoes, without a parish grumbling about it*." Young as she was, she was able to set her sense of personal freedom within the larger context of the reformed society. "The girls here that go out to doing house-work, *dress as well as any lady in Sedlescomb... You cannot tell the poor from the rich here*; they are dressed as good as the other."

Some of the emigrants realized that the egalitarianism of the new world depended on education and the law, then as now more readily accessible to the average American citizen than to the English equivalent. "The laws are excellent, within the reach of every man," wrote Edward Phillips to his father from Ohio in 1838, "and every man of 21 years of age has a vote in choosing the law givers. There is none to high that the law cannot reach him, nor none so low that it will not protect. The path to science, to wealth, and to honour is open to all." In *A Year's Residence* Cobbett too had praised the leveling influence of education:

> There are very few really *ignorant* men in America of native growth. Every farmer is more or less of *a reader*. There is no *brogue*, no *provincial dialect*. No class like that which the French call *peasantry*, and which degrading appellation the miscreant spawn of the Funds have, of late years applied to the whole mass of the most useful of the people in England, those who do the work and fight the battles.[8]

In other words, out of all the disorder of the liminal process, the disruption of social and political status of the old world, a new harmony had emerged. The new order into which the initiate was "aggregated" (to use Van Gennep's terminology) was both private and public. Like the Puritans on their transatlantic passage, the later emigrants felt their health improved when they reached the New World. "I have reason to thank God that I never was so well in my life as since I came to this country," James Whitelaw wrote to his father in Lanarkshire, Scotland, from New York in 1773. And he added, "the people in this country seem to be very healthy." "I have not had a fitt of sickness since I came into the Country," Alexander Cumine wrote to Alexander Ogilvie in 1766. "I myself am very well in body, mind, spirits, quite stout. I weigh 182lbs so you may think how I am, a man of my sise. Am very corpulent," wrote John Hesketh from Pittsburgh to his brother in Manchester in 1837, when "corpulence" was a badge of well-being.[9]

Personal appearance and behavior were transformed along with health. "Tell aunt she need not be in any trouble about her sons, for they are doing very well," Mary Jane Watson wrote to her grandparents in 1826. "Tell her she would not know [Uncle?] John if she was to see him; for he is altered both in speech, looks, and dress; *he is very polite*." Writing from Greenbush, New York, in 1828, James Parks reassured his father in Sussex that his younger son Joseph was doing well in Albany, just across the Hudson River. "I guess you would scarce know him. He is grown this year, and *dresses like a gentleman*; looks better than ever you see him; and I believe he is giving his heart to the Lord, and striving to please him."

Of course the emigrants did fall ill at times. But they could admit to this and other misfortunes when the discourse shifted to the reformed community relations in America. All society was at peace in the New World, and extended warm hospitality to the new arrivals. James Parks's sister, Martha Turner, and her husband wrote their father from Brooklyn in 1828 that

> We have had no parish to apply to for relief; but you would be astonished at the friends we have found, or rather, that have found us: for people that were quite strangers have called to know if a *sick Englishman lived here;* and one kind gentleman sent for a doctor, and another good old methodist gave me leave to *go to the grocer's for any thing* in his name, and others were equally kind.

A letter from Thomas and Hannah Boots confirms this impression. Writing to their children from Oswego County, New York, in the same year, they observed that "We have good laws, as good as they are in England, and much better attended to. For if a man comes to America with a family, and falls sick or lame within 6 months, the county must take care of them... *for we are all as one, and much more friendly*."[10]

So if various emigrants described America as "paradise," or a "goodly land," a "goodly country" or a "happy land," it was not just because they found it a garden set aside for the diligent planter.[11] America was also a paradise because it had worked a social and personal reformation in its inhabitants. But the emigrants' perception of their transformed condition could not easily be disentangled from their conviction that a reformation had taken place in their spiritual condition as well. Sometimes, as with the Puritan settlers in Massachusetts, this connection was acknowledged and explicit. "It pleased God not to let me run on always in my sinful way, the end of which is hell," John Hull wrote in his diary for 1647. "But, as he brought me to this good land, so he planted me under choice means, – viz., in Boston, under the ministry of Mr. John Cotton...and in some measure to increase and build me up in holy fellowship with him."

In other cases the sense of spiritual change was subliminal, but no less significant for that. "I never enjoyed my health so well in England as I have in this country," John and Margaret Griffiths wrote from Hancock County, Illinois, to her father and mother in Shropshire in 1850. But health was not all of it. "For this cause I have no desire to return to England as well as for many other reasons."[12] That apparently empty phrase, "for this cause," is used over a dozen times in the King James Bible, usually as a way of drawing attention to God's intervention in human affairs. "For this cause have I made thee to stand," God tells Moses (Exodus 9:16), "for to show thee my power, and that my name may be declared throughout all the earth." Prophesying His death, Jesus tells the Greeks who come to visit Him, "Now is my soul troubled; and what shall I say? Father, save me from this hour. But for this cause came I unto this hour" (John 12:27). But most significantly, since in this context it was also disseminated through the marriage service, the phrase marks the solemnization of the rite of matrimony: "For this cause shall a man leave his father and mother, and shall cleave to his wife; and the twain shall become one flesh" (Matthew 19:5).

Marriage, religious conversion, emigration: all three entail leaving "home" in some sense. All are imaged as crucial stages in development, out of which much good will come after the travail of familial dislocation. All three are celebrated in rites of passage. And like other initiations, the travail of emigration required a special breed of people willing to endure the testing process through which the new dispensation is earned. "Therefore good Sr. incourage men to come over, for heare is land, and meanes of lively hood sufficient for men that bring bodys able, and minds fitted to brave the first brunts, which the beginnings of such workes necessarily put men upon," Richard Saltonstall wrote to John Winthrop's brother-in-law, Emmanuel Downing, in 1631. In his first letter home in 1629, Higginson boasted that the transatlantic passage was not for "those that love their own chimney corner and dare not go far beyond their own town's end." They should "never have the honor to see these wonderful works of Almighty God" which he had encountered at sea. In his 1621 sermon Cushman criticized a whole "generation" of stay-at-homes: "Let the roof of the house drop through, they stir not; let the field be overgrown with weeds, they care not; they must not foul their hand, nor wet their foot." Such people are "idle drones...intolerable in a settled commonwealth, much more in a commonwealth which is but as it were in the bud."[13]

Emigration could be expressed in terms of adolescence or coming of age. Its adepts somehow became adult; those who would not venture it, or who tried it and failed, had no one but themselves to blame. This was a handy formula, because it served to discredit any adverse reports that might have sifted back from the New World. Do not be put off by some "of our company" who returned with discouraging reports of Virginia from the voyage financed by Sir Walter Ralegh, the mathematician Thomas Hariot wrote in 1588. Some of them, "after gold and silver was not so soon found as it was by them looked for, had little or no care of any other thing but to pamper their bellies." Others "were of a nice bringing-up, only in cities or towns, or such as never (as I may say) had seen the world before. Because there were not to be found any English cities, nor such fair houses, nor...any of their old accustomed dainty food, nor any soft beds of down or feathers, the country was to them miserable and their reports thereof according."

"They say the country is good for nothing but to starve so many people as comes in it," Christopher Levett wrote in his *Voyage into New England* of 1628, "but where was the fault, in the country or in themselves?" Take Thomas Weston's short-lived settlement near Plymouth for an example (also mentioned with contempt in Bradford's History of Plymouth Plantation). "When they came there," Levett continues, "they neither applied themselves to planting of corn nor taking of fish...but went about to build castles in the air, and making of forts...When winter came their forts would not keep out hunger...many were starved to death, and the rest hardly escaped." Why did a Londoner called Chapman die "miserably" five months after arriving in New England? Because on their way west he and his company stopped off at the English Plymouth, where they "spent seven or eight pound a week in wine, tobacco, and whores." Finally Chapman's capital was so reduced that "he was glad to become servant to one of his servants," who then put him on a strict ration of "one biscuit cake" a day. That was "if he would work"; if not, then the allowance would be halved. "He made choice of half a cake, without work; and so a base, lazy fellow, made a lamentable end. Where was the fault now, in the men or in the country?"

Those bringing home bad reports of New England "heard it was a rich land, a brave country," William Wood wrote in *New Englands Prospect* in 1634, "but when they came there they could see nothing but a few canvas booths and old houses, supposing at first to have found walled towns, fortifications, and corn fields, as if towns could have built themselves or corn fields have grown of themselves without the husbandry of man. These men, missing of their expectations, returned home and railed upon the country." But in truth, "the root of their want sprung up in England." Let none blame the country, he added, who are not willing to work. Let those "that are of weak constitutions...keep at home, if their estates cannot maintain servants. For all New-England must be workers in some kind."[14]

If the New England colonists seem to have rejected criticism of their venture particularly strenuously in the earliest months and years of their settlement, then there were reasons enough for their vehemence. They felt exposed: politically, to Arminian reaction at home; physically, on the frontier of a vast forest. They were chronically short of skills to build the material and social fabric of complex civilizations like those they had left behind them. They were uncomfortable, sometimes in danger, frequently bored. No wonder their mood was defensive.

Above all, they were short of population. It had been hard enough to persuade the faithful to risk their lives and savings on the American adventure, but now something worse was happening to affect their numbers. Once uprooted, people got into the habit of moving on in search of fresh opportunities. Ten years after it was settled Plymouth began to lose population to the more prosperous (and better connected) Massachusetts Bay Company as its colonists began to arrive in Boston. That is one of the reasons why Bradford began to write his history of Plymouth in 1630 – to proclaim the Plymouth Separatists' primacy in the mission of American settlement and conversion at the moment when Winthrop's fleet of around a thousand settlers dropped anchor in Boston Harbor. But no sooner had the Bay Colony got itself established than, to Winthrop's chagrin, Thomas Hooker set off with his followers, first for Cambridge, then Connecticut. Most wounding, and threatening, of all, many of the Massachusetts settlers began to return to England. For whatever reason – their uncomfortable living conditions, their exposed position, the increasing likelihood (given the growing resistance to Crown and Mitre by Puritans in England) that the millennium would begin there rather than America – no fewer than 7,000 of the 21,000 emigrants to Massachusetts Bay returned home in the first decade of the Colony's history.[15]

So in the early days the leaders of the Bay Colony paid particular attention to arrivals and departures from their precarious settlement. "We held a general day of thanksgiving throughout the whole colony for the safe arrival of the ship which came last with our provisions," deputy governor Thomas Dudley wrote to the Countess of Lincoln in 1631. On the other hand, "not much less than an hundred (some think many more)" colonists had already returned, "partly out of dislike of our government, which restrained and punished their excesses, and partly through fear of famine, not seeing other means than by their labor to feed themselves...And glad were we so to be rid of them." He seemed not displeased to have heard of "the death of many of those who went from us last year to Old England," because those who "went discontentedly from us last year...have raised many false and scandalous reports against us."

Governor Winthrop put the drama of migration and back-migration more starkly and schematically. His journal notes every ship that arrived in Boston carrying supplies and – most importantly – new settlers from England. Typically, the westbound vessels, their passengers and livestock arrive safely "through God's mercy" after "a very tempestuous passage." But with equal regularity these same ships get dismasted or attacked, with the loss of hands and passengers, on their return voyages, or if the back-migrants escaped the hazards of the return voyage, they sicken and die in due course.[16]

Sometimes this vindictive reaction to those discontented with the new dispensation reached as far as the courts. One of the first uses of a legal instrument against a dissident American (an early precursor of hearings held by the House Un-American Activities Committee) involved one John Pratt, who in 1635 was hauled before the Massachusetts Court of Assistants to be questioned about a letter he had "wrote unto England," as Winthrop reported in his journal, "wherein he affirmed divers things, which were untrue and of ill report, for the state of the country, as that here was nothing but rocks, and sands, and salt marshes, etc." Pratt apologized in a letter saying that he had been misled by the more optimistic tracts boosting New World planting, and agreeing that the soil, "being maunered and husbanded doth bring forth more fruit than I did expect." The Court pardoned him and let him go without further comment.

Ten years later, however (perhaps tiring of canvas booths and old houses), the Pratts finally gave up on New England and sailed for home. En route their ship fetched up on the notorious lee shore of the Bay of Biscay and was wrecked with the loss of many lives. This is how William Hubbard, in his *General History of New England* (ca. 1680) tells the story of their end:

Amongst them that were lost, was one Pratt and his wife, that had lived divers years in New England in much discontent, and went now to provide better for himself in his old age, fearing he might come to want afterward; but now he wanted nothing but a grave, being buried in the rude waters amongst others that needed not to have gone so long a voyage to have hastened their death...[17]

It is impossible to miss the note of religious fervor in this unpleasant dismissal. Pratt is perceived as an apostate, a traitor to the sect. His death is told in the same gallows-humor tone, and the irony of his "wants" framed in that same mechanism of reciprocal punishment, that Bradford uses for the story of the mocking sailor who boasted he would throw the Puritans' bodies over the side, only to get dumped over himself, as a corpse. If God worked His mercy (or the Lord His providence) to liberate those journeying westwards, He vented His justice to trap those going home, in the very words they had used in another context. If they ran from fear of illness in Massachusetts, they would meet, not the illusion, but the reality in England. If they "wanted" in the New World, they would want much more on returning to the Old.

Yet how strange to find God's attributes invoked here. Bradford's diptych of the two men lost overboard was a way of illustrating the contrasting conditions of saved and damned, as dramatized by the crucial transatlantic passage. But no one has alleged that Pratt, or the other back-migrants so despised by Dudley and Winthrop, were anything short of devout Puritans, secure in their faith. What they had trangressed was not the law of God, but the law of nature. To go home was to fail a crucial test that made them eligible to populate the new and better land. In the more fevered imagination this failure was somehow unnatural, as though the back-migrant had tried to reverse his or her adolescence. Rites of passage "travail" one way only. This is the religion of emigration.

Yet it would be a great mistake to represent the Massachusetts Puritans as unique in their contempt of failures, back-migrants and those who would not try the venture of emigration in the first place. For the discourse of emigration has always masked the reality that a significant proportion of American immigrants have turned around and gone back the other way. So if disaffection and back-migration once posed a material threat to vulnerable New England, they have always stood as an embarrassment to the dominant rhetoric of emigration.

That is why later, non-Puritan tracts promoting American emigration, like the Glasgow broadside of 1684, applied the same contempt to "our Commons so besotted with the love of their own misery, that rather then quit their Native Countrey, they will live in much toyl and penury so long as they have strength." George Poulett Scrope's tract reported that emigrants' letters home all agreed that "those *who are foolishly homesick* may be dispirited for the first few weeks, and those *who will not work* are not likely to be better off in that country than in any other." But he added, "*any labourer or mechanic, who is willing to exert himself, may be sure of obtaining full employment at high wages, and the very best of living.*"[18]

For the emigrants too the decision to emigrate was a test of manly strength and character: "Tell William we are astonished at him doubting the truths of our letters...America is as good as we have stated before; and he would find it so if he had heart enough to come"; "If Richard and Thomas was to come into this country, it would be the making of them," are typical comments. Perhaps George Martin expressed the choice most explicitly in terms of an initiation when he wrote to his brother near Sevenoaks, Kent, from Rochester, New York, in 1851:

Why don't folks ask themselves the question? Am I fit to emigrate? Am I fit to go to a new country to leave my old ways behind me, and begin life anew with everything strange about me, new manners, new customs, and I wedded strongly to my old customs! And if answered in the affirmative why not go manfully to work with a strong determination to go through thick and thin "never say die."

Like the Puritans before them, these later emigrants also felt compelled to attack back-migrants. Along with the failures and the dispatchers of adverse reports of the New World, the returnees had to be robbed of meaning. "*We cannot think what makes so many of them go back*," John and Mary Watson wrote to his parents from Indiana in 1825, "*for we would not come back again for Mr. Tilden Smith's farm and all he has got.* The poor home-sick things! were it not for their poor children, we would not care if they went to bed without supper all their lives." Another back-migrant aroused George Martin's contempt, when he wrote to his brother in 1850. "If you wish to succeed, you must learn [the Americans'] ways and conform to them as soon as possible. I really have no patience with such chicken-hearted people. Henry Clarke is one of that kind. He came braging what he would do...got scared and went home without trying any thing."

"There was two men that was passengers in the same ship as us that seemed to be in great spirits about America and after talked what great things they would do when they got to America," Andrew and Jane Morris wrote to their brother-in-law, John Birchall in Lancashire, from Germantown, Pennsylvania, in 1831:

but when we landed the first thing they got drunk instead of looking for work. They stayed in Philadelphia about two weeks and got drunk almost every day and then began to curse the country and all that was in it. They went back. They had not money to pay their passage, so they sold themselves to the captain untill their father come to Liverpool and pay their passage. So I leave you to guess what tales they would tell when they got home...[19]

Every aspect of this denunciation is significant. The back-migrants fail through their own moral lassitude. Their return journey is rendered in terms of bondage, like Levett's account of Chapman, and the construction put upon the return of Pratt and other defectors from New England by Dudley and Hubbard – that the journey back to the Old World subjected them once again to the constraints of Old Testament justice. Most significant of all, perhaps, their adolescence and independence are undone, when they have to fall back on their father to bail them out.

The back-migrants' failure could be narrated, though hardly with sympathy, but their return and the motives for it, being somehow against nature, were literally indescribable. In Cobbett's revealing formulation, there were no paupers in the New World, except for the men who have become "debilitated from a vicious life; or who, like the Boroughmongers and Priests, finds it more plesant to live upon the labour of others than upon his own labour." Or, as William Wood put it, "The root of their want sprung up in England." The only evils in the new dispensation were throwbacks to the old. Apart from references to the deprivation and social injustice he had encountered in England, Cobbett had, literally, no language to describe American poverty.[20] And when the back-migrants arrived home, they would find any story they had to tell pre-emptively effaced by rumors of their unreliablity. They would be written out of history.

9

The momentous choice to emigrate; psychological barriers to reversing the decision; "no desire to return"; pessimism about the Old Country's future development; writing home after a long silence: the letter as the badge of the initiate; "I will not persuade"

In order to understand the emigrants' strong feelings about those who "failed" – emotions conditioned by their feelings about themselves, of course – it is necessary to step outside the letters and promotional tracts for a moment, and to try to imagine the choice facing prospective emigrants.

They were confronted by an awesome decision. If they stayed home, they continued in a relatively settled network of family and custom that both constrained and comforted; if they went to America, they risked losing their capital, perhaps their lives, for the chance of greater economic, social and (in some cases, at least) political freedom. Unless they managed to emigrate as part of a community or extended family, or went over only temporarily to raise cash for their use at home, they would certainly have to abandon all but a few of their closest social contacts. Even today, when quick and relatively cheap transport keeps the family in touch with frequent visits back and forth from both parties, the emigrant has to pull up roots to move: give up a job, perhaps sell a house, say goodbye to informal contacts with a circle of family, neighbors and friends.

Before the 1960s – that is, before the introduction of jet aircraft whose size and quick turnaround left the airlines with excess capacity they needed to discount – the choice must have been even starker. Either the sailing voyage was so tedious or dangerous that it could not easily be conceived as repeatable, or (and this applied to later travel on scheduled steamships too) the reverse process could simply not be afforded. The necessary capital, whether saved, collected from family and friends or disbursed by the Poor Law commissioners, could not be raised again. As Robert Holditch commented, having quoted Goldsmith's lament for "the duteous son...and the blushing maid, / Forced from their homes" and Birkbeck on the conditions endured by the English tenant farmer, "Powerful indeed must be the motives which thus induce men to abandon their native soil, endeared to them by the ties of kindred and connections, and by the numberless associations which they form from infancy to manhood."[21]

But already we are back with rhetoric. Was the journey literally irreversible, or only perceived as such? Historians have established that a sizeable minority have always back-migrated. Even during the earliest, most difficult period of Atlantic travel, the Massachusetts settlers went back and forth on public and private business. And to illuminate the psychology of the choice itself we have little evidence (apart from Puritan journals and letters, which will be discussed more fully in Part III), since few emigrants wrote anything down until they had already made their decision to leave, when their distance away began to call for letters home.

What is clear is that having been made, the decision to go was conceived and presented as both inevitable and irrevocable, just as though it were a rite of passage. And the the choice to leave home, along with its attendant (perhaps necessary) mental adjustment, might be made well in advance of actual emigration. The Puritan James Cole moved to Massachusetts in or shortly after 1635, then to Connecticut, but at least a year before had left his wife and family in London, first for Ipswich, then for a sympathetic congregation in Warwick. It is not clear why: he may have feared persecution; he certainly mentions debts, "the great losse of my creditors" left behind, and the threat of imprisonment. His friend and spiritual counsellor Nehemiah Wallington made neat italic copies of his letters home, as well as of the various attempts to persuade him to stay, in a little bound volume of "Profitable and Comfortable Letters" relating to Puritan affairs in England and America.

Writing from Ipswich, Cole lamented "the doleful heauiness and sinking sorrows which my sinnes have brought me vnto." But he added, "to returne I do beseech you not to desire me." Instead, he advised his wife to divide his estate equally between members of his family, and to "caticise my children."

Nehemiah Wallington wrote to his friend to say how shocked and disappointed he was at his departure. How could "such a valliant champion in the Lords quarrell" and a "Job in bearing of many sorrows" have fled his responsibilities? His wife was grieving; so were his parents and "loving friends." He had "made the hearts of the righteous sad":

> Returne, returne. It is not much spred abroad. It is no shame to come hoam again; it was a shame to goe from home. Consider what Sollomon saith. He that wandreth from home is like a Bird that flieth from her nest... Youre Mother takes your going away to heart and is very sick, I feare it will be her death. Therefore I pray you return.

But no kind of appeal would work – to his faith, manly responsibilities or family feelings. Cole too could quote scripture to support his case. "David fled to Gath," he reminded his wife in a letter from Warwick, "and those that were in debt resorted to him, yet I doubt not that they were in as good a case as Shimei which reviled David." He wished most fervently that he had the faith and strength of character to make "pouerty, shame, persecution, banishment, debts and all troubles not dredfull but vsefull and serviceable to mee." But he had it not; circumstances had overwhelmed him. "My Lord's desier is to imploy me for New England," he announced abruptly.

When this news got around, Wallington's father took over the case. "You should be at White Chapell with your wife," John Wallington wrote Cole in June, 1635, "and dwell with her as a man of knowledg and instruct her and your children and saruants in the wayes of God . . . It is not unlawfull to take a journey farr off and to tarry long so we haue a good warrent from God's word . . . What secrett call you had from God I know not."[22]

Cole's distressed friends, being against his departure, had one view of a man's responsibilities to his family. Propagandists for American emigration had a very different one. For Cobbett the "shame" would attach to staying at home. Any man of spirit would be willing enough to take the chance, he thought, but the little woman might take a bit of persuading:

> A man ought to consider, that women, and especially women with families, have been long bound to their homes; to their neighbourhood; to their small circles; most frequently much in the company of their mothers, sisters, and other relations; and that, to tear themselves from all these . . . and to begin their departure on the wide ocean, the dangers of which are preverbial, and perfectly terrific to female minds; for a woman to do all this . . . is too much for any reasonable and just man to expect.

Here Cobbett back-forms the "manliness" of emigration from the general human values of independence and courage to the gender-specific attributes of the male. "He" is open to new experience, expansive of concept (while remaining "reasonable and just"); "she" is constrained by family connections, contented with "small circles."

What remedy did Cobbett advise, then? Well, tell her that she would cut herself from her family and friends just as decisively if she were to move from London to Canterbury, or from Sussex to Warwickshire. Besides, the dangers of the sea voyage are exaggerated; we never hear of all the safe passages, which are "too common, too uninteresting, even to form the subject of a newspaper." Finally, if all persuasion fails, he will have to get up and go on his own. "The law would prevent her husband from taking her out of the King's allegiance by *force*; but the law will not compel the man to *stay himself*."[23]

For Cole's friends being a man meant staying home to "dwell" with one's wife, to "instruct" her, the children and the servants. For Cobbett the man reached his fullest stature, and served his household best, when lighting out from them. On each side of the argument the wife is equally possessed by her husband, but Cobbett inscribes manhood and responsibility within the paradigm of the rite of passage.

In any case the emigrants and those they left behind thought that the break they had made with their families and friends was permanent. A common refrain in the letters speaks of their meeting again only in heaven. When Nehemiah Wallington could finally bring himself to resume contact with James Cole, in a letter he wrote to Connecticut in 1642, he reminded him that they had once been as inseparable as David and Jonathan. Now, though they might hope to be reunited in friendship, "I much feare I shall neuer see you againe here in this life but ever comfort myself in that I hope to see you in the world to come." "We should be very happy to see you," John and Mary Watson wrote to his parents in 1825, "but as we do not expect to see you this side of Eternity, we beseech you to prepare for the awful day, when we must all give account of the deeds done in the body." "Adieu, my dear Mother," John Fisher wrote from Franklin, Michigan, in 1832. "I fear I shall not see you again in this world. If not, may God grant that we meet again in the realms above..."[24]

But what is equally clear (as the letter from John and Margaret Griffiths put it) is that the emigrants had "no desire to return to England." This they affirmed often – sometimes out of context, sometimes as though half aware that they were denying their feelings – but always with vehemence. "Henry was sea sick at times above a Week tom was not all the pasage but Catchd Cold & was poorly for about a Week but is very well now," Burgess wrote to his son on arriving in New York in 1794, adding immediately, in case there was any doubt, "they dont so much as express a desire to return." Kate Bond wrote to her sister and brother in Lancashire that she "could never go to England to live now after being here in Kansas." Why? Because "the air is so light here." It is more a figure of speech than a material reason: even the air she breathed seemed transformed. Having expressed a great and continuing wish to see his "friends in England once again," John Fisher sidestepped quickly into a different stylistic register, the sort of escape into general formulation usually encountered in a letter from the bank manager: "I am so situated that I could not come to England."[25]

Something odd happens to their rhetoric when the emigrants write of returning. The journey is always desirable, never possible. But wish and fulfillment seem never to be opposed on the same logical plane. Reasons are not given, or they are evaded, or they become metaphors. The emigrants sensed that their passage to the New World could not be reversed, but to those who had never made that passage they couldn't explain why. Perhaps they couldn't explain it to themselves. And nothing expresses this confusion so well as those occasions on which they expressed their regret at the inevitable, permanent separation, frankly and revealingly, alongside their determination to sustain it forever. "*I never was so happy in my life as I am now*," Elizabeth Watson wrote to her mother from Albany. "*I never wish to go back to England*. Do not grieve for me: if we never meet in this world, we will meet in the world to come, to part no more." Kate Bond's sister had just lost her husband in Lancashire, and wanted to reach out to her distant family. So did Kate, when she answered, "I would like to see you, but I shall never leave Kansas. This is my home as long as I am on this earth so we must look forward to the meeting in a better world."[26]

In the emigrants' letters, then, the passage is irreversible. And if they seem to have been unaccountably happy with their life in the New World, they were often inexplicably pessimistic about the future of the Old. The particular public-affairs content of this feeling varied according to period, of course. "I see the Reform

Bill has had a second reading in the House of Lords by a majority of nine," John Fisher wrote to his brothers in 1832. "I am affraid it will not pass." Five years later he noted "that your good King William is dead and you have a *Queen*. I must say that it seems strange that among so many great and able statesmen as you have, a girl of eighteen should be called to rule the destinees of a hundred and fifty millions of free men, but so it is." "I cordially wish you out of that nook of Terra Firma, you at present reside in, where the prince of Darkness, hath sown such deadly feuds & animosities, between the landed Gentln. that it is impossible for a man of Candor...to live amongst them," John Campbell wrote to William Sinclair from Maryland in 1772. "The cordial and inveterate hatred of one party against another is now too deeply rooted, ever to be eradicated...As to the Decision [of the court?], I am prepared to hear the worst, & knowing whom you have to deal with am well convinced, that...your punishment will be Severe."

A century and a half earlier Nehemiah Wallington had resumed his correspondence with James Cole in New England to inform him that "The whole land [of England] was over runne with Idolatry & popery and all manner of abominations...which many of you did forsse which did make you fly to New England as to a city of refuge." But now in 1642, and for the last two years, despite personal tribulations and civil unrest, "the lords hand is open in giving"; though "many great metings of vs in priuate fasting and prayr" have been held, "and so many pursuants abrod to catch them, yeet I know not one company taken." "By Prayr" are many things accomplished. "By prayr we have a parliament. By prayr good men chose for the parliament. By prayr the policy and proiects of the wicked is brought to nought...By prayr we have got the ouerthrow of Gods and our Enemies."

Answering Wallington from Hartford, Connecticut, Cole reaffirmed his old friendship, but added, "hearing of the forlorne conditions of England it striketh sadnes into our hearts and palenes in our faces...I cannot discerne but that God will force many of his out of old England to furnish New England till the cuppe of his indignation be ouerpast."

Possibly. Meanwhile what was actually happening was that the Long Parliament was beginning to open up occasions for advancing the Puritan faith and the republican cause. As a result the more thoughtful and public-spirited New Englanders began to return home in increasing numbers. "The pacing and timing of their return were roughly synchronized with the receipt of good and bad news from old England," David Cressy has written in a recent study of migration to and back-migration from New England in the seventeenth century. "Among university-educated men there was a surge of returns in 1641 and 1642, then a falling off until a new peak in 1650."[27]

It is obvious why the letters home needed to declare such pessimism about England. The trauma of emigration was bearable only if the old life could be remembered as unreformed, stuck in the past. You moved, and felt the pain of it. They didn't. How unbearable if the old country should turn out to have a future after all: if after you had crossed the sea to live to make the millennium in canvas booths on the edge of a vast and threatening forest, the great moment should arrive in the relative comfort of England instead; if the bill to widen the franchise should become law, and Queen Victoria grow in her position until she came to reign over the most powerful empire in the world's history.

Were many emigrants also pessimistic about their future in America? Apart from the shadowy statistics of back-migration (themselves open to other interpretations beside that of disillusionment) we have no way of knowing. Certainly explicit, unqualified statements of disenchantment with their new life are rare. So powerfully was the emigration discourse conditioned by the rite of passage that people tended not to write home at all until they could approve the success of their venture. A long silence – sometimes of several years – often elapsed between their departure and their first letter home. The excuses proffered for their reticence were seldom convincing. Alexander Allison, writing from Logan

County, Illinois, reassured his uncle in Bathgate, west of Edinburgh, that he had thought of writing him almost every week for the last five or six years, but "never could set about it for I never was much of a hand to write anyhow."

Some family correspondents edged around to the real reason after trying out various verbose substitutes. Richard Mighell's first letter home to his parents in Brighton, from Zanesville, Ohio, in 1831, apologized for not writing sooner, "but wishing to give you a more correct account of what I have been doing or I might say what I am doing now [h]as prevented me till I could give a favourable acct. which I think I am now capable of." Still others came right out with it, as did Kate Bond, when she first wrote home to Lancashire: "We have had two very bad years out here, but we have pulled through them and this year is better so far. We are very busy harvesting wheat." "Dear Mother, – I would have wrote before this, but could not write you pleasant news, as Stephen has been *so unhappy* in a strange country," Elizabeth Watson wrote from Albany in 1823, "but is now contented and doing well."[28]

And even then, misfortune could only be confessed if it was recuperated in a good harvest or improved health, just as mercy recapitulates justice in the Puritans' accounts of the voyage over. This pattern of good news following bad was very common in the emigrants' rhetoric. "At Present I am very lame on account of a cart running on the side of one my feet," John Burgess wrote to an old Sussex acquaintance in 1807; but "it now begins to mend hope in a few days to make some use of it and in a week or two to get it well."

Sometimes the recourse verged on the desperate. "I hurt my thumb with a large piece of timber: this is the first day I have been unable to work with it," wrote John Parks to his father in 1827. "But tomorrow is Sunday. I think I shall be able to work on Monday." One way or another, they had to wring good news out of their misfortune. Otherwise they fell silent, or never began to write in the first place. John Ronaldson spoke for nearly all of the correspondents when he wrote to his wife from New York State in 1852: "If I am successfull you will soon hear from me again." And if not? If they failed, or could not contain their failure within a subsequent plausible success, they were willing to eradicate themselves from the memory of even their closest families. Nothing illustrates more clearly the crucial connection between the rite of passage and the discourse of emigration. The act of writing was itself the proof of their success, the letter home the badge of the initiate. It was not only the despised back-migrants they were willing to write out of history but all those who had failed – even themselves.[29]

But even emigrants who felt they had succeeded in the New World were careful not to extend that sense of achievement into a general rule for others to follow. Paradoxically one of the commonest features of the rhetoric of emigration is an explicit refusal to persuade. John Griffiths, who emigrated from Shropshire to Hancock County, Illinois, in 1840, wrote numerous letters home approving his enterprise and testifying to a sound adjustment to the new country. "You asked me in your last [letter] if I would advise you to come to this country," he wrote to his brothers and sisters some twenty-five years after he had moved to America, "but I could not then as I did not know how things would settle. And now I leave to yourself to choose for yourself." "This country with all its disadvantages is a great deal better country than England," wrote Nathan Haley from Jefferson County, Missouri, to his father in Yorkshire in 1823, but he added, "I wish not to give any encouragement to any person to come to America. If I did before they did get settled they would wish me all the bad wishes that men could wish."[30]

A historian might account for these apparent contradictions by reference to one or more of the various British laws passed to prevent people in crucial trades from being enticed out of the country. These regulations were well known, and even referred to in some of the promotional tracts as (slightly disingenuous) disclaimers and pitfalls to be avoided by the emigrants themselves. John Knight cites one of them verbatim in his *The Emigrant's Best Instructor* of 1818:

"If any person shall contract with, entice, or endeavour to persuade or solicit, any manufacturer or artificer of, or in wool, iron, or steel, brass or any other metal: clock-maker, watch-maker, or other artificer or manufacturer of Great Britain, to go out of this kingdom into any country out of his Majesty's dominion...the persons so convicted shall be fined in any sum not exceeding £100 for the first offence..."

Charlotte Erickson offers the more subtle explanation that the emigrants eschewed persuasion and forbade their families from showing their letters around the community in order to demarcate their letters home from the promotional tracts, which prospective emigrants had come to distrust. Besides, "they took the view that if...they gave an invitation to immigrants to come to them, they would be obliged to be their hosts when they arrived."

All this is perfectly true, and will serve as an immediate account of historical cause and effect. What it will not explain, however, is why John Smith should have written something very similar in his *A Description of New England* of 1616: "My purpose is not to perswade children from their parents; men from their wives; nor servants from their masters: onely, such as with free consent may be spared." Or why Emmanuel Altham, having assured his brother in 1624 that "if any man wants to adventure money to have land...I will make sure to them 10,000 acres [around Plymouth, Massachusetts] of as good land as any in England," but to "conceal it 'till others have reported the like." This was long before England was to worry about losing its clockmakers and steelworkers, and Smith and Altham, visitors only to New England, had nothing to fear from freeloaders turning up on their American doorsteps.[31]

However trifling the litany of "I will not persuade," it is an important clue to the psychology of emigration, and to the larger discourse of American self-definition which it helped to condition.

For what the refrain expresses is the utterly personal nature of the individual choice. For the rite of passage to work, it had to be self-motivated. An actual reformation – if not of the spirit, then at least of the individual consciousness – had to take place before the process could be registered as authentic. That is why the back-migrants had their stories retold (whatever the truth of their circumstances) as cases of consciousness unawakened, or puerile attitudes not outgrown; and why the "successful" emigrants wrote home of reformed states of personality and society, fortune and nature. The alternatives were stark; they were also, ultimately, a matter of personal choice. Emigration, fully understood in its psychological as well as its material transformations, was something you had to do for yourself.

10

Individual reformation as a model for the reformed community; the figure of the collective singular: sovereignty of "We the People"; the "American character"; Whitman's "Song of Myself"; how Old- and New-World values are distributed by generation in immigrant fiction: parents and children in Mary Antin, Anzia Yezierska, Henry Roth; the American drama of captivity and adolescence; back-migration and migration refusal as a personal failing: Our Old Home *and* Redburn

So the American rite of passage conforms to Victor Turner's pattern: the departure from Great Britain and the transatlantic passage disrupt established hierarchies of property, power, class – even of interpretative and linguistic style; the period of adjustment to the New World includes a temporary sense of *communitas*: hospitality, charity and equal opportunity. Yet the permanent, dominant value of the new dispensation is self-reliance: the doctrine that the only worthwhile achievements are those ventured and gained on one's own initiative.

This change – roughly speaking, from a feudal to a bourgeois social system (for many then a new model) – was as profound a shift as those entailed in other rites of passage. The new order had some obvious consequences, and some not so obvious. One is that you could take pride in your material accumulations and improved social status (even if, in fact, others helped you to it). But you also had to take responsibility for your failures. More surprisingly, perhaps, was the tendency to take the blame for disasters for which no individual could be held responsible.

In his absorbing autobiography *Timebends* (1987) Arthur Miller recalls how "often [it] has been said that what kept the United States from revolution in the depths of the Great Depression was the readiness of Americans to blame themselves rather than the system for their downfall," and how vainly he tried to convince his father "that it was not his fault that he had failed." The Depression haunts that autobiography and hovers over several of his plays – *The Man Who Had All the Luck*, *Death of a Salesman*, *After the Fall*, and *The American Clock* – but it is *The Price* (1968) that explores the theme of responsibility for the tragedy. Significantly, the play avoids the wider public arena; the question of blame is focused instead on the collapse of a family's fortunes following the stock market crash. Who (not what) was finally responsible for the various personal misfortunes suffered by members of the family? The successful son who lit out for a brilliant career as a surgeon? His brother who stayed home to support their failed father? Or the father himself, who gave up looking for alternative work when he lost his money, then turned out to have a tidy sum laid by after all? The answer, teased out in a microcosm of the plot of emigration, as seen from the vantage points of both leavers and stayers, seems to be that we all invent our own lives, and can blame no one else for the stories we tell about them.[32]

This strange dynamic in which the one assumes the burdens of the many is very American. Joyce Appleby has shown how Americans have always used the phrase "self-government" so as to embody a "radical double-entendre," to mean both an independent polity free of monarchical and hereditary prerogatives, and also the power of the individual to shape his or her own destiny.[33]

Indeed the figure is built into the very basis of the country's founding law. The first three words of the Constitution – "We the People..." – concentrate the whole population of American citizens into a single, sovereign power. Whitman imagined a poet (so did Wallace Stevens, with his "major man" in "Notes toward a Supreme Fiction") who would be both commonplace and exceptional, both individual and "en masse." The classical epic begins by establishing the triangular relationship between the "I" narrator, his material (say, the Trojan War) and the muse he invokes to help him tell the story. "Song of Myself" subverts this tradition, collapsing the triangle to an egocentric point – the American writer writing about writing about himself – and excluding the muse (of European convention) altogether: "I celebrate myself, and sing myself." But immediately the "I" involves the rest of us: "And what I assume you shall assume, / For every atom belonging to me as good as belongs to you." To put this idea even more pithily, he began the fourth edition of *Leaves of Grass* (1867) with a number of "Inscriptions," of which the first was (and still is):

One's-self I sing, a simple separate person,
Yet utter the word Democratic, the word En-Masse.

It is an impossible construction, a sort of Möbius strip of English usage, yet it works. It is an exact analog of the legal fiction of the sovereignty of the people.

American cultural historians have been perfectly at ease with generalizations about the American character – as though 200 million people of highly diverse origins could be described as a single personality. Books on the "American Character" abound. Here are a few titles of just the best known: *The Lonely Crowd: A Study of the Changing American Character*; *American Humor: A Study of the National Character*; *And Keep Your Powder Dry: An Anthropologist Looks at the American Character*; *American Tough: The Tough-Guy Tradition and American Character*. A relational sort routine on a representative bibliographical database – say, the catalog of a good university library or *Books in Print* on CD-ROM – will show more books dealing with the American, than all the other national "characters" put together. The current (1991) issue of *Books in Print* lists no fewer than 53 titles of books on the American character. "You might think that with such a varied nation there couldn't be...one character," as President Ronald Reagan (or one of his speechwriters) put it on April 30, 1984, "but in many ways there is...We're idealists...We're a compassionate people...We're an optimistic people...Like you [he was speaking in Shanghai, China], we inherited a land of endless skies, tall mountains, rich fields, and open prairies. It made us see the possibilities in everything."

This (workable) fiction of what might be called the collective singular is very different from the polity that authenticates the invisible British Constitution. In Great Britain, it is the monarch, not the people, who is sovereign – or more properly, the monarch in Parliament. Even today this sovereign power is vested in a real person in a real time and place. The Queen can be seen in her proper function every time she opens Parliament surrounded by the descending ranks of her subjects – Lords and Commons. Even when she is absent, when the real work is done, she is present by metonymic extension, in the throne on which she sits when she opens Parliament, and to which all Peers bow when entering or leaving the chamber of the Upper House.

Yet anglophone migrants to the American colonies, and their descendants – not to mention millions of British emigrants to the United States after its Constitution was formed – encountered no difficulty in conceiving and adjusting to the fiction of the collective singular, the sovereign people. Why not? The answer rests, I believe, somewhere in the nature of the reformation (whether spiritual or emotional) entailed in that rite of passage that so many emigrants experienced on settling into their new country.

As a capitalized proper noun, "Reformation" refers to an event in history, the Protestant separation from the Church of Rome. But as a common noun, as compared with its sister word "reform," for example, it takes on the paradox of the collective singular inherent in all those books about the American character and in the doctrine of the sovereignty of the people. Reform is a political act, instigated perhaps by one or a few progressive people, then debated and enacted in legislation, addressing a particular civic institution. One talks (or reads) of the "reform" of the franchise, or of the Civil Service. But reformation is both public and private, communal and individual. Of course, it had to be promulgated by one or more originators: Luther, Calvin, the many British and American evangelists from the eighteenth century to the present day. But in order for it to happen, it had to be taken up by millions of individuals. The Reformation as proper noun was actually the sum of countless personal reformations in the common sense. How could it be otherwise, given the Protestant theology of man's direct access to God, without the mediation of church structures, the parish priest, liturgy, the mechanism of salvation?

"Auto-American-biography," that peculiarly American narrative form in which an individual's life is posed as representative of the community in which he lives, has been traced to the Puritan doctrine of conversion in its New England setting.[34] The American Puritan's sense of his or her reformation was certainly a powerful influence on the idea of the collective singular, but only (I think) because it was the most articulate expression of what other emigrants were experiencing too, whether or not their psychology was encoded in a specifically Protestant ideology. And the persistence of "auto-American-biography" – say, in Franklin's autobiography, the writing of Emerson, Thoreau and Whitman – had less to do with the increasingly attenuated influence of the Puritans than with repeated impulses from the psychology of emigration.

Emigration was itself a conversion experience: a mass movement at times, but one motivated by a multitude of individual decisions, acts of forward planning, achievements and setbacks, endurance and imagination. As with religious reformation, you had to do it for yourself. Every emigration, however commonplace when considered statistically, was charged with intense drama. And even today every American life seems to replicate the founding process. The American emigrant makes – literally *makes* – his or her country by going there. The individual rite of passage is also that of the country. The founding of a new life is also the founding of a new country. And this drama of the individual transformation is, in turn, reinforced by the sense that the enterprise of the individual and the country are somehow coterminous.

If people tell stories to make sense of their lives, then these narratives, properly examined, will tell us something about the people who tell and hear them. The emigrants' letters home are stories of a sort. The more extended autobiographical narratives written by Jewish immigrants – or to be more accurate, their children who came to the United States with them – during the first third of this century unfold anxieties and exhilarations very like the experiences conveyed more fleetingly in the earlier letters home. As in the letters, the passage across upsets – sometimes even inverts – traditional cultural values. Qualities held in high esteem in the Old World become worthless in the New, and disruptive tendencies in Europe become engines of progress in America. In her autobiographical *The Promised Land* (1912) Mary Antin remembers how useless her father's painstakingly acquired rabbinical learning was in his new environment. "'Give me bread!' he cried to America. 'What will you do to earn it?' the challenge came back. And he found that he was master of no art, of no trade; that even his precious learning was of no avail, because he had only the most antiquated methods of communicating it."

Conversely Old World abuses proved acceptable when replicated in the New. Antin recalls rumors of how agents of the Czar would kidnap boys of seven and eight from the Jewish villages, settle them on peasant farms, give them "false names, so that they were entirely cut off from their own world," try to convert them to Christianity and finally, when they were old enough, conscript them into the army. Yet when she and her family emigrated to America, they were happy enough to divest themselves of their "despised immigrant clothing" and to "shed also our impossible Hebrew names."

As one might expect, these reversals of value are rendered as a rite of passage achieved or unachieved. To Antin her father's arrival in America was a thwarted adolescence: "In his maturity he awoke, and found himself poor in health, poor in purse, poor in useful knowledge, and hampered on all sides." Instead of attaining the increased power and freedom of adulthood, her father relapsed into an arrested infancy that vitiated his authority as her parent. The same dynamic "hampers" her mother's aspirations too. In the Old World she "entered on a career of higher education" at the age of fifteen, an ambition which her daughter would triumphantly fulfill for herself in the New World. But in Europe her mother could not effect the break with tradition, could not resist the family pressure to get married early, and in America her marriage subjected her to a man who "rated the intellectual capacity as only a little above that of the cattle she tended."

As these immigrant narratives tell the story, the children can always make the adjustment to the new life, their parents never. Anzia Yezierska's novel, *Bread Givers* (1925) also expresses the rite of passage theme through the dialectic of generation and gender, though with sharper irony. Sara Smolinsky, her sisters and mother are required not only to perform all the household tasks but even to go out to work to support the family, while her father stays at home to pursue his Talmudic study. But Sara too is an intellectual, equally ambitious, and as careless as her father about the effect her plans for self-improvement will have on her family. Why are her aspirations approved when her father's are not? Because she is a woman and a member of the "American" generation, for which getting ahead is the cultural norm. How is her selfishness made acceptable to the reader? By being projected onto the American plot of the rite of passage. When she departs the family for college, her journey is likened to the voyage of Columbus. When she gets there, one of her teachers calls her a "pioneer." Meanwhile Reb Smolinsky's intellectual ambitions, even though he actually crossed the Atlantic as Columbus had, are relegated to the "old" way of life, the repressive patriarchy from which Sara must escape in order to develop.

Henry Roth's *Call it Sleep* (1934) renders the immigrant experience even more elaborately, within an envelope of at least four initiations apart from that of the general adjustment to the habits and values of a new culture. As a new boy in the neighborhood David Schearl must make friends with others of his own age, learn the street geography of the Lower East Side. As the son of Yiddish-speaking parents he must learn a new language; accomodate to, or at least recognize, strange eating habits (to David, oysters are "rocks" which the gentiles "bust...open with a knife and shake out ketchup on the snot inside"). As a Jewish boy, he attends cheder to prepare for his Bar Mitzva. Though he is only about five when the novel begins, he is becoming aware of sex. A crippled girl tricks him into playing "dirty" with her; some of the other boys see his mother taking a bath, forcing David to recognize her as an object of desire apart from but also related to his own love for her. (As befits the period in which the novel was written, the conflict between generations – David, his bullish father and passive, loving mother – is rendered in heavily Freudian notation.)

All these rites of passage are effected simultaneously at the book's crisis, when David thrusts an iron ladle down into the central split between the streetcar tracks, to short out the power cable. He does it as a dare, to impress the boys; as an unfocussed act of aggression against his parents; as a displaced sexual act; as a reanactment of the moment when the seraph purifies Isaiah's lips with a coal taken from the altar of the Lord. David is not killed by the current, but the shock knocks him out. When he awakens, he begins to hear the voices of the concerned onlookers, speaking in the various accents and languages of the urban melting pot. And when his mother is called to the scene, her voice is only one of them:

"David! David!" His mother's screams pierced the reeling blur. "David! David! Beloved! What is it? What's happened?"

"Take it easy, missiz! Take it easy!" He could feel the policeman's elbow thrust out warding her off. "Give us a chanst, will yuh! He ain't hoit! He aint a bit hoit!"...

"Genya!" his father started..."Genya!" He exclaimed in Yiddish. "Stop it! Stop it! He says nothing's wrong..."

The intern had undressed him, pulled the covers down and tucked him in. The smooth sheets felt cool on his throbbing foot.

"Now!" He straightened, turned decisively to David's mother. "You can't help him by crying, lady. If you want to help him go make some tea. A lot of it."

"Kein gefahr?" she asked dully, disbelievingly.

"Yes! Yes! That's right!" he answered impatiently. "Kein gefahr! Now make him some tea."

At the beginning of this passage David hears his mother's Yiddish as the neutral medium, always rendered in an accent-free English, through which he and his parents have communicated throughout the novel. But then, after the (Irish-American) policeman and (Anglo-American?) intern depreciate his mother's over-protective panic, he begins to hear her in untranslated Yiddish. As her voice becomes only another patois amidst the babel, so the claustrophobia-inducing emotions of the Schearl family are distanced from David's concerns and set within the normative social context. Whereas before the novel was told from within his bewildered, sometimes even hallucinatory, point of view – a consciousness so intense and self-reinforcing that sometimes it is hard to make out what is happening in the story – now it relaxes into a more conventional realism. David has completed his rites of passage; his parents have become another generation from another world.

The theme of initiation is not confined to books expressly about immigration, however. In fact the idea of a passage through an ordeal into a higher state of awareness has had a perennial attraction for American readers. The long history of the American "western" is part of this subject, since its characteristic passage is to the *limen* of the geographical frontier, where the initiate is tested by the physical isolation and danger of the marginal state.

Another popular form, one which combines adolescence with initiations of other sorts, is the story of the good-bad boy, the innocent rebel at odds with grown-up society, like Mark Twain's *Huckleberry Finn* (1884), J.D. Salinger's *The Catcher in the Rye* (1951) and Philip Roth's *Portnoy's Complaint* (1969): dramatizations of adolescence prompting the child to light out from constraints of family life and often, in mimetic displacement, to kill his father in the process.

In the longest-running of these popular narrative types the testing ordeal is registered in the form of captivity. The captors may be Indians, as in Mary Rowlandson's account of her kidnapping by the Wampanoags during "King Philip's War," published as *A Narrative of the Captivity and Restoration of Mrs. Mary Rowlandson* in 1682, and in Fenimore Cooper's *The Last of the Mohicans* (1826). Or they may be South Sea Islanders, as in Melville's *Typee* (1846); or white planters (*Uncle Tom's Cabin*, 1852), or even the ancient Romans of *Ben Hur* (1880). Properly typed, even the bestsellers set in or around the Second World War come into this category, for in *The Naked and the Dead* (1948), *From Here to Eternity* (1951), *The Caine Mutiny* (1951) and *Catch-22* (1961) the protagonists are imprisoned, in one way or another, by officers and men of their own military forces.

All of these books were American bestsellers[35] (some of them in a period long before the Book of the Month Club and movie tie-ups worked so as to lead the market), so there is a strong probability that they represent versions or fragments of the story Americans wanted to be told about themselves. Yet the rite of passage pops up even in less popular books, and in texts apparently devoted to other topics. Hawthorne's *Our Old Home* (1863) is (as its title suggests) about England, but it starts with some striking anecdotes of how the author dealt with some of his compatriots seeking his help while he served as American Consul in Liverpool from 1853 to 1857.

One of the Americans applying to the Consul was a country shopkeeper from New England who had named his two children after Queen Victoria and Prince Albert, and had sent this information to the Queen, along with "photographs of the little people," after which "the Queen had gratefully acknowledged the favor in a letter under the hand of her private secretary." Having long imagined, "like a great many other Americans," that he was heir to a substantial English estate, and encouraged by "Her Majesty's letter and the hopes of royal patronage which it inspired," the man sold his shop and invested the proceeds in a voyage to England, during which he was defrauded of all his surplus cash by a German fellow-passenger. Forced "to pawn all his clothes except the remarkably shabby ones in which I beheld him," the shopkeeper applied for money – not to return home, but to smarten up his appearance and continue onwards to London and his rendezvous with royal fortune. "I never had so satisfactory a perception of a complete booby before in my life," Hawthorne comments, "and it caused me to feel kindly towards him, and yet impatient." Refused all consular assistance except for "the pittance that I allowed him in the hope of gradually starving him back to Connecticut," the poor man finally disappeared altogether, "and whither he had wandered, and whether he ever saw the Queen, or wasted quite away in the endeavor, I never knew."

The predicament of another supplicant Hawthorne found less comic. He was a "very ragged and pitiable old fellow, shabby beyond description, lean and hungry-looking," who claimed to have been born in Philadelphia and wanted help to return there. Twenty-seven years before he had come to England "in the hope of bettering himself, and for the sake of seeing the Old Country." For most of that time he had drifted around England, working sometimes as a jobbing printer and at others living on "such charity as he met with in his wanderings." Hawthorne decided that should he have been helped to return, he would only have been disappointed in, or unable to cope with the changes that had occurred in his native environment since his youth; then, like Melville's Israel Potter, died "among strangers" after "a year or two of dry and barren sojourn in an almshouse." So "I contented myself with giving him alms, which he thankfully accepted." But, Hawthorne adds:

> how very strange and sad was this old man's fate! Homeless on a foreign shore, looking always towards his country, coming again and again to the point whence so many were setting sail for it...losing, in this long series of years, some of the distinctive characteristics of an American, and at last dying and surrendering his clay to be a portion of the soil whence he could not escape in his lifetime!

So Hawthorne engages the discourse of emigration, casting the values of initiation into a definition of American national identity. Though, in discussing these retrograde Americans, he is gentler and more humane than the more strident propagandists of emigration, and strictly speaking, neither of his cases is a back-migrant, it is hard to escape the echo of Christopher Levett's denunciation of Thomas Weston, who spent his capital on liquor and whores in England, or William Hubbard's for the hapless John Pratt, or George Martin's dismissal of "chicken-hearted" Henry Clarke, or Andrew and Jane Morris's of the two improvident men who got drunk for two weeks in New York, then returned discouraged to England. Both Hawthorne's applicants are "shabby"; both have frittered away their capital; one of them, besotted with nostalgic, snobbish fantasies of royal approbation and feudal status, miscarried on the eastward voyage across the Atlantic. The other, equally out of touch with reality, has been away from America so long that his accent and manner have changed, and he would be unable to imagine, let alone face, the rough reality of the developments that have changed his native city, "the weed-like decay and growth of our localities, made over and anew," as Hawthorne puts it. For him the only future is continued captivity in the Old World, until his eventual death in it. Above all, both fade from notice. Through their politics, or fancies, or their moral lassitude, they have turned their backs on the progressive future of the New World. So they die or disappear in the Old – subject to God's justice, as it were, rather than His mercy, and lost forever to history.

Something analogous happens in Herman Melville's own narrative of Anglo-American comparisons. At first glance, *Redburn* (1849) looks to be the complete opposite of *Our Old Home*. Although part of it also takes place in Liverpool, that nodal point of anglophone emigration, the book concerns a young American whose father, like Melville's, had died in bankruptcy, and whose adolescence consists of a spell before the mast on a passage to England. As Wellingborough Redburn's ship leaves New York Harbor, passing through the Narrows between Staten Island and Long Island, he sees "a great castle or fort, all in ruins," "a beautiful, quiet, charming spot" which he had visited as a boy. He remembers a grove of trees on the side away from the water, and inside the castle, "cows silently grazing, or ruminating under the shade of young trees; and perhaps a calf frisking about." It is his last look at his boyhood happiness. The passage to England will form the testing ordeal of his initiation into manhood, and in Liverpool he will confront, not the Old World past but the commercial future of transatlantic trade: capacious docks of solid masonry (not rickety wood, which would have been the contemporary norm in an American port), with locks of the most modern design to keep the water deep right up to the wharf side, and a vast city whose sprawl and squalor outrun the maps in his father's old guidebook, even as they overwhelm Redburn with their rough reality.

Financial failure and death in America; America (*pace* Irving) as the site of the picturesque and of past associations; England as the future; and an *eastwards* rite of passage to maturity: these hardly sound like ingredients of the dominant discourse of American emigration. Yet that is precisely what is inscribed within the novel. In the first place, the topic gets an explicit airing – connected to the book's discourse by place rather than plot – when in the midst of his description of the Liverpool docks, Redburn begins to muse on European emigration to the United States. Redburn's thesis is the melting pot. "You can not spill a drop of American blood without spilling the blood of the whole world," he reflects. "Be he Englishman, Frenchman, German, Dane or Scot; the European who scoffs at an American calls his own brother *Raca*, and stands in danger of the judgement." Redburn has lost his father, but now he gains the realization that "Our ancestry is lost in the universal paternity; and Caesar and Alfred, St. Paul and Luther, and Homer and Shakespeare are as much ours as Washington, who is as much the world's as our own." His meditation finally moves him to a vision of his country's future, as millennial a projection as anything by John Winthrop. "Not a paradise, then or now," America "will be made so, at God's good pleasure, and in the fullness and mellowness of time. The seed is sown, and the harvest must come... Then shall the curse of Babel be revoked, a new Pentacost come... [and] there shall appear unto them cloven tongues as of fire."

In other words, Redburn's passage to England has been a voyage of discovery about America. To reinforce this idea, Melville has him befriend a young Englishman, Harry Bolton, who ships out with him on Redburn's return journey, intending to emigrate to America. Harry is reminiscent of Redburn when he first left New York – awkward, fastidious, genteel, inappropriately dressed for the job of a sailor – but unlike his American friend, he fails the test of manhood set for that particular passage: he refuses to climb the mast to set sail. "*He could not go aloft*; his nerves would not hear of it." When Redburn hears this damning confession, his response is even more shocking: "'Then, Harry,' said I, 'better you had never been born.'"

So far as I know, there are only three places in the Gospels where Jesus says His mercy will, or might, be refused. They are: "whosoever shall say to his brother, Raca, shall be in danger of the council; and whosoever shall say, Thou fool, shall be in danger of hell fire" (Matt. 5:22); "whosoever shall speak against the Holy Spirit, it shall not be forgiven him, neither in this world, nor in that which is to come" (Matt. 12:32); and "woe unto that man through whom the Son of man is betrayed! good were it for that man if he had not been born" (Matt. 26:24). The first of these warnings Melville uses for Europeans who scorn Americans; the third for a European who fails the crucial test of his passage over (and incidentally, refuses to pay his way with the full performance of his duties).

Harry wonders what he will do in the United States (where, after all, you are what you do, not who you are). He is a bit vague about this. Perhaps he will go round the houses of gentlefolk singing for money. Or his penmanship might qualify him to work as a clerk. Or perhaps not, after what ropes and tar have done to his fingers' ends. Though Redburn remains sympathetic, Harry is beginning to vanish from his attention. When the ship docks, Redburn receives "some letters" whose "purport compelled my departure homeward." They part, then "circumstances beyond my control, detained me at home." The story offers no reason for this strange alienation, and the language in which it is registered is evasive. Finally another friend writes to say that Harry has disappeared. To compare Harry Bolton to Judas Iscariot may seem a bit heavy. Nevertheless, in the discourse of emigration, he is, like the sailor who scorned Bradford's Puritans, as good as damned.

11

Narratives of initiation, raw and cooked: I
The first western: John Smith's General History*: why Henry Adams thought it was not history at all; how the text evolved so that social processes were displaced by a journey of self-discovery*

Whatever their differences, Hawthorne, Melville, Mary Antin, Anzia Yezierska and Henry Roth all defined the process of becoming American as a passage out to the edges of experience, a life-changing transformation in physical and emotional condition – a process from which any backsliding was a revolt against nature. To become American was to be tested by the unfamiliar – perhaps even the threatening: initiated into higher state of existence.

But it was the western, of all the popular American literary and dramatic forms, that treated this initiation most schematically. Actually, the word "form" is wrong here, since the western is more of a topic than a genre. American westerns can take many forms, from John Filson's fictionalized biography of Daniel Boone in his *Discovery, Settlement and Present State of Kentucke* (1784) and James Fenimore Cooper's *Leather-Stocking* Tales (1823–41), through the popular almanacks and dime novels, down to western movies of the 1940s and 1950s. What they have in common is a region – or more precisely, a condition of being in or on the border between culture and nature, the familiar and the alien, which Americans have called the frontier.

Though all American westerns may be said, loosely speaking, to have "mythic" elements, not all have been set out as fiction.

The longest-lived type is an apparently factual personal narrative of one person's encounter with the American wilderness lying beyond the western frontier. It is this kind of western that bears the closest relationship, in subject, style and tone, to the emigrant's letter and the settlement tract. Indeed, in a sense, that is what it is: a first-hand account of how one person left his or her traditionary culture for a voyage to the margin, and returned to reaggregate into a distinctly American dispensation.

Of course the frontier moved westwards throughout almost the first three centuries of American history – as long as it took to settle the continent – yet the larger topic of the "western" personal narrative remained the same. America was found, founded, invented, defined over and over again – every time the story was told of how someone found America for him- or herself. These last two chapters in Part II are about two such narratives, and about how the evolution of their texts paralleled the process of their initiations.

The earlier of these stories is very early indeed, yet it is undoubtedly America's first western. It has been so perennially popular with American readers that (though it cannot be said to have been about America as a nation) it has become part of the national folklore, and been turned into a foundation narrative of the American difference.

John Smith's narrative of the settlement of Virginia, and of the exploration of the wilderness surrounding the camp at Jamestown, was published as *The General History of Virginia* in 1623. But that was only his final version of the story. Earlier accounts had appeared as *A True Relation of Such Occurrences and Accidents of Noate as Hath Hapned in Virginia* (1608), and *The Proceedings of the English Colonie in Virginia* (1612). To the *Proceedings* Smith seems to have contributed little – possibly just parts of the first two short chapters. *The General History*, though compiled by Smith, is also the work of many hands, and even incorporates large excerpts of Richard Hakluyt's *The Principal Navigations...of the English Nation (1598 – 1600)*. But Book III, the expanded narrative of what happened to the English planters in the first year of their settlement, is Smith's own, according to the most recent editor of the complete works, Philip Barbour.[36] In other words, apart from the notional and conjectural fragments in *The Proceedings*, Smith wrote two versions of his adventures in Virginia. To compare the two is to be allowed a fascinating insight into how the discourse of American initiation developed.

The *True Relation*, covering the settlement and first year of the Jamestown colony, is arranged as a series of sorties out into the wilderness: to trade with the Indians for immediate provisions, and to explore rivers like the Chickahominy for evidence of a Northwest passage. Smith himself goes on all nine of these excursions, sometimes by himself, sometimes as the leader of a small band.

Typically what happens on these trips is that Smith encounters Indians from whom he anticipates hostility but actually receives generous hospitality and gifts of profuse natural bounty, "the people in all places kindely intreating us, daunsing and feasting us with strawberries, Mulberries, Bread, Fish, and other their Countrie provisions whereof we had plenty." When he returns, he finds the camp in some dissension – sometimes minor, often serious. Sometimes he has been suspected and falsely accused in his absence.

If a single idea emerges from these exploratory ventures, it is that Smith gets along better with the Indians than with his English confederates. But even that is to suggest more shape than the account conveys. There is not much to connect the episodes; they do not add to each other in theme or event. The story does not develop; indeed, there is not much of a story at all. Nor does Smith glorify his role as explorer. By his own admission, he is sometimes wrong about the Indians' motives. At one point he falls into a quagmire.

In a long central passage Smith may or may not (it is not clear) become the Indians' captive. In any case, he is led around the country to meet various "kings," with whom he exchanges scientific knowledge for information about their tribal and religious ceremonies, until they come to the camp of the great "Emperour" himself, Powhatan. Here he is made welcome. He and Powhatan also discuss religion, and the geography of their respective home regions.

Later, relations between the English and the Indians deteriorate, though characteristically in this account, no reason is given for this. The English capture some Indians and shut them up in the fort. "Pocahuntas," first described here as Powhatan's daughter, "a child of tenne yeares old" of great "wit and spirit," and not even named when first mentioned, is sent to plead for the Indians' freedom. The English grant her request, "in regard of her fathers kindnesse in sending her."

It is the *General History* that gives us back our familiar Pocahontas. In this version Smith's sorties into the wilderness are reduced to three, though others are mentioned, and the story develops as each exploration proves more lengthy and crucial than the one before. In the first, Smith and twenty men set out to discover the head of the river. They are treated with kindness by the "people in all parts," until they return to within twenty miles of Jamestown, when the Indians begin to act suspiciously. On returning to the camp, they find "17 men hurt, and a boy slaine by the Salvages." Before this Smith and the "President" of the plantation, Edward Maria Wingfield, have argued over whether to surround the camp with a stockade, Smith considering it prudent and Wingfield provocative. Now Wingfield agrees "the Fort should be pallisadoed."

Smith's first return to the English settlement also resolves another long-standing quarrel with Wingfield and the other aristocratic members of the Council. Falsely accused of mutiny while the fleet had been replenished in the Canary Islands, Smith had been clapped in irons on the way over, and denied membership of the Council when they landed. Now, having proved himself in exploration and Indian trade as in his estimate of the efficacy of pallisades, he is allowed to join the Council. Shortly afterwards, when caught out in a plan to escape the colony and head back to England, Wingfield is deposed as "President," a post to which Smith himself would eventually be elected.

On the second excursion Smith and "some of his workmen" set out to trade with the natives for food. At first the Indians scorn them by offering only "a handfull of Corne, [and] a peece of bread, for their swords and muskets." When his friendly approach fails, Smith gets tough and opens fire. The Indians retreat, then emerge from the woods to attack the settlers "with a most hydeous noyse" and carrying "their *Okee* (which was an Idoll made of skinnes, stuffed with moss, all painted and hung with chaines and copper)...before them." Smith and his men answer the assault with "muskets loaden with Pistoll shot, [so] that down fell their God, and divers lay sprauling on the ground," and the rest run away. When they return to "redeeme their *Okee*," Smith suggests some serious trading this time: beads, copper and hatchets, in return for provisions. The Indians agree, and bring him "Venison, Turkies, wilde foule, bread, and what they had, singing and dauncing in signe of friendship till they departed."

On their return, the trading party find Wingfield and others preparing once again to set sail for England. When Smith's unexpected return has "the plot discovered to him, much trouble he had to prevent it, till with store of sakre [small cannon] and musket shot he forced them to stay or sinke in the river." But now with the Indians offering more corn than the English have ever asked for, and with

> winter approaching, the rivers became so covered with swans, geese, duckes, and cranes, that we daily feasted with good bread, Virginia pease, pumpions, and putchamins, fish, fowle, and diverse sorts of wild beasts as fat as we could eate them: so that none of our Tuftaffety humorists desired to goe for England.[37]

But, as Smith puts it, "our comædies never endured long without a Tragedie." Criticized for not accomplishing the exploration of the Chickahominy, Smith is ordered again out into the wilderness. This time, with Smith away up river, his men are attacked by the Indians without warning, and one of them is killed. After a fight, Smith is captured, then taken around various Indian camps, where "many strange triumphes and conjurations [are] made of him." At one camp the Indians "cast themselves into a ring, dauncing in...severall postures, and singing and yelling out...hellish notes and screeches, being strangely painted." At another he is sitting in the long house, "when came skipping in a great grim fellow, all painted over with coale, mingled with oyle; and many Snakes and Wesels skins stuffed with mosse...[followed by] three more such like devils." After this ordeal "the Kings brother" invites him to his house, "where, with as many platters of bread, foule, and wild beasts, as did environ him, he bid him wellcome."

Finally he is brought to the "Emperor," Powhatan, who prepares to kill him as a sacrifice. They fetch two large stones, on which they force Smith to lay his head, preparing to beat out his brains with their clubs. This is when Pocahontas enters American mythology. "Pocahontas the Kings dearest daughter, when no intreaty could prevaile, got his head in her armes, and laid her owne upon his to save him from death: whereat the Emperour was content he should live."

At length, Powhatan sends Smith back to Jamestown to trade the "Country of Capahowosick" for "two great gunnes, and a gryndestone." Their return to the English settlement finds it once again "all in combustion, the stronger preparing to run away once more with the Pinnace; which with the hazzard of his life, with Sakre falcon and musket shot, Smith forced now the third time to stay or sinke." He also thwarts a plot to put him to death for the loss of two of his men, taking "such order with such Lawyers, that he layed them by the heeles till he sent some of them prisoners for England." These tensions resolved, Pocahontas arrives "ever once in foure or five dayes" to "bring him so much provision, that saved many of their lives, that els for all this had starved with hunger."

Henry Adams could not understand how so many Americans could have come to believe such rubbish for so long. While living in London to assist his father, the American Minister to the Court of St. James during the Civil War, Adams took time off from his duties at the Embassy to check the *General History* against the *True Relation* and other accounts of the Jamestown settlement in *Purchas his Pilgrimage* (1613) and William Strachey's *The Historie of Travell into Virginia Britannia*, which the Hakluyt Society had published in 1849. In a celebrated essay published in the *North American* after the War, Adams notes how in *The General History* Smith aggrandizes his role in both the leadership of the Virginia Colony and the exploration of the surrounding wilderness. All those feats of arms with saker falcon (small cannon) and musket shot are missing from the *True Relation*. If anyone deserves credit for making the colony a success, it is not Smith, Adams argued, but Sir Thomas Dale, who assumed the governorship of the colony in 1611.

As for Pocahontas, if she was only ten years old in the *Relation*, how could she have been Smith's paramour in the *History*? Other accounts tell how she was captured by the English, married to John Rolfe in 1613, then taken to England, where she was presented at court and became an exotic exhibit in fashionable London. On her way back to Virginia she died at Gravesend in 1617. According to Adams, Smith built his relationship with Pocahontas into the *History* in order to recruit her fame to his service. After his return to England following a gunpowder accident in 1609, "the Virginia Company, notwithstanding his applications, never employed him again." Now he was exploiting her reputation to get taken on as advisor to the venture to New England. "In the absence of criticism," Adams concludes acidly, "his [*General History*] has survived to become the standard authority on Virginian history. The readiness with which it was received is scarcely so remarkable as the credulity which has left it unquestioned almost to the present day."[38]

It is a brilliant essay in historical "criticism," even if

speculatively ungenerous about Smith's motives. Yet even today, over a century after Adams blew the whistle, the American people prefer (or rather, know only) the second, more heavily plotted and more fictitious of Smith's two narratives. The diligent historian would need to explain that phenomenon too. That is why a closer, more analytical look at the two stories is appropriate here.

The *Relation* cannot be defined in terms of a dominant theme, but it does present the repeated motif of Smith's fear of, or uncertainty about, the Indians' intentions, followed by their friendliness and hospitality. Nature suspected grants its gifts unasked. The English respond in turn to the Indians, when they yield up their Indian captives "in regard of her fathers kindnesse" in sending Pocahontas for them. In this version the only hostility that remains is that between Smith and Wingfield's party.

In other words the contemporary genre to which the *Relation* most closely approximates is the pastoral. The English and Indians set up a pastoral dialogue between culture and nature (even, at one point, as in *As You Like it*, exchanging the "science" of the city for the natural lore of the country). There is the same surprise when civil behavior is unexpectedly encountered in savage settings (again, see *As You Like it*, especially II, vii) and vice versa; and the same sense of harmony, at the end of each sortie, in the natural bounty of food offered unexpected and undeserved – a kind of natural grace – ratified, just as at the end of a pastoral romance or comedy, with "dauncing and feasting."

If the *Relation* is a pastoral, the *History* is a foundation epic. It begins *in medias res*, at its furthest point from home (literally and figuratively) and greatest state of disorder, from which the hero's quest leads the discourse back to a normative order which is also the birth of a new *ethos*. Although the action ends in harmony ratified by dancing, its resolution is not granted unexpectedly as in the pastoral version, but earned through struggle. It's not that Smith is uncertain about the Indians' motives, fearing them without justification; in the *History* the Indians really are dangerous and unpredictable, and have in each case to be subdued before they will grant their natural benisons. Initiated into the mysteries of life beyond the pale, able to respond to immediate stimuli, impassive in the face of noisy threats, Smith wins the Indians' respect, finally their friendship and the natural bounty which they dispense. On the third and most trying of his exploits, tested by the ordeal of captivity and the threat of death, he wins the heart of the Indian maiden who represents the New World.

The dispute in camp about the need to fortify it, and the proof of Smith's perspicacity when the Indians attack in his absence, are not just there to establish him as a man of action in contrast to the "Tuftaffety humorists" who stay behind. Smith is able to learn from New World experience; they are (again, literally) clothed in the habits of the Old. They want to do things by the book; he wants the English to adapt their behavior to the novel conditions of the New World. In addition, Smith represents Wingfield and his party as aristocrats; his quarrel with them is a matter of class as much as of policy. In their snobbery and authoritarian mode of government, just as in their tradition-bound strategy for settlement, they remain unreformed by the rite of passage across the Atlantic to the margins of civilization in the wilderness of Virginia.

As with other epics, *The General History* enfolds the human plot within the plot of the gods. The divine purpose is not mentioned in the *Relation*, but the *History* alludes to it with linking phrases like "But almightie God (by his divine providence) had mollified the hearts of those stern Barbarians with compassion." And Smith himself is God's agent. There is probably nothing significant in his reducing his forays into the wilderness to three, the number of the Trinity, but his return journeys to disorder and resistance in the camp are certainly represented so as to remind the reader of Moses rejoining the Israelites after sighting the Promised Land and receiving the Ten Commandments. In Chapter 32 of Exodus Moses comes down from Mount Sinai to find the people he has led across the wilderness fallen into apostacy, paying homage to the idols of the old dispensation, reversing their reformation.

When he finds them worshiping the golden calf, Moses orders the idol to be ground up, mixed with water and given to the Israelites to drink. Then, he orders the sons of Levi to "slay every man his brother, and every man his companion, and every man his neighbour," "about three thousand men" in all.

This may be why Smith added his punishment of Wingfield's party with "sakre falcon and musket shot" to the *History* version of his story: not just to boast of his courageous action but also to reinforce the parallel between Moses's mission in the wilderness and his own. He has gone to spy out the lie of the land, to get food for the English, to discover how to deal with the Indians – as it were, to receive the "law" by which the English were to survive in the new dispensation – only to find on his return that the English have fallen into apostacy. Even after their life-changing transatlantic passage, they are still obsessed with fine distinctions of rank and status, still conducting the planting and defense of the fort according to theories brought over from England. Now, worst of all, they are seeking actually to reverse that passage, to turn tail and run home rather than confront the invigorating challenge of the new. Smith's reaction, like Moses's, is violent, because he is fighting to defend a reformation hard won.

Henry Adams was right. *The General History* is fiction, not fact. It is also America's first foundation narrative – earlier even than Bradford's more specialized History of Plymouth Plantation – and the world's first western. It is a "western" because it reads man's experience on the American frontier as a struggle between the opposing forces of civilization and barbarism. It is an American foundation narrative because in it a representative individual finds out about himself even as he explores the topography around him. To become American is to to undergo a second adolescence beyond the biological and social process through which every human being passes, in order to discover a distinctive landscape both within and outside the American character.

12

Narratives of initiation: raw and cooked: II
The evolution of Francis Parkman's The Oregon Trail*; how the English out West fail to adapt to the new environment; how Parkman's health improves as he achieves a controlling prospect of western topography*

Americans and others who went west to settle – say, along the Oregon Trail to California or the Pacific Northwest – also called themselves emigrants, and their letters written to their families further east show rhetorical features similar to those examined earlier in this study.[39] For educated easterners the West was more a resort, or an outward-bound school, than a place of residence. They went out and back, and were very articulate about what the experience meant, both to themselves and to their country. But for them too the journey west replicated that first experience of emigration to America. The encounter with the frontier was an initiation into American manhood. It toughened their character, made it self-reliant, but reflection on the experience also sharpened the distinct outline of the American character in the public sense.

Mention of easterners proving themselves in the West even as they sought to define what made their country distinct puts most Americans in mind of Theodore Roosevelt and his friend Owen Wister, author of *The Virginian* (1902) – and above all, of the thesis outlined by Frederick Jackson Turner in his seminal lecture given to a meeting of the American Historical Association at the Chicago World's Fair in 1893.

In fact, narratives of western discovery and personal initiation began early in the 1800s and by mid century had become almost a national project. The *History of the Expedition under the Command of Captains Lewis and Clark*, edited by the President of the Second Bank of the United States, celebrated Jefferson's popular Louisiana Purchase by which the French were bought out of a vast tract of land across the middle of North America in 1803. Washington Irving's "A Tour on the Prairies" marked his farewell to Europe after seventeen years of living and working there. His widely reported speech in New York in June, 1832 advertized his return in glowing patriotic terms that a recent immigrant was delighted to crib when writing home in the same month to justify his decision to become American.[40] In the autumn he went off to rediscover his country on a voyage to the frontier. John Charles Frémont's *Report of the Exploring Expedition to the Rocky Mountains*..., published by the US Government in 1845, was widely used by forty-niners crossing the country in search of adventure and California gold in 1849 and 1850.

As the American character developed through its initiation on the frontier, so did the text in which that process was defined. Twentieth-century editions of journals, diaries and other early drafts of popular books of discovery, like Reuben Thwaites's eight-volume edition of the notebooks and journals of Lewis and Clark (1904) and John Francis McDermott's *The Western Journals of Washington Irving* (1944), afford a fascinating insight into this double development of text and character on the margin of experience.

When historians and literary critics began to compare the raw notes with the cooked texts as published, they came to the same conclusion as had Henry Adams when comparing John Smith's *Relation* with his *History*: the earlier the better. They preferred the rough versions to their later, more formally plotted elaborations. Nineteenth-century American writing on the West, they thought, had suffered a dilution in immediacy and vernacular pungency as the fragmentary diaries and journals, so richly full of material details about events as they happened, were edited, bowdlerized, rhetoricized (whether by the author himself or by editorial hands) in order to market the product to an eastern readership.[41]

Sometimes even the scholarly editors of the journals themselves shared this critical judgment. In 1846 Francis Parkman traveled through Missouri, along the River Platte to the camp of the Oglalla Sioux, in what is now Wyoming, keeping a journal of the expedition. He published a narrative of the trip in the *Knickerbocker Magazine* from February, 1847 through February, 1849, under the title, "The Oregon Trail. Or a Summer's Journey out of Bounds." The book version, substantially the same as that in the *Knickerbocker*, though adding a chapter and correcting a number of typological errors, came out in 1849 with a new title to catch the forty-niner trade, *The California and Oregon Trail: Being Sketches of Prairie and Rocky Mountain Life.*

Mason Wade, who edited Parkman's original journal of the expedition, thought that "The journal lost much...in the process of...being transmuted into book form." Parkman's companion on the journey, his cousin Quincey Adams Shaw, read the notebooks aloud to Parkman as the latter underwent medical treatment, then took down the version Parkman "dictated after recasting the narrative in his head." "Shaw made the Oregon Trail trip for sport, adventure, and his health," Wade adds, and his "outlook helped to shape the book into an adventure story." Then "still more of the original quality was lost" when Charles Eliot Norton revised the *Knickerbocker* pieces for book publication "in accordance with the literary amenities as then understood by right-thinking Bostonians."

The Oregon Trail had been enervated not only by this disastrous mediation but also by Parkman himself, who when he wrote (or dictated, or collaborated in producing) the book "had yet to shed the rhetorical impedimenta with which Harvard had encumbered his style, and...was self-consciously trying to be literary under the influence of his own literary idols, Byron and Cooper," according to Mason Wade. And "more serious than this Bowdlerizing [by Shaw and Norton] was the attempt to make literature out of history, for which Parkman himself must bear the ultimate blame."[42]

The implication is clear enough. The "real" West – like the emigrants' New World, the domain of nature – had been falsified by effete Brahmin culture. Yet pass over that confident distinction between "literature" and "history" and admit that (regrettably or otherwise) the *Oregon Trail* is indeed a kind of literature. The serious question is, how does the *Oregon Trail* work in its own right? As in Smith's case, a comparison between Parkman's raw and cooked versions of his frontier experience will yield an important perspective on the process by which the text evolved into a statement about a distinctive American character.

An early clue comes in the way the journal and the book treat a party of three English adventurers with whom Parkman and his friends traveled for a while. On the journal the English make no very profound impact; references to them are brief and fairly balanced in tone. On May 11, 1846, Parkman's party arrived at Fort Leavenworth, on the Missouri River above what is New Kansas City, and "in a level meadow by a wooded stream we saw the horses and tents of our English friends – a welcome sight." Three days later, on the way west, "[The Englishmen's] waggon stuck badly in the mud several times and had to be unloaded." On May 19, "The Englishmen, as usual, were impatient to get on the moment they had snatched a dinner – we chose to remain, as our mules were much tired. So the parties were again separated." One of the English party seemed "jealous of his authority and desirous of having all his own way," but "Capt. C[handler] and his brother [were] of a different stamp – very good-natured, sociable fellows."

Parkman had not always been so relaxed about the British. Three years before his Oregon Trail journey he had gone on the grand tour of Europe, and of this experience too he kept a journal. In Rome on February 22, 1844, the American holiday prompted a comparison of national manners:

the birthday of Washington. The Americans here must needs get up a dinner, with speeches, toasts, etc. It was like a visit home. There they sat, slight, rather pale and thin men, not like beef-fed and ruddy Englishmen; very quiet and apparently timid; speaking low to the waiters instead of roaring in the imperative tone of John Bull. There was not a shadow of that boisterous and haughty confidence of manner that you see among Englishmen... There are a number of American artists here, some of them fine fellows. In fact, it is some consolation, after looking at the thin faces, narrow shoulders, and awkward attitudes of the "Yankees," to remember that in genius, enterprise, and courage – nay, in bodily strength – they are a full match for the sneering Englishman.

He liked the Scots, but hated London. St. Paul's, "which the English ridiculously compare to St. Peter's, is without exception the dirtiest and gloomiest church I have been in yet." Looking down from its cupola, he saw "tiled roofs and steeples, half hid in smoke and mist – a filthy river covered with craft running through the mist... All was dirty and foul; the air was chilly and charged with fog and sleet, though it is the genial month of May" (May 18, 1844). Arrived home in Massachusetts from the "cursed hole" of London, he celebrated another national holiday with a train ride out to Concord:

July 4th, 44. The Celebration at Concord. The admirable good humor of the people in the cars, during some very vexatious delays, was remarkable...

The cheerfulness, the spirit of accomodation and politeness, was extraordinary. Perfect order, in the most difficult evolutions of the day. An hundred soldiers would not in Europe have ensured such quiet and unanimity... And I remembered, this is *our lowest class*... If we have not the courtly polish of the European upper circles, the absence of their stupid and brutal peasantry is a fair offset.

So like Irving, whose return home was wrapped in a patriotic contrast to pre-reform Britain "lowering with doubt and danger, where the rich man trembles and the poor man frowns," Parkman came back to America with a renewed sense (especially on the nation's birthday) of what made it politically and socially distinct. And also like Irving, he would build that new feeling of the American character into an exploration of that quintessential New World, the American West.

This may explain why the English tourists in *The Oregon Trail* are registered in a tone so different from the references to them in the Oregon Trail journal. In the book they are freighted with their national nickname, and with a lot else besides:

> The reader need not be told that John Bull never leaves home without encumbering himself with the greatest possible load of luggage. Our companions were no exception to the rule. They had a wagon drawn by six mules, and crammed with provisions for six months, besides ammunition enough for a regiment; spare rifles and fowling-pieces, ropes and harnesses; personal baggage, and a miscellaneous assortment of articles...telescopes and portable compasses, and carried English double-barrelled rifles of sixteen to the pound calibre, slung to their saddles in dragoon fashion.

Their ridiculous duplication of equipment is mirrored in Parkman's near-redundant phraseology: "*spare* rifles and fowling-pieces"; "ropes and harnesses." Like Smith's "Tuftaffety humorists," Parkman's English are encumbered by precedent. They bring the Old World with them – physically but, it is implied, mentally too. Unable to adapt to the novel conditions, they simply sink under the freight of their anxious overprovision. So of course later in the journey "our English companions broke the axle-tree of their wagon, and down came the whole cumbrous machine lumbering into the bed of a brook! Here was a day's work cut out for us."

Oddly enough, in the journal Parkman's and Shaw's wagon also gets stuck in the mud (May 14, 1846), an accident not mentioned in *The Oregon Trail*, and the only breakage recorded there occurs (again) to Parkman's party, when the "Axle of [their] waggon broke short in crossing, and we stayed for a new one to be put on" (May 25). Yet in *The Oregon Trail* the West becomes the arena for a contest between Old World and New World values.

The treatment of the English party puts this dialectic in the context of national comparisons, but the greater part of the book dramatizes the struggle as an American easterner's initiation into the rough mysteries of his country's nether regions. The West was also the proving ground for the more personal side of the American character. The process of Parkman's initiation is registered in terms of two kinds of response to which the text of *The Oregon Trail* pays continuing attention, and which may be said to form themes in the book. One is his physical health; the other is his sense of perspective, or ability to compose geographical and social landscapes out of his raw experience on the frontier. To both themes his perception of the Indians plays a crucial part.

To begin with the idea of perspective in its commonest sense, it is clear from his language in the journal that Parkman knew something of conventional landscape description. From the way he scrambles the terms, though, it is equally obvious that he is not interested in using them with any precision. Mountains are both "wild and picturesque"; Pike's Peak is both "sublime and beautiful"; the view from a summit is a "savage prospect" (July 28, August 19, July 29). Landscape is not an issue in the journal, simply a matter of stock epithets, routinely used: the sort of empty "rhetoric" which Mason Wade found more typical of *The Oregon Trail.*

But in the book Parkman's ability to compose a landscape certainly becomes a subject. For one thing, *The Oregon Trail* makes it clear that Parkman found it impossible to join in the chorus of praise by eastern and European travelers for the picturesque aspect of the prairies. His reader "need not think to enter upon the paradise of his imagination," whatever "preconceived ideas of the prairies" he may have picked up from "picturesque tourists, painters, poets, and novelists, who have seldom penetrated further" than the "wide and fertile belt" lying immediately beyond the Missouri frontier. Even there, though the scenery is "not wholly devoid of interest," the "plains [are] too wide for the eye to measure." Beyond that region, the traveler's "wagons will stick in the mud; his horses will break loose; harness will give way, and axle-trees prove unsound. His bed will be a soft one, consisting often of black mud, of the richest consistency." Though game is surprisingly scarce, "he will find himself beset with 'varmints' innumerable": wolves, "legions of frogs," a "profusion of snakes," and "unnumbered mosquitoes." Parched with thirst after a day's ride over "some boundless reach of prairie, he comes at length to a pool of water, and alights to drink," only to discover "a troop of young tadpoles sporting in the bottom of his cup." Insects, snakes and tadpoles were a nuisance, but words and phrases like "innumerable," "unnumbered," "boundless reach," and "too wide for the eye to measure" present Parkman's problem also as a failure to gain perspective. In *The Oregon Trail* the prairie is too big to see as a whole; so it cannot be comprehended as a landscape.

He also had trouble composing a single vantage point on the American Indians. Common to criticism of *The Oregon Trail*, from Melville's review of the book in *The Literary World* of March, 1849 to the editor of the latest edition, is the opinion that Parkman was unfair to Indians. A recent scholarly article has gone so far as to call his attitude ethnocentric, even racist: not just in *The Oregon Trail* but in later books like *The Conspiracy of Pontiac* (1851) and *The Jesuits in North America* (1867).[43]

During the six months of the tour, hunting buffalo and generally roughing it "out of bounds," Parkman's party encountered various Indian tribes, but became closely acquainted with just one of them, the Oglalla band of the Teton Sioux, with whom they camped in the Laramie Basin. This was an unusual privilege, granted because Parkman's chief guide, Henry Chatillon, was married to the daughter of the Chief, Bull Bear; so it is hardly surprising that despite occupying such a brief part of his journey, Parkman's experience of the Sioux Indians forms the major focus of interest in both journal and book.

In the journal Parkman's comments on Indian life and culture are reportorial and low-key. He offers no great general observations about the Indians, so develops no particular theme. When invited by the Indians to share their meal of "puppy dog," the strangeness of which dish is made much of in the book, he remarks, simply, "It was excellent" (June 20), and after that (July 3, July 15) swallows the entrée without further comment. In the journal Parkman takes Indian culture seriously, recording details of the elaborate dress of their warriors, of their etiquette of feasting and the exchange of gifts, but he is also alert to the less ceremonial side of Indian life, the comic incongruity of their appearance and behavior on occasion: their greedy feeding, the old squaws who looked like witches, their laziness, their superstition, and the "gross indecencies" of some of the men's names (July 2, 5, 6, 9, August 7).

The more complex information on Indian culture – for example, their "mystic association," or the ritual behavior of their religion – the journal reports in indirect speech, as conveyed to Parkman by one or another of the experts who traveled with him: Chatillon, or Reynal, another "squaw-man." "Raynale [sic] speaks of the legendary tales of the Sioux"; "Raynale says as follows..."; "The Sioux, Crows, Arapahos, according to Henry [Chatillon], have every year or therebouts medicine ceremonies, similar to the Mandans" (June 21, August 12). In the journal the Indians are called by "white" names, like Bull Bear (the young warrior son of the Oglalla Chief) and Old Red Water, the old man who befriends Parkman.

In *The Oregon Trail* this judicious distance is much reduced. Bull Bear reverts to his Indian name, Mahto-Tatonka, and Old Red Water gets a much expanded role as Mene-Seela, as though Parkman has no further need of a translation. Here too the cultural lore is presented without mediation, as what the narrator knows for himself. As the Indians become more intimate, more attention is devoted to making the various aspects of their behavior vivid and telling. There are fascinating accounts of their dreams and how they act on them; their initiations through self-torture; their regulations for councils and feasting; their belief that animals had human personalities and could understand human speech; and the compulsive behavior of an old man who believes he has to wake in the middle of every night to sing a particular song.

But the closer Parkman comes to his material, the less he can comprehend it. Again, perspective eludes him. The narrative point of view is not ethnocentric or racist; simply unable to make up its mind as to whether the Indians constitute a part of human culture, or no culture at all. In the journal this double view was a tendency; in the book it is a formal device. Almost every patient description of an Indian cultural practice is balanced by a corresponding antimasque undermining it. Indian dignity is set against Indian comedy; arcane custom against savagery.

So at one point the narrator takes great interest in Mene-Seela's store of the "legends and traditions of the village," and regrets not being able to draw more of them out, while at another he complains of the Indians' "endless stories." One day he comes across some children "playfully tossing up one of their number in a buffalo-robe, an exact counterpart of the ancient pastime from which Sancho Panza suffered so much." Then he notices another group further out on the prairie "pursuing birds and ground-squirrels with their bows and arrows; and woe to the unhappy little animals that fell into their merciless, torture-loving hands!" At one moment the children can be contextualized within "ancient" custom – and one celebrated in European literature too – to establish that they are like children everywhere throughout history. Immediately afterwards they are the prototype of savage nature, not part of any civilized tradition.

In the same way the young Sioux warrior Mahto-Tatonka is rendered both dignified and comic:

> As among us, those of highest worth and breeding are most simple in manner and attire, so our aspiring young friend was indifferent to the gaudy trappings and ornaments of his companions. He never arrayed himself in gaudy blanket and glittering necklaces, but left his statue-like form limbed like an Apollo of bronze, to win its way to favor. His voice was singularly deep and strong. It sounded from his chest like the deep notes of an organ. Yet after all, he was but an Indian. See him as he lies

there in the sun before our tent, kicking his heels in the air and cracking jokes with his brother. Does he look like a hero?

And so the tone goes on oscillating. An instant later Mahto-Tatonka is not only upright again, but mounted, "in the hour of his glory... gorgeous as a champion in his panoply, [as] he rides round and round within the great circle of lodges." One minute his tact in dress and deportment can be compared to the subtlest behavior "among us," and his stature hypothesized within references to classical form and chivalric romance. The next, he is "but an Indian." This failure to incorporate Mahto-Tatonka's boisterous tumbling about within a sense of tradition is too restless and temperamentally contradictory to be called the "rounded portrait" of a "complex character." Parkman's narrator comes close here to admitting that even with all the intimate knowledge he can deploy about the Indians – perhaps even *because* he has now become friendly with them – he cannot match the facts of Indian life to any conventional representation of them.

The other theme of *The Oregon Trail*, Parkman's health, demarcates the book from the journal at least as clearly as does the issue of his various perspectives on the experience with the Indians. About Parkman's actual state of mind and body before, during and after his tour there is a degree of confusion. According to Mason Wade, Parkman returned "to Boston from the West a sick man," with "his already strained sight weakened still further by exposure to the pitiless glare of the sun and to the harsh alkali dust of the Plains," with "an impaired digestion," "insomnia," the onset of arthritis – not to mention "an obscure mental disorder," in the wake of which came "a hypochondria, which haunts the book, while the journal possesses an entirely different spirit." David Levin cites Parkman's own description of his ailments as "'a hellish racing of the heart'" and also mentions "dysentery," "a terrible pressure on the brain and threats of blindness, and finally . . . a crippling arthritis." After the western trip, Parkman "was never again free of sickness."[44]

About all that can be said for certain is that Parkman did indeed suffer badly from arthritis later in life, and that his eyesight was sufficiently weakened for him to wish to dictate at least some of the text of *The Oregon Trail* rather than write it out himself – a process which Wade thinks also weakened the book's prose. As for the other ailments – insomnia, impaired digestion, dysentery, racing of the heart, pressure on the brain – these are hardly rendered in the terms of precise diagnosis. Another way of putting these "symptoms" would be sleeplessness, upset stomach, diarrhoea, palpitations and headaches: disorders common enough when people undergo intense physical effort in hot weather, while sleeping rough and eating strange food. (Not for nothing was travel first called "travail.") In any case, that last symptom on the Wade's list, hypochondria, puts the others, if not in doubt, at least in a new light.

Whatever the truth about Parkman's health, the important point, already noticed by Mason Wade, though he considers it yet another sign of the book's relative weakness, is that while *The Oregon Trail* makes an issue of the narrator's health, the journal hardly mentions it. On July 20, Parkman was "Too languid to hunt with spirit," but that condition might occasionally have affected others too, since hunting buffalo often required riding great distances, then suddenly breaking into a furious gallop amidst a thundering, bruising, dust-raising herd of wild animals. Besides it was "my horse" that was "very sick." But the book is punctuated with references to various disabilities. "Having been slightly ill on leaving camp in the morning, six or seven hours of rough riding had fatigued me extremely." "I had been slightly ill for several weeks," but on reaching Fort Laramie "a violent pain [of 'dysentery'] awoke me, and . . . in a day and a half I was reduced to extreme weakness." Having "taken six grains of opium" to no effect, he resolves to throw himself "upon Providence for recovery, using...any portion of strength that might remain to me."

In *The Oregon Trail* these themes of the narrator's failing – in health and in perspective on landscape and Indians – are brought together in a long, moving passage at the end of Chapter 18, "A Mountain Hunt." It is not the end of the book – the return journey south to the Santa Fe Trail and back east to Missouri is still to come – but it is certainly the culmination of his main focus of interest, his residence with the Oglalla Sioux.

What happens is that the narrator, bored with time on his hands, sets out to explore the mountains surrounding the camp. He passes through "many deep and gloomy gorges, choked with trees and bushes." He sees "Indians stalking along the edges of the woods" and "boys whooping and laughing on the mountain sides," "following birds and small animals and killing them with their little bows and arrows." Then thinking himself alone, he comes suddenly upon "the black head and red shoulders of an Indian among the bushes above."

"The reader need not prepare himself for a startling adventure," the narrator continues, "for I have none to relate." It was old Mene-Seela, "my best friend in the village," meditating in the wilderness:

> I saw him seated alone, immovable as a statue, among the rocks and trees. His face was turned upward, and his eyes seemed riveted on a pine-tree springing from a cleft in the precipice above. The crest of the pine was swaying to and fro in the wind, and its long limbs waved slowly up and down, as if the tree had life. Looking for a while at the old man, I was satisfied that he was engaged in an act of worship, or prayer, or communion of some kind with a supernatural being. I longed to penetrate his thoughts, but I could do nothing more than conjecture and speculate.

A number of the book's ideas are recapitulated here: the children busy at play and torture, the Indian as art work, the narrative disconfirmation of "the reader's" romantic preconceptions. But whereas earlier (in Chapter 9) he had delivered himself of the stunningly impertinent opinion that the Indians' souls are "dormant," here the setting, the Indian's dignified deportment and his own openness to new experience force him to acknowledge something like the opposite conclusion: that their souls are responsive to a "supreme being" working through the subtlest impulses of living nature. His admission is the more gracious because of its negative capability: he can't claim to know whether Mene-Seela is engaged in "worship, or prayer, or communion of some kind," but he recognizes the seriousness of the act. Hence, he continues, "Whatever was passing in the mind of the old man, it was no part of sense or of delicacy to disturb him." Mene-Seela is no savage now, but an equal in the human community, however different, to be accorded the most sensitive expression of customary respect. And this time the dignified aspect of the Indian sticks in the frame; it is not cancelled by a subsequent reference to behavior that is wild, comic or otherwise demeaning.

So he leaves Mene-Seela undisturbed. "Looking up, I saw a tall peak rising among the woods. Something impelled me to climb." What? And how, given his weak condition? He gives no answer, but simply affirms that:

> I had not felt for many a day such strength and elasticity of limb. An hour and a half of slow and often intermitted labor brought me to the very summit; and emerging from the dark shadows of the rocks and pines, I stepped forth into the light, and walking along the sunny verge of a precipice, seated myself on its extreme point. Looking between the mountain peaks to the westward, the pale blue prairie was stretching to the farthest horizen, like a serene and tranquil ocean. The surrounding mountains were in themselves sufficiently striking and impressive, but this contrast gave redoubled effect to their stern features.

Robert Edson Lee, who shares Wade's opinion on the relative merits of raw and cooked accounts of the West, accuses Parkman of turning the rough, vernacular immediacy of the journal into a weak book about the picturesque, replete with references to

Salvatore Rosa, and so "passing his descriptive problem off in terms of a second-rate painter."[45] Whether or not one shares this opinion of Rosa (I don't, as it happens, but it doesn't matter), one must resist the cheap dismissal of Parkman. The picturesque is certainly a subject in the book, as in many nineteenth-century accounts of travel in America. It was a sort of code word for what Irving called "association": that is, the quality of compositional contrast in a social and physical landscape, between ancient and modern, rough and smooth, cultivated and natural. The general opinion was that America didn't have it, though those who wanted to praise the country argued that it possessed many compensating political and geographical virtues. Mrs. Trollope certainly understood the code when she wrote, in *Domestic Manners of the Americans* (1832), "Who is it that says America is not picturesque? I forget," and then goes on to praise the picturesqueness of a "point of particular beauty" between Utica and Albany, New York, which, however, she discovers is owned by an Englishman![46]

The picturesque in *The Oregon Trail* is part of this debate over whether America can be composed, comprehended. Oddly enough Parkman uses the technical word more often in the rough, raw, vernacular, immediate, etc. journal than in the effete book, where on at least one occasion (as we have seen) it is part of a satire on literary and painterly preconceptions of the prairie. In this passage, where he doesn't use it at all, he nevertheless achieves something at least approaching a picturesque perspective on the prairies. Here is the pictorial contrast – not between cultivated and natural, of course, because it would be pushing the reader's credulity too far to suggest a gazebo or ruined abbey in Wyoming – but between the cool, light colors of the distant plain and the warmer, darker mountains framing it; between diagonals and horizontals, rough textures and smooth.

The conclusion that Parkman intended to express the picturesque in this passage is rendered even more probable on comparison with the *Knickerbocker* text of *The Oregon Trail*, where two long sentences, deleted from the book version, originally stood between the words "...seated myself on its extreme point." and "Looking between the mountain peaks..." The deleted passage (here relieved by a few elisions) reads:

A wilderness of mountains lay around me, their ridges bristling with rocky pinnacles, avalanches of rock thrown around their bases... There were black chasms, deep clefts and ravines... and here and there, in the midst of the desolation, small green glens and valleys... in the largest of [which] I could discern... the encampment of the wild and impetuous people with whom I was associated.

E.N. Feltskog, who cites this deletion in his edition of the 1892 edition of *The Oregon Trail*, thinks it provides additional support for his thesis that Parkman was out to disabuse the world of its exotic apprehension of the American Indian as a noble savage. "Parkman juxtaposes the Indian's veneration for Nature's spiritual power with the savagery of the landscape (particularly in the canceled passage)," he writes, "to undermine... the image of the Noble Savage paying devout... reverence to a beneficent Nature. Both landscape *and* Indian are savage."[47]

Yes, usually, but not here. Authors cancel passages because they feel them to be out of keeping with what they want to express, after all. What Parkman takes out is everything that would disturb the tranquil perspective he has achieved through the effort of his mountain ascent and his vision of Mene-Seela praying. Above all, he removes every word that would render both the scene and the Indians within it as savage and terrible: "wilderness... bristling... pinnacles... black chasms, deep clefts... ravines... wild and impetuous." He cancels the sublime and preserves the picturesque.

Properly understood, *The Oregon Trail* extends the narrative of emigration into its fullest definition of American identity. Here is a statement about what gives America its character, and a story of how an individual character became truly American. The book begins with an adversarial address to the preconceived notions of

European and eastern culture – an attack on Old World baggage – and it proceeds through a trial by physical and emotional travail on the bewildering margins of personal experience and national geography, until finally the narrator regains his health even as he achieves his long-sought-for perspective on prairie and Indian alike: a new dispensation of body and mind, person and nation, without the terminology of the old.

Part III

Falling away

13

Emigrants (some "successful," others not) disappointed in the contrast between the New World as they found it and as represented in the promotional propaganda: their accounts fragmentary, hesitant, few in number

Less than a year after writing home to his friends in Leicestershire that he felt "in perfect health, and freed from paine and vomiting," able "to digest the hardest and coarsest fare," when before he "could not eat finest meat," the Revd Francis Higginson died in Massachusetts. His wife was left nearly destitute, having "10 Acckers of ground to inclose," as she wrote to Governor Winthrop asking for help, and no "menns to do it"; owing money on her house, her "prouisiones grow[ing] skant: though I husband them the best I cane."[1]

It would be too slick to claim that Anne Higginson's brief appeal tells us more about conditions in early New England than all her husband's effusive praises put together, but at least she affords us a glimpse of the risks of New World settlement to set alongside its exhilarations. The reason why the discourse approving the enterprise of emigration and settlement has been called "dominant" is because by far the greater proportion of the personal accounts now extant testify to the success of the venture – and in characteristic terms and tropes that formed an important constituent of America's definition of itself. The question of whether the emigrants were "really" satisfied, in such great numbers, with their choice to remove to the New World is now unanswerable, and may always have been, except (admittedly crudely) in the fragmentary statistics of movements over and back across the Atlantic. It may be that an invisible, disinterested observer, a bug on the wall of the frontier cabin, would indeed approve the general tone and tenor of the emigrants' letters home. We can never know, since our access to the experience of emigrants and immigrants is limited by the process of vernacular publication outlined in the Introduction.

Even within these constraints, however, a few alternative views on American emigration have been preserved, through vernacular publication or the conventional kind, either disagreeing with the positive findings of the majority or less willing than they to dispense with what they all had to leave behind. Some express temporary discontents later to be incorporated within a larger plot of approval. Others are consciously adversarial, addressing the dominant discourse as though already familiar with it and wishing to negate it point by point.

Both these responses may be said in one sense or another to depend on the dominant discourse – being either enfolded within it or constructed by its terms and arguments. But others, like Anne Higginson's, stand right outside it, addressing different subjects in quite another tone of voice – or in some cases with a vague sense that they have lost their voice altogether. In the great tide of emigration, these fugitive countercurrents are the most intriguing of all.

Though the dismissal of culture could be exhilarating in prospect, even the public promoters of American emigration felt its relative paucity in American landscape and society. What they missed was not so much the high culture of book-learning and the fine arts. It was as easy to bid farewell (as Benjamin Franklin did in his *Information to Those Who Would Remove to America*) to "Belles-Lettres . . . Paintings, Statues, Architecture and other Works of Art that are more curious than useful," as it was later for Samuel Clemens and other western humorists to sell sketches to the newspapers lampooning grand opera and productions of Shakespeare.

Less dispensable to the British settler were the homely, traditional conventions and spatial dispositions informing everyday living. Cobbett missed the "*dwellings and gardens*" of farm laborers in southern England – the "warm little cottage...and the garden, nicely laid out and the paths bordered with flowers, while the cottage door is crowned with a garland of roses or honey-suckle." On Long Island "we...see the labourer content with a shell of boards, while all around him is as barren as the sea-beach." Birkbeck deplored the state of American court houses, which were "also made use of as places of worship," in which "filth of all kinds has been accumulating since they were built." The very nodal points of civil and spiritual law seemed corrupted. Lacking also a "central focus of fashion," American culture was, paradoxically, no better on the local level, where the inhabitants were "strangers to rural simplicity." Democratic classlessness removed the contrast that demarcated and defined the prince and the peasant, the metropolitan and the provincial. The Americans fell short even in their personal culture: "Cleanliness in houses, and too often in person, is neglected to a degree which is very revolting to an Englishman."

On the subject of American egalitarianism, both Cobbett and Birkbeck – as had, and would, many other English travelers both before and after them – found American "domestic servants" a great trial. "They are *honest*: but they are not *obedient*," wrote Cobbett. Birkbeck agreed that Americans had "a bigotted aversion to domestic service," though he attributed the trait as much to the stigma of southern slavery as to a general spirit of equality.

But in all cases these objections are qualified, or even justified, by admiring references to American democratic and republican sentiment: to the enlightened social and geographical decentralization of American political authority. An American servant "will not wear a *livery*, any more than he will wear a halter around his neck," writes Cobbett, adding that willing domestics are in short supply because "people in general are so comfortably situated." "To be easy and comfortable here," Birkbeck adds without apparent disapproval, a man should know how to wait upon himself."[2]

As for the actual emigrants, even those who ventured general comments on American social and physical culture stuck to what was closest to their condition. John Burgess noted that American farmers often "plow without shoe or Stocking" and that their wives "never ware any Stays very Seldom any cap & common without Shoe or Stocking when they are at Work." American farmers know nothing of English traditional farmcrafts like hedging, ditching and faggoting, "for there is not a bush hedge to be seen," only "pales...made of rails & some with Stones Laid together rufly...they Burn no spray wood except what they Burn out in ye woods to get rid of it." Nathan Haley, writing from Cincinnati to his father in Yorkshire on December 9, 1823, recalled that it was the day of the Bradford Fair. "There is no fairs in this country," he lamented, nostalgic for the interludes in the European vernacular calendar, "and I...see or hear but only in thought about shows and other things." James Grayston wrote from West Virginia to his sister in Lancashire, "I have not heard a good band of music since I left old England."[3]

For the most part, though, the emigrants expressed discontent at the sparseness of American cultural forms only by implication, in their requests for the occasional artifact to be sent to them from home. Sometimes these were humble physical needs – ryegrass seed, needles, nets for caps, James Roberts's "berry tree seed" – and sometimes vernacular formulae, as for herbal cures. George Martin wrote to his brother from Rochester, New York, to ask at various times for a root of "that pure flavoured rhubarb," a "recipe" for a medicine to cure rotten gums, a diamond to cut glass for windows, a formula for French polishing solution, some violin strings, books and magazines.

As the length of his list indicates, Martin was the least contented of these emigrants. At one point, in a particularly black mood, he envisions a whole vista of dissolution opening before him. "You cannot imagine what the feeling is to think that you will die," he reminds his brother, "the last of your race, in a foreign land far from your kindred and home, and no friendly hand to close your eyes." How can we account for his divergence from the norm? It may have something to do with the fact that, like James Grayston, he was writing to a sibling, not a parent. Then as now, letters home are characteristically more candid to brothers and sisters than to parents. From the mother one wants to hide bad news to keep her from worrying; from the father a son especially wants to maintain that show of manly independence with which he set out so publicly, often challenging paternal authority in the process. Also, as Erickson notes, Martin "did not succeed in achieving [his] goal of independence," and "became increasingly defensive about his failure to go into business for himself." Remaining the (albeit valued) employee of another carpenter until his death, he put all his savings into the construction of his American house, which was still unfinished when he died and had to be completed for his widow with a grant of $500 from his family in England. Possibly connected with his failure to establish his independence was his prolonged expectation of a modest fortune due to him on the death of his father, and from which, in the year he himself was to die, he wrote a bitter letter home to say that he had been robbed by one of his brothers. Great expectations erect a fantastical barrier to personal responsibility. In terms of the emigrant's psychology, the lingering hope that one may inherit a place in the old country – a competence, a job, a rank in society, or whatever – has typically been a factor in the emigrant's decision to return, because it forestalls that emotional and conceptual break with the past so crucial to the successful adaptation to new circumstances.

Yet George Martin did not return. Indeed, he is one of the most vehement in Erickson's collection in his approval of the new political dispensation in America: "It is about time you had a revolution in England," he wrote his brother in the incandescent year of 1848, "and pay no such expensive salaries to have a little woman reign over you and... keep her and her husband and all her young rats that will be eternally gnawing holes in your pockets". It was he who scorned the "chicken-hearted people" who "went home without trying any thing," and he too who was most eloquent about the need of prospective emigrants to ask themselves, "Am I fit to go to a new country to leave my old ways behind me, and begin life anew with everything strange about me, new manners, new customs... [to] go manfully to work with a strong determination to go through thick and thin and 'never say die'?"[4]

Still, a few documents remain from emigrants who, whether through bad judgment or worse luck, remained unaccomodated; for whom a deficiency of Old World culture was too high a price to pay for a liberation into New World nature; for whom indeed even nature itself had gone wrong. "*O if I was back to Scotland again*," wrote Janet Johnston to her sister, from Beverly, Upper Canada, "*I would say fareweel with the greates of glee to the old pine Stumps in Beverly*." That was in April, 1846. The following January found her even less jolly, now beyond the consolations of rhyme:

> *Dear Jane I never was in a place under the sun I liked worse* I helped James with the turnips hoying I was like to fall down with the heat and when taking them and the patatoes up I was al shaivering of cold... James has 15 acrs to plough if he is aible I thought he would been killed in summer with the heat and heard work togather... it was good of you to tell us to put our trust in god but you forgot that faith an works goes together you are something like me with our sheep James said he would like to have the Sheep in four he was afreid fore the wolf and I said there wear no – ? – up their but in the marning when we arose we found foure of them killed with the wolf.

This is very bleak. Here stripping nature of culture does not free it for greater productivity, as in the dominant discourse, but removes from it all governing principles, so that nature is forced to work against its own purpose in ever wilder oscillations of extremes. New World experience does not modify Old World precept in such a way as to authenticate it through experimental data; instead the savage forest breaks in on faith to destroy it. For though works may reinforce faith in a person's spiritual life, the example chosen by Janet Johnston – the prudent care of one's livestock – has nothing to do with the way in which works and faith collaborate to produce the individual spiritual career. In terms of the example she uses, "faith" and "works" are simply incompatible. What she really means is that the wolf, and the wilderness for which it stands, have destroyed her faith.

Rebecca Butterworth kept her faith at least, though not much more; and it's hard to understand how she saved that. All that remains of the account of her emigration is a single, long letter written from Outland Grove, Arkansas, to Rochdale in July, 1846, asking her father to help her and her husband to return home. Three years earlier Rebecca had left a comfortable enough existence in that growing Lancashire town to try farming in the "Back Woods of America," as she called it. "In spite of the help of her husband's family, settled nearby," Charlotte Erickson writes, "the Butterworths were ready to give up. Mrs. Butterworth was physically and temperamentally unprepared for the dangers and hardships of farming in such a region." Like other emigrants from urban regions, they had been used to relying on doctors when they fell ill. Also typically, they were a nuclear family, stripped of the sisters, aunts, mothers whose accumulated experience might have helped the young woman in childbirth.

When pregnant with her fourth child, she fell ill of a "bilious intermittant fever," for which she was treated with mustard plasters and "I cannot tell you what kind of medicine," followed by steamed bricks applied to her feet to warm them up, and "nearly 60 grains of calomel," which left one of her "cheeks cut half way through." According to Erickson, these were typical prescriptions of "an old-fashioned doctor of her day, contrasted with the botanic remedies used by working-class immigrants, who had not been accustomed to consulting doctors."

The fever induced premature labor and because she was in such pain anyway, she started having the baby without realising what was happening:

I suppose I had a dread few hours still not knowing I was in labour beside having ben so prostrated a whole week with fever. However I suppose about 3 oclock on Monday morning my dear baby was born. Not 5 minutes before they say I forced myself out of bed and from sister and run round the bed to a pallet on the floor. Well our little Wm Barton was born and crying like a child at full time. Thos did not like to help me as he had not studyed midwifery much. I had to remain in that situation for two hours before the doctor could be got...Doctor Howard came when he took the little darling and gave it to sister. In about ten minutes after he took his flight to heaven above to join my other 3 little angels. I know it is the Lords will. We are quite resigned. Both Doctor Howard and Thos said I may be very thankfull I am spared myself, for if I had lived to come to my full time the child was so large I could not of borne it. You would have been astonished to see. He is laid beside Polly and Rebecca. She would often tell tacky they were going to have another little broder Billy. So they have and seen him too. I felt when I heard him crying so if I could have him in my arms and put him to his breast I would be glad, but the Lords will be done and not ours.

The passage oscillates movingly between will and resignation. The terrible sequence of events is accepted as "the Lords will" and her bodily salvation; then the alternative sequence is invoked ("I felt...if I could...I would be glad"), only to be silenced – this time with only the barest hint of contest – in "the Lords will be done and not ours."

Rebecca Butterworth may just have saved her personal faith, but her confidence in the enterprise of emigration had been shattered. By now the New World was no land of plenty. With her health destroyed ("You would hardly know me now. I am so pulled down") and their stock of animals and vegetables reduced to the point where the couple were within days of the last square meal, the family's American time was running out:

What little corn we had the cattle as jumped the fence and eaten it so that it will not make even cattle feed. We are [dammed?] up in a corner. We have no bread to last above a week and no meat, very little coffee, about 1/2 lb of sugar. John can milk one cow which makes us a little butter but the other wont let him.[5]

In the nearly sixty letters from early New England collected by Everett Emerson, just two dissent from the approving chorus. And even that small minority seems lucky to have gained a foothold in the collection, since their provenance is so doubtful. Authors and/or dates have not been established with any certainty, and their process of transmission and preservation has been irregular. One was written in 1631 to William Pond, a workman on Winthrop's estate in Groton, Suffolk, by one of his sons – possibly John. Emerson conjectures that the letter was saved only because it "contains so much information that it was probably given to John Winthrop, Jr., who brought it back to America with him." The other, anonymous and undated (but thought to be sometime around 1637), was collected in the *History of Massachusetts Bay*, (1764) by the last royal governor of the colony, Thomas Hutchinson. A third critical letter, also collected by Hutchinson and ascribed to "a gentlewoman, a few years after" – that is, around 1640 – is mentioned by Emerson but not reproduced in *Letters from New England*.

Partly effaced though these dissenting opinions may have been, they lack nothing in the vehemence of their deliberate reversal of the standard view on American settlement. Johnston and Butterworth give no evidence of confronting a prior discourse advocating emigration and settlement, but Hutchinson's anonymous correspondents – early as they wrote – were already consciously engaged in dialogue with the propagandists. We had been sent "report of so rich a soil," wrote the first of Hutchinson's authors, "but we that came after found, by dear experience, that affection, not judgement, was the author of it." The "gentlewoman" put it more colorfully: "When I remember the high commendations some have given of the place, and find it inferior to the reports, I have thought the reason thereof to be this, that they wrote surely in strawberry time."

Of these three, it is she who is the most balanced in her assessment. At least she admits, albeit laconically, that "as it hath the means of grace...if you please, you may call it Canaan." The other two express blunter, more systematic inversions of pro-settlement propaganda. Pond refutes the standard view almost point by point, as though squaring off against that sense of delight in New England's material richness expressed by his contemporaries Francis Higginson and Thomas Welde. The trans-atlantic voyage was anything but a passage to a transformed life. "We ware wondurfule seick as we cam at sea with the small Poxe," he wrote his father and mother from Watertown, Massachusetts. Fourteen died on the way. "No man thought that I and my leittell cheilld woolld a liveid, and my boye is lame and my gurell too." Though twenty-five passengers came over, "fouer skore and od" returned by the same ship, "and as maney more wolld a cume if thay had whare withe all to bringe them hom." If for Winthrop and Higginson the simplicity of their food and the bracing purity of New England water were part of their passage to *communitas*, for Pond they were a bore that he prayed his father to relieve by sending him a small barrell of butter and a larger one of unground malt for making beer out of, for here "we dreinck notheinge but walltre [water]." Without commodities, they had nothing to trade with the Indians, "for her[e] whare we liue her is no beuer and her is no clothe to be had to mack no [ap]parell and shoes ar at 5*s* a payer for me and that clothe that is woorthe 2*s* 8*d* a yard is woorthe her 5*s*." Though there is some open ground for planting, the soil is very shallow. As for livestock:

Cattell threiue well here, but they giue small stor of mylck...here is good stor of feishe. If we had botes to goo 8 or x leges to sea to fish in her are good stor of weield foule but thay are hard to c[o]me by it is hardur to get a shoot then it is in ould eingland and Peple her ar subjecte to deicesesse for her have deyeid of the skurueye and of the bur[n]inge feuer too hundreid and ode...and prouisseyones ar her at a wondurfule rat[e] wheat mell is xiiij*s* a bushell and pese x*s* and mault x*s* and eindey seid wheat [Indian corn seed] is xv*s* and...buttr xii*d* a pound and chese is 8*d* a pound and all kind of speyseis uerey de[a]r and allmoste non to be got.

Pond inverts the dominant discourse in both matter and manner. Health, soil, material resources are all worse than in England, and the prices higher; but also, as in Butterworth's "not bread...no meat, very little coffee," the positive catalogs are negatived – either simply ("no beuer...no clothe...no parell") or arranged in an anti-redemptive pattern, reversing the recuperations of the majority account. Here the good news (the open ground, the thriving cattle, the bounty of fish and game) is inevitably swallowed up by the bad.

The other anonymous correspondent in Hutchinson's *History* reverses the standard recuperations even more thoroughly than does Pond's letter. The New England soil is "mixed; the uplands rather...sand than clay, yet our rye likes it not" because it is "both cold and barren." When manuered it "yeild[s] some increase, but not to answer expectation." It is most "like your woodland in England, best at first, yet afterwards grows more barren." It might be improved by "marl, lime or other manure," but "as yet we are destitute of these supplies":

For the present, we make a shift to live, but hereafter, when our numbers increase and the fertility of the soil doth decrease...what shall become of us I will not determine, but it is probable we must either disband ourselves, like beasts straitened in their pasture...or else, continuing together, be made the subject of some fearful famine...[6]

Here no faith, even in the eye of a ludicrous beholder, remains to redeem the fall. Things are generally getting worse, and no mistake.

14

Back-migrants who turned themselves into travelers: Boucher, the other John Fisher, Shepperson's returnees; their texts more numerous, more articulate; the gain in confidence as the voyage back gathers momentum

It is not known whether Pond and Hutchinson's correspondents returned to England. The Butterworths almost certainly did, because her letter home discusses detailed arrangements for the passage, by steerage, from Philadelphia. No one knows for certain either how many British settlers back-migrated to the United Kingdom up until the end of the nineteenth century, but a conservative estimate would place the figure at well over a million. From all these, only a handful of letters are known to have survived through the process of vernacular publication. A greater number of back-migrants, however, managed to publish their impressions in the conventional way, usually in Great Britain, and thus to give them wide currency through the rapidly expanding market for books and articles about the United States during the course of the nineteenth century. In his *Emigration and Disenchantment* Wilbur Shepperson discusses the writings of seventy-five British back-migrants published during that period. His exhaustive survey includes some authors, like Mrs. Trollope, more often classified as travelers than migrants.

There are good reasons for running these categories together. In the first place, as Shepperson points out, "Immigrants, tourists, businessmen, and others aboard a vessel were commonly lumped together as migrants" in British and American official records of movements between the two countries. Secondly, a man or woman might have belonged to more than one of these groups, if not at once, then certainly in succession. Many so-called migrants had always intended their sojourn to be temporary, to last only so long as it took them to accumulate, say, a planned sum of money. Others were recalled by circumstances external to their intentions, like the illness of a close relative at home, or a sudden economic collapse in the host country. (In the year running from July, 1931 to June, 1932, the worst of the Great Depression, only 2,155 British aliens entered the US while 12,311 left it.)[7]

Some emigrants remained tourists, however long they stayed in the New World. The Revd Jonathan Boucher emigrated from Cumberland to Virginia in 1759, settled as an Episcopal minister in the Carolinas, then as a schoolmaster in Annapolis, Maryland. He married an American, bought a small plantation, lived well, was friendly with the Governor of Maryland, Robert Eden, and with George Washington, whose stepson attended the school he ran. Yet in 1775, sixteen years after he first came over, he returned to live permanently in England. Why? The reason he gave was that he could no longer reconcile the increasing likelihood of American separation with his royalist convictions.

Yet letters he wrote throughout his period in America to the same two correspondents in Cumberland, a Revd and Mrs. John James, suggest a more complex weave of reasons for his return. For one thing, his politics had not always been quite so opposed to American aspirations. In July, 1769, reproving the Revd James for his "True-Blue" contempt of the colonials, Boucher added, "Seriously, I do think the American Opposit'n the most warrantable, generous, & manly, that History can produce...and being a virtuous one, it will certainly, in the end, be successful." Before his departure the politics that put him out of sorts with the Americans had more to do with Church than State. Though in 1767 he rejoiced in an American Church "much less under the Controll of dogmatic'l Superiors than you are" and rejoiced at not having to say the Athanasian Creed as often as at home, four years later he reported that his attempts to establish an American episcopate had made him very unpopular with dissenters in the North.

Perhaps the immediate cause of Boucher's decision to return was the same as Crèvecoeur's: the threat posed by the general uncertainty of the times to both property and livelihood. But for underlying reasons one has to search out the psychology of the man. From the start he was a traveler. "My letters are my Historians," he wrote to the Jameses shortly after he arrived in Virginia. "I flatter myself I shall one Day return Home not a little benefitted by my Peregrination." He may have settled in body, never in mind. As his American fortunes rose and fell – as an engagement was made or broken off, a vocation found or lost, or the hope flowed and ebbed of preferment within the Church – so he kept restlessly changing his mind about whether or not to return. The death of his elder brother in England put him in line for his father's modest inheritance. "What is Cumberland to me now more than Cornwall?" he mused in 1766. "Yes, there is something w'c, independent of Relations & Friendships, attaches me even to its miry Plains & rugged Hills. And should it ever happen, as now alas! it is probable it may, that I should posess a small Pittance of Property in it, I am persuaded, no Consideration whatever c'd ever induce me to alienate it."

Yet less than a year later, responding to a practical proposal that he actually move back, Boucher refused the plan in evasively over-profuse rhetoric:

> W'd to God I c'd longer amuse myself with the pleasing Hope of joining you in the Accomplishm't of that Plan you have so happily pourtrayed But alas! my Friend, this World, this vile World, at w'c We neither can, nor perhaps, ought to be totally indifferent, whilst we are in it, begins to take such fast Hold of me, that, at present, I see not how I shall, in this Particular, ever make Inter[est] & Inclina'n unite.

And three months later, when the vile but irresistable world was treating him less well (a woman had just refused to marry him because he was too "unsettled...giddy & fickle"!), he was ready to return: "if you or any other friend," he wrote to the Revd James, "can only point out to me any Thing like a comfortable Provision...I assuredly will relinquish all my American views, and embrace it." Yet five months later, "America...is the Country for Me." And so on.

The dominant ideology of American national identity, informed and reinforced by the discourse of emigration, would encounter no difficulty in explaining Boucher's eventual back-migration. From the vantage point of the dominant discourse there is a connection – though admittedly it is unclear which is cause and which effect – between his mental restlessness and the source to which he looked for the condition of his worldly fortunes. A member of an international bureaucracy, he always sought preferment (or, as we would say, employment and promotion) from a metropolitan authority. He lived in expectation of a small inheritance. Every "living," "place," "competence" he sought was from another power – fate, his father, the Bishop, the Governor of the colony – anything but his own exertions. The nearest he got to self-reliance was when, disgusted with "the unworthy Condescensions daily imposed upon the Candidate for Preferment," he concluded that he could "see no moral Turpitude in this terrible Crime of Simony." This reversion to the medieval crime of buying one's own living is certainly a novel variation on the American way of enterprise, and somehow fitting for an eventual back-migrant.[8]

So Boucher started for America as a traveler and psychologically speaking, he remained one after he settled there. But it could work the other way round. Someone setting out as an emigrant, a settler or a speculator in a business venture might be thwarted in his or her enterprise and wind up as a professional traveler: that is, someone who returns to write up the experience for the metropolitan audience. Almost from the beginning of American settlement the London publishing world had been avid for news of the New World, since, apart from its intrinsic fascination for British readers, America has frequently stood for a thesis or antithesis in the British domestic political debate: as a positive or negative example of republicanism, or the reform of the franchise, or a rights-based democracy with a written constitution – or whatever else, depending on historical period.

So those who were literate among the ones who "failed" in America, according to whatever definition and for whatever reason, could always entertain the hope of redeeming lost ideals, energy, capital and face by writing up their American adventures for the London literary market. Their books would be widely noticed – possibly the *Quarterly* or the *Edinburgh Review* would peg a long essay on them – and widely sold. They would make money.

This was what happened to Frances Trollope, who, captivated by Frances Wright's radical vision of a community for freed slaves in Nashoba, Tennessee, emigrated to Cincinnati in 1827, to recoup the family fortunes, first in a "Western Museum" of Barnum-like curiosities, then in a grand emporium offering the latest European fashions. When both enterprises failed, the second catastrophically and to the ungallant amusement of the westerners whose benighted taste she had sought to improve, Mrs. Trollope made her way home, by way of Baltimore, Washington, Philadelphia, Niagara Falls and New York. By now she was a traveler and knew the way to make good. It was *Domestic Manners of the Americans* (1832) and a literary career in London. The rest, as they say, is history.

But Mrs. Trollope was only one of many to follow this sequence of careers. Among other back-migrants turned authors were William Clark (*The Mania of Emigrating to the United States*, 1820), Richard Weston (*A Visit to the United States and Canada in 1833; with the View of Settling in America*, 1836), Francis Wyse (*America, Its Realities and Resources*, 1846), James Burn (*The Beggar Boy: an Autobiography*, 1882), and many others – indeed most of the seventy-five returnees surveyed in Shepperson's book covering the better part of the nineteenth century.

What is most striking about these books is how little they differ in matter and manner from the few unpublished accounts remaining in letters from back-migrants, or indeed from the published impressions of out-and-out, self-declared travelers, like William Faux (*Memorable Days in America*, 1823), Dickens (*American Notes for General Circulation*, 1842) and the Captains Marryat and Hall (*Diary in America*, 1839; *Travels in North America*, 1819). They all, roughly speaking, express the same kinds of disappointment in the American physical and cultural environment, in the same ringingly defensive tones.

Which is to say that all are susceptible to that reaction formation common to most travelers, however sophisticated, by which the British (or the Americans, or the French, or whatever) suddenly become strident representatives of what they take to be their home culture when confronted with the manners and customs of "abroad."

And the obscure, unpublished back-migrant could construct his case against the dominant discourse with equal force (if not equal articulacy), reacting against both the propagandists and also his own opinions before emigrating. Writing from New York in November, 1834, John Fisher was ready to return to England. He had been in the States for at least two years, because in one letter he mentions the re-election of President Andrew Jackson in 1832. Almost nothing else is known about him, and even his letters are fragmentary, missing either their first pages (along with the addressee's name) or their last. On November 30, 1834, he wrote someone that "However Owen and Cobbett may Boast of the Country, I have no Cause to Boast of it." Clearly both men could be dismissed as equally visionary:

> I may be [called?] an Unenlightened Foreigner, that may Be, But experience tells me that Mechanics are Better Paid in the Land of Taxes than they are here, However Owen and Cobbett may write and talk. it is quite evident they only do it to Delude the Mechanic by telling him how well they may improve their Circumstances here and at the Same time they are talking they are only doing it for the Purpose of Picking their Pockets and then Laugh up their sleeves to think how easily Englishmen are deluded by Paying their Hard earnd Sixpences to Support Such Characters...

So it goes on and on, like a letter written to the papers in green ink. "If this Country is what they have said it is," he adds, drawing at least a spot of blood this time, "why did not they stay here and enjoy it?" "For my part," Fisher continues, "i shall return to old England very well satisfied that England is still a Place where a steady man may live as comfortable and much more [h]appier than he can here."[9]

So an ordinary "mechanic," with no apparent ambition to, or much chance of having his impressions published in the conventional sense, writes of his disenchantment with America in much the same confidently voiced address to public affairs as any "literary" traveler or back-migrant. Because in their self-image back-migrants could reconstitute themselves as travelers, they could escape the shame of having committed themselves to the American venture, only to be suckered out of their capital; or to give up before the crops came in, or the land had been properly cleared, or transport to markets developed; or to fail in one of a hundred other ways. In their revised image of themselves, they had never really been trying after all, just looking. They were disinterested observers of an exotic land, reporting back their bizarre adventures to a metropolitan audience whose political and cultural values they shared.

That would explain their confident tone. Having converted themselves into travelers, the back-migrants no longer needed to adjust to the socially and culturally puzzling ways of the Americans – so free and frank at times, yet so oddly pompous or prissy at others; so unpredictable in their humour; so aggressively egalitarian yet so besotted with rank that they carried military titles into civilian life. They no longer had to scratch a living from an uncleared wilderness, or find a job in the midst of a financial panic. Whereas before their letters home had to cover up their social and physical unease, to defend their original choice to emigrate or risk ridicule from those they left behind, now they could convey their American news from the critical, distanced perspective shared by their correspondents at home. They were, in other words, newly confident of an audience which now seemed always to have been a majority culture from which they had separated themselves only temporarily; which would get their jokes, share their (revised) politics, understand their allusions.

From the point of view of the "successful" immigrants, the back-migrants may have written themselves out of the dominant discourse. Their criticisms of American physical and social culture may have been discounted in advance. But the back-migrants now had another, more familiar audience to address – whether a single friend, parent, or sibling, or the whole metropolitan reading public – and though that constituency was more than willing to hear the prodigal's recantation, the back-migrants didn't really need the prospect of conventional publication to authenticate their stories. They were going home, and one of the comforts they anticipated on their return was the mutual understanding of their reception.

15

The politics of back-migration and anti-emigration

It would be futile, therefore, to attempt to distinguish between writings of back-migrants and travelers, or between those that were published in the conventional way and those that were merely "preserved." They all constructed themselves in confident refutation of the dominant discourse on emigration, and so they all – almost irrespective of historical period – share certain characteristic topics and modes of address. Above all else, what they had in common was that their political opposition to America was expressed through an assessment of that country's culture – political, social, economic and literary – as a suitable environment for the British emigrant. So once again the topic of emigration stood in for domestic politics – only this time not for the advocates for reform, but for its enemies.

Only a few of the critics, as had Pond and the correspondents in Hutchinson, challenged head-on the assertion that America would afford the emigrant an improved standard of living. Thomas Lechford, a solicitor of Clements Inn, emigrated to Massachusetts when he incurred the enmity of Bishop Laud after defending the Puritan William Prynne, and was "thrown out of [his] station in England." In Boston he worked as a notary, drawing up depositions and other legal documents for people at a shilling a letter. Suspect both because of his profession (lawyers being generally mistrusted in Massachusetts as "caterpillars on the commonwealth") and also for his doctrine (he believed that the function of the Apostolic Succession had not yet ceased – that the church still required a hierarchy), he soon fell out with the authorities of the Bay Colony, and returned to England in 1641. In *Plain Dealing, or Newes from New-England* (London, 1642) Lechford challenged the promoters' promise of material advantages to be found in the New World. "Money is wanting," he wrote, "by reason of the failing of passengers these last two years..." "It is very cold in winter, so that some are frozen to death, or lose their fingers or toes every yeere...Winter begins in October, and lasts till Aprill," and the cold would be felt all the more keenly, because "Here wants a staple commodity to maintain cloathing to the Colony." Or if the trouble wasn't the Massachusetts winter cold, it was the heat of summer in the American South. In one of his low moods Boucher complained of "heart-sickening Fevers" which "have fully determined me at length to quit these burning Climes, & return to Peace and Health in some quiet Corner of England."[10]

In the period following the Napoleonic Wars, when Birkbeck, Cobbett and others advocated emigration to the United States as part of their agitation for domestic reform, their conservative opponents felt compelled to dilate much more fully on the deficiencies of the American physical environment. In 1817 Henry Bradshaw Fearon spent nine months examining the prospects of migration to Illinois, on behalf of thirty-nine farming families in Essex. His discouraging report, published as *Sketches of America* two years later, attacked Birkbeck, Cobbett and other optimistic projectors of the emigrant's material prospects. Fearon found a carpenter recently arrived who now earned ten shillings more a week than he had in Hull, but who found "great difficulty in getting his money from his employer" and who judged the cost of living in America "as nearly like that in England as possible." The climate on the western prairie outran even the combined extremes of Massachusetts and the Carolinas, ranging between 85 to 105 in summer, and "from 10 below to 20 above zero" in winter. And "the disturbance of a great body of surplus vegetable matter, upon the first settling of land, together with the dampness arising from stagnant waters, frequently produce bilious fevers and agues."

Any Englishman "of small fortune, who cares little about politics" (that is, who doesn't bother his head about new-fangled notions of reform) would do better to stay at home, Fearon writes, or else emulate the family who arrived in New York, took one look around, and went back on the same vessel that brought them over. "They went to America in the cabin, they departed from it in the steerage."

William Savage did not emigrate himself, though he claimed to have formed "a serious design...of going to America, and residing in Kentucky," and to have received numerous extensive reports from those who tried the venture to their dissatisfaction. As a result of these researches, he felt compelled to write an admonishing pamphlet priced within the reach of "those who are most interested in the subject." A Kentucky farmer may expect "to labour more, and to suffer greater hardship," he wrote, "than any cottager in England, till his constitution is broken, and his spirits depressed." He recalls a friend of his who died a little over a year after his arrival on the frontier, "whether it was owing to the unhealthiness of the Grant, or some other cause." Since the backwoods are without roads, the settlements are generally on rivers, "and if they be on flats, the inhabitants are almost certain to be subject to dangerous fevers."

Reports like these were pushed to the point of parody by an anonymous pamphlet, also published in 1819, by a disappointed emigrant newly returned to Belper, Derbyshire, from New York City. Attacking "the crafty, scurvy, spleenish, coarse, and mercenary Cobbett," and Birkbeck's "false and fascinating account of swamps, morasses, or mud-fields, swarming with croaking bull-frogs and everlasting filth," the author turns rapidly to the physical depredations of the city he has just left. New York swarms with animals of other kinds: stock jobbers, failed businessmen and hogs ("There have been three different instances...within the last two months, of sows being met in the public streets with young children in their mouths"). The heat is so scorching that "drinking cold water when in a state of perspiration, carries off great numbers; they seldom live many minutes when they swallow it." "People here are taken ill very commonly after breakfast," he adds, as if his measure were not overflowing already, "and are in the grave the same evening."[11]

But if the politics of reform gave back-migrants and their conservative allies a motive to write and an audience to write for, the myth of America's material promise was too powerful to be much affected by doubts cast on the emigrant's expectations of his health and wealth on arrival. In any case, heat, frost, swamps, agues and famine could not plausibly be blamed directly on a republican government. Texts confronting the dominant discourse have always functioned more seriously and extensively when their attentions turn from American nature to American culture. Even the most fervent proponents of settlement acknowledged that the emigrant would have to give up his or her accustomed physical landscape, as well as the familiar hierarchies and other dispositions of a traditional society. Some renounced "culture" with relish; others, like Cobbett and Birkbeck, with a touch of regret at a price worth paying for an invigorated "nature."

Sometimes this critique confined itself to what British travelers in America do so well – and so often – then as now: sharp observations on American manners. "The people [in Virginia] may boast a sort of apathy," Jonathan Boucher wrote to the Jameses, soon after his arrival in Virginia in 1759. "A sentimental Story is lost upon Them, & they Acknowledge themselves quite Strangers to that refind, delicate Sensibility w'c distinguishes a generous Mind." Henry Fearon came to a similar conclusion about the people of New York, where "there is, on the surface of society, a carelessness, a laziness, an unsocial indifference, which freezes the blood and disgusts the judgement."

Elsewhere he found abuses much grosser. Americans had no literature to speak of, poor schools, bad architecture, no "*haut-ton*" to match the English aristocracy, universal color prejudice. In their hotels they smoked "segars"; in the House of Representatives, they spat tobacco. Western inns and taverns served only whisky, and if their proprietors were "cold...unfeeling, callous and selfish," the hogs at least were friendly enough, coming in at night "for their due share of the log residence."[12]

Observations like these go along with other appalled reactions to local manners that form the staple of the nineteenth-century British traveler's account: dismay at the misuse of the English language in America, the aggressive competition for servings of food in American hotels and boarding houses, the curiosity of fellow-travelers on American trains and boats, the insolence of servants. But not all authors rested content with observations of American surface behavior. Bizarre manners spoke of a deeper disorder in American society. How could it be otherwise when the population was composed of such heterogeneous disposits of human character? Even Robert Holditch, he who lamented the emigrant's departure in the words of Oliver Goldsmith and was on balance a proponent of transatlantic migration, had to admit that alongside the "industrious, sober, skilful mechanic," the "ingenious manufacturer," the "indefatigable peasant" and the "respected farmer," America also attracted "adventurers from every part of Europe, – the visionary – the bankrupt in fortune and in fame – the idle and the vicious." Savage, naturally, shifted the balance towards the pejorative side of the scale: "The United States of America have...for many years...attracted the Disaffected in Politics – the Swindler – the Ruined Tradesman – and the Agriculturalist with small capital, who has been weighed down by the effects of the taxes of this country."

Of these motives for migration, the second and third would hardly have been admitted by the emigrant himself; the last frequently, and with apparently well-justified fervor; the first sometimes. Historians of emigration are still uncertain as to how frequently – and above all, how generally – politics could be said to have caused the typical individual or family to remove to the New World. I have argued that to emigrate because of high taxes and other material causes – to seek increased "independence," even if only economic – is itself a political act, and that to express a material motive for doing so is to make a kind of political statement. But the politics of Savage and the back-migrants for whom he spoke and wrote were both explicit and partisan. "The great mass of the [American] population is composed [of] the disaffected in politics and the traitors to their country, from all parts of Europe," he reiterates, "to whom England is obnoxious, on account of the noble and glorious stand she made for the preservation of social order."

In the early nineteenth century, that social order was the hierarchy of kingly government. The English emigrant "must, on landing [in America] discard every appearance of loyalty to his natural Sovereign, and abuse both him and his native land," Savage warns. When the sovereign principle is overthrown, so is everything "natural" and "native." Savage tells the story of his friend, an English widower who courted a Kentucky widow, the "proprietor of a farm and five negro slaves":

> she accepted him for a husband...but she secured her property to herself. Some time after the marriage, he began to lord it over his wife with a high hand, as he had been in the habit of doing before; but this behaviour did not suit the feelings of the republican dame; and one day, after a violent altercation, to shew that she would not be mastered by an Englishman, she ordered her negroes to seize her leige lord and master, and give him a good flogging, which they did with great glee and a cat-o-nine-tails.

It is difficult to keep up with the shifts in tone here. At first the phrases "lord it over," "high hand," and "her leige lord and master" seem to convey at least a degree of ironic detachment from his friend's behavior towards his wife, but soon it becomes clear that Savage takes his feudal jargon quite seriously: that what his friend "had been in the habit of doing" is justified on the grounds of tradition. Savage is outraged by what he calls "this violent breach of prerogative." The "republican dame" has overturned most of the hierarchical relationships that St. Paul could think of – the wife's subjection to her husband, the woman's to the man, the servant's to his master – plus some that he couldn't: sexual, racial, financial and national (for contributing to Savage's angry incredulity is the fact that an American was treating an Englishman in this way).

Frances Trollope was equally explicit about the contemporary politics dividing the United States and Great Britain, and even more vehement. The principal source of American social disorder, she thought, were the works (in both the published and Biblical senses) of Thomas Jefferson, which "would make of mankind an unamalgamated mass of grating atoms, where the darling 'I'm as good as you,' would soon take place of the law and the Gospel." As it is in America now, "The assumption of equality, however empty, is sufficient to tincture the manners of the poor with brutal insolence, and subjects the rich to the paltry expediency of sanctioning the falsehood." As for Jefferson himself, it was well known (of course) that he had betrayed his own principles, "when past the three score years and ten, [he] still taught young females to obey his nod, and so became the father of unnumbered generations of groaning slaves."[13]

Those who know and like *Domestic Manners* will detect something happening to Mrs. Trollope's prose here. Gone is that characteristic, cool irony; vanished too is even the pretense of meticulous observation based on evidence seen with her own eyes. Suddenly to stoop to the old canard that Jefferson had fathered "generations" of children by his own slaves, a staple of British anti-American propaganda since the beginning of the nineteenth century, is as serious a lapse in her normal standards of debate as is her choice to reiterate so feverishly the perennial conservative nightmare of an insolent poor and a compliant ruling class.

So if the enemies of American republicanism commonly expressed their adversarial politics through a critique of America as a site for emigration, those who "failed" at emigration, or refused it, frequently inscribed their disappointment with the American experience within a political critique of the country. In the dominant discourse the two dialogues, of emigration and party, were inextricable. As for the traveler, since issues of franchise and constitution divided the two nations so dramatically, the reaction formation to all things foreign in America, so common to the tourist's psychology, was bound to come out in expressions of political difference.

Confronting American politics, Dickens and Frances Trollope found themselves asserting opinions far more reactionary than those they upheld at home. So did many of the published back-migrants discussed by Shepperson. Andrew Bell (*Men and Things in America*, 1838) "grew up a radical republican" and "embraced a Thomas Paine type of egalitarianism," according to Shepperson, but "after a sojourn in America...gradually became more conservative and died a rigid traditionalist." Also inspired by Paine, the hatter Thomas Brothers sailed with his family for Philadelphia in 1824, where he prospered for six years or so, until the manufacture of hats by machine began to cut into the economics of his craft. Nine years later he returned to England convinced that "self-government...has no existence in the nature of things." The title of his book on America, published in 1840, neatly outlines his own political trajectory: *The United States of North America as They Are; Not as They Are Generally Described: Being a Cure for Radicalism*.

And John Fisher exhibited the same reaction:

> When I left England I was Certainly a Reformer but since i have been in this Country I have seen that a Democratic Government and a Reform Government are one and the same thing. I have seen that sudden experiments only end in a Panic without any real Good resulting...my own Political Principles have entirely changed and I shall return to England a Tory for i am now quite satisfied with the British Constitution and with Arthur Duke of Wellington as a Proper man to Defend it.[14]

With the words "Arthur Duke of Wellington" the handwriting actually opens out and grows larger, as though miming the pride swelling in his breast.

But the process was operating well before the nineteenth century, even before the United States had become a sovereign nation. Lechford's quarrel with Massachusetts Bay was not just ecclesiastical: "We are quite out of the way of right government," he wrote in *Plain Dealing*, "both in Church and Commonwealth." Not only was democracy dangerous in its own right ("A Monarchy is the best government for Englishmen; better to suffer some pressures under that kind of government, then to spoile one another with popular elections"), but since the Massachusetts franchise was confined to members of the Church, "many well-affected or affectionate people, but weak in sound experience, are...drawn thereunto." In other words, the enthusiastic and the dogmatic got to vote, while steadier men could not.

From a similar ecclesiastical standpoint, Jonathan Boucher also began to connect Puritanism with subversion of the secular government. In 1773, increasingly embattled for his advocacy of an American episcopate, unpaid "one Penny" of his church stipend for two years, he warned that

> The Bulk of the People are Dissenters, of the same Puritan, or rather Indepen't, republican Spirit. They plant Schools, Colleges & Churches in every Corner, where they openly teach & inculcate Principles subversive to all good Government...at a late Commencement at the College of Princeton in New Jersey...a student delivered some Oration on Government [and] w'th much shew of Erudition affected to draw it all from a Compact between King and People – that certain Conditions were stipulated for by each of the contracting Parties, on the Failure, or non performance of which, on either side, the contract became void...

Two years later he left America, having been banned from his Church. Back in London, in January, 1776, he wrote, "There is a Principle of Revolt innate in All Colonies."[15]

16

Fully-formed travelers' accounts of the United States; their notice in the quarterlies: "barbarizing" and degeneration; religion: incarnational and reformed

The more ambitious travelers' and back-migrants' accounts of the United States organize their observations of unruly manners and subversive politics into a comprehensive scheme of cultural regress. The sense that American society was degenerating enters the published literature from very early in the history of anglophone settlement in North America – by the middle of the seventeenth century at the latest. For Lechford the Church in Boston was not effecting an invigorating reformation but falling away from the ritual and minor offices it was accustomed to observe at home. "There are Lectures...in *Boston*, upon Thursdayes, when Master *Cotton* teacheth out of the *Revelation*... but no holy dayes, except the Sunday. In some Churches, nothing is read on the first day of the weeke, or Lords day, but a Psalme dictated before or after the Sermon."[16]

As we have seen, other members of the Massachusetts migration, like Pond and the correspondents in Hutchinson's history, feared that the New England soil would give out after a generation. But the thesis that American culture and society was degenerating really began to gather momentum after the Revolution. The proponents of emigration and the political allies of the new country believed American independence to be the logical, communal extension of the rite of passage undertaken by every individual in the process of becoming American in the first place. For the conservative opponents of the American political model, the Republic had begun irreversibly to decline as soon as it cut itself off from the mother country. Each side of the argument was based on a different organic model: that of the child reaching independent adulthood, or of the branch being lopped off the tree.

The tension leading up to and following the War of 1812, in which the two countries first squared off against each other as sovereign antagonists, prompted a flurry of references to American degeneration in the British quarterlies, as one side in the so-called "paper war" that preceded, accompanied and followed the shooting war. In his essay in the *Edinburgh Review* which asked "who reads an American book?" Sidney Smith reminded his readers that the "Franklins and Washingtons, and all the other sages and heroes of [the American] revolution, were born and bred subjects of the King of England," and that since then "they have yet done marvellously little to assert the honour of such a descent." A review in the *Quarterly* of Birkbeck's *Notes on a Journey in America* opined that while "man" may find it agreeable enough to return "to that state of nature in which he is accountable to no earthly tribunal for his actions...once he has thrown off the restraints which a state of civilization and a sense of religion impose, he feels little inclination to reassume them."

"'Retrograding and barbarizing is an easy process,'" another reviewer quoted from W. Faux's *Memorable Days in America*, in a notice that covered almost thirty-two pages of the *Quarterly* in 1823. "'Far from the laws and restraints of society, and having no servants to do that for us which was once daily done, we become too idle in time to do any thing but that which nature and necessity require.'" Not pausing to ask how the continued presence of servants might have discouraged idleness, the reviewer continued quoting the dire report: "'pride and all stimuli forsake us, for we find ourselves surrounded only by men of similar manners; hence the face is seldom shaved or washed, or the linen changed except on washing days. The shoes are cleaned, perhaps, never...'"

As the people, so their public buildings. "'Every edifice, saving the college, a beautiful building, seems filthy, neglected, and in ruins, particularly the court-house, the temple of justice, in the best square, which, with its broken windows, rotten window-frames...all ruined and spoiled for lack of paint and a nail, looks like an old abandoned bagnio, not fit to be compared with any workhouse in England.'" Religion, too, was degenerating, the *Quarterly* reviewer continued, now under his own steam: "The want of an established national religion has made the bulk of people either infidels or fanatics...In the back settlements, here and there a frantic sectarian holds forth in a hovel or under a tree...The village church, with its spiry steeple, its bells, its clock, the well-fenced churchyard with its ancient yew-tree, and the numerous monumental records of the dead, are here utterly unknown."

The best joke of all greeted Faux when he reached the "English prairie" in Illinois Territory, to which Flower and Birkbeck had inveigled so many "degenerate English mechanics" five years before. There he found the son of the great agitator for reform, "Orator" Hunt, "'living in a miserable, one-roomed log-cabin, without servant...half naked and in rags,'" his land "'uncultivated, unsown and selling *for the payment of taxes*!'" The *Quarterly* reviewer could hardly contain his mirth:

> Avast reading there! Overhaul that article again! as old Trunnian says. *Taxes*, did you say? *taxes* in this last retreat of suffering humanity!...What a shock will this intelligence give to the great "Champion of Reform"...when he finds that he has sent his only son to America to starve...where "no power on earth can crush the citizen!"[17]

Savage, Mrs. Trollope, even Dickens, took their lead from this periodical literature on America, mainly of a Tory persuasion. For Trollope American religion was a fallen remnant of the proper institution in Europe, debased to the "atrocious wickedness" of a camp meeting "in a wild district on the confines of Indiana." Savage could think of the emigrant moving by boat to his new settlement only in terms of a descent to oblivion; the settler "fall[s] down the stream to Kentucky...convey[s] his family and property down the Ohio," only to succumb "with horror of the dreariness" of the way, along which "all is dull, solitary, gloomy – nothing to cheer, nothing to enliven the mind...nothing [to be seen] but the sky over the head, and the banks of the river bounded with trees."

Understandably, Dickens associated degeneration with the evil of slavery. "There is an air of ruin and decay abroad," he wrote in *American Notes* (1842), "which is inseparable from the system. The barns and outhouses are mouldering away; the sheds parched and half roofless." The Indian burial mounds along the Ohio, long a feature of intense interest to American and European travelers alike, filled him with "compassion for the extinct tribes who lived so pleasantly here, in their blessed ignorance of white existence, hundreds of years ago." As for "white existence" on the frontier, he noted that the newer a settlement was, the more likely it was to be decrepit, with "broken windows, patched with worn-out hats, old clothes, old boards, fragments of blankets and paper." So powerful was that distinctive tendency of his imagination to caricature a social atmosphere through its inanimate objects, that it extended the connection even to the morally neutral features of a natural topography, unmediated by any human settlement. Where the Ohio River had washed away its banks, "stately trees [had] fallen down into the stream," some of which were "mere dry, grizzly skeletons."[18]

Of course, there is another way of looking at it. New seedlings replace old trees; rivers wash soil away only to deposit it elsewhere; a frontier settlement is a harbinger of the future as well as a midden of discarded clothing. "Democratic peoples do not bother at all about the past," as de Tocqueville pointed out, "but gladly start dreaming about the future, and in that direction their imagination knows no bounds, but spreads and grows beyond measure." The western land speculator could ignore the swampy wastes of the present in his vision of their future promise. The eastern defender of the republic's young culture could counter

Irving's lament for lost "association" by arguing that the American's proper association should be with the future rather than the past. In Query II of *Notes on Virginia* Thomas Jefferson could describe American rivers in terms of their present allure as well as their future promise: "The *Ohio* is the most beautiful river on earth. Its current gentle, waters clear, and bosom smooth, and unbroken by rocks and rapids"; "The *Missisipi* [*sic*] will be one of the principle channels of future commerce for the country westward of the Alleghaney."

This habit of the imagination Morris Birkbeck called the "figure of anticipation": that is, "the use of the present indicative, instead of the future subjunctive" in describing an area in the course of development. Birkbeck's not unfriendly comment, arising from his having heard that Pittsburgh was "the Birmingham of America" and his subsequent disappointment in the pokey manufacturing town (as it then was) that he actually found there, was picked up and turned into a sneer by the *Quarterly Review*. Dickens had a good time with the joke in *Martin Chuzzlewit*, in the form of "The thriving City of Eden" – so spacious in prospect, but a couple of derelict log cabins in fact. Yet Pittsburgh did come to surpass Birmingham in the production of steel, just as surely as the Mississippi became – and remains – a "principle channel of... commerce."[19]

But Mrs. Trollope's river is nothing less than a symbolic landscape of American desolation. *Domestic Manners* does not begin with the conventional emigrant's account of the voyage across the Atlantic: no passage to a fresh experience – let alone to a new life – for her. As she tells it, their landfall was first signaled by the "deep blue of the Mexican Gulf" being sullied by the brown alluvial waters of the Mississippi. Whereas others entered America through its mouth, Mrs. Trollope came in through its cloaca. The entrance of the river is, by an explicit allusion to Dante's *Inferno*, turned into the gates of Hell. The reader enters both text and country through a whole landscape symbolic of decay, solitude and disruption. "The mast of a vessel long since wrecked" stands as "a dismal witness to the destruction that has been, and a boding prophet of that which is to come."

As they move up river more of this Heart of Darkness becomes visible: "monstrous bulrushes," "a huge crocodile luxuriating in the slime." Occasionally a tree "of enormous length," uprooted by the "frequent hurricane," floats past them:

> Sometimes several of these, entangled together, collect among their boughs a quantity of floating rubbish, that gives the mass an appearance of a moving island, bearing a forest, with its roots mocking the heavens; while the dishonoured branches lash the tide in idle vengeance: this, as it approaches the vessel, and glides swiftly past, looks like the fragment of a world in ruins.

Here in these first two astonishing pages is everything Mrs. Trollope wants to say about America. It has no decorum; everything is out of scale, "monstrous"; the climate violent. There is a hint also of the sexual license she thought she witnessed at the frontier camp meeting, since the Latin root of "luxuriating" means lust, and "dishonoured" was conventionally applied to Victorian heroines who had been seduced and abandoned. Above all, the country is a fragment, uprooted, topsy-turvy, literally "The World Turned Upside Down." (Burgoyne's regimental bands played that old radical anthem, slowly and ironically, when the British surrendered at Yorktown.)

Analyzed under the old headings of narrative analysis, the writings of back-migrants and hostile travelers could be said to share a tone, a content and a structure. They were confidently expressed because their authors knew their audience and could both allude to its preconceptions and anticipate its reactions. They were conservative because they were written by travelers abroad, who saw themselves as representing a traditional order at home, and because an influential force in metropolitan literary production was avid for evidence that the radical American experiment had failed. Their structure was governed above all by the imperative to subvert or negate the propaganda – both perennial and contemporary – in favor of American emigration.

So Mrs. Trollope, like Fearon, Pond, and Hutchinson's correspondents, inverts the redemptive pattern of the successful emigrant's narrative – only she does it systematically and repeatedly. Throughout *Domestic Manners* the bad news follows the good, instead of the other way round. At one point she rivals Jefferson in her praise of the beauty of the Ohio River: "sometimes it is bounded by perpendicular rocks; pretty dwellings, with their gay porticoes are seen, alternately with wild intervals of forest." "Yet," she does not fail to add, "these fair shores are still unhealthy." The market in Cincinnati "can hardly...be surpassed in any part of the world," yet "the fruits...are very inferior to any I have seen in Europe." Once on a walk for pleasure they climbed "a certain noble-looking sugar-loaf hill, that promised pure air and a fine view," only to find the brook at its base turned "red with the stream from a pig slaughter-house," and their feet "entangled in pigs' tails and jawbones: and thus the prettiest walk in the neighbourhood was interdicted for ever." Wherever she seemed on the point of establishing a perspective – whether a sense of ordered society or a picturesque landscape – she was disappointed by the eventuality. Like her high hopes for the Nashoba community, and for her own enterprise in America itself, her every optimistic expectation "was interdicted for ever." Significantly, when she finally managed to compose a picturesque scene, in a "sweetly wild...spot" on a road following the Mohawk River, she was on her way home, and the land turned out to be owned by an English Member of Parliament. Even that wasn't to last. He had just sold most of it to American commercial interests, which had already erected "a great wooden edifice, where, on the white paint, 'Cash for Rags,' in letters three feet high, might be seen."[20]

Savage undermined the propaganda for settlement by turning the chief trope of the prelapsarian vision, the negative catalog of cultural institutions with which the Golden Age had yet to be cursed, from beneficent to malign. His subject is a frontier clearing. The farmer in the "wilds of America," he writes, has:

no society, even to quarrel with . . . no social neighbour . . . no newspaper to inform him of the occurrences of that society of which he has ceased to be a mamber . . . no village feasts, weddings, or christenings . . . no market where he can go once a week . . . no interesting bustle with his fellow labourers . . . no mill to grind his corn . . . no joint of meat for his family's Sunday dinner; no means of education for his children . . . no medical assistance if he should be ill of a fever . . . no help but what himself can afford if his wife should be in "that situation which all women wish to be in who love their lords;" no sound of bells from the parish church to summon him on Sundays to worship the Almighty.

Trollope works the same vein:

These people were indeed independent, Robinson Crusoe was hardly more so, and they eat and drink abundantly; but yet it seemed to me that there was something awful and almost unnatural in their loneliness. No village bell ever summoned them to prayer . . . When they die, no spot sacred by ancient reverence will receive their bones – Religion will not breathe her sweet and solemn farewell upon their grave; the husband or father will dig the pit that is to hold them, beneath the nearest tree; he will himself deposit them within it, and the wind that whispers through the boughs will be their only requiem. But then they pay neither taxes nor tythes, are never expected to pull off a hat or make a curtsy, and will live and die without hearing or uttering the dreadful words, "God save the King."[21]

Aspects of these important passages are very unpleasant: Trollope's substitution of "pit" for "grave"; Savage's sexual politics, betrayed by the coyly feudal way he tiptoes around the word "pregnant." Yet there is much that is serious here too, and diagnostic of issues more general than the individual psychology of the two authors concerned. Trollope's ending, sardonically catching up the beneficent negatives of the emigrant's stock apology, show the extent to which her narrative is controlled by the dominant discourse. The frontier settlement could almost be called a trope of the hostile traveler's report, so often was it described and quoted in lengthy quarterly reviews, as though it stood for the values of a whole people: cultureless, restless and solitary.

Yet opinions apart, the American and European physical landscapes were objectively as different from each other as were their social structures – and especially outside the cities. The characteristic European farming community was organized along cooperative lines, symbolized by the walled town to which the farmer returned at sundown – as one can see in France even today – or in Italy by the *fattoria* (perhaps originally a fortified manor house, or even a Roman villa) to which the farmers in the outlying *case coloniche*, or colony-farms, repaired to share out their produce, and for shelter in times of danger.

By contrast the characteristic American model is the freestanding, wooden farmhouse – perhaps (in time) surrounded by outbuildings, but all owned by one family, and sharing little until the arrival of later settlers. The architecture and geography of the American farm expressed independence, an idea which both preceded and was reinforced by its settlement. The emigrant made his decision, set out on his own to develop an isolated tract. Firearms made fortifications redundant, which was just as well, since stones were hardly lying around dressed ready to be made into walls. Besides, the urgent need to get something in the ground made time spent even on constructing a fence of log palings more of a risk than a defense. (Some of the bitterest quarrels between early settlers in Virginia and New England were over whether first to plant or build stockades.)

A more specific objective contrast between Europe and America lies in ideas of religion. The descriptions given by Savage and Trollope of American frontier settlements display a perhaps unbridgeable gulf between what it means to be American and British – or perhaps here, English. The frontier settler, were he granted a voice (which he seldom is in these accounts), might respond that he and his family do indeed have access to "religion": that their God they carry always with them, in their Bible and their prayers and their personal sense of His grace in their daily lives; that therefore they had no need of formal weddings, christenings, funerals, or other external rituals to mark the stages of their physical and spiritual lives. But for the English commentators such a faith, without the social and institutional relations inextricably bound up with religion at home, was literally unimaginable. For the English middle classes the Church of England, however uncertainly they may attend its services or fathom its doctrine, stands for a whole culture – perhaps for culture itself. In *As You Like It*, when Orlando is trying to tell whether Duke Senior and his band in the Forest of Arden are truly civilized, he asks them if they have "ever been where bells have knolled to church."

This difference between English and American perceptions is, therefore, also that between a Catholic, incarnational sense of the everyday world and a reformed Protestant one. (The difference has also divided classes and regions within Great Britain, but that is another subject.) From the incarnational standpoint, the "horizontal" connections – physical and social – between men and women mediate the "vertical" relationship between people and their God. The Protestant, like the emigrant (who in the American paradigm of settlement *was* a Protestant) was willing to forgo the neighbors, the newspaper, the market, the village pub and the parish church, along with the political and ecclesiastical hierarchies, and the tythes and taxes that supported them. But, says the other voice, consider what you are giving up when you cast "culture" off. Lechford's objection to the shortage of holidays in Puritan Massachusetts, as he explains in a footnote, was that it was a way of exploiting labor: "And sure enough, at New-England, the Masters will and must hold their servants to their labour more then in other Countries well planted is needfull."[22]

So even when most unlikable, Trollope and Savage tell a kind of truth. Stripped of its nauseating mode of expression, even Savage's point about the difficulty of a frontier pregnancy would find an echo in the experience of Rebecca Butterworth. But though the truth is expressed as universal, it is not. It is partial: socially and politically constructed – rhetorically constructed too, since it is in dialogue with the advocacy of New World settlement. The truth in sight here is what it feels like to be English when confronting the United States of America.

Similarly, it would be perfectly "true" to point out that crossing the Atlantic in the 1840s was, on balance, more pleasant when going from North America to Europe than the other way round. Before steam, a ship heading west had to tack against the prevailing winds, or in the mid-nineteenth century, when steam was used as auxiliary power to enable a service to keep to schedule, punch the wind and waves unsteadied by the force against full sails. Going to America took longer than returning, and was much less comfortable.

But look at the values Dickens inscribes on the two transatlantic passages in *American Notes*. Unlike Trollope, he does have something to say about his voyage across, but the experience is presented as the exact opposite of the emigrant's liberating passage to a new life. Going aboard to get to his quarters, Dickens found himself "descending into the bowels of the ship" through "a long, narrow compartment not unlike a gigantic hearse." His berth reminded him of a coffin. The trip across was very rough, with the ship "staggering, heaving, wrestling, leaping, diving, jumping, pitching, throbbing, rolling and rocking," and the "state-room...standing on its head." The passengers were lethargic, when not actively seasick, so there was no good company. Progress was laborious, the "prospect" of the ocean dull; the food, produced by a druken ship's cook, an atrocious mess of "pig's face, cold ham...and hot collops." They shipped water, drowning several of the bunks. Running into Halifax harbor they grounded on a bank of mud. Later, making their way down the coast to Boston, they got lost altogether.

His return to England was entirely different. Instead of the new-fangled steam packet in which he crossed over to America, he returned, running before the wind, in a traditional full-rigged sailing ship. Instead of the confinement, darkness, dulness, death, and disorder of the outward voyage, they weighed anchor with a "Cheerily men, oh cheerily," and the ship, "spreading her white wings...soared away upon her free and solitary course." En route their "select association" enjoyed "an abundance of amusements," with "banquets," music, lively company, and diverting sights from the ship's rail. "Dolphins and porpoises...rolled and leaped and dived around the vessel," and "those small creatures ever on the wing, the Mother Carey's chickens...flutter[ed] about the vessel's stern."

Meanwhile, down in the steerage, regarded with benign curiosity by the happy band of cabin passengers, were "nearly a hundred" miserable failed emigrants, returning in ruins from their American adventures:

> Some of them had been in America but three days, some but three months...Others had sold their clothes to raise the passage-money, and had hardly rags to cover them; others had no food, and lived upon the charity of the rest; and one man...had had no sustenance whatever but the bones and scraps of fat he took from the plates used in the after-cabin dinner, when they were put out to be washed...The history of every family we had on board was pretty much the same. After hoarding up, and borrowing, and begging, and selling everything to pay the passage, they had gone out to New York, expecting to find its streets paved with gold; and had found them paved with very hard and very real stones. Enterprise was dull; labourers were not wanted; jobs of work were to be got, but the payment was not. They were coming back, even poorer than they went.

And that was true too, as the statistics of back-migration suggest. Or was it? Like Fearon – like most of us perhaps – Dickens assumed that the only passengers traveling eastbound in steerage were failed back-migrants. It was not the thought of British emigration that so dismayed Dickens, it was British emigration to the United States. This was, after all, the same man who was soon so warmly to approve Mrs. Chisholm's scheme to assist emigration to Australia. And the same author who would collect, verify, edit and publish in the first issue of his family magazine the letters of apparently contented emigrants to Australia, here mocks the form with parody, standing the good news on its head when it comes from the independent republic across the Atlantic:

> One of them was carrying an open letter from a young English artisan... "This is the country, Jem," said the writer. "I like America. There is no despotism here; that's the great thing. Employment of all sorts is going a-begging, and wages are capital. You have only to choose a trade, Jem, and be it... *At present I haven't made up my mind whether to be a carpenter – or a tailor.*"[23]

Charles Dickens's meditation as he mused over the passengers in steerage is part of the dominant discourse of American emigration. Indeed, so influential was it – so witty and imaginative – that *American Notes* can be said to have contributed to the construction of that discourse, even as it epitomized and typified it.

17

The alternative voice and how it was preserved, 1: The Puritan debate before departure

One of the strongest impulses behind the dominant discourse was the emigrant's need to justify his or her life-changing venture to family and friends left behind – and through that process, to define his or her new identity in the New World. Obviously, emigrants began to write only when they had left home and had news to communicate from afar. And since overwhelmingly the largest body of written evidence of how the emigrants felt about their move (and of why they went in the first place) comes from letters written home, it is impossible to distinguish what they "really" felt (assuming they could have articulated their feelings in a form we could accept as convincing) from their need to establish their success for those who loved and supported them, and for those who had been skeptical about the idea from the beginning.

But as it happens, there is another body of evidence apparently quite free from this self-justificatory imperative. The reason we have it to examine is that it was produced and preserved within that most literate and articulate community of self-examiners, the American Puritans. It comes in two forms: conscientious writing (journals, letters written by people still at home to those who had already gone over) agonizing over the decision of whether or not to emigrate; and communications between those who had settled in Massachusetts. Neither discourse was produced either to promote or deprecate the enterprise. Either the decision had still to be taken, so had no need to be defended, or the recipient of the communication was another emigrant, not a father or friend at home from whom the emigrant had to assert his independence.

These data lie outside the field of the dominant discourse. Are they thereby more neutral? Do they illuminate the psychology of anglophone emigration more directly and tellingly than the promotional tracts, emigrants' letters home, and the adversarial response they provoked from British travel journalists?

Let us consider, first, the letters and journals of those at home, still trying to decide whether or not to go over. Between 1636 and 1638 Lucy Downing wrote a series of letters to her brother and sister-in-law, John and Margaret Winthrop, expressing a wide range of doubts – private and public, natural and cultural – over whether to join them in New England. "For ould enlan and London, whoe that knowes them can deny the desireablenes of them as they are in them selues: and for my owne part, changes were euer irksome to mee: and the sea much more." Besides, had God truly called her to join them? He seemed now "to hould forth Christ" as "gratiously and gloriously" in England as ever before. Later, "my present condition [now she was pregnant] is vnfit for changes," though in another letter (and mood) she added, "big as I am, I should rather wish to bring an Indyan then a coknye into the world."

More generally, she worried about the material conditions to sustain life in New England: the shortage of "subsistance" for God's people, the apparent lack of staple commodities for them to trade. And what about her eldest son's education? "Poor boy, I fear the journie would not be so prosperous for him as I could wish, in respect you haue yet noe sosieties nor means in that kind of education of youths in learninge."

Yet in 1638 Lucy Downing and her husband Emmanuel emigrated to New England. Why did she go? She doesn't say directly. The obvious answer, that he was determined on the venture and that she was his wife, won't wholly fit the case of such an intelligent, articulate and spirited woman: a devout Protestant schooled to find out and follow the path of her own salvation. If she finally went simply because her husband did, she wasn't going to acknowledge the fact. "But now," she wrote her brother in 1636, "you may saye I take to much upon me, I am but a wife, and therfore it is sufficient for me to follow my husban." It was true that she had objected to the idea "by way of caueat...for I thought it my duty," but her resistance was never absolute, nor would he have proceeded if it had been. "Yet if he likes to goe...I shall endeuer to be with you as sone as I maye." Finally her choice may have had as much to do with the fatigue of indecision as with conjugal obedience: "I doe not apprehend it aduantagious to vs to be apon such vncertainties either for soule or body. I could earnestly wish a more settled condition in new or ould; but what shall I saye. It hath bine the lot of many far more deseruing then my selfe, to be in greater exigents then I haue yet felt." Even so, her consolation was more of one bereaved than spiritually invigorated.[24]

More puzzling is the case of John Bailey, whose letters from Limerick to Increase Mather in 1682 and 1683 consist largely of reasons for not emigrating to Massachusetts, yet who went over less than a year later. Having begun to preach in Chester, England, when he was twenty-two, Bailey moved to Ireland, where he and his congregation lived in "quiet and in peac, enjoying our libertys as formerly," though characteristically this anguished conscience feared their good fortune as a great temptation to sin. What of New England, though? Like Lucy Downing, he could not "tell what the mind of God is in it." Though "satisfyed abundantly" that Mather's praise of Massachusetts was justified, he wondered whether New England wasn't greatly fallen away from its original "purity, humility & holiness." Yet he went, possibly fatigued with anxiety that "Our turn to suffer [in Ireland] will come," and "our case is likely to be very badd in this place, tho at present we have our libertye."[25]

Others traced the opposite trajectory, giving themselves (and others) numerous reasons for going over, then unaccountably deciding against it. Samuel Rogers, one of an influential family of

English Puritans, heard "good news from New England" and began to examine his soul for evidence of "the Lord's mind beckoning me towards that place." In England he perceived "the church of God held under hatches, the walls of Jerusalem beaten down." At length God and America became interchangeable: "The more of New England I have, the more of God I enjoy," he wrote in his diary on April 1, 1636. "The more I have of God, the more I sigh after New England." Yet for all his private and public assurance in his calling to Massachusetts, he stayed behind. Why? The modern editor of his diary suggests several reasons. His father and brother seem to have opposed the idea. He was worried about his "future accomodations," which appears to have meant a New England ministry as much as food and housing. Ultimately he gained a place in the household of the Puritan patron, Lady Mary Vere.[26]

Writing from Bristol to Thomas Dyer of Weymouth, Massachusetts, in 1663, John Retsolloh listed a whole catalog of contemporary abuses against the dissenting Churches, that put him in "no minde to this land" of England. Meetings of both Independents and Baptists had been broken up, their pastors imprisoned. Some had been fined forty shillings, others five, ten and even fifty pounds, then forced to "lie in prison tell they have payd it." Examining a Quaker, the Mayor of Bristol

> asked him a reason of his beeinge at such meetinges contrary to the kinges lawes the man touled him hee came in contiens to the command of god the mayor answered sir you must know that the kings lawes is the supreame judg of constience: by which answer you may understand his soundnes knowledg and godlynes; but this is to let you see what...magistrats god doth permit to be set up over us.

Yet for all his outrage at the persecution of the reformed Churches in his home town, Retsolloh stayed behind. "I doe talke every year of cominge to you," he wrote, then adding a condition as ingenious as it was difficult to fulfill, "but I thinke I shall hardly come tell a waymoth vesell come to cary mee." And then, parenthetically, almost at the end of his long letter: "Brother pray remember mee to...all the rest of my friends with you and tell them I longe to see them, but my wife will not goe to NE and I locke at it as a difficult thinge to part and leave her behind." This latter, at least, is a real reason, yet the embarrassed way he sets the case against going at the margins of his letter's substance, suggests that he feels it as an excuse.[27]

The longest, and also the funniest, series of letters from such waverers was written from England by Edward Howes to John Winthrop, Jr., in Boston. "I haue sould all and meane to followe," Howes wrote his old friend, in November, 1631, adding the significant qualification, "Deo iuvante" (if it please the Lord). By the following March, the Lord had yet to be pleased, so Howes was "yet confined within the lymitts of my natiue soyle." The next year he began to study law, moving first to chambers in Clifford's Inn, and then to the Inner Temple. A year later he had secured his "mothers good will...to goe ouer when I will," adding in the margin, "it was since my admittance" (to Clifford's Inn, so now a new disincentive had taken the place of her disapproval). Three months later he thought of another impediment. Though unmarried and "as farre from marrying as euer I was," he was "loath to goe to N: E:" without a wife. Two months later still he seemed keen enough to ask the younger Winthrop to get him some "cow calues of a yeare old or older," for "I desire to haue some stock there." But three years on he was still in London, even though "there dyed...of the plague this weeke 181." As for Massachusetts, "The Lord knowes when I shall gett thither."

Why did Edward Howes stay behind? Apart from the reasons he offered almost as he thought of them, he may have had genuine doubts about the physical and spiritual viability of the infant colony. Was it not working "a too palpable seperation...[from] our church gouernement"? What about the widely reported severity of the Massachusetts government – the story "about cuttinge off the Lunatick mans eares, and other grievances"? Was it true that many of them were coming home, or moving to Virginia? Weren't they worried about this learned opinion that the New England diet of fish would cause leprosy? And so on.

Of these various adverse reports of the Massachusetts settlement, some were true. One Philip Ratcliffe really did have his ears cut off, was whipped and banished "for vttering mallitious and scandalous speeches against the gouernment and the church of Salem." Others, like the imputation of Massachusetts separatism, were at least an entertainable suspicion. Still others were scaremongering, or just silly.

The question is whether Howes believed them, and whether they constituted the real reasons for his staying behind. Perhaps they were a way of expressing fears he had always entertained about settling in the New World, while protesting his faith in the enterprise. Always attributed to "knaues" and other mischief-makers, the objections prompted quick rebuttals from him. To the rumor that Massachusetts was falling away from Anglican Church practice, for instance, Howes replied, "it is not any outward will worship that god requires, but god being a spirit ought to be worshiped in spirit and truth." On the punishment of Ratcliffe he commented, "there are here a thousand eyes watchinge ouer you to pick a hole in your coats, yet feare not, there are more with you than against you, for you have god and his promises."

In other words, it was a good thing that he remained behind to counter the false assertions that its enemies might invent against Massachusetts. "Your plantation hath need of some hartie and able friends to back you vpon all occasions, which must remaine here; and have friends at Courte," he wrote to John Winthrop, Jr., in March, 1632. And who better to maintain this defense than Edward Howes? The adverse reports of New England may have kept Howes at home, but not just because they frightened or filled him with disapproval. They also provided a handy justification for his remaining behind, while still appearing a "hartie" supporter of the venture.

Howes's messages to the Massachusetts settlers had always been salted with helpful advice, especially of a practical nature. He told them how to make mortar from soap ashes, lime, loam and sand, passed on the recipe of a "wholesome and savorie drinke" made of white wine and potatoes "for such as are sick, weak, or cannot drinke water," offered to send books on the management of silkworms, sent an "engine...to boyle in wooden vessells" which "wee tryed...in our Parlor" and found to work "verie well."

The Lord knows (as Howes would say) what Winthrop, his father and the other settlers made of these hints and contraptions. Could they really have found much use for the sort of Swiss Army knife Howes sent over ("a knife or what you will; together with a small sawe and steele hammer, and a bodkyn and a forke all in one Case")? Were they much relieved when, in 1634, he informed them how to kill wolves with pieces of sponge hidden "in such flesh or garbage they feede on" or with steel hooks "put within theire meate"? It is not very likely. Howes's hints have an air more of camping out – of an exciting adventure into the romantic outback – than of practical reality. They bear as much relation to the everyday needs of Massachusetts as do the reasons he offered for staying at home to what really kept him behind – and for the same reason. Properly read, both the reported objections and the helpful hints tell us all we need to know of his feelings about New England. It was unhealthy, melodramatically dangerous, finally impossible. It belonged to a world of exotic fantasy, not reality. No one could really live there on a permanent basis. It was not to be taken seriously.[28]

So though they may have covered a wide range of concerns – physical and spiritual, individual and social – not even the Puritans' deliberations over whether or not to emigrate were wholly neutral. The most striking feature of their discourse is that whatever their ultimate decision, the reasons they set out supported the opposite course of action. The letters and journals tell us only why they didn't do what they did.

This may reflect nothing more than a well developed taste and aptitude for the dialectic. Conscientious belief required constant testing against its opposite. Psychologically too, a rehearsal of objections before the event may fortify the courage when it happens: forewarned is forearmed.

This may be what is happening in Lucy Downing's and John Bailey's letters. But it won't account for the absence of reasons for going over, or for their lack of enthusiasm for the radical reformation of the spirit both required and prompted by thoughts of the project. There is no trace in Downing and Bailey of Cushman's radical thesis of portability – "but now we are all in all places strangers and Pilgrims, travellers and sojourners" – or of John Winthrop's reminder to Margaret that if God does not watch over us in England, we have no need to travel overseas to seek our destruction.

Perhaps those arguments were taken as already understood. Or perhaps both had grown weary of exhortation, and needed now to examine the practical implications of the venture. Bailey had already "removed" once to Ireland and may have dreaded another uprooting. Lucy Downing was burdened with family commitments: a growing boy to educate and another child on the way. In addition, her motives were mixed up with her obligations as a wife, an issue she herself foregrounded in her anticipation of her brother's objection.

Whatever their evasions, whatever reasons for going they may have suppressed (even assuming that "evasions" and "suppressed" are appropriate words in this context), Downing's and Bailey's arguments against their emigration at least have the sound ring of authenticity. One feels them as their real concerns, even if they were finally overcome by weary resignation to the inevitable rather than by enthusiastic conviction. The same cannot be said for the various reasons given by Rogers, Retsolloh and Howes for staying behind. Their letters and journals are full of various kinds of enthusiasm, including the radical thesis of the God we have always with us. They embraced, and expressed the

Puritan thesis of the movable faith. But Rogers stayed behind for causes at which his modern editor can only guess. As for Retsolloh and Howes, scattered through their writing, unconnected to the main line of their arguments, are reasons for remaining that read as *ad hoc* justifications for decisions taken on other, unmentionable grounds. Here we can infer suppression and evasion with more justice.

What were these other grounds and why were they unmentionable? I think chiefly something that is simple to state but hard to describe, a love of the metropolis: that is, a developed taste, not only for the complex social and professional life in a large city, but also for the sense of being in the midst of things, where history was being made. Howes may have been enthused by the idea of Massachusetts, and full of spurious advice and help for the colony, but he couldn't disguise his excitement at living in London: its news and gossip, the progress of his law career, the building of Covent Garden, even the plague. For Puritan emigrants to New England this attraction of the center grew especially acute during the period of the Commonwealth. They had fled the depredations of Arminianism in England to make the millennium in America, only to hear that the event was taking shape at home. History was going on behind them. "The early 1640s may have been the only time in New England history when immigrants were outnumbered by people returning in the opposite direction," writes David Cressy, "when vigorous settlers abandoned Massachusetts to take part in the revolutionary developments at home."[29]

Some of the most enthusiastic promoters of Massachusetts settlement, like Thomas Welde, whose letter home to his parishioners in Essex is almost a foundation document of the dominant discourse, returned at this time. So did friends of the Winthrop family, and even members of it. Stephen Winthrop, John Jr.'s half brother, came over on the Arbella, made several trips back and forth across the Atlantic between 1638 and 1645, then finally returned for good to fight in Cromwell's army in 1646.

A letter he wrote in 1650 to John Winthrop, Jr., gives a sense of the swirl of events from which the New Englanders must have felt excluded:

I am in Wales and am Left with some horsse to keepe quiett those partts: my Lord Cromwell is made Lord Genll. of all the forces (my Lord Fairfax Laying down his Commision:) and is marching into Scotland with all speed... France very full of Disturbance... the Prince of Orang and the States differences grow wider and Like to break into a flame. Noe perfect peace in Germany: though the Prince Electer hath much restored to him: Litle Ishue of the Warre betwene the turke and Venetian.

And so it continues, with references to the Portugese, Prince Rupert, General Blake and his prize of five ships coming from Brazil, the likely reaction of the Spanish to this action, and much else.

In the same year Robert Child wrote a similarly newsy letter to his old friend John Winthrop, Jr. Child, another back-migrant (he would die four years later in Ireland), had been one of the authors of the Massachusetts Remonstrance in 1646, trying to limit the autonomy of the Bay Colony to that of an ordinary English corporation and petitioning the General Court for the rights of freemen. Back in England, he reported excitedly that "The Venetians still continue to mayntayne Candy against the great Turke... the Spaniards will not restore Frankendale... The Palsgrave is lately married either to the Langsgrave of Hessen sister, or to Brandenburgs I know not: the Emperour of Russia scarcely permitteth our merchants to live in his Country... Sweden, Poland, Denmarke and all the Princes of Germany are in Peace and promise assistance to the King of Scotland," and so on for another page or so. If he was right in guessing that Winthrop would be interested in all this, how cut off Winthrop must have felt. Even more so, when Child summarized recent scientific scholarship, like the work of a "famous Chymist in Germany – named Glauber, who hath written a very excellent book about all sort of Chymicall things, but at this time a booke is not to be had." Denied even the portable culture of a book sent over to New England, Winthrop would have to remain ignorant of the very excellent chemical things discovered by the wonderful Glauber. "I, for my part," wrote Child, "am more than halfe weaned from New-England."[30] This is an interesting reversal of the dominant metaphor: now to grow up is to get out of Massachusetts and into the real world.

So much, then, for why Howes, Rogers and others might have been reluctant to leave England, whatever the spiritual attractions of Massachusetts. The second question is why they should have suppressed this reason for staying behind. The answer is already before us, in the form of Cushman's portability thesis. Puritanism left them with no vocabulary for asserting their attraction to the metropolis. Someone like John Pory, the Anglican Secretary of Virginia to Sir Dudley Carleton, and as exotic a traveler as ever visited the early English colonies in North America, could praise Plymouth, Massachusetts, because "Amongst these Christall rivers, & oderiferous woods I doe escape muche expense, envye, contempte, vanity and vexation of minde," adding an immediate plea to his employer. "Yet good my lorde, have a little compassion upon me, and be pleased to sende me, what pampletts and relations of the Interim since I was with you..." That is, he could act the part of Duke Senior in Arden, "these woods / More free from Peril than the envious court," where "feel we not the penalty of Adam," and yet solicit gossip and news from the very court and city from which his exotic imagination was in flight. But for a Puritan the metropolis, and all imperial power structures based on a metropolitan center, were not only disposable, but positively to be cast off, left behind. This impulse was the chief Puritan contribution to that phase of the propaganda for emigration that valorized the stripping away of Old World culture, and insofar as Puritan correspondents were constrained to suppress the attractions to themselves of metropolitan living, they can be said, for all their apparently neutral, explicit rehearsal of the pros and cons of going to America, to have come under the penumbra of the dominant discourse.

18

The alternative voice and how it was preserved, II: spiritual autobiographies; the anticlimax of arrival

Of all the testimonies to American emigration, no body of writing departs more completely from the optimism in which advocates of the enterprise generally presented the experience than those confessional narratives spoken and written by the Massachusetts Puritans shortly after their arrival in the New World. Yet these people were not confronting and challenging the dominant discourse, as had the travelers and back-migrants. They were not answering the positive arguments of the propagandists, point by point, so as to discourage further settlement for political or other reasons, any more than they were trying to sell land, or to populate their new communities, or to justify their venture to friends and relatives back home. They were speaking to a local audience – to themselves and to their contemporaries. In these documents the dominant discourse plays no role whatsoever.

There is no doubt that this material reads as a chronicle of anticlimax, disappointment, disillusion – perhaps in some cases despair would not be too strong a word. What does it prove? That a sizeable minority – perhaps even a majority – of early settlers in New England were disenchanted with their move to the New World? That other new Americans, had they written to themselves and their neighbors, and had their accounts been preserved, would have conveyed a similarly dispirited message?

Recent good books by literary critics like Patricia Caldwell and Andrew Delbanco have seized upon this material as evidence to challenge the standard view that the Puritans converted the narratives of their settlement into a confident assertion of

America's exceptional status as a "redeemer nation."[31] Yet an important caveat must be entered here. Most of the narratives in question are spiritual autobiographies of one kind or another. Either they are journals of an individual's progress in the faith, or "relations" – public confessions – spoken by someone seeking entrance to a local congregation, then taken down in dictation.

In other words, these data do not constitute a neutral account giving the lie to the official propaganda in favor of settlement, but an alternative discourse with rigid conventions of its own, enjoining the practitioner to a public display of his or her humility. No such narrative would be more likely to fail in its purpose than one detailing a confident assurance of the applicant's election to grace. Similarly, spiritual autobiographies (Bunyan's *Grace Abounding* of 1765 is a late but still representative example) are not plotted like novels or detective stories, with a rising action and a single climax or dénouement. The subject does not encounter conversion once only, after which his or her life is changed forever; but instead experiences many moments of hope, or glimmers of election, from each of which he or she falls into a renewed slovenliness of spirit. The plot and rhetoric of spiritual autobiographies compose the very model of anticlimax, disappointment, backsliding; that is how the genre achieves its air of authenticity.

Even so, there may be something in Caldwell's and Delbanco's case. Another way of putting the issue is that the discourse of the spiritual autobiography provided an acceptable voice to Puritan discontents: gave them a way of complaining about their translation to the New World that would not undermine the vulnerable frontier community. This would explain why so many of the relations seem most dispirited when recalling the experience of "coming over."

Seeking membership of the Reverend Thomas Shepard's congregation in Cambridge, Massachusetts, Edward Hall claimed that "since the Lord brought him to this place...he hath found more enmity of his heart against the Lord than ever before."

"Hence I did think to enjoy more of the Lord," Golden Moore told the same assembly, "and so coming hither and being in fears of my estate and that if my life was gone I had no promise to support. And I coming hither I found my heart in a worse frame than ever..." In more stripped down syntax, "Brother Jackson's maid" told the same story: "When I came hither first Sabbath affected but afterward left to a dead blockish frame and knewe nothing." In Old England, John Stansby:

seeing ordinances polluted, my soul desired to be there where Christ is feeding of His flock in this place. But saw many stumbling blocks yet prized, yet since I came hither my heart hath been straightened for God. I have been under vines and fig trees but Lord has been as a stranger to my soul.

It might be argued with some justice that Shepard was of a nervously introspective, perhaps even neurotic disposition, whose example encouraged such revelations from applicants to his congregation. Certainly Shepard's theology of conversion was such as to induce doubt in his flock – indeed, positively to construct a culture of spiritual uncertainty. He taught that there was no objective test of conversion, not even such as could be narrated in a convincing and affecting way. As the modern editors of the relations put it, "Grace came in no momentary Pauline wrenching of the will during an inspiring sermon or while 'taking a pipe of tobacco,' but rather emerged from a prepared-for conclusion to a lengthy regenerative process. Viewing conversion in this way, Cambridge parishioners had no immediate assurance of their salvation."[32]

Other pastors, while still adhering to the Puritan doctrine that conversion was the crucial test of election, allowed at least subjective criteria by which the sense of conversion could be confirmed and expressed. The Reverend Peter Bulkeley, minister at Concord from 1636 until his death in 1659, seems to have provided his parishioners with assurances to stem their spiritual anxieties – or at least that is how they told the story when they moved to Wenham and sought admission to the congregation of the Reverend John Fiske. In his relation to the Wenham church Thomas Hincksman remembered having felt "sadly" about the condition of his belief, "till what time Mr. Bulkeley...handled that question, how may one know whether he hath faith or no? And among other things he answered if the soul satisfaction be placed above on Christ...Hereupon his soul was drawn to take to Christ and riches of God's grace in Him alone."

Bulkeley's influence, and Fiske's willingness to let his assurances stand as tests of membership, may account for the generally less anxious tone in the relations given to the Wenham church. Still, that sense of disappointment on "coming hither" persists even in the Fiske collection. "In coming to New England," the pastor's wife, Anne Fiske, was "some[what] discouraged" on hearing the "opinions in New England (when in ship)." Joan White felt "Her heart being drawn to New England because good people came hither," but "at last by a providence coming over she was shut for a long space of time living far in the woods away from the means."[33]

Whatever their differences in mood, these various narratives have at least two features in common. The first is that, unlike the optimistic reports of other Puritans such as Higginson and Welde, they cannot reconcile the material and spiritual benefits of New England. For Joan White the woods are not an invigorating site of initiation, much less a desert retreat in which she might renew her faith, but a solitary place in which she has been denied the solace of her minister and other fellow religionists. The dominant discourse might well have used John Stansby's "vines and fig trees" as a figure for both the material and spiritual promise of the New World (not least because the Book of Zechariah catches up that image of Israel's felicity in 1 Kings as a type of the Promised Land), but for Stansby these delectable blessings kept "the Lord a stranger to my soul."

So much might be explained by the severely contemplative demands of the relation form, and the religious context of the utterance. But these reasons won't wholly account for the prevailing mood of disappointment in the act of emigration itself, the uprooting, voyage and resettlement in Massachusetts. It is as though, despite being trained not to expect a single, irreversible moment of conversion – or at least not to hope to identify and describe that experience with absolute confidence – they had, after all, expected a fundamental transformation of spirit to accompany their migration westwards.

Of course, that is exactly what the dominant discourse promised them. The promise went unfulfilled. Travel, especially travel leading to resettlement, was and is immensely fatiguing and distracting. A thousand details of sorting, packing, household management, the competition for land and housing in the new home and the disposition of property in the old – all have to be managed alongside the social and emotional upheavals of changing countries. The world and its vanities they had always with them – more so than ever. The notarial records of early Massachusetts show just how taken up the new settlers were with securing land and other goods, and how preoccupied they were still with their affairs back in England. As late as 1644, nearly a decade after he told Shepard's congregation that he "sensed a spirit of enmity" in New England, Nathaniel Sparrowhawk was inditing a letter of attorney "to Thomas Adams Alderman of London to recover a debt of £16 – 2 – 10...for clothes, diet, books & other necessaries unto his son."[34]

◇◇◇◇◇◇◇◇◇◇◇◇◇◇

"For many of New England's founders," writes Sacvan Bercovitch in *The Puritan Origins of the American Self*, "the embarkation was a literal one. Figurally and structurally, the migration to America displaces conversion as the crucial event." This was true of that point at which Puritan narrative inserted itself into the dominant discourse: when the new settlers wrote home to persuade members of their old congregations to follow them; and later, when the "founders" and (more particularly) their offspring began to write, not for themselves and their contemporaries, but for posterity. Certainly Puritan historiography, starting with Bradford's account of Plymouth Plantation and culminating in the monumental company history of Cotton Mather's *Magnalia* of 1702, caught up the optimistic millennarian tone of letters home from early settlers like Higginson and Welde, and worked it into a whole myth of American exceptionalism.

But in their personal relations most of the early Puritan settlers expressed something approaching the exact opposite of Bercovitch's generalization. They may have expected their migration to displace their conversion as the crucial event in their lives, but they were disappointed in that expectation. Emigration to New England promised teasingly to fulfill certain types of conversion, like crossing the Red Sea and travailing through the wilderness to the Promised Land, with literal enactments of these figures. In the event, at least as they told their stories to themselves and their neighbors, their lives remained unchanged, and "coming hither" was just a transatlantic crossing.

To prove his point, Bercovitch cites Thomas Shepard's own spiritual *Autobiography*, in which the New World becomes his new life into which he is baptized by the Atlantic as a greater Red Sea: "After his extraordinary adventures at sea, he feels certain that he has in fact undergone a 'heavenly translation...come and risen from the dead.'"[35]

In fact, Shepard was writing here of the North Sea, not the Atlantic, and endured these particular adventures while anchored off the coast of East Anglia. True, they had set off for New England, but a severe storm aborted the voyage, and Shepard would have to wait the better part of a year before sailing for Massachusetts again. Nor was this the only occasion when he felt his life renewed by the baptism of tempestuous waters.

Shepard's memoir is a classic spiritual autobiography, alternating from beginning to end between hope and disappointment, the progress and regress of the attentive soul. From the "profane, ignorant town of Towcester where I was born," he went to

Cambridge, where he "had many good affections," only to "join loose scholars of other colleges," get drunk and spend the Sabbath hiding in a cornfield. But "I never went out to meditate in the fields but I did find the Lord teaching me somewhat of myself or himself or the vanity of the world I never saw before," he wrote. So "when I was worst, [the Lord] began to be best unto me," confronting him with the sense of his own unworthiness, but sending him good instruction in College, and later the fellowship of Thomas Welde and Thomas Hooker in Essex.

If Shepard experienced many moments of conversion (or at least conviction and its renewal), from which he relapsed equally as often, so also he "removed" within England more than once – to Cambridge, Essex, Yorkshire, Newcastle, Harwich, Great Yarmouth and London – before crossing the Atlantic. With Welde, he confronted Bishop Laud in Essex and, barely escaping the pursuivants, made his way into Yorkshire. It rained heavily all the way. At Ferrybridge (just northeast of Pontefract) they found "the waters were up and ran over the bridge... Whereupon my heart was so smitten with fear... that had not the Lord immediately upheld me... I had certainly perished." Finally they reached dry land, "and went to prayer, and blessed God for this wonderful preservation of us. And the Lord made me then to profess that I looked now upon my life as a new life given unto me."

So Shepard felt baptized into a new life more than once. This time it was the waters of the tiny River Aire that did the trick, not the North Sea – much less the Atlantic. But characteristically, no sooner had he reached his destination than he found his spirits slumping once again. In York he found himself lodging in a house where he found "divers... at dice and tables" and immediately felt "never so low sunk in... spirit... far from all friends... in a profane house... unknown... and my sins were upon me."

Compared with his experiences on the Great North Road, and off Great Yarmouth, Shepard's transatlantic voyage was figured rather less as a converting experience. No very great providence was shown them. The ship sprung a leak, which "the Lord discovered...unto us," but his wife caught a cold, of which she was to die soon after they reached Massachusetts. Shortly after they arrived in Boston, the community was vexed (as he tells it) by Anne Hutchinson's apostacy, "by means of which division by these opinions the ancient and received truth came to be darkened." It is true that he looked back on the experience, six years after crossing over, as a rite of passage "to a land of peace, through a place of trial," but even that brief expression of satisfaction is clouded by the death of a second wife (Joannah, eldest daughter of Thomas Hooker) and his concluding reflection that

> God hath visited and scourged me for my sins and sought to wean me from this world, but I have ever found it a difficult thing to profit even but a little by the sorest and sharpest afflictions.

So anticlimax follows the narrative of the Atlantic voyage, just as it does Shepard's account of crossing the swollen river in Yorkshire. Compared with his treatment of the Atlantic crossing, Shepard's narrative of his thwarted departure from East Anglia devotes great time and energy to both the technicalities of their predicament and also the devout affections it aroused. Having set sail from Harwich, their ship had to anchor off Great Yarmouth in the teeth of a westerly gale. They prayed; "immediately after prayer, the wind began to abate, and the ship stayed." All the anchors broke except one, which was

> drawn along, plowing the sands with the violence of the wind...And so we rid it out; yet not without fear of our lives though the anchor stopped the ship, because the cable was let out so far, that a little rope held the cable, and the cable the little anchor, and the little anchor the great ship, in this great storm.

Here is "figuration" enough: the anchor as *spes*, the emblem of hope (while never, for a moment, ceasing to be an anchor); a man lost overboard and later revived who they declared a type of their deliverance; Shepard calling, like the Psalmist, *de profundis*, "out of these depths of seas and miseries" and receiving a "deliverance...so great, that I then did think if ever the Lord did bring me to shore again I should live like one come and risen from the dead."[36]

But even this masterly passage, as full of accurately rendered nautical detail as it is of passionate devotional prose, is followed by the characteristic downward plunge in the cycle of spiritual autobiography. They had set off for New England, only to get stuck in the Old. On landing at Yarmouth, they felt their fortunes ebb almost immediately. His eldest son fell sick and died. Always dodging the pursuivants, Shepard and his family would not undertake another voyage for America for another ten months.

In other words, the only way to make Shepard's *Autobiography* a document of American exceptionalism is by recasting the text so as to make the Atlantic crossing itself appear exceptional. But the spiritual relations of early Puritan migrants cannot be made to work like this. If anything, they become both more depressed and at the same time less articulate about the reasons for this mood when they move to consider the author's life after coming over.

John Dane, a tailor from Bishop's Stortford, Hertfordshire, emigrated to New England sometime in the 1630s, settling in Ipswich, Massachusetts, by 1638. Two years before he died in 1684 he wrote two narratives of his spiritual life, one in verse and one in prose, "in waie of preparation for death." When dealing with his life in England, the prose account follows the oscillations of Puritan spiritual autobiography between conversion and backsliding, conviction and doubt. Though born of "godly parents," he "was giuen mutch to play and run out without my fathers Consent." He thinks himself in a good spiritual "condishon" because he prays and listens to sermons, but is also "giuen to pastime and to dansing." Beaten by his father for staying out at night, he leaves home "to seke my fortin." "*Goe whare you will*," his mother warns, "*god he will find you out.*"

His travels are punctuated by, among other events, three temptations to sexual pleasure: one by a woman who stays late in his shop, another by his landlady, who waits up for him "by the fyer, in hur naked shift, houlding hur brests open," and the third by "a fine lase" awaiting him in the bed of his lodgings. All three invitations he manfully refuses by polite excuses, but he can take no satisfaction in his spiritual strength: "Here I toke no notes of the goodnes of god in Restrayning me, but Ratther ascribd it to my self." Like Shepard, he skips out on church meeting to spend the Sabbath in a field "close by a meadow sid." There he too meets with God's justice, in the form of a bee sting on his finger, which produces, as had Christ's wound, "watter and blod" and "pained me much. I went up to a hous and shoud it, but thay knew not what a sting I had at my harte. Now I thout of my mothers words, that god would find me out." Recovered from the sting to finger and conscience, he "did Reforme, and stod in aw of gods Judgments," though still hankering after his "former pastime." Another sting (on the same finger) pulls him round again. And so it goes on.

His decision to emigrate to New England is at first opposed by both parents, but unlike Samuel Rogers, Dane persists in his plan. Opening the Bible at random, he shows them the first text that catches his eye. It was (as he remembered it) "Cum out from among them, touch no unclene thing, and I will be your god and you shall be my pepell" (a version of II Cor. 6:17). From then on his parents withold their objections, and indeed follow him to Massachusetts in due course.

Dane's narrative covers just over seven pages of small print in its published version. Though he says nothing of his birth date, he lived around fifty years – say around two thirds of his life – in Massachusetts. Yet only a page and a half of his seven relate to his life in the New World. His first recorded experience there is such as to reinforce the exceptionalist thesis. Weary and thirsty, he comes to a spring in a street in Roxbury, "and went to it, and drunk, and drunk againe and againe manie times; and I neuer drounk wine in my lyfe that more Refresht me." This might almost be Francis Higginson writing home about the restorative benefits of New England water, and not even the sacramental connotations of Dane's drink – of baptism or the Lord's Supper – can be excluded from his range of reference.

Yet almost immediately, in the sequence of his narrative, Dane is moved to record his disappointment in his new home. Though he has brought with him about a year's supply of food, he soon gives it to others in need. When down to his last bushel, he is visited by a neighbor who "said he had no corne" and "made great complaints." Dane gives him half of his remaining store, only to discover later that the neighbor has a bushel of his own at home:

> It trubled me to se his dealings, and the dealings of other men. Manie trobles I past thorow and I found in my heart that I could not sarue god as I should. What they ware, were two teadus to menshun. But uppon a time walking, with my Gun on my shoulder charged, in the myle brok path, beyond Decon goodhewes, I had seauerall thouts cam flocking into my mynd, that I had beatter make away with myself then to liue longer...I cock my Gun, and set it one the ground, and put the musell under my throte, and toke up my fote to let it of. And then thare cam manie thing into my head; one that I should not doe euell that good myt cum of it. And at that time I no more scrupld to cill myself then to goe home to my oune house.[37]

It is important to recall that though silence – the cult of the inexpressible – was much prized in Quaker relations, it had no part in the Puritan spiritual autobiography. John Dane, for all his lack of sophistication, could be perfectly explicit about his spiritual doubts and exhilarations in England. He had the abstract vocabulary to analyze the conflicting forces within his conscience, and sufficient skill at plotting to reinforce these conflicts by paralleling the two bee stings and three sexual temptations, and by setting out his mother's warning about God finding him out as prophecy and fulfillment. Only in New England does he encounter a crisis of the spirit sufficient to lead him to the brink of suicide. Yet grievous as these "troubles" must have been, he is unable or unwilling to specify them. They are "two teadus to menshon." More tedious than a bee sting?

Something subverts Dane's narrative in New England. Like that of the dog that didn't bark in the night, his silence is expressive, significant. This is true of the relations collected by Shepard too. Though occasionally, like Dane, they voice their disappointment that the New England saints were as worldly as their persecutors back home (if not more so), their overriding tone of fatigue and wan inability is negative – an absence, the expression of inexpressibility. John Sill "lost that frame I had" when his "heart began to be troubled"; his wife Joannah "found no presence of God"; "she could not believe indeed and she knew not where she was." Asked whether "she had assurance," Mary Angier "said no but some hope." Barbary Cutter, who "saw [her] condition more miserable than ever" since she "came hither," "knew not what to do, and spoke to none as knowing none like [her]."[38]

As in Dane's case, their terrible demoralization, even despair, is vivid enough; what remain unspecified are the "troubles" that caused it. All that can be said with any degree of certainty is that though the Puritans may have expected the voyage across the ocean to join the community of the elect in Massachusetts to be a transforming event in their spiritual lives, that was not how they told the story to each other when they got there. John Dane's verse narrative puts best what all the rest had to face in time:

But when that I cam here
I found it did apere
I brout a rutched hart
I find 'tis not eth place
will help on in the rase
unless we with sin parte
and holy doe Rely
on Christ our surety[39]

19

The alternative voice and how it was preserved, III*: New England falling away from its first love; the privatization of Plymouth; passage not a rite of passage; narrative as ritual;* A True Picture of Emigration*: story of a migration out and back*

The last chapter raised the question of how it was that the Puritans managed, outside the dominant discourse of emigration, to voice their disappointment in New England. Did the conventions of the spiritual autobiography and the "relation" before the congregation encourage expressions of depression and demoralization? Or did they merely provide the occasion for conveying such emotions already formed? Outside the boosters' optimism of the first reports home, and apart from spiritual relations and letters from those trying to decide whether to remove to New England, the main clues to how the Puritans felt about their migration come from fraternal communications between fellow-believers. The evidence is sketchy, but such as it is suggests that the sense of anticlimax after the crossing and the feeling that New England was somehow falling away from its original purpose were not just generic demands imposed by the form of the spiritual autobiography.

Writing home in 1637 to answer fears expressed by his fellow English clergymen that Massachusetts was beginning to show alarmingly separatist tendencies, the New England Puritan John Cotton confessed that "Our native country...we have left not in affection but in place, but our native corruptions and selves we still carry with us." Now forced to defend their theological position, the Massachusetts Puritans had to adopt a more "realistic" stance than that taken in the dominant discourse: migration to the New World did not guarantee a reformation of the spirit.[40]

Robert Cushman expected the migration to New England to work a reformation that would reach down to the social and economic structure of life in the New World. The people in Plymouth, he hoped, would so love their fellow-settlers that they would consent to hold their land in common. For the first two years or so after they landed, the Plymouth settlers did follow this plan, until finally, in 1623, Bradford (as he tells it in his history of Plymouth Plantation) was forced to agree to their demands that "they should set corne every man for his owne perticuler." This reversion to private enterprise "had very good success; for it made all hands very industrious, so as much more corne was planted then other waise," and even "the women now wente willingly into the feild, and tooke their litl-ons with them to set corne."

And so child labor came to America. Marx himself could not have expressed the impact of the capitalist imperative on family life so succinctly. Cushman was bitterly disappointed. While in Plymouth for a month at the end of 1621, when the issue was already being discussed, he had given a sermon warning against the social and spiritual effects of private property. "When some withdraw themselves, and retire to their own particular ease, pleasure, or profit, what heart can men have to go on in their business?" he asked. "Nay, you must seek still the wealth of one another, and inquire, as David, How liveth such a man? How is he clad? How is he fed? He is my brother, my associate." St. Paul tells us that "men in the *last days* shall be lovers of themselves; but it is here yet but the *first* days, and, as it were, the dawning of this new world."[41]

After Plymouth's decision to go private, and hearing reports of dissention among the settlers, Cushman wrote to Bradford to warn the settlers once again that they risked falling away from their "first love" of one another. "If any amongst you...have still a withdrawing heart, and will be all to himself, and nothing to his neighbour, let him think on these things." Let them remember

God's providence in bringing them to the new settlement together, and in preserving them there. Let them recall their hopes for their future spiritual and physical health, and for that of their posterity. Finally let them think of "the woful estate of him which is alone, especially in a wilderness, [and] the succour and comfort which the generality can daily afford."

The spiritual and social danger of ignoring these concerns Cushman expresses so powerfully that a fuller quotation is warranted here:

> But as they will be a commonwealth alone, so alone they must work, and alone they must eat, and alone they must be sick and die, or else languishing under the frustration of their vain hopes, alone return to England, and there to help all cry out [against] the country and the people; counting the one fruitless and the other merciless; when indeed their own folly, pride, and idleness is the cause of all, which never weigh either the providence of God, the conscience of their duty, nor care for their neighbours, or themselves; further than to grate upon their friends; as if other men owed them all things, and they owed no man anything.[42]

It is a testament of the strength of the dominant discourse (to which other exhortations from Cushman subscribed whole-heartedly, of course) that this appeal to Plymouth's sense of responsibility looks so like the warnings of the successful emigrants against the back-migrants' fecklessness, and the adverse reports they might carry back to England. But one must be quite clear about what motivates Cushman's disappointment here. The failure of the imagined immigrant – his or her torpor, self-pity, "folly, pride, and idleness" – will result from a lack, not of self-reliance but of communal responsibility. This is a moral environment in which "care for themselves" is not just inextricable from, but consequent upon "care for their neighbours." And from this ideal Cushman feared that Plymouth was greatly fallen.

Some time around 1654, about three years before he died, Bradford himself would express a general anxiety about Plymouth's decline, in his verse history of New England. Though full of justified boasts about the colonies' material achievements, and their trials bravely borne, the poem laments Plymouth's loss of population:

O poor Plymouth, how dost thou moan,
Thy children all are from thee gone,
And left thou art in widow's state,
Poor, helpless, sad, and desolate.

Many of these "children" had gone to the better-supported settlement of the Massachusetts Bay, at Boston. But the rest of New England had suffered similar losses:

Methinks I see some great change at hand,
That ere long will fall upon this poor land;
Not only because many are took away,
Of the best rank, but virtue doth decay,
And true godliness doth not now so shine,
As some whiles it did, in the former time;[43]

Already American Puritan writing was moving into its jeremiad stage, and these warnings may have been intended at least as much as a vigorous exhortation to the conscience of the present as a dispirited, nostalgic lament for past glories.

Even so, many "of the best rank" were "took away," and by back migration as well as by death. How difficult it was for the dominant discourse to accomodate the critique of these disappointed returnees can be gauged from Winthrop's journal. Sir Henry Vane, Governor of Massachusetts Bay from 1636 to 1637, convened the Court of Deputies to allow his return to England, where (he said) urgent business matters required his personal attention. Responding to the Court's plea that the loss of his leadership would greatly imperil the colony "in a time of such danger as did hang over us, from the Indians and French," Vane blurted out he wouldn't have wanted to leave even if "the utter ruin of his outward estate" were threatened; that what really repelled him from Massachusetts was his fear that "God's judgments [would] come upon us for these differences and dissentions...and the scandalous imputations brought upon himself." (He had supported the cause of Anne Hutchinson against the majority led by Winthrop.)

But the Court was unwilling to allow him to depart "upon these grounds":

> Whereupon he recalled himself, and professed, that the reasons concerning his own estate were sufficient to his own satisfaction for his departure, and therefore desired the court he might have leave to go; as for the other passage, it slipped him out of his passion, and not out of judgement. Upon this the court consented, silently, to his departure.[44]

Vane's private business they could accept as a cause for his return, but not any reason that would threaten the reputation of the vulnerable settlement in Boston. In the event he went, and stayed, to play such a full part in the Commonwealth that he was excuted for high treason after the Restoration.

Perhaps because he was of lower rank and could therefore do less to damage the reputation of Massachusetts, John Pratt was allowed to return after only partly retracting his criticisms of New England's physical, social and spiritual environment. But even he was brought before the Court of Assistants in 1635, to explain a letter he had written home (and which the Massachusetts authorities had intercepted, presumably), complaining that Massachusetts consisted of nothing but rocks, sand and salt marshes. The letter is now lost, but Pratt's deposition to the Court gives a sense of how comprehensive his indictment must have been, as well as the kind of apology he had to make in order to be let go. That business about the soil, he claimed, had been taken in the wrong sense (perhaps it had even been heard as an echo of the Biblical house built on sand, a metaphor sweeping far wider than the fitness of New England for the planting of crops). What he meant was that he had been misled by the propagandists for emigration who "had made larger reports into England of the country, than I found to be true." "Being manured and husbanded," he allowed, the land did "bring forth more fruit than

I did expect," especially rye and oats, "but as for other kinds of grain, I do still question, whether they will come to such perfection as in our native country from whence they came."

So even his apology reserved a trace of that sense of degeneration expressed so feelingly in letters from Pond and the correspondents collected by Hutchinson, a feeling that Buffon would later turn into a scientific thesis. But he had been even more concerned about a decline in the spiritual environment. Though (he is quick to add) he meant it only with regard to "some particular occasions and apprehensions of mine own, not intending to lay any secret blemish upon the state," still he had sensed

> the danger of decaying here in our first love... how hard it is to keep our hearts in that holy frame which sometimes they were in, where we had less to do in outward things, but not at all intending to impute it as necessary to our condition, much less as a fruit of our precious liberties.[45]

They let him off, and in due course he and his wife set sail for England, to end their lives in that tragic wreck on the coast of Spain which Hubbard so relished. Yet though, like Vane, Pratt excused his critique as a private matter, not wishing now to impugn the general condition of the young colony, enough remains of his original indictment to underline what Cushman, John Dane and Shepard's congregation expressed in other rhetorical contexts. New England had fallen away from its "first love." Even after their translation across the sea, the affairs of the world were always with them: "'tis not eth place / will help on in the rase."

Does this feeling of general decline explain the weary tone of those few letters remaining outside that great body of reports sent home to extoll the benefits of New England? In 1647 John Woodbridge left for England carrying with him the manuscript of a remarkable collection of poems written by his sister-in-law, Anne (Dudley) Bradstreet, which he would publish in London as the first volume of one woman's verse to appear in the English language. A year later he sent for his wife and family. Governor Dudley was at first unwilling to let his youngest daughter go, "thinking she could with no safety go with 5 children, one of them sucking, for if she went sick at sea and the children or some of them so also, it might probably cost divers of them their lives."

But when he heard "that Mrs. Gardiner and her children were to go in the ship," he changed his mind, and sent her with his blessing, and this letter:

> She is my beloved daughter with whom (had I not married again) I meant to have ended my days in this world, but God to whose will I must and do submit hast now otherwise ordained it, and I am like to see neither your nor her face again till we meet in heaven: Yet as long as I remain in this decayed tabernacle I shall daily pray for your self and her and all your pretty children.[46]

Dudley sensed that their separation was permanent, and he was right. In the event Woodbridge remained in England for sixteen years, serving as chaplain to the Parliamentary Commission treating with the King on the Isle of Wight, and later as a minister and schoolteacher, returning to New England only when pushed out of his employment by the Act of Uniformity, 1662.

There are objective reasons enough for Dudley's mood, without reading into it any dissatisfaction with New England. He was already seventy-two years old (the "decayed tabernacle" was his body, not the colony); his youngest daughter and her children were about to leave on a voyage sufficiently hazardous to prevent his ever seeing them again, even if they had not decided to stay in England. Yet even an old man saying goodbye to a beloved part of his close family might have seen the event as a beginning as well as an ending. There is something in his depression that is almost fatalistic, as though New England is decaying along with him, its lifespan to be measured on the scale of the human forescore and ten. As I will attempt to show in Part IV, that odd conflation is another aspect of the myth of the collective singular.

Certainly as the various New England settlements reached their communal middle age, then their sixties and seventies, their inhabitants' sense of falling away became more acute. The prolonged disputes over who should be admitted to the Lord's Supper, the recurrent threat to the Massachusetts charter, the wars with the Indians, the widespread fears that the community of saints was being progressively diluted by the immigration of worldly non-believers bent on everyday business: all these concerns and the apocalyptic jeremiads they prompted are staples of American Puritan historiography.

◇◇◇◇◇◇◇◇◇◇◇◇◇◇◇

So when they addressed themselves and their fellow-emigrants, some American Puritans expressed a sense of anticlimax following their remove to the New World. We know this because the Puritan obligation of self-investigation prompted the relevant documents to be written and preserved. Would other emigrants who were not part of this articulate culture have given similarly dispirited accounts of their experience after coming over, had they been sharing their feelings with their fellow-migrants, instead of putting on a brave face for parents, supporters and other well-wishers back home? On the other hand, did members of Shepard's congregation also write optimistic, booster letters to their families back in England?

My guess is that the answer to both these questions is yes. That is, other emigrants whom we know only through their participation in the dominant discourse might also have expressed a sense of anticlimax, had they had occasion to record their everyday feelings, and had those opinions been preserved, and it is quite possible that at least some of Shepard's congregation and other spiritual autobiographers also wrote home in the exhilarating spirit of the boosters' approbation venture.

That answer is only a guess, because to date, little or no positive evidence has emerged to support it. And yet that very absence of data may be a clue. Though some of the large majority of eighteenth- and nineteenth-century emigrants did not write home until they had good news to report, most of them also broke off communication as they settled down to ordinary life, or moved on within the country and lost contact with their origins. The dominant discourse of emigration draws the attention of the home audience to the drama of moving to America, not to the long process of adjustment to everyday life in the New World – and certainly not to disappointment with it. As for Puritan communications homewards – both private and public – we have ample evidence in the letters and tracts written by Cushman, Bradford, Higginson, Welde, William Hilton, Winthrop, William Wood, Edward Johnson and many others, of their whole-hearted participation in the dominant discourse: the willingness to strip away Old World cultural deposits; the celebration of America's rich natural profusion; the plot paradigm of initiation into a higher spiritual and social state. But records also expressing disappointment in the venture survive from only a handful of these writers: Cushman, Bradford and (only implicitly) Winthrop. As for Shepard's communicants and other spiritual autobiographers, nothing, either relishing the move to Massachusetts or despairing of it, has yet turned up in the relevant collections in England.

The reason for that may not be hard to find. The most assiduous preservers and collectors of the relevant Puritan manuscripts were those to whom the Massachusetts experiment was especially important: the contemporary settlers and their prosperous, influential, tireless and meticulous posterity, organized in the numerous historical and genealogical societies still flourishing in New England. And obviously these curators would be more likely to receive letters and other documents written to and for other settlers living locally, than letters sent to England.

In England, on the other hand, interest in the American Puritan experiment would have been reflected mainly in collections made by supporters of the Puritan cause, like Nehemiah Wallington, but would hardly be replicated generally. This may be one reason why English county records offices have so little material from the American seventeenth century, and why the counties from which

Shepard's communicants departed, or where they had family connections, have nothing from any of them.

Still, exceptions prove – that is, test – the rule. In 1688, just over three years after he arrived in New England, John Bailey wrote home to his brother to say that he had been thinking of returning to England. He had been sick, his wife sicker, and their other brother, Thomas, sickest of all. Massachusetts "is growing very poore," Bailey wrote, and "many feare that ministers will be starved out of it." The recent war with the Indians had added to the settlers' sense of exposure and danger, because "The Indians...play no fair play, but ly in bushes and shoot...[and it is] an easy thing for them...to cut us all off, by reason of being scattered in the woods, all our houses are made of wood, their way is to fire the houses, to kill all as they run out." This country has not recovered since the war, he added, and "there is a great degeneracy" in it.[47]

And yet John Bailey did not back-migrate, but stayed in New England – as did his brother Thomas, who recovered from his illness. From his ministry in Watertown John moved to become minister of the First Church of Boston in 1693. He died in 1697. Might the depression communicated to his brother in England have been typical of the feelings of thousands, even millions, of other emigrants to America, Puritan and otherwise?

All we can say is that circumstances exceptional to that process of vernacular publication which husbanded the dominant discourse attended the production and preservation of his gloomy letter. For one thing, it fell into the hands of a friend and patron of the Bailey family, the Lancashire minister, Thomas Jollie – like John Woodbridge, one of the dissenters from the Act of Uniformity. For another, John was writing to a sibling, not a parent; so he could be franker with bad news that had to be kept from a mother to prevent her worrying (Bailey asks his brother to give his love to theirs, who was now very frail), or from a father, to save the face of a son who might have set off originally with a show of manly independence.

At any rate what is clear is that the mood prevailing in spiritual autobiographies by Dane, Shepard and his congregation and others – that emigration had betrayed its promise of a crucial transformation in their lives – proceeded from a confusion between prophecy and fulfillment, figure and actuality, vehicle and tenor. And from this follows what is at least the strong supposition, that though other emigrants may have been less interested than were the Puritans in prophecy and fulfillment, they faced a version of the same problem.

The problem is this. Though characteristically imaged as a rite of passage, emigration – if it succeeds – is only a passage. There are two reasons for this. First, in rites of passage the participants go out to the *limen* (to a remote place or a social inversion remote from their ordinary lives) *and back*, whereas the successful emigrant goes out only. Second, rites of passage are rituals – symbolic representations of fundamental changes of state – whereas the successful emigrant's passage, as distinct, say, from the traveler's, is both actual and literal.

It is this confusion, I believe, which explains the spiritual autobiographers' disappointment with life in the New World. It certainly explains Cushman's resistance to the Plymouth settlers' suggestion that they privatize their land. Though quick to distinguish Plymouth's mission from that of a Popish, "retired, monastical course," Cushman's sermon of December, 1621 charges the young community with responsibilities very like those of a monastic order. They are "in league together" as "brothers" as well as "associates." They must "cleve together in the service of God"; Because they "ventured [their] lives together here, and had a hard brunt of it," they must look out for each other's interest, sharing their "sorrows," "sickness" and "welfare," yielding up their surplus to those in need.[48]

This condition is what Victor Turner calls *communitas*: the liminal phase in the ritual passage, in which the initiates abolish gradations of class, property and wealth in order to live communally. But though Turner allows that monastic orders have attempted to turn "transition" into a "permanent condition,"[49] his general observation of rites of passage in most human communities is that the stage of *communitas* is precisely that: a stage in a three-part process that ends with the return from the *limen*, to aggregation into everyday life. Cushman was clear enough that he didn't want Plymouth to be a monastic society, but he enjoined upon it a pattern of behavior that would have to be just so institutionalized if it were to be made permanent. Since Plymouth was an "ordinary" settlement after all, not a monastery, its period of *communitas* had to remain only a temporary stage in its development. Cushman's mistake lay in thinking it would last forever, and in trying to impose a symbolic representation upon literal life. Since both undertakings were impossible, Plymouth was bound to "fail" and he to despair.

Of course one way to ritualize a passage – or any experience – is to turn it into a narrative. I have argued that it is the psychology of emigration that has made stories of initiation through travel "westwards" such a popular American genre. But significantly the geographical particulars of these narratives, and their protagonists' situation, have always been arranged so that the passage is out and back. We have seen how this convention works in John Smith's *General History* and Francis Parkman's *The Oregon Trail* – both of them "ritualized" versions of earlier, less tidy accounts of the same events.

Another popular American genre, closely related to the western tale of initiation and indeed sharing many of its features, conforms to the same paradigm. It is the narrative of captivity. Here too the dreadful experience is inscribed as an initiation for the protagonist: a voyage to the *limen*, where ordinary prerogatives and hierarchies are inverted; then back to normal life, renewed and strengthened by the ordeal on the margins of experience. In Mary Rowlandson's *Captivity and Restoration* of 1682, the Indians attack the small town of Lancaster, Massachusetts, killing some of the settlers and kidnapping others. Mary is carried away with her infant daughter, who has been shot in the attack and who dies later of her horrible wound. Grieving for her daughter's death, disoriented by the Indians' constant movement from place to place within the wilderness of central and western Massachusetts, and constantly anxious for her physical safety, the narrator comes to question the very foundations of her faith. Of all the ways in which her captivity inverts her normal life's pattern, this spiritual perplexity troubles her most. Much of the narrative's energy is devoted to trying to interpret the catastrophic events in the light of God's assurances for His elect.

Usually the struggle to reconcile her personal misfortunes with God's providence ends happily in the recollection of a comforting Biblical text. Not always, though. On one occasion the Indians manage to get across a river by "cutting dry trees to make rafts," then sit down to sup on broth made of "an old horse's leg," while the pursuing "English" are held back by the river. "And here I cannot but take notice of the strange providence of God in preserving the heathen," Rowlandson writes. "The greatest number...were squaws, and they traveled with all they had, bag and baggage, and yet they got over this river aforesaid...On that very day came the English army after them...and yet this river put a stop to them." This was a shocking reversal of the type of Exodus: the "heathen" fed in the wilderness and crossing the water dry shod, while the saints, like Pharoah's soldiers, are stopped in their tracks. To such a strong challenge to her sense of election, Rowlandson can say only, "We were not ready yet for so great a mercy as victory and deliverance." Even her interpretative energy seems to have run out here. For an American Puritan accustomed to investigating every aspect of ordinary life for the light it throws on God's plan for both individual and community, this interpretative failure was Mary Rowlandson's sorest trial. Yet despite – or rather because of – her spatial and spiritual disorientation in the wilderness, Rowlandson's return home effects a reformation in her spirit. As she tells it, everything she cares about is "restored": God's prophecies, the Biblical types through which He speaks to the elect, her consciousness of her place in the elect community, even (perhaps most importantly, since it governs her skill at interpretation) her sense of proportion:

> Yet I see, when God calls a person to anything, and through never so many difficulties, yet He is fully able to carry them through and make them see, and say they have been gainers thereby. And I hope I can say in some measure, as David did, "It is good for me that I have been afflicted." The Lord hath shown me the vanity of these outward things...If trouble from smaller matters begin to arise in me, I have something to hand to check myself with, and say, why am I troubled? It was but the other day that if I had had the world, I would have given it for my freedom.

As for narratives of the experience of emigration itself, we have seen that plenty of them express the experience as a *partial* initiation, dramatizing the act of stripping away old culture and embracing new nature, then falling silent at what ought to be the third stage of aggregation. Others, written by failed emigrants who become travelers of sorts, rejoice in returning home without always embracing the idea that home comforts and conventions have first to be dismissed before they can be reassumed. But there remains at least one emigration story that goes both "out" and "back," even though it is about a woman whose venture succeeded and who died, apparently contented, in Pike County, Illinois, where she had originally settled.

Rebecca Burlend's *A True Picture of Emigration*, first published in London in 1848, is much cited by historians of anglophone migration to America. One can see why. No narrative expresses more completely the whole range of mood and experience, the traumas, exhilarations, disappointments and satisfactions of migrating to the New World.

Hence her passage over is both providential (after a terrible storm, the captain appears "like one of those celestial visitors" to reassure the passengers that the danger is past), but also tedious and frightening in turn. The full moon glimpsed from deck makes her feel both vulnerable and desperately homesick.[50] When they join an English friend in Illinois, an immigrant who had gone before them and written home to promise "a land flowing with milk and honey," they find his appearance as degenerate as any planter's in Faux or Savage: "as ragged as a sheep...and his house...more like the cell of a hermit...than the cottage of an industrious peasant" (51). Like Mrs. Trollope, Mrs. Burlend was repulsed by the violent passions of religious camp meetings (144-7) and felt the want of regular church services she could attend conveniently (115).

There is even a scene that might have been prompted by Dickens. She and her family first set foot in Illinois at a remote river landing called Philips Ferry, where

> we were utterly confounded: there was no appearance of a landing place, no luggage yard, nor even a building of any kind within sight...In a few minutes [we] saw ourselves standing by the brink of the river, bordered by a dark wood...as the evening shades were rapidly settling on the earth...It was in the middle of November, and already very frosty. My husband and I looked at each other till we burst into tears, and our children observing our disquietude began to cry bitterly. Is this America, thought I, is this the reception I meet with after my long, painfully anxious and bereaving voyage? (42-3)

Six years before this was published, *American Notes* offered a nearly identical vignette, seen from the point of the disappearing steamboat. The settlers land on the bank and "stand where they landed, as if stricken into stone; and look after the boat." As the steamer pulls away, "There they stand yet, without the motion of a hand...in the distance and increasing darkness they are mere specks to the eye: lingering there still."[51]

Yet her imagination could also celebrate the fecundity of American nature. Long passages catalog the profusion of wild and cultivated fruit and vegetables available to them in Illinois, the beauty of flowers and birds, the astonishing variety of animal life (94-106). Her health improves; "asthmatic symptoms" chronic in England leave her altogether in America. Season by season they become "better situated" (113), begin to accumulate enough to save for seed, even a surplus to sell (129-31). Finally their wealth in stock, housing, land and equipment becomes such as to allow them to invite visitors to stay, and to take pleasure in their amazement. Nor was her pleasure in their accumulations merely material; they were a sign of the ordeal through which they had passed: "I make no boast of our possessions; but having told the difficulties we experienced at our commencement, I ought in fairness to state what our success has been" (151-2).

Yet though she draws on both sides of the dominant discourse, Burlend also provides a store of details of the sort the promoters note only by the way, if then, and of which the hostile travelers were largely ignorant: the countless practical difficulties of settling and farming on a frontier. She documents the nuisance of mosquitoes (82), the violence of thunderstorms (80), what it means to the struggling farmer to be cheated by the miller (88), to be short of working capital (79-80), even to lack a whetstone to sharpen axes and scythes (123). Once her husband cuts his knee on a sickle. The infection almost kills him, then lays him up for several weeks, during which she has to cut and gather in the wheat harvest, aided only by a small child (89-92). Later part of the crop is destroyed in a fire. Insights like these into the everyday concerns of the ordinary frontier settler are among the qualities that recommend Burlend's book to the historian of emigration.

On reflection, though, the book seems an odd authority for an historian to cite. For Rebecca Burlend did not write *A True Picture of Emigration*. She was not illiterate – much less unintelligent – but she was an English peasant woman of little education, happily unschooled in the mid-Victorian literary diction and redundant phrasing units in which the book is written. This is no primary document of first-hand experience, but a ghosted "as-told-to" job – much more heavily inflected by another hand than the collections of letters from happy settlers published by British promoters of emigration to the United States. It was Rebecca's eldest son who wrote the book, a schoolmaster and the author of *Village Rhymes* (1858) and *Amy Thornton; or the Curate's Daughter* (1862). Plagued by recurrent illness and unlikely to be of much help on a frontier settlement, Edward had stayed behind when the rest of his family set off for Illinois in 1831. He might have learned of his mother's experiences – or some of them – by letter, but the main point of transmission seems to have been Rebecca's return visit to England in 1846, two years before the book was published, when she got the chance to tell her son the whole story.

Who can say for certain how many of the events related in *A True Picture of Emigration* really happened to Rebecca Burlend, much less how many of the book's more leisurely reflections were really hers? Savage, Trollope, Dickens and many others had already published their reports on the American scene by the time Edward began to write up his mother's adventure, and there is no reason why a young literary gent interested in American emigration might not have read at least some of these books and incorporated elements of them in his own. Even so, the historians are right. Despite its style and the other extraneous influences which may have invaded the text, *A True Picture of Emigration* lives up to its title. Even today, it convinces.

Why? Because the book is so inclusive, catching up the whole range of the emigrant experience. It contains strands of the promoters' dominant discourse, and of its antithesis posed by the travelers and journalists; it has Lucy Downing's skepticism about the practicalities of living in the New World, and the spiritual autobiographers' sense of anticlimax after coming over. In addition it offers observations and insights not available in other accounts of emigration. The reader is constantly learning something new about the experience.

What facilitated this openness to all the moods and experiences of emigration? What kept *A True Picture* from being just another incomplete or partial record of the venture? I believe the book succeeds in this respect precisely because it has been filtered through another consciousness and other possible versions of the story. Above all it succeeds because Rebecca's migration has been ritualized into a narrative of a voyage out and back, just as the adventures of Smith, Parkman and Rowlandson were. It is as though this completion of an archetypal cycle has allowed the text to relax: to surrender a defensive position, to allow alternative discourses alongside each other. For it ends, not with her inviting guests to inspect their prosperity in Illinois, not with her apparently contented old age in America, but with her happy return to England. The last paragraph does not hide the fact that her return was only for a visit ("she" writes of "a prosperous voyage" to "a few short summer weeks, in my own country"), but it is with the image of Burlend happily "restored" to her native land that the reader is left. Only Edward, breaking cover at last as the true writer of the book, documents Rebecca's return to America. But he does so in a footnote, after the narrative is done.

Part IV

"Ruins so soon!"

20

Going home in fancy; reveries of European culture; daydreams of American antiquity; future association; sublimity of American scenery; romantic solitude; why all these remedies collapsed of their own improbability and mutual contradictions

The optimistic rhetoric of American emigration and settlement – the ideology of initiation, of culture satirized and nature embraced – was faced with two kinds of opposition, therefore. One was the attack voiced by the political enemies of the American Republic, back-migrants and travelers. This confronted the boosters' claims head-on. It was the antithesis of their thesis, and therefore part of the dominant discourse. The other kind of opposition – the feelings of frustration, anticlimax, even boredom, occasionally implied by emigrants who remained in America – would more properly be called an alternative to the dominant discourse rather than its antithesis. Because the discourse of emigration was dominant, this alternative was scarcely "voiced" at all, was not really a discourse. Because it was felt as somehow subversive, it was hardly preserved by the process of vernacular publication, and were it not for the unusual circumstances governing the productions of the Puritans' letters and journals, we might have encountered little direct, personal expression of the complex of feelings that make it up.

Yet traces of both the antithesis and the alternative to the discourse of emigration are evident in American writing. The "successful" emigrants counter-refuted the antithesis when they tried to get their families to discount the adverse reports of back-migrants, and made occasional – though usually fragmentary and oblique – references to the disillusion entailed in the alternative view. Or perhaps it might be put this way: because American writers could not help internalizing the antithesis, they expressed the alternative covertly, sometimes unconsciously. And the same is true of what we more conventionally allow as "American literature": itself a rhetorical construct of the dominant discourse. The strata of American literature are cut across by the alternative – by oblique fractures, indirect expressions of the anxiety of separation. This section explores some of these fault lines.

Rebecca Burlend's *A True Picture of Emigration* was exceptional. Other successful migrants did not manage to ritualize their movements into fully developed, out-and-back narratives of initiation. In a sense, because their letters so often broke off after they got settled, their stories were always unfinished. And however exhilarating the idea of process may have seemed – however useful as a distinguishing characteristic of American self-definition – its less comfortable side was a sense of incompleteness, of not having brought things round to a conclusion.

Though this feeling could not be accomodated within the positive rhetoric of emigration, Americans, even of the second and later generations, would continue to try to "go back," though (as Hawthorne's *Our Old Home* makes clear) they would accomplish this ambition more successfully as tourists than as claimants to a lost birthright.

Others could go back in their imaginations. On her way from Boston to New York in 1704, Sarah Kemble Knight "found great difficulty in Travailing, the way being very narrow, and...it being so exceeding dark." Bewildered in "the dolesome woods," her "company next to none, Going I knew not whither," she suddenly breasted a hill and caught sight of the full moon just rising above the distant horizon. The light much reassured her, not least because coming through the branches of some distant trees, it "fill'd my Imagination with the pleasant delusion of a Sumpteous citty, fill'd with famous Buildings... Grandeurs wch I had heard of, and wch the stories of foreign countries had given me the Idea of." She was even moved (later, presumably) to formalize the spectacle in verse:

Here stood a Lofty church – there is a steeple,
And there the Grand Parade – O see the people!
That Famous Castle there, were I but nigh.
To see the mote and Bridg and walls so high –
They'r very fine! sais my deluded eye.

A hundred and fifty years later Susan Fenimore Cooper, the novelist's daughter, performed a strikingly similar trick of her imagination on the American landscape. Seated on the trunk of a fallen pine in "the softening haze of the Indian summer," that season when (she says) "Images, quaint and strange, rise unbidden and fill the mind," she waved a sprig of wych-hazel across the view before her and pretended to erase the village below. Instantly the wooden bridge, the court house, the churches, the "seven taverns," the "dozen stores" and the "hundred dwelling houses" all "vanished like the smoke from their own chimneys." In their place stood the primeval forest, "the trees in full maturity" as before the first settlers had entered the scene.

"But even this... did not satisfy the whim of the moment." Another sweep of the wych-hazel, and an English village appeared where the American had been: "low, picturesque, thatched cottages... a large stone cross, beautifully designed and elaborately carved, doubtless a monument of some past historical event... the church... evidently very old... the bridge... of massive stone... the ruins of a tower" – and so on, down to an old priory built on the site of a Roman villa. Then just as suddenly and capriciously, she waved the wand again, and the scene "resumed its every-day aspect."[1]

Faced with a scene either wild or banal, both authors express a yearning for the solid architectural deposits of ancient culture. Yet in both texts the European scene proposed is admittedly unattainable, insubstantial. Cooper's village has been conjured up out of the autumn mists and can be wiped away in an instant. Knight's "Sumpteous citty" belongs to publicity, not experience. It is composed of "Famous" artifacts which she has read about in books, not seen – let alone lived with. As she goes on immediately to say, her "pleasant delusion" was confected of nothing more than a thought "of thoughts themselves." That is why it deconstructs itself in self-mockery. To borrow Coleridge's old distinction, both visions come from the fancy rather than the imagination.

Still other Americans tried to disinter a classical past out of the physical materials available in the landscape around them. There has always been a receptive audience in the country for reports of the indistinct deposits left by Viking explorers, Welsh princes and other Europeans supposed to have settled on the continent long before Columbus landed in the New World. Early in the nineteenth century this appetite of the imagination centered on the burial mounds discovered in Illinois and elsewhere. Were these mysterious remains a sign of a complex, "classical" civilization, now vanished, or were they just a pile of dead Indians?

As so often in that period, the phenomenon inscribed itself on British politics: on the domestic debate about the viability of the American republican example. Tory journals like the *Quarterly Review* needed to prove that America had degenerated since becoming independent, so they favored the vanished-civilization hypothesis. In its very first issue, reviewing Patrick Gass's *Journal of the Voyages*...[of] *Lewis and Clark* (1808), the *Quarterly* said that the mounds clearly indicated a vanished culture greatly superior to that of the present-day Indians, who are entirely indifferent to the mounds, and among whom "even the voice of tradition is silent with respect to their origins." But in the same year the Whig *Edinburgh Review* took Thomas Ashe's *Travels in America* (1809) apart for its "maukish enthusiasm and inept speculation" on the topic of the mounds. They were not, the reviewer insisted, the "venerable relics of once polished, but now degreded nations"; they were not even "antiquities," properly speaking. What kind of civilization "records itself in no language of tradition – in no monument of higher art than a mud wall – and in no instrument more perfect than a hatchet of stone"?[2]

Among Americans too, the politically more progressive were inclined to discount the ancient-civilization construction put upon the Indian burial mounds. In *Notes on the State of Virginia* Thomas Jefferson, keen to counter inferences of New-World degeneration, claims to "know of no such thing existing as an Indian monument: for I should not honour with that name arrow points, stone hatchets, stone pipes, and half-shapen images." He excavated a burial mound near his home in Virginia, to find only a haphazard heap of bones, "some vertical, some oblique, some horizontal...entangled and held together in clusters by the earth" (Query XI).

But Americans of a more poetical profession could not rest content with so unromantic a conclusion. In "The Prairies," written after a visit to his brothers in Illinois in 1832, William Cullen Bryant erected around the burial mounds a whole edifice of suppositions about the people who built them. They were a "race, that long has passed away," "disciplined and populous," more ancient than the classical Greeks. The prairies were the "ample fields" where

their herds were fed,
When haply by their stalls the bison lowed,
And bowed his maned shoulder to the yoke.
All day this desert murmured with their toils,
Till twilight blushed and lovers walked, and wooed
In a forgotten language, and old tunes,
From instruments of unremembered form,
Gave the soft winds a voice...

What happened to them? "The red man came – / The roaming hunter tribes, warlike and fierce, / And the mound-builders vanished from the earth." Perhaps one among the ancient race survived to marry the daughter of an Indian chief, though never able to forget "the wife / Of his first love, and her sweet little ones / Butchered, amid their shrieks, with all his race."

It is an alluring poem, highly evocative and deeply dishonest. On one level its evasiveness is political. The only hunters, warlike and fierce known for certain by Bryant to have butchered the indigenous peoples of the prairies were his white fellow-citizens, and their victims were the Indians. To obscure that fact, he needs to invent a fairy-tale culture for the Indians to wipe out, a civilization so advanced that it had learned to domesticate the American buffalo; then to plot their catastrophe against a general backdrop in which all "form of beings" pass away: a scheme in which, however, the "red man" is not "butchered" in turn, but merely "leaves the blooming wilds he ranged so long." (As Huck Finn said about *Pilgrim's Progress*, it is about a man that left his family, it didn't say why.)

After the various "races" go their ways, the poet is left in the "solitude" of the prairie. No human beings now grace the scene, but at least the "great solitude is quick with life": insects, flowers, "gentle quadrupeds," "reptiles.../ Startlingly beautiful," "the bee," "the graceful deer." Then suddenly, quite without warning, the poem ends in a different tone:

> All at once
> A fresher wind sweeps by, and breaks my dream,
> And I am in the wilderness alone.

That is, not just the mound builders and the Indians pass away, but also the lively scene before him, and the very scheme of things that has brought all these in sequence before his mind's eye. There is no order after all, not even a degenerative succession of pathetic events: no history. Space, too, ceases to exist, because he is now simply "alone" in the "wilderness." Reality, unmasked at last, is beyond explanation, because time and space – which provide the coordinates by which the individual fixes himself in his society, the perspectives necessary to the analysis of self and community – have been revealed as illusions.

It is important to recognise how this greater erasure of order at the poem's conclusion is related to Bryant's lesser evasions over the "red man" and the ancient race. Bryant invents his paleo-classical civilization in order to provide moral cause for the Indians' own disappearance; but also because, like Knight and Susan Cooper, he hungers after the ancient, rooted artifacts which good Americans (for good reasons) have had to put behind them. If only we could have the freedom, the self-reliance, the sense of infinite possibilities offered by the American dispensation, while retaining that secure perspective afforded by centuries of European history lying around and beneath us. Maybe we can imagine it. Maybe we can excavate it here, however obscured. Maybe, like William Randolph Hearst or Henry E. Huntington or J. Paul Getty, we can carry it bodily over to a *Kunstkammer* in California. No, we can't. Because we are talking here not of two places, but of two contrary states of mind. We can't retrieve the "culture" we discarded any more than did the Indians massacre the tender suitors, with their lovely tunes and serviceable buffaloes. So the fanciful project of the ancient civilization collapses – of its own absurdity and of the emotional and intellectual shallowness motivating its invention. With it collapses, first, any accurate examination and discrimination of present and past reality; next, the bland, degenerative scheme that is offered as a substitute for such analysis; and finally, even the concrete scene presently before the observer. When the reverie of fancy evaporates, it takes everything else with it.

So the loyal American could not go back in imagination, or sustain faith in a classical past discovered at home. This is what Washington Irving meant when he said America lacked "association," and why American landscape was so commonly said to be deficient in "the picturesque." (*The Home Book of the Picturesque*, the collection in which Susan Cooper's essay first appeared, tried – as its very title proclaimed – to refute this critique, though with only limited success in her case.)

But bolder responses suggested themselves. One was a restatement, in aesthetic terms, of the "figure of anticipation." Americans' imaginative associations should be with the future, not the past, as N.P. Willis wrote in his introduction to a collection of landscape sketches by the American artist, W.H. Bartlett (1840). "Instead of looking through a valley...in which live lords and tenants...whose fields have never changed landmarks or modes of culture since the memory of man, [the American]...sees a valley laden with virgin vegetation...and his first thought is of the villages that will soon sparkle on the hillside, the axes that will ring from the woodlands, and the mills, bridges, canals, and railroads, that will span and border the stream that now runs through sedges and wild flowers."

Or as the Hudson River painter Thomas Cole had put it in his celebrated essay on "American Landscape" (1836), no American observer looks over a valley to see the "ruined tower to tell of outrage" or the "gorgeous temple to speak of ostentation." But denied these European advantages, he can, at least, cast "his mind's eye...far into futurity. Where the wolf roams, the plough shall glisten, on the gray crag shall rise temple and tower – mighty deeds shall be done in the now pathless wilderness; and poets yet unborn shall sanctify the soil."

But just in case the future-association argument failed, Willis, Cole and others had another up their sleeves. Irving's Preface to *The Sketch Book* had used it too. What America lacked in associations with the past that constituted the traditional picturesque, it could make up for in its natural topography: its vast plains, steep mountains, plunging "cataracts," and so forth. Delivering the graduation speech at Bowdoin College in 1825, Henry Wadsworth Longfellow prophesied a native "literary prosperity" (significant phrase) to be extracted from "the scenery of our country...so rich as it is in everything beautiful and magnificent, and so full of quiet loveliness or of sublime and solitary awe." America's "language is in its high mountains, and in the pleasant valleys scooped out between them," or (as Willis put it) in its "lavish and large-featured sublimity...quite dissimilar to the picturesque of all other countries." "Those scenes of solitude from which the hand of nature has never been lifted," wrote Cole, "affect the mind with a more deep toned emotion than aught which the hand of man has touched."

In other words, as Irving had already confessed, "never need an American look beyond his own country for the sublime and beautiful of natural scenery." Yet the prestige of the European cult of Romantic solitude in nature, and the massive scale of American topography that most clearly distinguished it from the European, meant that the mode of the sublime would take precedence over the beautiful in the enterprise of American self-definition. Even by 1816 Edward Tyrell Channing (later Professor of Rhetoric and Oratory at Harvard) had become sufficiently familiar with the Romantic sublime to turn it into a prospective American aesthetic. "We have exact scholars who require a sustained faultlessness and elegance in every thing," he wrote in the *North American Review*. "They never look at gleams or regions of clear azure in a sleepy sky. They laugh at foolish simplicity." And we have, too, a "middling crowd of readers whose vocabulary of criticism extends little further than to '*unnatural*, *out-of-life*,' &c...against every man who ventures upon the marvellous, wild, and unreal." "A heavy day it will be for poetry when society is made the school of genius instead of solitude."[3]

Solitude, not society: this defense, drawn immediately from Wordsworth, from whom Channing quotes at the head of his essay, chimed perfectly with the ideology of emigration, in which nature displaced culture. It would serve very well as the aesthetic branch of American self-definition. So would the hypothesis of future association, exploiting as it did the emigrants' valorizing of process.

But neither argument could be made to work. The idea that the observer's imagination could be stimulated by associations with future developments was vitiated by the same weakness that caused Knight's, Cooper's and Bryant's fancies of an ancient civilization to collapse. For a metaphor to succeed, both the thing and the thing compared – however distant they may be – have to be believable, verified by experience. A metaphor's power lies in the ingenuity with which it ties two disparate ideas together while still convincing that the comparison is justified, not in confecting one or more of those ideas out of whole cloth. But the shape of the future is no more knowable than were (to Knight, Cooper and Bryant) the rooted artifacts of European culture or the history of the burial mounds. These visions belong to fancy, not the imagination – to reverie rather than meditation.

And Romantic solitude? What follows is more difficult to demonstrate, because it arises from a subjective response, but "solitude" feels very different in its contemporary British and American contexts. In Wordsworth solitude is a temporary condition, deliberately evoked as an environment for reflection. One returns to Dorothy, the fireside, the community. Similarly, the "solitaries" encountered in the *Lyrical Ballads* or *The Prelude*, though perhaps impaired psychologically or physically – and permanently so – are seen in the context of, as much as in contradistinction to, a wider community, to which the enquiring narrative voice also belongs and speaks.

When Bryant writes that "Still this great solitude is quick with life," he achieves something of Wordsworth's feeling, even if the "life" to which he refers is inhuman. But *his* poem ends, not by returning from that solitude, but by effacing even what life he senses there. With his realization that he is "in the wilderness alone," Bryant has descended to a bedrock of "solitude" from which, if he ever felt it, Wordsworth was quick enough to return to the solicitations of society.

A similar mood descends at the end of Fenimore Cooper's *The Deerslayer* (1841). Fifteen years after the events that form that novel's action, Natty Bumppo and Chingachgook revisit Lake Glimmerglass, to find the scene deserted, the few remnants of Hutter's settlement now fallen into decay. An old canoe bumps up against the shore. "Wild beasts" have rooted up the bodies of the Indians who fell in the climactic battle, leaving "human bones...bleaching in the rains of summer." Hutter's floating castle is now grounded on a shoal, unroofed, open to the seasons, which "rioted in the place, as if in mockery at the attempt to exclude them." Piles and palisades alike are rotting, "and it was evident that...a few more gales and tempests would sweep all into the lake, and blot the building from the face of that magnificent solitude." Cooper does his best to connect the scene with European landscape conventions. He even calls the "castle" a "picturesque ruin." But "real" ruined castles survive for the associative imagination to build on – however fallaciously – whereas this one will have vanished utterly in a (very) few more years at most. Even now, there is little the visitors can "associate" with events only fifteen years in the past. Try as they might, they cannot find the graves where old allies and enemies lie buried. "Either the elements had obliterated their traces, or time had caused those who looked for them to forget their position." The landscape is reverting to topography. Already insufficient artifacts remain to orient human memory. And that memory will itself fade, becoming less human on that account. This "solitude" (the word is used twice in this short passage) is degenerative, terminal, absolute.

In truth, it was not the solitude of the American wilderness that was eroding human cultural deposits, but the other way round. Both defenses of the American scene as an aesthetic environment – the hypotheses of "future association" and of sublime topography – contained their own inherent contradictions. Even more cruelly, they contradicted each other. The more the imagination was enflamed by the energetic, republican enterprise of settling farms, towns and factories on the scene below, the less wilderness was left in which to take pleasure in the solitary sublime. Cole himself was aware of this paradox, though unable to resolve it. His lavish paragraphs praising the "magnificence" and "sublimity" of the American "solitudes" give way to visions of future culture, when "the plough shall glisten, on the gray crag shall rise temple and tower, [and] mighty deeds shall be done in the now pathless wilderness." He doesn't say how the new towers and temples will escape the "outrage" and "ostentation" of their European prototypes, but he admits that you can't have the development and the sublime wilderness as well. "Yet I cannot but express my sorrow that the beauty of such landscapes are [*sic*] quickly passing away – the ravages of the axe are daily increasing – the most noble scenes are made desolate, and oftentimes with a wantonness and barbarism scarcely credible in a civilized nation." The dream of enterprise, in which the plow "glistens," is inseparable from the nightmare of despoliation, in which the axe "ravages." Yet moral qualities inhere in neither plow nor axe (Willis's axe "sings," remember); they are neutral metonyms for clearing and cultivation. Cole's nightmare does not qualify his dream, or somehow round it out; it simply cancels it. Or, as he puts it himself, "an enlightened and increasing people have broken in upon the solitude." Both as a convention and as a real condition actually to be experienced, European solitude could somehow tolerate other people, if only because it would be beyond European imagining to shut them, wholly and permanently, out of the landscape. But to American solitude, as an idea and as a real wilderness, any incursion was an invasion. People – any people, enlightened or otherwise – destroyed it utterly.[4]

That is why the tone of Cooper's *The Prairie* (1827) comes as such a surprise. To American poets and European travelers alike, the prairies were the most famous distinguishing feature of North American topography: the Appalachian Chain, even the American Rockies, might fall short of the precipitous rises and falls of Alpine peaks, but the prairies, at least, were a proper topic for the sublime. Whitman thought they embodied the American character itself: "broad, patriotic, heroic, and new."[5] Furthermore, *The Prairie* is set in the year when Lewis and Clark were busy surveying the Lousiana Purchase, preparing for the greatest, fastest spatial expansion and era of democratic hope in American demographic history. Yet, even as it begins, the novel puts it readers in mind of endings: "The harvest of the first year of our possession had long been passed, and the fading foliage of a few scattered trees was, already, beginning to exhibit the hues and tints of autumn." Much else is autumnal too: the Indians are vanishing; the game is getting scarce – the hunters of deer now catch bees, and even Natty has had to learn to trap beaver. It is in this book that the great Leatherstocking finally dies, facing west, answering his God as he once did Judge Temple, nostalgic for the passing of the royal colony of which he was once such a loyal servant. And the cause of all this degeneration? The very "people" of whom Cole warned, "breaking in upon" the American solitude. Only in this book they aren't so enlightened. They are the restless, aggressive Ishmael Bush and his numerous family, and many thousands like him: the immigrants rushing into the newly opened territory and destroying it forever.

21

The American looks at immigrants; how restless, degenerate immigrants warp the narrative of initiation; the immigrant as "the other" by which the American self is defined

If *The Prairie* seems to invert the spring of Jefferson's populist vision into an autumn of nostalgia for America's colonial past, it is because its author thought the emigrants' restless, thrusting invasion of the prairies to be a retrograde step. He felt even more strongly about strangers on his own turf. Though a stout defender of American republican principles, and a supporter of revolutionary causes abroad, he fought a series of legal battles to keep his extensive property around Cooperstown inviolate from settlers and even casual pleasure-seekers. (He sent a barbed message on this topic when, in *The Deerslayer*, he set the camp of the wicked Hurons on Three Mile Point on the shores of Lake Glimmerglass – or Lake Otsego in real life – which the Cooper family owned but the local people had taken to using as a picnic ground.)

This odd mixture of radical and conservative impulses was not confined to Cooper, and elsewhere it was even more sharply focused on the issue of emigration. Benjamin Franklin must be counted among the most vehement propagandists for European emigration to America. To Franklin, what motivated the emigrants would define the country's character. Emigration was a mutual benefit: to the prosperity of America and to the happiness of hard-working European artisans and tenant farmers seeking financial and political independence. Yet in another mood, or looking at the process from another angle, he could take the opposite position. Writing to Peter Collinson, the English Quaker scientist, in 1753, he complained of English immigrants whose "Industry seems to diminish in equal proportion" to the better pay they were getting for their labor. But the Germans were even more of a threat, because they worked *too* hard, piling up wealth and influence, increasing in numbers, and making their own laws, so that "all the advantages we have will not...be able to preserve our language, and even our Government will become precarious."[6]

The reversal of opinion between Franklin's *Information to Those Who Would Remove to America* of 1782 and this much earlier letter can not be explained as a change of mind over the course of time. Others of his writings composed both earlier and later than the Collinson letter supported the need and desirability of mass emigration to the New World.[7] No, the difference is one, literally, of viewpoint. Seen as *em*igrants – that is, as venturing their livelihoods to escape the feudal tyranny of the Old World – these brave people seem to bear with them the hopes of America itself: they are the distillation of what it means to be American. Seen as *imm*igrants, they are a disorderly mass invading our native space, threatening to swamp it with alien tongues and cultures. Once arrived, they become the very antithesis of what it means to be American.

At least Franklin's strikingly divergent views on emigration/immigration are expressed in separate places – indeed in different kinds of discourse: the one public, the other private. But other American texts are less consistent within themselves. In 1631, in a journal so anxious to celebrate English migration to Massachusetts that it recorded every ship bringing settlers to the colony, John Winthrop made this strange entry:

> The poorer sort of people (who lay long in tents, etc.) were much afflicted with the scurvy, and many died, especially at Boston and Charlestown; but when this ship came and brought store of juice of lemons, many recovered speedily. It hath been always observed here, that such as fell into discontent, and lingered after their former conditions in England, fell into the scurvy and died.[8]

The tone of this short paragraph reverses itself twice, and it confuses in other ways too. Is he talking of physical or psychological causes? Did the settlers sicken and die of the scurvy because their diet lacked vitamin C, or because they hankered after their old homes? The latter reason will serve the propaganda for emigration as well as the lamentable departure of the Pratts. People fail in the enterprise of resettlement because they somehow lack the courage to break with the past and venture new experience: "The poor home-sick things!" "I really have no patience with such chicken-hearted people."

Yet Winthrop cannot ignore the physiological cause of scurvy, for how else could he dramatize the timely intervention of citrus fruit? Fortunate arrivals strengthening their enterprise at crucial moments form a chief constituent of Winthrop's propaganda for New World settlement. But another cause, equally physical to their vitamin deficiency, lurks behind the the poor settlers' distress: the fact that they lived in tents. Here again Winthrop's tone is hard; he blames the victim for the crime. The trouble with the poorer sort (despite God's providence in showering lemons upon them in the wilderness) is that they are poor. And, it is implied, rootless and feckless with it. What can you expect of people who live in tents rather than houses, and can't stick to it when the going gets rough? In this way, so as to still their own sense of guilt, the better off have often characterized "the poorer sort."

So even in Winthrop's project for a reformed community vestiges of the Old World social and economic hierarchies linger on. Even more surprisingly, since it happens in a more egalitarian environment than that of early Massachusetts, something very similar occurs in Parkman's *Oregon Trail* and Thoreau's *Walden* (1854). Both texts were written and read as excursions into the wilderness (though Thoreau admitted that Walden Pond, only two miles from Concord, Massachusetts, was rather a "laboratory version of the West"). Both were constructed as initiations in which the narrative consciousness goes out to the margin and returns to aggregate with the society left behind. The initiation experienced in the wilderness resolves tensions in the narrator's world: for Parkman, between eastern and western landscapes, Christian and Indian cultures; for Thoreau, (roughly speaking) between technology and commercialism, on the one hand, and natural self-sufficiency on the other.

Which is to say that, via the extended metaphor of their narratives, both books approve the trajectory of risk and resolution, the learning process central to the emigrant's rite of passage. Yet unexpectedly (given their focus on the development of the central narrative consciousness) both also address the issue of emigration literally and explicitly. More strikingly still, the values both ascribe to the experience of emigration is exactly the opposite of those promoted by the narrative of initiation.

Parkman's attention was arrested by the desperate condition of the Americans who were moving west to try their luck in Oregon. He recalls coming across abandoned graves on the prairie. "The earth was usually torn up, and covered thickly with wolf tracks...Nothing could speak more for the hardihood, or rather infatuation, of the adventurers, or the sufferings that await them upon their journey," he comments.

That correction of "hardihood" to "infatuation" is significant. In mid-sentence Parkman is switching from the positive to the negative case in the debate over emigration – from the propagandists' boast to the hostile travelers' critique. Parkman's emigrants are every bit as rootless, degenerate, socially and politically unstable, as any frontier settler in Faux, Savage, Trollope or Dickens. And in the same language. When Parkman and his party overtake an emigrant party on the trail, they notice how "care-worn" appeared the "thin-featured matron, or the buxom girl" whose faces peeped out of the covered wagons:

It was easy to see that fear and dissension prevailed among them...Many were murmuring against the leader they had chosen, and wished to depose him; and this discontent was fomented by some ambitious spirits, who had hopes of succeeding in his place. The women were divided between regrets for the homes they had left and apprehension of the deserts and the savages before them.

Two points about this curious passage require immediate comment. First, how can Parkman, riding past their wagons, possibly infer what is going on in the women's minds? Second, what are the men up to, if not (in other words) something approaching the democratic process? But it is the words that are important. What Parkman wants to stress in this vignette is division, "dissention," "discontent." It's as though he were recalling Milton's preamble to the Fall in Book IX of *Paradise Lost:* "foul distrust, and breach / Disloyal on the part of man, revolt, / And disobedience." Or more immediately, as though he had been infected with the conservative rhetoric of the English travelers in America, for whom political opposition to the established government was always the work of "ambitious spirits" "fomenting" rebellion, and the act of voting out an *elected* leader, tantamount to "deposing" him.

Thoreau's reference to emigration is even more unpleasant, perhaps because he is discussing immigrants rather than emigrants. "Wilderness" though it may have been – and as "solitary" as "on the prairies" – the country around Walden Pond was paradoxically replete with the ruins of earlier human habitation. Hikers in the hills of Massachusetts today are used to coming across the sunken pits of what were once the excavated cellars of farmhouses, now covered (like the fields their inhabitants once cleared and worked) in second-growth forest. But it comes as something of a surprise to learn that some 125 years ago Thoreau too commonly encountered "these cellar dents, like deserted fox burrows, old holes...all that is left where once were the stir and bustle of human life."

When out fishing one day, as he tells it in *Walden*, he is caught in a thundershower and seeks shelter in another abandoned farmhouse, a hut that has "long been uninhabited," only to find a family of immigrants there, an Irishman called John Field, his wife and

> several children, from the broad-faced boy who assisted his father at his work...to the wrinkled, sybil-like, cone-headed infant that sat upon his father's knee as in the palace of nobles...not knowing but it was the last of a noble line, and the hope and cynosure of the world, instead of John Field's poor starveling brat. There we sat together under that part of the roof which leaked the least, while it showered and thundered without. I had sat there many times of old before the ship was built that floated this family to America. An honest, hard-working, but shiftless man plainly was John Field.

Thoreau sets up this scene in order to contrast Field's way of life with his own: the Irishman has to dig a farmer's field at $10 an acre to pay his rent and pay for his food, whereas Thoreau "lived in a tight light and clean house, which hardly cost more than the annual rent of such a ruin as his," and "did not use tea, nor coffee, nor butter, nor milk, nor fresh meat, and so did not have to work to get them." This comparison is hardly worth considering, since it ignores the difference in their family commitments, the fact that Thoreau's shelter was built on land loaned him by Emerson, and his freedom (so to speak) to walk over to Concord every once and a while so that Mrs. Emerson could cook him a Sunday dinner and do his laundry. What is interesting is why Thoreau should want to make the comparison in the first place, and the language in which he sets the scene. What is that description of Field in his hut doing there? Why the painstaking evocation of old age in youth on the baby's face? What aggression prompts him to call the child a "starveling brat"? Why is the best hope for the child – and even that a preposterous illusion – to be "the last of a noble line"? The answer is that Thoreau resents the Field family, and the other Irishmen recalled in *Walden*,[9] because they are late arrivals on his pitch. He had sat there "many times *of old*" (the archaic construction reinforces his relative antiquity); they were merely squatters. Though it would not suit his tactics here to admit to being descended from emigrants himself, the implication is that the first American Thoreaux made their way there through courage, hardihood and enterprise, while the Fields merely "floated" over. It seems an oddly leisurely verb to apply to people who were probably starved out of Ireland by the potato famine, forced to save and beg the money to pay for six weeks or so of transatlantic passage in steerage. But then they had no will or energy of their own, no "hardihood," as Parkman would say. They were "shiftless," even if they had to work hard for the luxuries on which they so foolishly insisted, and – like Savage's and Trollope's frontier settlers – rootless and degenerate.

If Parkman and Thoreau seem to turn temporarily into Tory travelers when confronting their feckless migrants, that may be because *The Oregon Trail* and *Walden* are also kinds of travel narrative. Travelers are able to choose whether they go to places newer or older than – settled before or after – their starting points. In American cultural geography they can go west to the frontier or east to Europe. Both directions serve to reinforce the values of the home culture – but different values in different ways. Parkman's journal of his European grand tour in 1843-4 shows a rush of pride in the republican simplicities of his native country. When he went west two years later, the scaleless landscape and the bizarre behavior of the Indians (as first encountered) made the Christian culture of New England seem settled, even traditional by contrast. Similarly, Dickens and Frances Trollope were not immune to the stress caused by the rapid pace of social and political change in Victorian Britain, but a trip westward to America – both geographically and culturally speaking – rendered the home culture reassuringly staid and stable by contrast. Even today, as films like Woody Allen's "Annie Hall" make clear, New Yorkers like to travel to California, especially southern California, to laugh at its outlandish manners and feel good about New York.

This contrast between home and abroad can be brought into the text of the narrative itself. At the end of a Shakespeare comedy, when almost everyone is getting married, a lone malcontent – say, a Jacques or a Malvolio – is left to slink off into the outer darkness without a partner. So the happy resolution of all the play's tensions is celebrated not only through the symmetries of dance and music, but by contrast to the isolated *idiotes* who cannot be accommodated within the harmony of the play's conclusion. This is exactly what Dickens is doing, at the end of *American Notes*, when he and his "select association," happily returning to England, are juxtaposed to the desperate emigrants returning in steerage. Not only have the back-migrants failed to achieve their fortunate resolution, but they are going home to nothing – to even less than they left behind them.

So a possible explanation for the contrary currents in Winthrop's journal, *The Oregon Trail* and *Walden* is that they serve to reinforce the "return" phase of the rite of passage. What is less likely is that the Americans share a secure belief in the possiblity of resolution. The migrants encountered by the Americans certainly function as *idiotes* figures in these narratives, yet they are treated with a harshness, even an accusatory tone, not suffered by Jacques or Dickens's back-migrants. In English uses of the *idiotes* device, at least a degree of compassion is allowed into the contrasting tableaux. The Americans are more vehement. It is as though they felt that if they couldn't "go home" themselves – or doubted the possibility of such a resolution – they could at least send someone else even further out into the wilderness than they. That way anxieties about falling away, about drifting forever rootless as an outcast from substantial social and physical architectures, could be offloaded, and their own security buttressed by contrast. Winthrop's "poorer sort," Parkman's Oregon emigrants and Thoreau's Irish are not just Malvolios; they are also scapegoats for the authors' anxieties about degeneration, and one way of strengthening the new dispensations on which their narratives insist elsewhere.

22

Death in life, old age in youth; Indian graves and settlers' cabins; how Cooper, Hawthorne and James use the motif to interrogate the American character

The intensity with which Winthrop, Parkman and Thoreau banish their unsettled settlers is established partly by the motif on which they insist in their tableaux, the paradox of death in life, or old age in youth. It is actually on the face of John Field's infant, and implicit generally in the suggestion that the newest arrivals, the mobile and vigorous emigrants, were also the most degenerate. Common to all three, like a *memento mori*, is the theme of death and loss: the lonely grave on the Oregon Trail, the ghost of the farmers haunting ruined huts and cellar pits (a lost generation supplanted by the degraded Irish), and Winthrop's poor settlers perishing of scurvy, exposure and homesickness.

However, the surprising discovery of death in life, or decrepitude in youth, is not confined to the narratives of Winthrop, Parkman and Thoreau. From almost the beginning of American exploration (as opposed to discovery) settlers and travelers alike, whether approving or critical of the American venture, had been taken aback by the same apparent contradiction. What was "new" about the New World, after all? The trees, rocks, mountains and rivers were as old or young as those of Europe (the phrase "New World" was coined long before science had established a belief in geological history – of some formations being literally younger than others). America was new because it lacked what history was about: human culture. It was a blank page on which "history" had still to be written.

Here the distinction must be restated between narratives of

discovery, on the one hand, and of exploration and settlement, on the other. If the early settlers and travelers in the American continent had been reading nothing but the paradisal projections of New World discoverers like Vespucci, they might well have expected to be greeted on arrival by a settled, developed society of Amerindians. But for the most part, what they had actually been reading were promotional tracts of colonial exploration and settlement, from which the Indians had been largely effaced and replaced by catalogs of material nature awaiting the processes of culture – of extraction and manufacture – or if mentioned at all, then as a sort of cultural and spiritual equivalent of the other American raw materials, passive *tabulae rasae* awaiting their inscriptions of European religion and society.

So the first surprise registered by settlers and travelers was that the indigenous Americans had a culture of sorts. Early settlers' narratives like *Mourt's Relation* exhibit a naive, sometimes even benignly open-minded curiosity about Indian customs and artifacts. And the second was that the Indian cultures were old enough already to be ruinous in places. Writing to the Earl of Southampton in 1623, John Pory explained how the early separatists happened to settle in Plymouth. "It pleased almighty God...to plant them on the seat of an old town which divers [years] before had been abandoned of the Indians." In *Mourt's Relation* the Plymouth planters first set foot in the New World on Cape Cod, where their first discovery is an Indian burial ground, with "heaps of sand, one whereof was covered with old mats and had a wooden thing like a mortar whelmed on the top of it, and an earthen pot laid in a little hole at the end thereof." Elsewhere they find abandoned baskets of Indian corn, some of which they take for their own needs, but the graves they leave "untouched, because we thought it would be odious unto them to ransack their sepulchres."[10]

In fact, there was an objective basis to these observations of deserted Indian communities, and a terrible one. Even before the Plymouth settlers landed in Massachusetts, the Indians had died in huge numbers after catching diseases like smallpox, to which they had developed no immunity, from fishermen and other Europeans who had been reconnoitering the coast and trading with the natives. But there was also a subjective reason, supporting the ideology of the western planting. If the Indians had vanished, the Europeans could take their place in good conscience, and emigrants could be encouraged to come over without the fear of Indian reprisals. So, as Pory wrote, the Plymouth settlers "both quietly and justly sate down without either dispossessing any of the natives, or being resisted by them, and without shedding so much as one drop of blood."

Yet this theme of old culture discovered in new nature persists beyond accounts of the Europeans displacing the Indians. Dickens noted that the newest frontier settlements in America were also the most decrepit. A decade earlier, while traveling in western New York, de Tocqueville had come across a deserted lake, in the middle of which a small wooded island tempted a visit. Borrowing an Indian canoe, he crossed the water to discover "one of those delightful New World solitudes that almost make civilized man regret the savage life." Its vigorous vegetation "told of the incomparable wealth of the soil"; the "deep silence of the North American wilderness" was broken only by the cooing of a wood pigeon and "the tapping of green woodpeckers on the trees' bark." Nature seemed to have been left to herself. But as he approached the very middle of the island, he began to notice traces of human settlement:

> I was soon convinced that a European had come to seek a refuge in this place. But how greatly his work had changed appearance! The logs he had hastily cut to build a shelter had sprouted afresh; his fences had become live hedges, and his cabin had been turned into a grove... For some little time I silently contemplated the resources of nature and the feebleness of man; and when I did leave the enchanted spot, I kept saying sadly: "What! Ruins so soon!"[11]

The surprising discovery of old age, or death, where one might expect to find youth and life, also had its objective basis in the American social and physical landscape, where the inherited psychology of emigration combined with the availability of cheap land until almost the end of the nineteenth century. De Tocqueville's "Ruins so soon!" comes at the end of his comment on how easily and quickly American settlers moved on further westwards, before they had completed the work of developing their first point of settlement. It was, he suggested, as though once the emigrants had made the break from their native country, they could rest nowhere ever again, had become addicted to a process of incessant movement as to a game of chance.

A European expecting to encounter a reformed pastoral agronomy in America might well be taken aback by this fresh decay. A ruined farmhouse in Europe might betoken a major economic, social or natural upheaval – say, the wholesale enclosure of common lands, or the Highland clearances, or the Irish potato famine. In America it was a much more routine occurrence, and often less catastrophic. Still, de Tocqueville's text is not unduly disturbed by this curiosity of American social behavior. He registers it, and moves on. And Dickens's observation that the newest settlements were also the most shabby and run down is also a passing comment in *American Notes*, though it blends easily into the sentiment that he knew a generation of Tory travelers had conditioned his metropolitan audience to expect: that for all its novelty in politics and manners, America had fallen away since separating itself from the mother country.

American authors and readers, however, shared no such sentiment. Indeed, conditioned by the psychology of emigration, America defined itself around exactly the opposite ideology: that the New World represented the last best hope of mankind. The discovery of ruins in the virgin wilderness was not, therefore, a specific case to be slotted casually into the general condition of American degeneration, nor even an interesting socio-economic phenomenon neutrally to be noted. In some American texts the motif of old age in youth, or death in life, is symptomatic of a narrative pathology. In *The Oregon Trail* and *Walden*, particularly, one feels that the author has been so fixed by the paradox that it has begun to warp the line of his story, claiming a disproportionate demand on the energies of both author and reader, and distracting attention from the main business of the book.

So far this chapter has dealt with American writers for whom the paradox of death in life was an unconscious or partially realized anxiety cutting across their narratives, and running counter to what they "wanted to say," and Chapters 23, 24 and 25 will pick up on anxious fault lines of different sorts and later dates. But other authors used the motif, apparently deliberately, as figure or complex of figures to interrogate an aspect of the American difference. These were Americans who had lived and worked in Europe, and whose relationship to the antithesis of the dominant discourse was at once more complex and more assured than that of, say, Winthrop, Thoreau and Parkman. Cooper, Hawthorne and James knew all about the antithesis – had encountered it and countered it in print, and had even deployed its negative catalogs of missing cultural deposits as part of a semi-ironic critique of the American literary environment. But precisely because they had engaged in this debate, they knew the antithesis for what it was: part of a discourse between interested parties, not a hidden and unspeakable fact of American life.

So in Cooper's *The Prairie* the figure of death in life is not just a passing motif or a device for closing the narrative; the sense of degeneration evoked in the first chapter is quite consistent with the novel's thematics throughout. Cooper wanted to confront head-on the popular ideology of cheap land and western expansion – the emigrant's dream of endless process. He questioned the promise of the Louisiana Purchase. Like it or not, it was a point of view, evoked sometimes movingly, sometimes merely melodramatically. Unlike Dickens, who played on their prejudices, he wanted to say something surprising to his readers: to challenge their (as he thought) unthinking optimism about the future with a nightmare of accelerating settlement overrunning the continent and displacing everything native to it; to pose Cole's warning in the last few sentences of his essay on American scenery, that the wilderness was fast disappearing, ravaged by the axe.

The trope is more elaborately deployed in *The House of the Seven Gables* (1851), in order to pose – and also, as usual with Hawthorne's novels and stories, to problematize – an entirely different meaning. Three years before Thoreau published his description of John Field's "poor starveling brat," the "sybil-like, cone-headed infant that sat upon its father's knee…not knowing but it was the last of a noble line," *The House of the Seven Gables* had already produced a chicken (and also an egg, because this is Hawthorne, and nothing is simple) exhibiting the same contrary characteristics. The narrative is discussing the curious flock owned by the Pyncheon family:

> All hens are well-worth studying…but by no possibility can there have been other fowls, of such odd appearance and deportment as these ancestral ones. They probably embodied the traditionary peculiarities of their whole line of progenitors, derived through an unbroken succession of eggs…Queerly indeed they looked! Chanticleer himself was…hardly bigger than an ordinary partridge; his two wives were about the size of quails; and as for the one chicken, it looked small enough to be still in the egg, and, at the same time, sufficiently old, withered, wizened, and experienced, to have been the founder of the antiquated race… Its mother evidently regarded it as the one chicken of the world, and as necessary, in fact, to the world's continuance.

Nor are the novel's human characters exempt from the contradictory condition. The little boy who buys gingerbread animals from Hepzibah Pyncheon's shop, though he "looked almost as youthful as if he had been just that moment made," was "the very emblem of old Father Time" in the way he devoured the types of nature's creation. Hepzibah is a "rusty-jointed maiden" in "rusty black silk," who lives in a "rusty wooden house" with doors hung on "rusty hinges," yet at over sixty years of age[12] she is embarking on the new venture of a cent shop, stepping "down from her pedestal of imaginary rank" to "earn her own food, or starve," transforming herself from "patrician Lady" to "plebian woman."

The idea of transformation is central to the novel. Not only is Hepzibah, two centuries after her family first came to America, finally facing up to American social and economic realities, but also the Pyncheon's hidden guilt and the curse laid upon them by their victim is at last to be uncovered, laid bare, understood and atoned for – and the ancient hostility resolved by a marriage uniting the families. Holgrave's crucial part in this process of discovery is made possible by his occupation of daguerrotypist, and by his amateur interest in mesmerism. Both his hobby and his job were modern interests at the time of writing, thought to be at the forefront of scientific knowledge, yet together they interpret the whole truth – produce an accurate portrait of the whole person, the surface of the face and the inner workings of the personality. (Holgrave's name is derived from the Greek for "to write" and "the whole.") As a scientist of surfaces Holgrave can provide the first rational, naturalistic explanation of Maule's curse on the Pyncheons – the physiological basis of "God will give them blood to drink!" – but as a scientist also of the human psyche, he does not allow the medical explanation, the Pyncheons' hereditary tendency to haemorrhage in the throat, to efface the moral dimension of the family's condition. They really are guilty.

So *The House of the Seven Gables* is constructed around pivotal moments, all of them involving surprising conjunctions of death and life, antiquity and modernity. The Pyncheons abandon their aristocratic pretensions to earn their living in the real world. Hepzibah and Clifford flee their captivity in the House of the Seven Gables in the most modern of conveyances, the railroad, only to wind up at an inconsequential way station with a wooden church "black with age" and a derelict farm "in the old style." Does science destroy the ancient faith of our fathers and their agrarian traditions, or can it be enlisted in a humane cause, to break into the dark old house to illuminate the malevolent superstition lodged there, to interpret and finally resolve the ancient curse of the settlers' acquisitiveness?

In other words, is this death in life, or life in death? As so often in Hawthorne, the ambivalence is much foregrounded, and might almost be said to constitute the tale's chief source of suspense. But I believe the narrative does come down, finally, on one side. It is life in death, and therefore a deliberate reversal of the American anxiety. Unlike Winthrop, Parkman and Thoreau, Hawthorne assigns his symbols of degeneration to the aristocratic hangovers from the Old World, the benighted, unregenerate Pyncheons of old. The chickens are degenerating because, like Hepzibah until she opened the door on her new enterprise, they have come over from Europe, never to adapt to New World conditions. The same is true of the declining white rose bush in the garden, carefully tended but "propped up anew against the house," and of the "few species of antique and hereditary flowers, of no very flourishing condition, but scrupulously weeded."

And so the novel enters the old dispute over whether transplants from Europe degenerate in America. But unlike Jefferson and others, who were anxious to deny the proposition lest it impugn the reputation of the New World's natural fecundity, Hawthorne has the confidence to press the dominant discourse to its logical conclusion. The break from Europe had to be absolute – animal and vegetable as well as social and institutional. *The House of the Seven Gables* is, among other things, the story of how the Pyncheons belatedly became Americans. And almost untended by them, the natural process was already going on in the Pyncheon's garden before the novel's action begins. Alongside the failing Old World flowers a riot of New World plants – humble but eatable – flourishes rampant: "summer squashes, almost in their golden-blossom; cucumbers, now evincing a tendency to spread away from the main-stock...string-beans...about to festoon themselves on poles; tomatoes...already gigantic, and promis[ing] an early and abundant harvest." And in time the very presence of Phoebe, the young, innocent – and so first truly "American" – Pyncheon, who is associated with flower imagery throughout the novel, will make even the flowers blossom forth "in full bloom." American art will at last ornament the material plenty of American nature.

If the conjunction of youth and age finally confirms the ideology of American settlement in *The House of the Seven Gables*, it is deployed more equivocally – though no less deliberately – in the work of Henry James. Like Cooper and Hawthorne, James uses the figure to interrogate aspects of the American character, but he is shyer than either of the others of answering his own questions. In *Daisy Miller*, an early, short and somewhat schematic story (subtitled "A Study" by *The Cornhill Magazine*, where it was first published in 1878) the trope is used to interrogate the nature of the American type in Europe. How "old" is Randolph C. Miller, Daisy's precocious little brother? "The child, who was diminutive for his years, had an aged expression of countenance, a pale complexion, and sharp little features." On tour in Switzerland, his mother has tricked him out in what she supposes to be the adult dress of mountainous regions, replete with knickerbockers and an alpenstock – an implement he uses childishly, however, to spear "the flowerbeds, the garden-benches, the trains of ladies' dresses." His "sharp, hard little voice" is "immature, and yet, somehow, not young."

Despite a few touches of highly amusing characterization, Randolph is really more of an emblem than a fleshed-out character in a novel, like the Pyncheons' young-old chicken and the boy who devours the gingerbread animals like old Father Time. The puzzle over Randolph's age introduces and focuses attention on the central mystery posed about Daisy's innocence, and also on the question of the nature, function and value of American innocence in Europe generally. "Was she simply a pretty girl from New York State?" Winterbourne wonders; "were they all like that, the pretty girls who had a good deal of gentlemen's society? Or was she also a designing, an audacious, an unscrupulous young person?" Winterbourne can't tell. By now, he has lived too long in Europe to receive the American social signals; as his aunt says, this long absence has rendered him (in quite another sense) "too innocent" on his own part.

On the wider canvas of *The Bostonians* James invokes the paradox of age in youth in more complex form. Though first published in 1886, the novel is set two decades earlier. As seen by the Mississippi lawyer Basil Ransom, Boston just after the Civil War ought to be the epitome of modernity. The most progressive city in America, home of all the most advanced causes, Boston was the intellectual and moral home of abolitionism and the center of all those social and economic values that had discredited and displaced the outmoded fuedalism of the Old South.

But as seen and described (Basil's perceptions and those of the narrator are intertwined early in the novel), the reality is very different. The "progressive" reformers – even those promoting advanced causes, like feminism, not yet effected – are actually very old. Miss Birdseye is so faded as to have become almost transparent. The immediate environment too has become run down. When Verena Tarrant and Olive Chancellor look out of the window over the Back Bay late on a winter afternoon, they see

> the long, low bridge that crawled, on its staggering posts, across the Charles; the casual patches of ice and snow; the desolate suburban horizons... There was something inexorable in the poverty of the scene, shameful in the meanness of its details, which gave a collective impression of boards and tin and frozen earth, sheds and rotting piles... loose fences, vacant lots, mounds of refuse, yards bestrewn with iron pipes, telegraph poles, and bare wooden backs of places.

Though references to disorder and decay are very insistent here, this passage is not one of those narrative warps like Parkman's and Thoreau's descriptions of the degenerate migrants. In the first place, however curiously, Verena "thought such a view lovely";

so there is some agreement between the mood inside the house and that evoked by what lies outside it. How is the scene connected with what is going on in "Miss Chancellor's strenuous parlour"? The two women spend their time reading "a great deal of history together," and they do so "ever with the same thought – that of finding confirmation in it for this idea that their sex had suffered inexpressibly." But, objects Verena, what about the "wicked queens" and "profligate mistresses of Kings," the women in the past who "had been instrusted with power and had not always used it amiably"? Somehow (it doesn't say how) "these ladies were easily disposed of between the two, and the public crimes of Bloody Mary, the private misdemeanours of Faustina, wife of the pure Marcus Aurelius, were very satisfactorily classified."

The "meanness" of the winter scene outside is posed, then, as an index of the women's occupation within: their use of history as a dead encyclopaedia, filleted to feed their ideology. For James this is clearly the wrong use of history. The past is raided to provide support for the latest fashion in thought; what will not serve the moment is simply discarded. The crucial point to remember about the exterior scene – one which James and his readers knew well, and a process that had been completed by the time the novel came out – was that the Back Bay looked so desolate because it was being filled and reclaimed to provide land for some of the newest and most fashionable residences in Boston. But as with the deserted frontier cabin that de Tocqueville discovered on the island, the progressive impulse had no need, or time, for the structures of the past. They were simply left to decay to be built over – excrescences to be discarded, superseded, by progress.

23

The past as lost, East and West; Crèvecoeur's escape from history; immigrants and framing narratives in Willa Cather; history as trace; the past splits into "the classics" and a nostalgic recollection of youth lost forever; the missing middle distance of space and time

And so *The Bostonians* circles back on that old American preoccupation, expressed at least as early as Washington Irving's "Author's Account" introducing *The Sketch Book*, that America had no "association": that its collective imagination, being formed of an ideology of uprooting and rebellion, and inhabiting a landscape without concrete remnants of the past, could make no living use of history. It is hardly worth pausing on the question of whether this concern was "really" justified, since American novelists, starting with Irving's contemporary Fenimore Cooper, have steadily disconfirmed the charge in their fiction, even as they repeated it in their prefaces.

But the anxiety was real enough, and so were the literary remedies brought in to deal with it. The program of American literature, as set out in prefaces and sometimes also in the thematics of poems and novels, has been infiltrated by the problematic of history: of whether and how it can be used both to enlighten and enliven the present; whether it can ever be anything other than what has been irretrievably lost. The most recent sustained attempt to solve the supposed problem – and probably the last – was the great modernist project of the second and third decades of this century, when young Americans like Pound and Eliot went to Europe – "backwards" in both history and cultural space – to reinvent the American present and invent its future: to raid the past to "make it new."

But as James suggests in *Daisy Miller* and *The Bostonians*, moving to Europe, or back again, could not resolve the difficulty, any more than could the American daydream of European culture, or a native antiquity, at home. That paradox of old age in youth, or experience in innocence, Americans carried with them wherever they went – unless, like Winterbourne, they ceased to be American – because for them the past remained a lost, dead thing. Once discarded in the crucial break with the old home, the past had to be deprecated thereafter in the dominant discourse: abandoned to decay like that settler's cabin de Tocqueville discovered on the pretty wooded island, rather than maintained as a living connection with a tradition on which the present could build.

If going to Europe couldn't assuage the anxiety, neither could moving around within the American continent. At first reading, it is easy to see why the community evoked in Sarah Orne Jewett's *The Country of the Pointed Firs* (1896) is so dispersed, and why the people are so nostalgic for the past. Their vigorous trade with the rest of the world is now reduced to hazardous journeys in an open boat from island to island. Families once numerous have now "died and scattered," so remaining individuals are "far from neighbors." Farming is declining. The stony land was recalcitrant at the best of times. Now the only vigorous growth it supports is of "them little peakèd-topped spruces an' fir balsams comin' up over the hill all green an' hearty," to reclaim the farmers' fields. "The farms all wore a look of gathering age, though the settlement was, after all, so young. The fences were already fragile, and it seemed as if the first impulse of agriculture had soon spent itself without hope of renewal."

Yet fragmentary links with the old country linger on. The people speak (we are told) an argot peppered with remnants of "Chaucer's English." An indistinct track, problematically inscribed "historically" in that it might once have been an Indian trail, leads to the isolated house of a woman who imagines she is the twin of Queen Victoria. "I had often been struck by the quick interest...[in] the royal house which one found in distant neighborhoods of New England," the narrator comments; "whether some old instincts of personal loyalty have survived all changes of time and national vicissitudes, or whether...the Queen's own character and disposition have won friends for her so far away, it is impossible to tell." Neither explanation will serve, of course. As with Madame Knight and Susan Cooper, as with Hawthorne's pathetic "American claimants" in *Our Old Home*, it is that very distance of New England from the metropolitan center that prompts such nostalgic fantasies.

The immediate explanation for this mood lies in the objective facts of American history and the geography of Maine. The community Jewett observed and so meticulously described was indeed dispersed socially, because it was physically so scattered in tiny hamlets settled on islands and rocky inlets connected only by poor roads. If maritime trade no longer connected it with Europe and the Far East, that was because Boston, New York, New Orleans, Los Angeles and San Francisco – now all connected by railroads – were bigger, deeper harbors, safer to get in and out of, than anywhere in Maine, including Portland. And if Maine's farming culture was declining in population and general vigor, that was because for half a century the young had been moving west in search of rich alluvial land at a price they could afford.

But how to explain that young-old farm with its failing fences, those problematic tracks and that uncertain connection with a European "tradition" that is half remembered, though wholly desired? These motifs do not belong to objective facts, minutely oberved. Hamlin Garland's father was one of those who emigrated from Maine, first to Wisconsin (where Hamlin was born), then Iowa, and finally Dakota Territory. So shouldn't young Hamlin's stories, set in the fertile "middle border" of the Mississippi Valley, express all the vigor and youthful hope drained away from New England?

They should, but they don't. *Main-Travelled Roads* (1891) is full of despair, degeneration and nostalgia for more settled communities further east. The Mississippi Valley communities are as dispersed as Jewett's in Maine:

> "Where's Rachel?" Howard inquired. Her smile faded away.
>
> "Shellie married Orrin McIlvaine. They're 'way out in Dakota. Shellie's havin' a hard row of stumps."
>
> There was a little silence.
>
> "And Tommie?"
>
> "Gone West. Most all the boys have gone West. That's the reason there's so many old maids"...
>
> "You don't mean to tell me that no young fellow comes prowling round – "
>
> "Oh, a young Dutchman or Norwegian once in a while. Nobody that counts. Fact is, we're getting like Boston – four women to one man."

There was, in other words, no end to "West" – not, at least, until Frederick Jackson Turner declared the process of westward expansion at an end. (How that announcement was connected with the ideology of emigration, and why it caused such consternation, will be discussed in the Conclusion.) In the fiction of Jewett and Garland people just went on moving. And so the women even of the middle border are left on the shelf, feel trapped, and daydream of escape eastwards. The men have managed this in fact. The characteristic story in *Main-Travelled Roads* is of a young man gone east – to college, or to make his artistic fortune in New York – returning to his western home, only to find it much decayed. In "A Branch Road" Will is shocked at how the little spring under the poplar trees has been left to "fill with leaves and dirt." The old family house, where "his mother had toiled for thirty years. A sort of prison after all," has reverted to "Old man Kinney," who has "let the weeds choke out the flowers and surround the bee-hives." Agnes, his old sweetheart now married to Kinney's loutish son, he finds "worn and wasted incredibly. The blue of her eyes seemed dimmed and faded by weeping, and the old-time scarlet of her lips had been washed away." In "Up the Coulé" Howard McLane returns to his home town to find "an unpaved street, drab-colored, miserable, rotting wooden buildings...the same, only worse." Freeme Cole, "a man who was the fighting wonder of Howard's boyhood, [has] now degenerated into a stoop-shouldered, faded, garrulous, and quarrelsome old man." Are there any trout left in the stream? asks Howard. "Not many," comes the answer, "little Fellers." When he finally reaches his house, he meets one of his nephews for the first time, "a boy of about fourteen...his bent shoulders making him look like an old man."

In the fiction of the West, then, America's newest regions are also its oldest. We come back to motif of old age in youth, to the prairie of Bryant and Cooper, about to be thrown open to the hopeful enterprise of fresh settlement, yet despairingly autumnal, the site for nostalgic reveries of a past irretrievably lost. No novel explores this ambivalent mood about the West more intelligently than Willa Cather's *My Ántonia* (1918), and it is significant that the settlement of European immigrants in Nebraska forms the armature around which the novel's action is wound.

In *My Ántonia* the fortunes of the various Bohemian and Norwegian families divide by generation. "'Yes, a new country's hard on the old ones, sometimes,' said Anna thoughtfully." Her Norwegian grandmother craves the fish she used to be able to buy at the waterside market. Tiny Soderball's mother "'ain't been so homesick, ever since father's raised rye flour for her.'" Ántonia's father lays aside the violin he used to play for village gatherings in Bohemia, declines into melancholy and finally commits suicide.

If the parents decline because they have been uprooted, their children, born in Nebraska, are more robust, healthy and cheerful than their contemporaries born of American parents. In time, their patient cultivation of the prairie yields abundant produce and ample prosperity. The third generation will even begin to reconstitute some of the "lost" vernacular culture of the old country. Ántonia's children can still speak Czech, and one of her sons has taken up Papa Shimerda's violin: "it was too big for him. But he played very well for a self-taught boy."

So on the face of it, *My Ántonia* is a full account of the emigration experience, fairly posing both sides of the debate. Like Rebecca Burlend's *A True Picture of Emigration*, it can admit the physical, cultural and emotional costs of uprooting and resettling, without undermining faith in the eventual outcome of the project. But *My Ántonia* is not just a story about the varying fortunes of successive generations of immigrants in Nebraska. The novel's narrator, Jim Burden, has a story of his own, the trajectory of which leads in quite another direction to that of the Shimerda family and Ántonia's children.

The contradiction can best be illustrated by comparison to a similar conflict in Crèvecoeur's *Letters from an American Farmer*. The better part of that book advances strenuously the manifold values of cultivation. In Crèvecoeur's moral geography, the hunters of the frontier degenerate into barbarism, the southern planters uphold a cruel feudalism, and the traders and fishermen of Nantucket – however ingenious and industrious – lack a secure basis for continued progress. Only the yeoman farmers of the Middle Atlantic colonies – New York, New Jersey and Pennsylvania – live and work so as to provide each generation with a richer environment than enjoyed by the one preceding it. Farming, according to Crèvecoeur's physiocratic economics, is the one certain way to improve on capital, because the investment is based on increases guaranteed by nature; hence farmers were the Americans most likely to overcome the degenerative effects of transplantation to the New World. But because the farmer improved the land physically – cleared it, drained it, allowed it to yield its natural increase – he also provided, in time, increased leisure fully to develop his mind and spirit. The plow is a central symbol in *Letters*, because it stands for cultivation in every sense of that word.

Yet because the farmer's wealth is immobile, vulnerable to

attack, and requires an orderly succession of generations to return the initial investment with interest, war and civil unrest threaten the farmer's project far more radically than they do the trader's or the hunter's, whose wealth lie as much in skills and business contacts (both exploitable in time of war) as it does in land. The coming of the Revolutionary War, then, directly confronted the values most feelingly advanced in *Letters From an American Farmer*. Faced with the challenge of the Revolution, Crèvecoeur simply ducked out of it. He himself did this, when he took off for Europe, leaving his wife and children to fend as best as they could on their farm. He did it in his text, when he has Farmer James light out for the frontier (perhaps the first, certainly not the last, American protagonist so to do), while proclaiming unconvincingly the exact opposite of the values championed so far in the book.

It is important to understand that Farmer James's late conversion to a hunter's life on the frontier does not enter into dialog with his earlier advocacy of farming in the Middle Colonies. The two positions belong on different planes of discourse; they don't engage at any point. The author "lighted back" to Europe – returned to the more secure, though less free, world he had left behind him, to publish his book. But to the level of settlement discourse, such a resolution *as an escape* could not be admitted, even if it could function, as in Burlend's book, as a triumphant return; in Crèvecoeur's argument, the break with Europe must be absolute, irreversible. So a wholly fanciful alternative has to be dreamed up: an escape that follows the logic neither of actuality nor of the book's moral geography.

Something very like this contradiction occurs in *My Ántonia*. On the storybook level the transplanted immigrants stay and succeed in the West, cultivating and procreating and providing increased leisure for their children to play the violin – the very process traced with such conviction in Crèvecoeur's first three letters, and the visit to John Bartram's farm. But on the level of the narrator's plot, the opposite happens. Jim Burden, like Cather herself, did not remain in his native Nebraska to work the land, but went east (culturally speaking, at least) to university to study, not animal husbandry or crop rotation or farm management, but the classics. They too "lit back," away from the frontier and back to the secure structures of time-tested, traditional civilization.

In fact, the classics play their part in *My Ántonia* – but most curiously, since they have little to do with the immigrants. Musing "listlessly" over his books one evening, Burden opens the *Georgics* at Virgil's "melancholy reflection that, in the lives of mortals, the best days are the first to flee. '*Optima dies...prima fugit.*'" Then he turns back to the First Book, which they studied that morning. "'*Primus ego in patriam mecum...deducam Musas*; for I shall be the first, if I live, to bring the Muse into my country.'" Burden's professor has already explained that "patria" means not a nation but the little rural community where the poet was born:

> Cleric said he thought Virgil, when he was dying at Brindisi, must have remembered that passage. After he had faced the bitter fact that he was to leave the "Aeneid" unfinished...then his mind must have gone back to the perfect utterance of the "Georgics," where the pen was fitted to the matter as the plow is to the furrow; and he must have said to himself, with the thankfulness of a good man, "I was the first to bring the Muse into my country."

The only thematic relevance of this passage to the interests of the immigrants comes through that metaphorical reference to the plow. And indeed that figure is at least as central to *My Ántonia* as it is to Crèvecoeur's *Letters*. Shortly before Burden's meditation over *The Georgics*, a symbolic little episode has already elevated the plow to the status, almost, of the novel's logo. One afternoon as they sit talking and looking over the country, Burden and the immigrant girls suddenly see "a Curious thing":

> On some upland farm a plow had been left standing in a field. The sun was sinking just behind it. Magnified across the distance by the horizontal light, it stood out against the sun, was exactly contained

within the circle of the disk; the handles, the tongue, the share – black against the molten red. There it was, heroic in size, a picture writing on the sun.

The point of the Virgil passage is clearly to unite the project of the immigrants and that of author and narrator. Through Jim Burden, Cather wants her readers to take her as the writing equivalent of the plowing immigrants. Before the United States split off from the British Empire an important constituent of the rhetoric of the western planting was a reworking of the early medieval theme of *translatio imperii*, *translatio studii*, or the proposition that imperial authority is carried from east to west (originally from Constantine to Charlemagne) on the wings of knowledge. Excited by the project (never achieved) of building an Anglican college in Bermuda to convert the "savage Americans," the philosopher George, Bishop Berkeley encapsulated the theme in his "Verses on the Prospect of Planting Arts and Learning in America" of 1752. Because it was virtually the figure of anticipation in verse, proclaiming the value of progress through western migration and the hope that new forms, appropriate to new physical and social landscapes, would supplant the old, the poem became enormously popular in America after independence: much quoted in celebratory orations, grandly illustrated by Thomas Cole, even lending its author's name to the westernmost plantation of American learning, the home campus of the University of California:

Westward the course of empire takes its way;
  The first four acts already past,
A fifth shall close the drama of the day;
  Time's noblest offspring is the last.

This is Burden's burden, and Cather's too. By recounting the events of his youth on the immigrant's frontier, he carries learning to the far western reaches of the empire, so as to extend its dominion. Like Ezra Pound, Cather wanted to reinvent America in the European cultural tradition. Like Hamlin Garland, she wanted to celebrate the unique social and physical landscape of the Great West in a native American literature. But whereas Virgil's expression of the same ambition became his most perfect utterance (or so we're told) – the pen fitting his matter as the plow the furrow – Cather's plow can stand only for actual plowing: that is, as a useful metonym for the emigrants' achievement of settlement and cultivation, as realized at last in Ántonia's marriage, her prospering on the land, and the health of her children. What the figure cannot be is a metaphor of the author's own achievement. The only way in which Burden, and Cather herself, can "fit the plow to the furrow" in their writing is to leave the actual plow and furrow behind.

And that paradox may explain the odd note of nostalgia in Burden's thoughts about his Latin homework. Since the only way he can gain the plow as a figure fit for his "country" is to lose it in actuality, even the figurative plow – the plow as logo – is part of a nostalgic recollection of a life already vanished. "Everybody thinks about the old times, even the happiest people," as Ántonia says to Burden towards the end of the novel. *Optima dies...prima fugit*. But whereas Ántonia means this to refer to the lifespan of the individual (everyone's imagination plays tricks of this kind about the golden days of his or her youth), the narrators of *My Ántonia* and another Cather novel, *A Lost Lady*, extend the sentiment to the sphere of public, communal history. Neil Herbert, Cather's narrator in *A Lost Lady*, thinks he has witnessed the passing of a whole era, which appears to have lasted only slightly longer than his own lifetime: "He had seen the end of an era, the sunset of the pioneer. He had come upon it when already its glory was nearly spent."

This odd illusion is due partly to the perception of settlement in a primeval topography. In laying claim to virgin land, the imagination links space and time relativistically. The further west you go to settle, the further back in time you seem to be traveling, until you come, as it were, to the edge of "time" itself. Indians and other "aboriginals" (inaccurately termed, since they had not been there from the beginning) are commonly thought to belong to a category of history quite distinct from the words and deeds to which we assign a chronological sequence in the schoolroom. They are called "pre-historical," as though nothing has happened to them and to their communities through time, and they had always been the same until discovered by rational Europeans with their own sense of their own history. This is why the American Indians have always converted so easily to legend, or even to myth: signifyers outside the time scale of ordinary chronology.

Of what does "history" consist in Cather's West? Where is it to be found? In *My Ántonia* the only suggestion of history in its conventional sense comes from the ambiguous traces in the land that so fascinate Burden and the immigrant girls. One is an indistinct line of sunflowers that may be a natural feature, or may have been scattered by the first Mormons en route to Utah, so that later parties of emigrants could find their way to Deseret. Another is a circle in the prairie sod where the Indians used to ride, that shows up only when picked out by the autumn's first flurries of snow. The third, mentioned just before the "logo" of the plow, is a sword and a stirrup, on which Spanish words can just be made out.

Like the faint track leading to the house of the Queen's Twin in *The Country of the Pointed Firs*, these remains are ambiguous – and not just because each is so faintly inscribed. Each poses its own mystery. The presence of the Spanish artifacts is puzzling because "At school we were taught that [Coronado] had not got so far as Nebraska . . . but Charley Harling and I had a strong belief that he had been along this very river." (The possibility that the sword and stirrup might have been stolen, or looted from a distant grave, and then brought west, doesn't occur to them.) The Indian track is "real" enough, but what does it tell them of what they did there? "Jake and Otto were sure that when they galloped round that ring the Indians tortured prisoners, bound to a stake in the center; but grandfather thought they merely ran races or trained horses there." As for the sunflowers, they might not even be an artifact at all – which is to say that they might have nothing to do with history.

Apart from this ambiguously inscribed archaeology, the past exists in *My Ántonia* in two forms only, personal memory and "the classics." Neither is history: the former because it has little communal reference, and the second because it is unchanging, inviolate, outside time – "classic" in the popular sense. History in the sense of a sequence of events in a community to which each individual is related, and by which each is limited – this kind of "history" has gone dead in *My Ántonia* and *A Lost Lady*. It is dead because "lost," and lost because it has been imagined, not as the public past, but as the personal, autobiographical past, which we all lose. History in this sense is always nostalgic in mood, because one's youth is always lost forever. So the past is no longer public. That is, it is not a context within which to live and to which the individual can allude so as to share a meaning with a wider community, or (as T.S. Eliot said a "tradition" should be) a standard against which to set the innovations of the present. The past is not a culture in which we share.

For the author worried about this deficit, the only recourse is a leap over the body of the middle distance of the past, straight to the timeless: legend, or myth, or "the classics." Eliot himself found this, as did Pound and the other great American modernists, among whom Cather herself is to be counted. American poets after the modernist movement – Robert Lowell is a good example – would discover how to dip in and out of the historical middle distance and bleed the personal into the public without embarrassment, but for the American modernists the only viable polarities were the self and the past far distant in time and place: German opera, snippets from Shakespeare, Homer, the events of the Italian Renaissance, Confucian statecraft, the Upanishads, or whatever. With them "history" goes straight into myth – or perhaps legend would be closer, since at least the Greeks believed the myths on which they based their tragedies to have approximated to historical reality. The fainter the traces remaining in the present, the more feelingly they evoke the legend, though (precisely because they are so faint) the less reliably they function as tracks back to the sort of history that is mediated through three-dimensional monuments and other more substantial artifacts, including writing. There is no mediating middle ground between "now" and "I" (on the one hand) and the legendary "anytime," or "alltime," or "notime."

24

The missing middle distance in the European and American novel: mirrors and windows

So the self-proclaimed American difference, in "American literature" as in other branches of the dominant discourse, elided the middle distance of the communal past and present. Nor was this feeling always foregrounded in the thematics of American literature – the "problem" as set out in the fiction of Cooper, Hawthorne and James, and in their prefaces and other critical marginalia. Sometimes it seeped down into the bedrock of narrative procedure itself, to the stratum of the controlling imagery.

There is, for example, a European convention for situating a novel's protagonist within the middle distance of the surrounding community, a device which fuses actual and moral sight through the symbolism of mirrors or windows. Mirrors frame the self in his or her surroundings, so provide a site for "speculation" (from the Latin for mirror), and of course "reflection." They may even transmit an otherwise inexpressible social message, as when Mme. Basile in *The Confessions* (1770) catches sight of the silently adoring Rousseau, prostrate on the carpet behind her, reflected in the mirror over the mantelpiece.

In the classic realistic novel a window is supposed to present a glimpse of things as they are; like the narrative surface itself, though "framed" and selective of its subject matter, it opens transparently onto the realities of ordinary life. Towards the end of *Middlemarch* (1871-2) Dorothea Brooke, exhausted by rage and humiliation at her treatment by Rosamond and Will Ladislaw, falls asleep on the cold floor of her drawing-room. Waking early, she opens the curtains and looks "out on the bit of road that lay in view, with fields beyond, outside the entrance gates":

> On the road there was a man with a bundle on his back and a woman carrying her baby; in the field she could see figures moving – perhaps the shepherd with his dog. Far off in the bending sky was the pearly light; and she felt the largeness of the world and the manifold wakings of men to labour and endurance. She was part of that involuntary, palpitating life, and could neither look out on it from her luxurious shelter as a mere spectator, nor hide her eyes in selfish complaining.

This is clearly the novel's crisis, because it is the pivotal moment in Dorothea's emotional, intellectual and moral development. Here at last she sets herself in perspective, accepting the world as George Eliot thought her readers should: in its humble and imperfect solidity, stripped of the illusions she had projected upon it.

Not all European novels valorize this kind of realism, in either method or theme. *Madame Bovary* (1857) is much more impressionistic than *Middlemarch*, and its protagonist a much less assiduous searcher after truth than Dorothea Brooke. In *Madame Bovary* mirrors and windows distort things as they are, reflecting Emma's subjective emotions. Yet epistemologically they still function as the window in *Middlemarch*, presenting the reader – whether directly or ironically – with an accurate index of the protagonist's delusions. Emma looks in her mirror, amazed at how her adultery with Rodolphe has transformed her appearance:

> Jamais elle n'avait eu les yeux si grands, si noirs, ni d'une telle profondeur. Quelque chose de subtil épandu sur sa personne la transfigurait.
>
> Elle se répétait: "J'ai un amant! un amant!", se délectant à cette idée comme à celle d'une autre puberté qui lui serait survenue. Elle allait donc posséder enfin ces joies de l'amour, cette fièvre du bonheur dont elle avait désespéré.

Of course she will not know, for long, those joys of love, that fever of happiness, of which she had despaired. Yet her emotion is powerful and real; so is that subtle transformation in her face, confirmed elsewhere in the narrative: the evidence of her eyes grown so large, so black, so deep.

Similarly, the novel's many vistas out of windows, or from hills overlooking the countryside, serve to demarcate Emma's moods from the realities of ordinary life, charting the ebb and flow of her fancies. Emma first sees Rodolphe from a window. Between their meetings while the affair is flourishing Emma stands typically before a window gazing over the middle distance of the town to a landscape dissolving in mist. To translate this tableau crudely into the moral sense of the novel, she foregrounds the middle distance because she is ignoring her reponsibilities to her husband and his patients, and the far distance of her future is flatteringly obscured by her reverie. When Rodolphe writes to end the affair, she reads his letter by an open window from which, "par-dessus les toits, la pleine campagne s'étalait à pert de vue," and "En bas, sous elle, la place du village était vide." Now the middle distance is empty and the open country stretches to a hard horizon, as far as the eye can see, unsoftened by comforting daydreams. A moment later the whole scene tilts crazily, and she is on the precipice of suicide.[13]

But consider what happens to mirror and window scenes in American novels. It's not that they are absent – far from it – but that they might almost have been posed in conscious, intertextual debate with their European equivalents. For American windows and mirrors look out on, or give back, a blank. They communicate nothing, except that there is nothing to communicate. When Verena looks out of Olive's window over Boston's Back Bay, what she sees reflects neither directly nor ironically on her moral, intellectual or emotional condition. It "tells" her nothing, and it "says" little more to the reader than that history is dead to her. In any case – and perhaps bodily movement is more important here than meditation – she turns her back on the scene, to resume her exertions in "Miss Chancellor's strenuous parlor."

Towards the end of *The American* (1875-6), after the Bellegardes have rejected him and shut their daughter up in a nunnery out of his way, Christopher Newman returns briefly to his native United States. He has the evidence he thinks will destroy the Bellegarde family, but his attempt to threaten them with the revelation has proved fruitless. Once back home, he becomes "a hopeless, helpless loafer, useful to no one and detestable to himself – this was what the treachery of the Bellegarde's had made of him":

In his restless idleness he came back from San Francisco to New York, and sat for three days in the lobby of his hotel, looking out through a huge wall of plate-glass at the unceasing stream of pretty girls in Parisian-looking dresses, undulating past with little parcels nursed against their neat figures. At the end of three days he returned to San Francisco, and having arrived there he wished he had stayed away. He had nothing to do, his occupation was gone, and it seemed to him that he should never find it again.

With some ingenuity, it might be possible to force an ironic contrast between the scenes on either side of that hotel window – the "unceasing stream" of Claire-Cintré lookalikes so freely available on the American market, when the European original is lost to him forever – but in truth it is the inconsequentiality of the vignette that should be remarked. Nothing happens to Newman here; for the three days he spends gazing into nothing he thinks nothing, and feels nothing. (In a sense, he *is* nothing, since Americans are defined by what they do, not who they are, and he has "nothing to do.") Sitting before the window is just one of the ways Newman fills his time, like crossing the country back and forth to San Francisco.

Incessant motion is also the predominant impression left by Poe's short story, "The Man of the Crowd." Here the window scene is central to the action, which begins with a man musing on passers-by in a London street, as seen through the window of a coffee house. At first it seems that the story's narrator is connecting most intently with the middle distance framed in his gaze, because he observes closely the representatives of every imaginable profession and social class. Noblemen, merchants and attorneys, junior clerks, women factory hands, pick-pockets, gamblers, pedlars, thieves and others are all classified with the minutest precision.

But "classified" is the word. These are museum exhibits, albeit highly mobile, viewed from a perspective of "scientific" detachment, without affection. And they themselves do not interact, except occasionally to bump into each other in the street. No imaginative effort is invited or expended on how they might work within a community, on how money, goods or love might circulate between them. That's the point: not only are they separate from each other, each locked in his own immediate concerns; to the observer they are isolated types, each representing a particular band of society. When the narrator finally notices an individual singular enough to arouse his curiosity, he follows him out of the coffee house, and across the whole of London all night long, only to watch him turn around at daybreak to retrace his steps without stopping. This is the "man of the crowd" – not just in it, but of it: the ultimate distillation of the urban population who, like the types viewed through the window (and like Newman), goes nowhere except back and forth.

This motif of meaningless reciprocal motion as an expression of urban alienation functions powerfully too in Dreiser's *Sister Carrie* (1900). When Carrie leaves him, Hurstwood sits stunned in their shabby apartment till past midnight, "still rocking" back and forth in his rocking chair, "staring at the floor." As the direction of his gaze indicates, Hurstwood has no view out onto the world. His awareness that other people in the city are as hard-up as he comes not through windows but via the newspapers:

> In his worry, other's people's worries became apparent. No item about a farm failing, a family starving, or a man dying upon the streets...but arrested his eye as he scanned the morning papers. Once the "World" came out with a flaring announcement about "80,000 people out of employment in New York this winter," which struck as a knife at his heart.
>
> "Eighty thousand!" he thought. "What an awful thing that is."[14]

Earlier in the story Carrie's first lover, Druet, anxious to oblige a "very prominent" figure in the "local branch of Elks" by finding the lodge a heroine for their amateur production of "Under the Gaslight," tries to persuade Carrie to take on the role. Her eventual agreement will be fateful, since her success will lead on to a professional career and away from Druet, then Hurstwood in turn. Uncertain at first what to do, she sits "down in her rocking-chair by the window to think about it." But instead of looking out of the window, she looks inward – not to her capacities or her inclinations, but to fantasies of the theatrical roles she might play:

> pathetic situations in which she assumed a tremulous voice and suffering manner... scenes of luxury and refinement, situations in which she was the cynosure of all eyes, the arbiter of all fates. As she rocked to and fro she felt the tensity of woe in abandonment, the magnificence of wrath after abandonment, the languor of sorrow after defeat.

If windows are unattended in *Sister Carrie*, mirrors remain blank. When first attracted to Hurstwood, Carrie is thrown into another flurry of indecision. After he leaves:

> She undid her broad lace collar before the mirror and unfastened her pretty alligator belt which she had recently bought.
>
> "I'm getting terrible," she said, honestly affected by a feeling of trouble and shame. "I don't seem to do anything right."
>
> She unloosed her hair after a time, and let it hang in loose brown waves. Her mind was going over the event of the evening.
>
> "I don't know," she murmured at last, "what I can do."
>
> "Well," said Hurstwood as he rode away, "she likes me alright: that I know."

Unlike Poe's narrator, Dreiser's is not in the least unaware of, or indifferent to, the complex relationships between individuals and their urban environment. Love and sexual attraction, the circulation of money (or the delectable goods and services it will buy), the search for social status and a sense of individual fulfillment: all these engage him as intensely as they motivate his characters. Yet the characters know nothing of the material forces governing their desires and aversions. The narrative insists on this division between subjective will and objective material base. Hurstwood may think the 80,000 unemployed in New York "an awful thing," but that sentiment does not prevent his seeking work as a scab motorman during the streetcar strike. "In his heart of hearts, he sympathised with the strikers" and also "felt the dignity and use of the police force," protecting the scab labor, while "never once dream[ing]" of "its true social significance."

This divorce from the socio-economic realities of his environment explains why Hurstwood needs the newspapers to tell him what is going on, and why his response to the news of unemployment – "what an awful thing that is" – is so blandly witless, so inadequate in its vagueness about the causes and effects of the human tragedy around him, in which he too is involved. Carrie too is unaware of what is really moving her towards Hurstwood, unable to assess or analyze the moral choice with which she is faced. She looks into her mirror, neither to situate herself within the middle distance of her social relationships, nor to discriminate between possible courses of action open to her. She doesn't "reflect" or "speculate"; indeed she makes no choice at all, moral or otherwise. Her only words on that occasion are clichés of passive fatigue: "I'm getting terrible"; "I don't seem to do anything right"; "I don't know what I can do." The important action is going on in physical gestures: her undressing as she speaks, "unloos[ing]" her hair and letting it fall in "loose brown waves."

The moral discrimination so central to *Middlemarch* and other novels of the "Great Tradition," the attainment of which marks the crisis in the heroine's development, requires a complex repertoire of linguistic skills: a vocabulary of moral abstractions, a sensitivity to levels of reference sufficient to admit ironic juxtapositions. But *Sister Carrie* subverts that tradition. "People in general attach too much importance to words," as the narrative informs us just before Carrie looks into the mirror. "They are under the illusion that talking effects great results. As a matter of fact, words are, as a rule, the shallowest portion of all the argument. They but dimly represent the great surging feelings and desires which lie behind." And as a revealing metaphor puts it, Carrie "was created with that passivity of soul which is always the mirror of the active world." In *Sister Carrie* mirrors, like the people who look into them, neither receive an image nor give it back.

25

Popular American novels of World War II: how the enemy within displaces the enemy outside; war novels as captivity narratives; historical conflicts inscribed as stories of personal development: leaving the nuclear family, achieving independence, attaining adulthood

If any historical experience were strong enough to impinge upon a country's literary imagination, it should be that of warfare. So it comes as a particular surprise to find American fiction still eliding the middle distance of public events when it reaches the subject of World War II. Perhaps the oddest expression of the dominant discourse of American emigration is the way in which the ideology of the individual initiation invaded the country's favorite war novels. This was, after all, America's first experience with a world conflict involving mass conscription to fight a foreign enemy. (By contrast the American involvement in World War I was a minor and short-lived affair.) History and the rest of the world had never seemed so pressing.

Yet consider the curious case of the following novels: *Mister Roberts* (1946) by Thomas Heggen, Norman Mailer's *The Naked and the Dead* (1948), *From Here to Eternity* (1951) by James Jones, Herman Wouk's *The Caine Mutiny* (1951) and Joseph Heller's *Catch-22* (1961). What, apart from their historical moment, do they have in common? First, they were all bestsellers. So this is a body of fiction validated by the marketplace. In one way or another all these books spoke to their constituency.

Secondly, since they are all realistic novels in the conventional definition of that category, one would expect them to conform roughly to the historical events on which they are based. The enemy, for instance, would be the one Americans actually fought: the Germans or the Japanese. But not in these books. Here the enemy is other American servicemen – usually superior officers, sometimes buddies in the ranks. And this is not because the authors lacked wartime experience, engaging the actual enemy, from which to draw their fiction. All of them served in the American Army, Navy or Air Force during World War II. James Jones was decorated.

In their books, though, the enemy is within. In *The Caine Mutiny* it is Captain Queeg who exercises the attention and arouses the hostility of the novel's main characters, and the book climaxes, not in a pitched battle with the Japs, but a court martial to decide the issue between Queeg and his junior officers. Private Prewitt in *From Here to Eternity* is an amateur boxer who refuses to fight in the divisional championships because he once accidentally blinded a friend in the ring. Harrassed for his obstinacy, he hits a non-commissioned officer and winds up in the company stockade. In *Mister Roberts* the enemy is Captain Morton and his petty regulations about tidiness aboard ship, and the only campaign a series of japes to embarrass him, for which the Lieutenant Roberts of the title even gets awarded a makeshift medal by a grateful crew. Yossarian in *Catch-22* is a bombardier in a wartime B-25 who would rather bomb his own Colonel Cathcart for sending him out on an endless series of dangerous missions over Italy. Indeed one of his fellow-officers (though typically no friend or ally to Yossarian) actually does bomb his own airbase when the Germans offer him cost plus 6 percent to undertake the mission.

How was it possible for the authors of these books virtually to ignore the real battles going on outside and credibly to present the fictional conflict as between the Americans themselves? They did it by taking pains to set the stories in an environment removed from the historical theaters of war. Though he published *From Here to Eternity* in 1951 and thus could have drawn on his experience in the real Pacific War, James Jones chose to set the book in the peacetime Army – but only just in peacetime, and on the very cusp of war, since the action takes place in and around Pearl Harbor and ends with the Japanese surprise attack which brought America into it at last. Most of the action of *Catch-22* is literally insulated from the historical war in Europe: set on the tiny island of Pianosa off the coast of Tuscany. It's a real place on the map, but curiously unreal in the novel – a kind of dream (or nightmare) retreat from the campaign on the mainland. The sailors and officers in *The Caine Mutiny* and *Mister Roberts* are also removed from the action as experienced by millions of their countrymen in the airplanes, and on the ships and beaches of the Pacific. *Mister Roberts* happens on a pokey little supply ship, marooned in a backwater, and the Caine is a dreary minesweeper made even more inglorious by its captain's cowardly failure properly to engage the ship in the one battle in which his ship is called to participate.

The isolation is made more credible by being imagined as against the wishes of the participants. The intramural aggression is often felt as a form of captivity. Private Prewitt is actually imprisoned by his own army. So, in a sense, are the officers of the Caine, kept by Captain Queeg's cowardice and paranoia from a relevant role in the war. Mister Roberts is desperate to get a transfer out of the supply ship onto a cruiser and into the fighting, but his applications to move are repeatedly disapproved by *his* captain, who (as Lyndon Johnson used to say) would rather have him inside the tent pissing out than outside the tent pissing in. Joseph Heller turned this neat system of double binds into the Catch-22 of his title. Catch-22 is a categorically distinct regulation that plugs all loopholes. For example, if a pilot can be judged medically unfit by reason of insanity, he can be excused from more of Colonel Cathcart's murderous bombing missions. But the catch is that in order to present himself as insane, he has to ask the doctor to release him from active duty. That request itself would be a mark of sanity; therefore, he can not be excused.

At first sight *The Naked and the Dead* seems an exception to this rule. In Mailer's novel the enemy is certainly the historical adversary, and the book is plotted around a convincing military campaign to secure a Pacific island. It's an ambitious book: ranging from high strategy to low motives, rounding out the issues of the immediate conflict with flashbacks that situate the characters in their peacetime social contexts, and discussions of the likely profile of American politics after the war. In the main outlines of its action it is in no sense insulated from the human issues – great and small – of World War II. *The Naked and the Dead* is no flight from history.

Yet the rising action, the climax and dénouement of this 600-page study – in other words, what might be called the conventional novelistic plot within the swirl of references backwards and forwards in time, up and down the ranks – is something apart. It is a pointless patrol into the mountains of the enemy-held island, a diversion from the main action, not a microcosm of it. Lieutenant Hearn has fallen foul of his commanding officer and as a result is detached from Combined Headquarters and "sentenced" (that is the appropriate word) to lead a pointless patrol into the mountains of the enemy-held island. He and his men are made captive by the tactical circumstances of enemy-infested jungle. They fall to quarreling, then to ugly interracial conflict. Through a complicated piece of treachery by one of his sergeants, the decent Hearn is killed in an ambush. At the point of scaling a summit, the survivors run into a nest of hornets, from which they tumble ignominiously down the mountain. When they finally get back, they find that the island has been all but taken, and the Japanese routed – that, as one of them says, "we broke our ass for nothin'." *The Naked and the Dead* is the exception that tests the rule, and confirms it.

There are various ways to explain this preoccupation with the domestic enemy in American war novels. One is the feeling that World War II forced the United States to act against its own deepest suspicion of "foreign entanglements" and a constitutional proscription against standing armies. Another is that America's first experience with modern warfare – civilian conscripts going into battle with mass-produced armaments – was a civil war, the utterly traumatic, life-changing conflict between the States from 1861 to 1865. The American novelists of World War II may, therefore, have been trying to give fictional expression to these tensions between American ideology and the innovations being forced upon the country by modern history. Whatever their own experience in the historical conflict with the real enemy, they may have felt that a more important struggle was going on within the nation's sense of itself as essentially anti-militaristic. Certainly the overt references to the country's future in *The Naked and the Dead* add some weight to the idea that the United States would face the threat of fascism at home, as a result of the war, an unwelcome importation of what was seen as an exclusively European political model. Less explicitly, when Mister Roberts finally wins his domestic struggle with Captain Morton and gets his transfer to a cruiser in the front line of the action, he is killed by a Japanese kamikaze plane – as though to suggest, in some roundabout way, that the insertion into history is lethal.

All this may convince. But it is also worth registering the obvious fact that all these books are narratives of captivity, a genre perennially popular with American readers, not only since before the United States had entered the diplomatic and military world arena, and before it had fought the civil war, but even before the country had constituted itself as a nation. From John Smith's *General History* right down to the Vietnam War movie *Platoon* (1986) crucial historical conflicts have been displaced by more private struggles – say, a crisis in personal development, like adolescence, or a spiritual or political conversion – in which captivity is posed as the central test of the protagonist's initiation. Typically the theater of operations is not the military or ideological conflict going on outside – the one we read about in the history books – but (more often than not) the protagonist's personal struggle against an alien family into which the larger conflict has forced him or her by adoption.

So although Mary Rowlandson's captivity is set against the backdrop of "King Philip's War," a series of historical skirmishes between the Massachusetts settlers and the Wampanoag, the Nipmuck and the Narragansett Indians, the narrative expresses its human relationships in references to natural families dissolved and artificial families refused. Initially her tragedy is expressed in terms of the break-up of the settlers' families: "the infidels" raid the village by "haling mothers one way, and children another, and some wallowing in their blood." Her sister and brother-in-law are killed, and her little daughter horribly wounded by – later to die from – an Indian bullet. The captivity itself is articulated in terms of family too: she is "adopted" into an Indian family, who take responsibility for feeding and sheltering her in return for odd jobs like sewing, but she refuses familial references to this surrogate social unit – never calling them "mother" and "father," but always the more formal "mistress" and "master."

What has all this to do with the psychology of emigration? Richard Slotkin, the acknowledged expert on American captivity narratives, has suggested that the way Mary Rowlandson tells her story "dramatizes and brings to the surface the ambivalent feelings of desire (for emigration) and guilt (for deserting England)... by casting her emigration as an unwilling captivity to heathens and by conceiving it not as a crusader's quest but as a sinner's trial and judgement."[15]

But I think that her tone, however complex about the state of her own soul, is somewhat simpler with regard to what she and her fellow New Englanders have left behind them in the Old World. Though her impulse to distance herself from her kidnappers is natural enough, the way she refers to her "adoptive" parents – as "master" and "mistress" – suggests that what she most resents about the social relationships forced upon her by her captivity is that they drive her back to a feudalism from which she thought she had escaped when the New World settlers emigrated from Europe.

John Smith, too, calls his captors by archaic, Old World titles – calling Powhatan "the Emperour," for instance. As "infidels," the Indians are part of an old, unreformed mentality. So were Jesuits and other Roman Catholics, another common source for the kidnappers in the American captivity story. For the American writer and reader, the nightmare of the captivity genre – what made it especially frightening – was its retrograde motion. To be captured was also to fall back into an Old World dispensation of rigid hierarchies.

As for the larger outlines of Rowlandson's narrative, there is very little attention given to what might be called the cinematic elements of her adventure: the danger she faces, the question of her survival and whether she will be rescued. Her struggle is focused on the tension between the promise of God's providence for her as one of the elect, and the facts of what is actually happening to her, and the narrative suspense concentrated on how she will resolve this apparent discrepancy through her powers of interpretation, rather than on whether she will be returned to the European settlement. And when she is finally restored to her husband and community, what she registers is a fundamental change in her world outlook – nothing less. The captivity has been to her as a rite of passage to a new quality of experience.

The same features, or most of them, can be found in the other American captivity narratives. *The Last of the Mohicans* (1826) takes place in the historical French and Indian War – a setting much insisted on by a sort of scholarly apparatus provided by the author – but the novel's action is taken up with the kidnapping of two English girls on the way to join their father, and their rescue by the fiancé of one of them; again, old family relationships are dissolved, a wicked Indian tries to claim a white woman for his wife, and she is restored – not to her father but to her proper intended husband – the next stage in her personal development. Her irreversible growth is a part of the story. In Melville's *Typee* (1846) the historical confrontation between hemispheres – the French and English navies and missionaries bidding for raw materials and native souls – is first established, then marginalized by the narrative. The central story is the protagonist's escape from his natural family and the surrogate "family" of the ship on which he serves, his "adoption" by a native family whose warm embrace he comes to find as restricting and even frightening, his escape – and the irreversible change this experience works on his personality.

Uncle Tom's Cabin (1851-2) is set in the midst of the furious contemporary debate between abolitionists and slaveholders, but in its political expression this issue comes close to being ridiculed, in an argument between the relatively humane slaveholder Augustine St. Claire and his strident abolitionist sister Ophelia from Vermont, in which he turns the tables and denounces slavery more contemptuously than any abolitionist Ophelia has ever heard lecture. What lacerated contemporary sensibilities about *Uncle Tom's Cabin* – and still moves the reader today – is what slavery did to black families: Uncle Tom separated from his wife and children when sold down the river; his virtual adoption by St. Claire, whose child, Little Eva, becomes Tom's surrogate daughter; the separation of George Harris and Eliza, with Eliza's winter escape across the Ohio River, stepping to freedom from ice floe to ice floe with her baby in her arms. And just as the plot is perplexed by families dissolved, so it is resolved by families reunited in a series of highly symmetrical coincidences.

If the issue of the family is not so salient in the novels of World War II, its ghost survives in the frequent references to real families left behind and to the military organization as an intolerable surrogate family, controlled by a detested parodic father in the form of a senior officer who exercises the authority of paternity without the love. But the theme of captivity is as strong as ever, and the plot of personal crisis still displaces the social or communal conflict; private development is still more important than the public evolution we call history. As the stories are written, Lieutenant Hearn's control of his platoon and Sergeant Croft's test of his own physical and psychic limitations in *The Naked and the*

Dead, Ensign Keefer in *The Caine Mutiny* learning what it means to be an adult, the evolution and revelation of Private Prewitt's courage in *From Here to Eternity*, the private campaigns of Yossarian and Mister Roberts – all these concerns occupy the foregrounds of stories, the historical setting of which might be almost anytime and anywhere.

It might be objected that this is what good novels should do: personalize the public issues, make them accessible to readers through the local incarnation of characters in a story. To take a British example for a moment, Nicholas Monserrat's *The Cruel Sea* and Alistair MacLean's first novel, *H.M.S. Ulysses* – both record-breaking bestsellers in their own right in the early and mid 1950s – also take place in the claustrophobic, all-male environment of a ship at sea. But however undistinguished the fighting unit represented (the first half of *The Cruel Sea* takes place in a tiny flower-class corvette), and however sour the interpersonal conflict on board, the action of the novel inserts them into the real war, the crucial battle of the Atlantic convoys. But what's missing in the American novels is just this connection between the personal and the historical; for how is the reader to extrapolate from the smaller to the greater conflict?

From the American point of view, no two wars could be less alike than World War II and the Vietnam War. One was a world-wide conflict between sovereign nations, the other a colonial police action (albeit grotesquely and catastrophically engrossed); one was just, and largely supported by the American people, the other not; one was won, the other lost. Yet how did the Vietnam conflict play back in the American aesthetic consciousness? To date, the Vietnam War's most popular representations have been in movies. Judging from a representative sample, the experience did very little to modify the stereotype of personal initiation through captivity. In *The Deer Hunter* (1978) war is once again a rite of passage, tucked into the bracketing image of the American male proving himself by tracking and shooting deer. Granted, in the film's central action the captors are not other Americans but a ludicrous fictional band of wicked orientals out of a children's adventure story, who force the American soldiers to play Russian roulette.

But by the time the (much better) *Platoon* was released, the genre had got fully back to form. This may come as a surprise, since *Platoon* is usually cited, along with *Full Metal Jacket* and *Hamburger Hill* (both 1987), as representing the most "realistic" stage of representation of the Vietnam War. Perhaps this means nothing more than that they weren't the fancifully heroic *The Green Berets* (1968) and *Rambo* (1985), which represent, respectively, the initial optimism of the American involvement in Indochina, and the last-ditch attempt to recoup some of the country's dignity along with its captive soldiers "missing in action."

A simple synopsis of *Platoon* will show just how completely the movie reverts to the type of the adolescent's rite of passage. Despite his parents' strong objections, Chris Taylor drops out of college to volunteer for service in Vietnam. Estranged from his mother and father, he has no one to write home to apart from his grandmother. "Nobody tells the new guys what to expect," says Chris's voice-over to Grandma as the new grunts get off the plane onto which the most recent war dead are already being loaded.

The "new guys," mainly blacks and working-class whites, "come from the end of the line, most of them." Unlike the idealistic Chris, who volunteered to escape from his parents' "goddamn world," they have been drafted. Though they have only "a factory job to go back to," they are fighting for their country and its proclaimed values.

It is with this group that Chris identifies, and into which he is initiated, through the ritual of smoking dope. They are "the heads." Another group, of white and (mainly) career soldiers, smokes tobacco. Their acknowledged leader is Staff Sergeant Barnes. The two factions first come into open conflict when on patrol to a Vietnam village. They shoot a pig, the first hit in the movie. Then Barnes kills an old woman, and threatens a little girl with his .45 automatic, until one of the adult villagers tells him where the North Vietnam Army are hiding. Elias, one of the heads, objects to Barnes's behavior, and fights him.

By now Chris is beginning to run out of "energy to write" his grandmother. "A civil war was in the Platoon – half the men with Elias and half with Barnes," he tells her. "I can't believe we're fighting each other, when we should be fighting them." Finally his words break off: "Tell Mom and Dad...well, just tell them." In a fierce firefight with the NVA Barnes pulls back, cutting Elias off, then shoots him in cold blood.

Chris's best friend is a sympathetic black soldier called King. "How come you ain't writing nobody?" King asks him. "What about your folks? That grandma you was telling me about? Girl? Got a mother and father, aintcha? They must be *some*body." "Na," says Chris, "there's nobody." In another battle, after King has been invalided out, Chris shoots Barnes with an NVA carbine, after Barnes challenges him: "Do it!" This fullfils the heads' prophecy that if "anybody kills Barnes, it'll be Barnes." As the wounded Chris is helicoptered out and away from the devastation, and the perspective widens, his voice-over offers a final comment on the action:

I think now, looking back, we did not fight the enemy. We fought ourselves. And the enemy was in us. The war is over for me now, but it will always be there the rest of my days – as I'm sure Elias will be – fighting with Barnes for...possession of my soul. There are times since I've felt like a child born of those two fathers.

Conclusion: lighting out

So we end with this paradox. The land of the free is very fond of stories of captivity. "Lighting out," the psychology of emigration so instrumental in the self-definition of the "American character," has always posed contradictory feelings: raised as many problems as it has solved, in fiction as in fact. Rupert Wilkinson, the cultural historian and a leading analyst of the "American character," has written of the "four fears" that haunt the American consciousness: the fear of being owned, of falling apart, of falling away (from which Part III of this book takes its title) and of winding down.[1] The first and last of these concerns must account for the perennial fascination of the captivity narrative, but "falling away" was certainly the preoccupation of Cushman, Vane and other American Puritans who feared that New England was turning its back on the "first love" that constituted its founding principles.

To put this "characteristically" American problem in another way, the dominant discourse of emigration, which formed the basis of the Americans' sense of what made them distinct, always contained its contradictions. Every invigorating leap into the future entails a loss of the past. To embrace nature is to forgo culture. To liberate oneself from convention is to deprive oneself of tradition. To break free from the prerogatives of familial and political power is also to rupture one's ties to a sustaining community. To speculate in one's own business is to give up the security of waged or salaried employment. To insist on defining oneself is to forgo the comfort of having one's place set in the scheme of things, and thus to be spared all that competition and self-assertion.

Emigrants to America experienced these, and other versions of the same binary opposition, however strenuously their discourse seeks to write bad news out of its script. American writing found or allowed itself to be invaded by the antithesis of the dominant discourse: those expressions of loss, of degeneration, disorder and rootlessness that formed the insistent themes of British travelers in, and articulate back-migrants from, the New World. Cooper, Hawthorne and James lamented the loss of European titles and prerogatives – the stuff, they thought, of the social novel – and their novels addressed these supposed deficiencies. Other American writers internalized the antithesis without wholly controlling it. Madame Knight and Susan Cooper pined for the substantial deposits of European culture, and William Cullen Bryant fancied an American antiquity on the Prairie – only to have their mirages vanish on closer scrutiny, leaving them in the wilderness alone. Winthrop, Parkman and Thoreau were disturbed and irritated by their unsettled settlers. Cather's Jim Burden needs the Latin classics to express the settlement of Nebraska. The inhabitants of Jewett's *Country of the Pointed Firs* still speak in fragments of "Chaucer's English," recalling a lost vigor of trade, travel and prosperity, and (like the back-migrants in Hawthorne's *Our Old Home*) fancying a relationship to English royalty.

Even the process of lighting out itself posed an insidious problem. To escape one kind of captivity might mean being subjected to another. Like the motif of death in life, this confusing feeling also had its objective basis. Traditionary communities in Europe, or on the American East Coast, might inflict one kind of claustrophobia on the restless or ambitious spirit, but the uncleared forest to which the settler took flight could induce another sort, at least as strong. Furthermore, once laboriously removed to the frontiers of civilized settlement, deprived of all but the most primitive facilities for travel and communications, the emigrant could do very little to relieve his or her condition, to vary the narrow repertoire of sights, sounds, company and experiences of the daily routine. Wherever you could move in those surroundings – in a day or even a week – would land you in much the same physical and social environment.

A few emigrants could admit to this feeling, but who and what sort are themselves highly significant. Rebecca Butterworth wrote of feeling "[dammed ?] up in a corner," but this was in a desperate letter to her father admitting to utter failure of health and prospects, seeking help and making arrangements to return to England: a rare enough sort of communication even in Charlotte Erickson's comprehensive survey of emigrants' letters home.

Susanna Moodie could look back on seven years spent in "the green prison of the woods" of the Canadian wilderness, now that she had moved to "one of the most thriving districts of the Upper Province," in a more "settled part of the country." She could also admit to homesickness, and shared the English travelers' scorn for uppity North American servants, the monotony of New World landscape, and the scurrility of its newspapers. But then she and her family emigrated to Canada, not the United States, in 1832, and so in a sense had never lighted out in the first place, always maintaining their ties to the imperial order. Her husband fought in the militia, and agreed not to stand down at the threat of a republican rebellion, aided by radicals from New York. In 1839, to effect their escape from their "green prison," Susanna petitioned the Lieutenant Governor of Upper Canada, Sir George Arthur, to offer her husband a government post. Grateful for Moodie's services, Arthur made him Sheriff of Victoria District in 1839.[2]

But few Americans could admit to feeling captive in their frontier settlements. The idea ran too strongly against the ideology of their emigration; the dominant discourse could not allow it – had no terms for it. Emigrants to the United States had burned their boats: not only left their neighbors and extended families, but also cut the apron strings of imperial hierarchy and the purse strings of government preferment. They had undergone a reformation of the spirit – of behavior, belief and expectation.

They had discarded the familiar in the uncertain hope of a better life. How intolerable, then, if the new dispensation for which they risked all should be as confining (albeit in a different way) as the old. So the dominant discourse had to displace claustrophobia in narratives of captivity, in which the perpetrators of confinement were agents of "the other" – Indians, Jesuits, or other Americans acting in an un-American way, like aristocratic slaveholders or authoritarian officers in a military bureaucracy. And unlike the Catholics and other "idolaters" and hierarchs of the Old World, these antithetical forces were not safely quarantined by 3,000 miles of ocean. They were close enough to subvert the new order for which the emigrants had risked so much. The enemy was within – or might be.

⋄⋄⋄⋄⋄⋄⋄⋄⋄⋄⋄⋄⋄⋄

As with lighting out, so with the other impulses of the dominant discourse. All entailed obvious corresponding losses, but also contained inherent contradictions less evident at first sight. The ideology of the Redeemer Nation, the shedding of Old World culture, the yearning for the endless material profusion of New World nature – even the figure of anticipation and the celebration of process: all these motives for emigration and defenses of the enterprise after the fact contain their own negation within them. Why? Because they are all species of the apocalypse. The revolution they all invite and defend is to take place once only, and to be the condition for the preparation of the last things.

This millennial dimension is not just a matter of John Winthrop's projection of a "Cittie upon a Hill." Of course the Massachusetts Puritans gave voice and spiritual authority to the vision (and so earned themselves a place in the pantheon of American "founding fathers," not to mention a large share of American cultural and literary history), but the image of America as the Promised Land was, and continues to be, far too widespread among emigrants of other faiths and from other countries to have been conditioned by a few Devonshire and East Anglian Puritans, however devout and articulate.

So even the more secular projections of American process found it hard to disentangle the idea of the Promised Land from its millennial context. "Westward the course of Empire takes its way" may sound exhilaratingly and unstoppably progressive, but even the ambition to extend learning so as to enlarge the Empire contains its own built-in limits, as Bishop Berkeley's enormously popular expression of the theme makes clear. Look again at the three lines following that optimistic opening:

The first four acts already past,
  A fifth shall close the drama of the day;
Time's noblest offspring is the last.

In other words, American progress was not to be endless after all. Berkeley's chronology here, like the time scale of the dominant discourse itself, is not a chronology, but a *kairology*. That is, it measures itself not in the recorded events of ordinary history, but in the four millennial eras of the Assyrian, Persian, Greek and Roman monarchies, and the fifth, or thousand-year rule of Christ and His Saints. Deep in the impulse to migrate westwards lies the end of the world. The Promised Land is the end of history, and death is buried in the trope.

This is why Frederick Jackson Turner's paper delivered at the otherwise strenuously hopeful Chicago "World Columbian Exposition" in 1893 made such a profound impression, not only on professional American historians but also in time on all custodians of the American character and on the popular consensus of the American identity. What Turner announced was nothing less than the end of the American process. The western frontier, once fully extended to the West Coast (the natural continental limits of Manifest Destiny), was now closed. That benign mechanism of ambitious expansion into free or cheap virgin land that had formed the American character had ceased to operate. To many, Turner's paper marked the beginning of the end of America as a distinct national identity. Since this is so decidedly *not* the way things turned out, it is worth asking why so many prominent interpreters of the American scene have been so disturbed by Turner's paper. The answer, I believe, lies within the essay itself: in its appeal to the widely shared psychology of emigration, and its inherent contradictions.

The point can be illustrated, first, by another look – not at the supposed end of the American process, but at one of the most popular and influential expressions of its beginning. Why, after all, did Tom Paine's *Common Sense* galvanize the American colonies into violent separation from Great Britain? How did the pamphlet move a whole community to such a momentous decision?

Of course, there was Paine's brilliant satire, drawn from the English radical tradition, against "Kingly Government." But other arguments appealed to his readers' sense of their condition as distinctly American. One was the unalterable dispensation proclaimed by "the simple voice of nature." Geography, for example, was a natural fact. How could a tiny island "of three hundred and sixty miles," preoccupied with "distinctions too limited for continental minds," continue to govern a whole continent lying 3,000 miles to the west of them across the great ocean? "Let Britain wave [waive] her pretensions to the continent, or the continent throw off the dependence." Another "natural" argument derived its strength from the development of the individual organism. If "America hath flourished under her former connexion with Great-Britain," wouldn't she continue so to benefit in the future? "Nothing can be more fallacious than this kind of argument. We may as well assert, that because a child has thrived upon milk, that it is never to have meat." And so, drawing on the ideology of the inevitable rite of passage, Paine naturalized what the eighteenth century considered to be the most unnatural of political acts, revolution.

But *Common Sense* begins with a different appeal, to the widespread belief in a dispensation to be found neither in nature nor in human history: a lost, paradisal Golden Age. "Government, like dress, is the badge of lost innocence; the palaces of kings are built on the ruins of the bowers of paradise." Could paradise be regained? "Let us suppose a small number of persons settled in some sequestered part of the earth," a community like the first American colonists, who "represent the first peopling of any country, or of the world." What would they do? "In this state of natural liberty, society will be their first thought." Then the process of nature would take over:

> Thus necessity, like a gravitating power, would soon form our newly arrived emigrants into society, the recripocal blessings of which, would supersede, and render the obligations of law and government unnecessary while they remained perfectly just to each other.

Of course, Paine was not so naive as to suppose that the colonists will be able to dispense with government forever. He goes on immediately to trace the "natural" evolution of elected representatives, a system checked by the people it governs. But unfortunately there is nothing either natural or inevitable about democracy; it doesn't grow on trees. And the contradiction lies buried in that figure with which he begins: the Golden Age. No government (of any kind) is needed in paradise; the condition of "innocence" does not require it. The Golden Age belongs to a discourse quite distinct from discussions of a possible political future in the fallen world of human history.

Turner's paper begins with a similar, equally vehement, appeal to the psychology of emigration, and to the Americans' sense of their distinct identity which it fostered. First, he evokes the primitivism so central to the myth of the Golden Age. In order to expand westwards, settle and develop the virgin land, the American "return[s] to primitive conditions": "strips off the garments of civilization" and puts on "the hunting shirt and moccasin." At first this new environment "is too strong for the man," but "little by little he transforms the wilderness," and "the outcome is not the old Europe...[but] a new product that is American."

This is nothing less than the emigrant's rite of passage, replicated in every generation – indeed, in every individual settler. The initiate strips away old culture, is tested in the anarchic conditions (or the rules of nature) on the *limen*, then aggregated as a "new product" in a unique, reformed society. Like Paine, Turner privileges nature over culture; so "history" takes on the necessity of a natural process: in Turner's case, the evolution of the species. Like Paine, too, he collapses the development of a whole people into the icon of the collective singular. As the individual evolves, so does the nation: "We, the people."

Nature supplanting culture; process; the rite of passage: Turner's argument spoke as powerfully as had Paine's to the American identity conditioned by the psychology of emigration. Yet even as he proclaimed and defined the American process, recapitulating the stages through which millions of emigrants had been motivated westwards, Turner announced its ending. Though confessing that "he would be a rash prophet who should assert that the expansive character of American life has now entirely ceased," his last words declare: "And now, four centuries from the discovery of America...the frontier has gone, and with its going has closed the first period of American history."

Yet history is just what Turner's discourse does not address. The process by which the individual strips away old culture, returns to nature, then attains a unique, reformed dispensation is neither historical nor (despite the imagery in which it is expressed) truly natural. Turner's apotheosis of the individual icon prevents the scrutiny and analysis of national institutions. These do not simply "evolve" as natural organisms; they are produced by social and economic forces operating in a complex field over long periods of time. The reason why 400 years pass in the blink of Turner's eye is that they are imaged as a timeless Golden Age in which nothing happened except the numberless rites of personal development that characterized "the first period of American history." The inevitablity of his system is not "historical" – not even in the Hegelian sense of a dialectic of social and economic interests working itself out deterministically – but (as Turner's revealing choice of word indicates) prophetic. Its ending is not governed by historical causes – not even the closing of the frontier. As he admits, other spheres for optimistic American expansion remain, and in any case there was still plenty of undeveloped land remaining in 1893, even if no longer lined up just ahead of the advancing tide of "civilization." The American process is at an end because an ending is buried in the complex of apocalyptic figures through which that process was proclaimed in the first place.

So the very ideas in the discourse of emigration that enabled America's self-definition could also disable it. What, after all, are the chief constituents of the American difference, as proclaimed by the interpreters of the "American character"? Equal access to education, wealth and the law (though bad luck, bad health or bad character will always defer their equal attainment); a government open to all – to observe, control and take part in; the willingness to take risks, to try new institutions and modes of living; a predominantly middle-class ethos of hard work, self-reliance and the discipline to defer gratification – to "invest" in the future – and a correspondingly hostile environment for communism, socialism, labor unionism and other collective institutions; a recurring sense of optimism, a faith in future possibilities. And finally (it must be added) the very hypothesis on which all these speculations are based: that something called the "American character" – the figure of the collective singular on which the very Constitution is based – exists, and is a dispensation exceptional among nations.

There is not one of these characteristics that cannot be traced to the arguments favoring emigration to the New World, if only because America internalized that ideology and deployed it to invent itself. And, as Frederick Jackson Turner would put it, "he would be a rash prophet who should" deny that these ideas have produced the most invigorating environment for potential human development the world has ever known. Yet prophecy is what it remains, not history: faith not fact. Like a religious sect, a nation that invents itself derives enormous cohesion from its shared ideals, and also perfects the machinery of invention itself, by which it can continue to modify its institutions to meet changing circumstances. Yet within this self-constructed dispensation the threat of the subversive "other" always seems to lurk. As Seymour Martin Lipsett (perhaps the most influential and thought-provoking of all commentators on the American character) has written, "if foreigners may become Americans, Americans may become 'un-American.' This concept of 'un-American activities'...does not have its counterpart in other countries...An American political leader could not say, as Winston Churchill did in 1940, that the English Communist party was composed of Englishmen, and he did not fear an Englishman."[3] It would be absurd to speak of an English dissident as "un-English," if only because he or she was born in England. "Americanism" is, finally, an ideology, not a natural condition. And this serves as a reminder of the dark side of American public life: the recurrent bouts of paranoia, the occasional loss of confidence in the viability of the exceptional state. In that sense too, the early Puritans of Massachusetts have served as both a model and a warning.

Like the rest of American culture, "American literature" is a synthetic construction of the ideology of emigration. Not, that is, any literature that happens to have been written and read in America, but the self-proclaimed canon that constitutes the subject as distinct from other literatures in English. In this sense, American literature has always been exceptional; it has "lit out" from the dead conventions of Europe, freeing itself for endless experiments in form and reference. It has pioneered the novel that interrogates its own narrative epistemology, and the open-field poem that breaks classical form to renew itself in a tireless process terminated only by its author's death. It displaces historical conflict in personal struggles between parent and adolescent child, in captivity threatened and escaped, and posed as a test of human fulfillment. Since its most radical impulses are autobiographical, it reinforces the dominant ideology of individual enterprise and self-reliance, even when most critical of that ideology, yet it famously refuses accommodation with the middle distance of contemporary society – often overlooks the middle distance altogether. As de Tocqueville predicted even before much American literature had emerged, "Human destiny, man himself, not tied to time or place, but face to face with nature and with God, with his passions, his doubts, his unexpected good fortune, and his incomprehensible miseries, will for these peoples be the chief and almost the sole subject of poetry."[4]

So the psychology of emigration has both enabled and disabled American literature, just as it has the country's idea of its own social and political character. In the hands of some authors the spatial, architectural and institutional rupture with a more traditionary culture has proved overwhelming: an occasion (at best) for nostalgic reverie. In others even the most unsettling fears of captivity and degeneration have been confronted – rendered and analyzed movingly as subjects.

Post-war American writing has even allowed the middle distance back in the frame. Whitman's great American long poem oscillates between references to the collective self and the universal "kosmos" (the types parading in between being about as substantial as silhouettes in a shadow show). The modernist epics of Pound and Eliot jump straight from the present, over the past to the timeless classics. But American poets after the war, like Lowell, Berryman, Ed Dorn, Sylvia Plath, Adrienne Rich and Frank O'Hara could admit allegiance to sub-groups of family, class, gender and coterie, without feeling embarrassed at their lack of "universality."

At first sight things don't look so good for the popular post-war novel. Perhaps the most extreme symptom of the elided middle distance is presented by William Styron's *Sophie's Choice* (1976), in which the whole of World War II, the Holocaust and a paranoid schizophrenic all seem to have done their murderous work so that Stingo, the novel's narrator, can lose his virginity and be initiated into manhood. The book modifies this vulgarity by investing Stingo with a hardboiled, self-ironizing voice, but the truly dreadful movie ("Handsome, doggedly faithful and astoundingly tedious" – *Variety*) ends with a long shot of Stingo walking across the Brooklyn Bridge towards Manhattan at dawn (crossing, passing) with his portentous voice-over saying:

> And so ended my voyage of discovery, in a place as strange as Brooklyn. I let go the rage and sorrow for Sophie and Nathan, and for the many others who were but a few of the butchered and betrayed and martyred children of the earth. When I could finally see again, I saw the first rays of daylight reflected in the murky river. This was not judgement day – only morning, excellent and fair.

All right for some. But *Sophie's Choice* is best understood as the decadence of a tradition. More experimental post-war novels have found ways of treating the immediate past of public events, even if obliquely. Thomas Pynchon and Don DeLillo have made a style out of American paranoia, bringing history into the novel's plot and thus problematizing it as only another fiction. In DeLillo's *Libra* (1988) Win Everett, the deep-deep-cover CIA man plans an assassination *attempt* on John F. Kennedy, in which a shot will wound a Secret Service man and put the frighteners on the President. But Everett has a "fear and premonition":

> Plots carry their own logic. There is a tendency of plots to move toward death. He believed that the idea of death is woven into the nature of every plot. A plot in fiction, he believed, is the way we localize the force of death outside the book, play it off, contain it... He had a foreboding that the plot would move to a limit, develop a logical end.

This is not "history" strictly speaking; or rather, it is history as an alternative synopsis. But by invoking the inherent American fear that death may be hidden in the trope of the Promised Land, *Libra* offers a highly inventive, yet still plausible motive for a catastrophic public event. The novel is full of neuroses, convincingly rendered through the most subtle modulations of dialogue (or more tellingly, monologue), and the particular pathology that killed President Kennedy could just as well be one of them.

Something different has happened to the Vietnam war story, though this transformation, too, involves reversal and indirection. If *Platoon* simply redeploys the conventions of the narrative of initiation, *In Country* (1985), by Bobby Ann Mason, turns them inside out. Here interest centers not on the military conflict abroad, but on the imprints it leaves at home: the veterans it has unmanned – literally rendered impotent – rather then proved through initiation; the young woman getting to know her father killed in action through his diary and letters from Vietnam. Significantly her fullest understanding of the concrete struggle of war comes through the abstract inscription of its documentary remains, in her father's journal and on the Vietnam Memorial in Washington with which the novel ends.

Similarly in *Machine Dreams* (1984) Jayne Anne Phillips multiplies the central drama of adolescence by two, and marginalizes it. That is, she treats two generations of men who went to war – against Japan in 1941-5 and in Vietnam – from the narrative consciousness of the wife of one and the sister of the other. No longer central and unique, the initiation of the male loses that spurious universality by which, in earlier war novels, it claimed to stand for general human value. Instead it becomes one of a series in time, conditioned by the preceding generation and limited by the gendered consciousness through which it is perceived.

As with *In Country*, the author's gender seems to have placed a minus sign in front of all the usual expressions of American war fiction. Phillips's men "fail" their initiations – die young, or go out of business, or go "missing in action" in Vietnam. The "action" of traditional war fiction is itself missing. Phillips does not send Rambo to get the boys back. Absence displaces the heroic presence of the individual test. The narrative is decentered. There is no linear narrative, no single rising action to a crucial climax, no dominant, narrative point of view organizing choices of subject and emphasis.

Of course, this may be to claim nothing more than that *Machine Dreams* and *In Country* are "art" – rather than popular novels of America at war. The country may still prefer to read, see and speak Vietnam in the dominant discourse. But I think something is changing – or rather, still the same in a deeper sense. The best American writing, like the culture of which it is a part, continues to reinvent itself, as always, by confronting its contradictions, turning in upon itself to address and analyze, as one of its legitimate subjects, its own inherited ideology.

Notes

Introduction

1 Cited in Dorothy Norman, *Alfred Stieglitz, an American Seer* (New York: Aperture Books, 1973), 75–6. I am grateful to my colleague Andrew Crozier for this reference, and for the information that Stieglitz took the photograph on his way to Europe.

2 The first federal immigration law of 1882 kept out lunatics, convicts, paupers; later regulations debarred contract laborers, prostitutes, polygamists, people with contagious diseases, anarchists and anyone advocating the violent overthrow of the US Government. For this information, and the figure of two percent turned back, see Maldwyn A. Jones, *The Limits of Liberty* (New York: Oxford University Press, 1983), 324.

3 William Forbes Adams, *Ireland and the Irish Emigration to the New World from 1815 to the Famine* (New Haven and London: Yale Historical Publications, Miscellany 23, 1932); Oscar Handlin, *The Uprooted*, 2nd edn. (Boston and Toronto: Little, Brown, 1973); John Bodnar, *The Transplanted: A History of Immigrants in Urban America* (Bloomington: Indiana University Press, 1985); David Cressy, *Coming Over: Migration and Communication between England and New England in the Seventeenth Century* (Cambridge: Cambridge University Press, 1987); Bernard Bailyn, *The Peopling of British North America: An Introduction* and *Voyagers to the West: Emigration from Britain to America on the Eve of the Revolution* (New York/London: Knopf/I.B. Taurus, 1987); David Hackett Fischer, *Albion's Seed: Four British Folkways in America* (Oxford: Oxford University Press, 1989); Thomas Archdeacon, *Becoming American: An Ethnic History* (New York and London: The Freepress and Collier Macmillan, 1983); Werner Sollors, *Beyond Ethnicity: Consent and Descent in American Culture* (New York and Oxford: Oxford University Press, 1986).

4 Oscar Handlin, *Race and Nationality in American Life* (New York: Anchor Books, 1957), 103.

5 Louis Hartz, *et al.*, *The Founding of New Societies: Studies in the History of the United States, Latin America, South Africa, Canada and Australia* (New York: Harcourt, Brace & World, 1964), 7; John Harmon McElroy, *Finding Freedom: America's Distinctive Cultural Formation* (Carbondale: Southern Illinois University Press, 1989).

6 Kerby Miller, *Emigrants and Exiles: Ireland and the Irish Exodus to North America* (New York and Oxford: Oxford University Press, 1985).

7 Sacvan Bercovitch, *The Puritan Origins of the American Self* (New Haven: Yale University Press, 1975), 134.

Culture and nature

1 "Amerigo Vespucci's Account of his First Voyage," *American Historical Documents, 1000–1904*, vol. 43 of *The Harvard Classics*, ed. Charles W. Eliot (New York: P.F. Collier & Son, 1910), 35–6; Hesiod, *Works and Days*, lines 90–2, 117–18, trans. Dorothea Wender (Harmondsworth: Penguin Books, 1973); Ovid, *Metamorphoses*, I, lines 80–103, *passim*, trans. Mary M. Innes (Harmondsworth: Penguin Books, 1955).

2 *A True and Sincere Declaration of the Purpose and Ends of the Plantation Begun in Virginia* (1610); Henry Robinson, *Englands Safety in Trades Encrease* (London, 1641); Sir George Peckham, "A True Report of the Late Discoveries" (1583), in Richard Hakluyt, *The Principall Navigations* (1589); Richard Hakluyt, *Discourse on Western Planting* (1584); all are cited in Klaus E. Knorr, *British Colonial Theories, 1570–1850* (London: Frank Cass, 1963), 42–4; Knorr's book is an indispensable account of the reasons advanced for colonizing North America up to 1660.

3 Details and figures for the eighteenth century come from Bernard Bailyn, *The Peopling of British North America: An Introduction* (London: I.B. Taurus, 1987), 9–10; and *ibid.*, *Voyagers to the West: Emigration from Britain to America on the Eve of the Revolution* (London: I.B. Taurus, 1987), 24–70; for the nineteenth century, see W.S. Shepperson, *British Emigration to North America*... (Oxford: Basil Blackwell, 1957), 257–8; and Charlotte Erickson, ed., *Emigration from Europe, 1815–1914: Selected Documents* (London: Adam & Charles Black, 1976), 121, 127, 131.

4 Charles Dickens, ed., "A Bundle of Emigrants' Letters," *Household Words*, **1** (March 30, 1850), 19–24; "A Carol on Caroline Chisholm," *Punch, or The London Charivari* **25** (1853), 71.

5 "Report of the Royal Commissioners in 1665...," British Library, Egerton MSS 2395, ff. 434–434b.

6 E.P. Thompson, *The Making of the English Working Class*, revised edn. (Harmondsworth: Penguin, 1968), 660.

7 These figures come from W.S. Shepperson, *British Emigration to North America*, 257–8. Shepperson warns that the statistics must be treated with some caution, since they do not discriminate between the emigrants' nationalities (some foreigners left for North America and elsewhere from British ports), nor do they identify those who left intending to return, or those emigrating for a second time. Another caution is that emigrants often went on from Canada to the United States, some without settling in Canada at all.

8 Morris Birkbeck, *Notes on a Journey in America from the Coast of Virginia to the Territory of Illinois*, 5th edn (London: James Ridgway, 1819), 8; Henry Bradshaw Fearon, *Sketches of America: A Narrative of a Journey of Five Thousand Miles through the Eastern and Western States of America*...3rd edn. (London: Longman, Hurst, Rees, Orme & Brown, 1819); [anon], *A Clear and Concise Statement of New York and the Surrounding Country*...(New York: printed for the author to be sold by John Wilson, No. 22 Williams St., 1819), 5, 1; William Savage, *Observations on Emigration to the United States of America, Illustrated by Original Facts* (London: Sherwood, Neely & Jones, 1819), 59, 10; William Cobbett, *A Year's Residence in the United States of America*, 3rd edn. (London: published by the author, 1828); William Cobbett, *The Emigrant's Guide: in Ten Letters Addressed to the Tax-Payers of England*...(London: published by the author, 1829), 43–4.

9 Charlotte Erickson, *Invisible Immigrants: The Adaptation of English and Scottish Immigrants in Nineteenth-Century America* (London: Weidenfeld & Nicholson, 1972), 8, 33, 22–31.

10 Cobbett, *The Emigrant's Guide*, 42–3; Benjamin Smith (of Mountfield, Sussex), *Twenty-Four Letters From Labourers in America to their Friends in England*; the British Library copy (8290.e.14) is a 2nd edn (London: Edward Rainford), 1829.

11 Erickson, *Invisible Immigrants*, 117–18; what Irving is reported to have said is:

> It has been asked, "Can I be content to live in this country?" Whoever asks that question must have but an inadequate idea of its blessings and delights...I come from countries lowering with doubt and danger, where the rich man trembles and the poor man frowns – where all repine at the present and dread the future...Is this not a land in which one may be happy to fix his destiny, and ambition – if possible to found a name? [A burst of applause, when Mr. Irving quickly resumed] – I am asked how long I mean to remain here?...I answer, as long as I live.

"Speech at the Irving Dinner," *New York Mirror*, June 9, 1832; cited in Stanley Williams, *The Life of Washington Irving*, 2 vols. (New York: Oxford University Press, 1935), **2**, 27n.

12 Other peak periods in the nineteenth century were 1826, 1830–2, 1839–42, 1846–54, and 1869; see Erickson, *Invisible Immigrants*, 16, and Shepperson, *British Emigration to North America*, 257–9; different immediate causes impinged on different sections of society; paradoxically the penultimate of these peaks may have been occasioned by the *repeal* of the Corn Laws in 1846, since it consisted largely of tenant farmers suffering from the resulting drop in the price of cereals; see William E. Van Vugt, "Running from Ruin? the Emigration of British Farmers to the U.S.A. in the Wake of the Repeal of the Corn Laws," *Economic History Review*, 2nd Series, **41**, 3 (1988), 411–28. Birkbeck's passage is cited in Robert Holditch, *Observations on Emigration to British America and the United States* (Plymouth Dock: W. Byers, 1818), 59–60; and in John Noble, *Noble's Instructions to Emigrants... [to] the United States of America... Particularly to those of the Poorer Classes*, (Boston, 1819).

13 Erickson, *Invisible Immigrants*, 8.

14 Cobbett, ed., *The Emigrant's Guide*, 81; John Burgess to his son John at Mr. Bridgens, Cuckfield, Sussex, from Westchester County, New York, North America, Sept. 18, 1794, East Sussex Record Office (ESRO), AMS 5853; also in Donald F. Burgess, ed., *No Continuing City: The Diary and Letters of John Burgess, a Sussex Craftsman, Between 1785 and 1819* (Redhill, Surrey: Published Privately, 1989), 89; further citations will be from this volume, hereinafter *NCC*. "York" is New York, not Toronto.

15 *Invisible Immigrants*, 121; *The Emigrant's Guide*, 52; *Invisible Immigrants*, 155.

16 Joshua Scottow, *Narrative of the Planting of the Massachusetts Colony...* (Boston: Benjamin Harris, 1694), reprinted in *Collections of the Massachusetts Historical Society* (*CMHS*), 4th Series, **4** (1858), 327; William Bradford, "[Verses]," *Proceedings of the Massachusetts Historical Society* (*PMHS*), **11** (1869–70), 469; "skirrets" were (in Europe) a species of water parsnip (*OED*), though it may be Bradford's word for the New World potato; "colewort" was a kind of cabbage; Thomas Welde to his former parishioners at Tarling, Essex, June/July, 1632, in Nehemiah Wallington, Copies of Profitable and Comfortable Letters, British Library, Sloane MS 922, f. 92.

17 Cobbett, *A Year's Residence*, para. 331; Birkbeck, *Notes*, 136–7; Noble, *Instructions*, 2–3; Holditch, *Observations on Emigration*, 16–17; John Knight, *The Emigrant's Best Instructor... Respecting the United States of America...* (Manchester: M. Wilson, 1818), 19–28.

18 *Invisible Immigrants*, 271, 273; Cobbett, *Emigrant's Guide*, 79; *Invisible Immigrants*, 322. "Berry tree" can mean the berry-bearing alder (*OED*) but it is hard to imagine what use James Roberts would have had for alder trees. Besides, his negative applies to berries in general.

19 "Sir John Eliot's Copy of the New England Tracts," [Massachusetts Historical Society], *The Winthrop Papers*, 5 vols., (Boston: 1929–47), **2**, 146; Francis Higginson, *New Englands Plantation, Or, a Short and True Description of the Commodities and Discommodities of that Country* (London: 1630), reprinted in Everett Emerson, ed., *Letters from New England: The Massachusetts Bay Colony, 1629–1638* (Amherst: University of Massachusetts Press, 1976), 29–38; Paul J. Lindholdt, ed., *John Josselyn, Colonial Traveler: A Critical Edition of "Two Voyages to New England,"* (Hanover, NH, and London: University Press of New England, 1988), 81–2.

20 For a literary analysis of the catalog, see Wayne Franklin, *Discoverers, Explorers, Settlers: The Diligent Writers of Early America* (Chicago: University of Chicago Press, 1979), 3–5; also Stephen Fender, *Plotting the Golden West: American Literature and the Rhetoric of the California Trail*, (Cambridge: Cambridge University Press, 1981), 217–19; and *ibid.*, *American Literature in Context: 1620–1830* (London: Methuen, 1983), 23–9.

21 John Burgess to his son John, Sept. 18, 1794, *NCC*, 89; Cobbett, *The Emigrant's Guide*, 51; Wallington, Letters, British Library, Sloane MS 922, ff. 92b–3. For the sons of Belial in the city of Gibeah, see Judges 19: 14, ff.

22 *Noble's Instructions to Emigrants*, 105; George Poulett Scrope, *Extracts from Poor Persons who Emigrated Last Year to Canada and the United States. Printed for the Information of the Labouring Poor, and their Friends in the Country*, 2nd edn. (London: James Ridgeway, 1832), 8; Cobbett, *A Year's Residence*, paras. 427–8.

23 [anonymous broadside], "Advertisement, to all Tradesmen, Husbandmen, Servants, and others who are Willing to Transport themselves unto the Province of North-East-Jersey in America..." (Glasgow, 1684), in *The Bannatyne Miscellany, Containing Original Papers and Tracts Chiefly Relating to...Scotland*, (Edinburgh, 1855), III, 387. The pamphlet was typical of boosters' promotions and emigrants' letters alike, promising endless catalogs of both agricultural increase and also natural bounty available without cultivation: "infinite quantities of Deer and rae [roe-deer], Elcks, Beaver, Hares, Cunnies, wild Swine and Horses, &c. and Wild-honey in great abundance...Wine-grapes, Peaches, Apricocks, Chastnuts, Walnuts, Plumbs, Mulberries, &c."

24 Barbara DeWolfe, "Discoveries of America: Letters of British Emigrants to America on the Eve of the Revolution," *Perspectives in American History*, New Series, **3** (1986), 62, 9, 41; *Invisible Immigrants*, 114; *The Emigrant's Guide*, 53.

25 [tract appended to] John Brereton, "A Brief and True Relation of the Discovery of the North Part of Virginia...made this Present Year, 1602, by Captain Bartholomew Gosnold," *CMHS*, 3rd Series, **8** (1843), 96; James Rosier, "A True Relation of the...Voyage made this Present Year, 1605, by Captain George Waymouth, in the Discovery of...Virginia, *ibid.*, 132; Captain John Smith, *The Description of New England*, in Philip L. Barbour, ed., *The Complete Works of Captain John Smith, 1580–1631*, 3 vols. (Chapel Hill: University of North Carolina Press, 1986), **I**, 343; Sydney V. James, Jr., ed., *Three Visitors to Early Plymouth* (Plymouth: Plymouth Plantation, 1963), 9.

26 *Invisible Immigrants*, 28–9.

27 See Stephen Fender "Retrospective Revolutions," in *The Third Dimension: Voices from Radio Three*, ed. Philip French (London: Stourton Press, 1983), 84–5; *ibid.*, *American Literature in Context: 1620–1830* (London: Methuen, 1983), 86–9, 102–6.

28 ll. 4–41, *passim*; the translation is by H. Rushton Fairclough, in the Loeb edition (London: Heinemann, 1920), 29–33.

29 Those arguing the radical case include Sacvan Bercovitch, *The American Jeremiad* (Madison: University of Wisconsin Press, 1978), Max Weber, *The Protestant Ethic and the Spirit of Capitalism*, trans. Talcott Parsons (London: Allen & Unwin, 1930) and Christopher Hill, *Society and Puritanism in Pre-Revolutionary England* (London: Secker & Warburg, 1964). The conservative side of the argument is presented by, for example, Darrett B. Rutman, *American Puritanism: Faith and Practice* (Philadelphia: Lippincott, 1970).

30 Theodore Dwight Bozeman, *To Live Ancient Lives: The Primitivist Dimension in Puritanism* (Chapel Hill: University of North Carolina Press, 1988), 13–18.

31 "[A Letter from New Plymouth]," *Chronicles of the Pilgrim Fathers of the Colony of Plymouth from 1602 to 1625*, ed. Alexander Young, 2nd edn, reprint (Baltimore: Genealogical Publishing Co., 1974), 250–1; the letter was also published in Captain John Smith's *New England's Trials* (London: W. Jones, 1620).

32 Robert Cushman, "Reasons and Considerations touching the Lawfulness of removing out of England into the Parts of America," in *A Relation...of the Beginnings and Proceedings of the English Plantation Settled at*

Plymouth in New England... ["Mourt's Relation," 1622], ed. Dwight B. Heath (New York: Corinth Books, 1963), 89–90.

33 *Letters from New England*, 129; Edward Browne to Nehemiah Wallington, Ipswich, MA, Dec. 10, 1644, British Library, Sloane MS 922, ff.144b–5; "New England's First Fruits," *CMHS*, **1** (1792), 248; Bradford, "[Verses]," 473.

34 *Winthrop Papers*, **2**, 151, 165, 209, 303, 312–13.

35 John Burgess to Thomas Hallett, Oct. 29, 1794, *NCC*, 92.

36 *Letters from New England*, 176; *Winthrop Papers*, **2**, 111–12; 110; Smith, *Complete Works*, **1**, 344.

37 Holditch, *Observations on Emigration*, 9; Goldsmith's "matron" is "modest," not "ancient"; his forests are "tangling," not "tangled," and his original of Holditch's last two lines has

> Through woods, where beasts divided empire claim,
> And the brown Indian takes a deadly aim. Cobbett, *The Emigrant's Guide*, 12.

38 *PMHS*, **5** (1860–2), 101–3; "Cushman's Discourse," *Chronicles of the Pilgrim Fathers*, 256; William Wood, *New Englands Prospect*, ed. Alden T. Vaughan (Amherst: University of Massachusetts Press, 1977), 68, 73; Christopher Levett, "A Voyage into New England, Begun in 1623, and Ended in 1624," *CMHS*, 3rd Series, **8** (1843), 179; Benjamin Franklin, "Information to Those Who Would Remove to America," in *The Writings of Benjamin Franklin*, ed. Albert Henry Smyth, 10 vols. (New York, 1907, rpt. Haskell House, 1970), **8**, 607.

39 *Letters from New England*, 30; *Observations on Emigration*, 11; *The Emigrant's Guide*, 6; "Morell's Poem on New England," *CMHS*, **1** (1792, reprinted 1806), 129; Thomas Hariot, "A Brief and True Report of the New-Found Land of Virginia" (1588), in Louis B. Wright, ed., *The Elizabethans' America: A Collection of Early Reports by Englishmen on the New World* (London: Edward Arnold, 1965), 126, 121.

40 John Cranch to Joseph Palmer, Axminster, April 12, 1783, Cranch Family Papers, Boston Public Library, Ms.Eng. 483 (112); John Cranch to Elizabeth Palmer Cranch, Axminster, June 12, 1784 (118); Elizabeth Palmer Cranch to John Cranch, Germantown [Quincey], Oct. 12, 1784, (410); Mary Palmer to John Cranch, Germantown [Quincey], Oct. 10, 1784 (414).

41 In his *Discourse on Western Planting* (London, 1584).

42 Smith, *Complete Works*, **1**, 390.

43 For a fuller discussion of the "degenerationist" thesis, see Gilbert Chinard, "Eighteenth-Century Theories on America as a Human

Habitat," *Proceedings of the American Philosophical Society*, **91** (1947), 27–57.

44 [Sidney Willard], Review of *A Vocabulary, or Collection of Words and Phrases which have been supposed to be Peculiar to the United States of America*..., by John Pickering, *North American Review*, **3** (1816), 360.

45 [J.G. Cogswell], "On the Means of Education, and the State of Learning, in the United States of America," *Blackwood's Edinburgh Magazine*, **4** (March, 1819), 647.

46 See Chinard, "America as a Human Habitat," 35–6.

47 [Edward Everett], "On the Complaints in America Against the British Press. An Essay in the New London Monthly Magazine for February, 1821," *North American Review*, **13** (1821), 31; Benjamin Franklin, "Information to Those Who Would Remove to America," **8**, 605–6.

48 William Tudor's Phi Beta Kappa address was given in 1815, and reprinted in *The North American Review*, **2** (1815), 18–32; the following year's address was by Francis Calley Grey, in *The North American Review*, **3** (1816), 289–305; Everett's "The Peculiar Motives to Intellectual Exertion in America" was given to the Society in 1824; all three papers are reprinted in Robert E. Spiller, ed., *The American Literary Revolution, 1783–1837*, 2nd edn (New York: New York University Press, 1969), 133–53, 163–74, 284–318.

Rites of passage

1 See Arnold van Gennep, *Les Rites de Passage*...(Paris: E. Nourry, 1909); Victor Turner's fullest general treatment of liminality comes in his *The Ritual Process: Structure and Anti-Structure* (1969). Chapter 3: "Liminality and Communitas"; Chapter 4: "*Communitas*: Model and Process"; citations here from the paperback edn (Ithaca: Cornell University Press, 1977), 107, 95, 111, 102, 135, 95; Turner develops his ideas with respect to religious pilgrimages in *Dramas, Fields and Metaphors* (Ithaca: Cornell University Press, 1974), and (with Edith Turner), *Image and Pilgrimage in Christian Culture: Anthropological Perspectives* (Oxford: Basil Blackwell, 1978).

2 *John Josselyn, Colonial Traveler*, 25–6; "Diary of Edward Taylor," *PMHS*, **18** (1880–1), 6, 8, 11, 10, 12, 14, 15; the conjectured reading is that of the contemporary editor.

3 John L. Nikalls, ed., *The Journal of George Fox* (London: Religious Society of Friends, 1975), 613–14, 621–2; [Robert Fowler], "A True Relation of the Voyage Undertaken by me, Robert Fowler...," in James Bowden, ed., *The History of the Society of Friends in America*, 2 vols. (London: Charles Gilpin, 1850), **1**, 63, 67, 64, 66.

4 Emmanuel Altham to Sir Edward Altham, September, 1623, in *Three Visitors to Early Plymouth*, ed. Sydney V. James, Jr. (Plymouth: Plymouth Plantation, 1963), 23; William Bradford, *Of Plymouth Plantation*, ed. Harvey Wish (New York: Paragon Books, 1962), 87; Higginson, *Letters from New England*, 23; *ibid.*, "New England's Plantation," *CHMS* **1** (1792, rpt. 1806), 120; Welde, British Library, Sloane MS 922, ff. 90b–1.

5 Higginson, *Letters from New England*, 16, 23, 20; Bradford, *Of Plymouth Plantation*, 57–8. Granted, "lustie" could have meant happy, pleasing and healthy, as well as lascivious, insolent and arrogant (*OED*). Perhaps the saint was the former and the sailor the latter. More likely, though, Bradford is making use of the word's double meaning to dramatize the complexities of human character between which it is God's prerogative to discriminate.

6 John Burgess to his son John, August, 1794, *NCC*, 86; John Pory to Sir Dudley Carleton, James City, Virginia, Sept. 30, 1619, "The Aspinwall Papers," *CMHS*, Series 4, **9** (1871), 12–14; "Cushman's Discourse," *Chronicles of the Pilgrim Fathers*, 264–6 (emphasis added). To "pill" is to rob or pillage (*OED*).

7 DeWolfe, ed., "Discoveries of America," 64; Jonathan Boucher to Revd. and Mrs. John James, Caroline County, Maryland, Nov. 28, 1767, ESRO, BOU/A/16; John Burgess to Thomas Hallett, Mount Pleasant, Westchester County, New York, Oct. 29, 1794, *NCC*, 92.

8 Cobbett, *A Year's Residence*, paras. 392, 393; *ibid.*, *The Emigrant's Guide*, 47, 59 (the emphases are Cobbett's); Erickson, *Invisible Immigrants*, 271; Cobbett, *A Year's Residence*, para. 356.

9 DeWolfe, ed., "Discoveries of America," 18, 21, 66; Erickson, *Invisible Immigrants*, 423.

10 Cobbett, *The Emigrant's Guide*, 62, 70, 71, 83 (emphases Cobbett's).

11 Higginson, *Letters from New England*, 21; Welde, *ibid.*, 96; "A Letter from New England by Master Graves, Engynere, now there resident," *CMHS*, **1** (1792), 124; Scrope, *Extracts from Poor Persons who Emigrated Last Year...*, 29.

12 John Hull, "Some Passages of God's Providence about Myself and in

Relation to Myself...," *Transactions and Collections of the American Antiquarian Society*, **3** (1857), 144–5; Erickson, *Invisible Immigrants*, 199.

13 "Richard Saltonstall to Emmanuel Downing," in Robert E. Moody, ed., *The Saltonstall Papers, 1607–1815*, 2 vols. (Boston: MHS, 1972), **1**, 117; (the Richard Saltonstall writing here is the son of Sir Richard Saltonstall, an enthusiastic supporter of the Massachusetts venture and Councillor of the Bay Company; by the time this letter was dispatched, he was already on his way back to England); Higginson, *Letters from New England*, 24; Cushman, *Chronicles of the Pilgrim Fathers*, 262.

14 Hariot, *A Brief and True Report*, *The Elizabethans' America*, 117; Levett, "A Voyage into New England," 182–3; Wood, *New Englands Prospect*, 67–8.

15 For a fuller discussion of Bradford's reasons for writing *Of Plymouth Plantation*, and an acute analysis of the book's rhetoric, see Jesper Rosenmeier, "'With my owne eyes': William Bradford's *Of Plymouth Plantation*," in Sacvan Bercovitch, ed., *The American Puritan Imagination* (Cambridge: Cambridge University Press, 1974), 77–106; the figures on back-migration from Massachusetts Bay come from David Cressey, *Coming Over: Migration and Communication Between England and New England in the Seventeenth Century*, (Cambridge: Cambridge University Press, 1987), 192.

16 Thomas Dudley, *Letters from New England*, 79, 72, 78; see *John Winthrop's Journal: "History of New England," 1630–1649*, ed. James Kendall Hosmer, 2 vols. (New York: Barnes & Noble, 1946, repr. 1959), **1**, 57, 70, 80–2, 92, 102, 166 (for providential arrivals), and 58, 59 (for disastrous returns).

17 *Winthrop's Journal*, 165; "Pratt's Apology," *CMHS*, 2nd Series, **7** (1818), 125–9; William Hubbard, *General History of New England*, *CMHS*, 2nd Series, **5–6** (1814–15); this citation from **6** (1815), 525.

18 *The Bannatyne Miscellany*, 386; Scrope, *Extracts*, 3.

19 Cobbett, *The Emigrant's Guide*, 61, 81; Erickson, *Invisible Immigrants*, 296; Cobbett, *The Emigrant's Guide*, 52; Erickson, *Invisible Immigrants*, 294, 152.

20 Cobbett, *A Year's Residence*, para. 392.

21 Holditch, *Observations on Emigration*, 61.

22 British Library, Sloane 922, ff. 94–103.

23 Cobbett, *The Emigrant's Guide*, 36–8.

24 British Library, Sloane 922, f. 104; Cobbett, *The Emigrant's Guide*, 53; Erickson, *Invisible Immigrants*, 117.

25 Burgess, *NCC*, 87; Erickson, *Invisible Immigrants*, 224, 124.

26 Cobbett, *The Emigrant's Guide*, 57; Erickson, *Invisible Immigrants*, 224–5.

27 Erickson, *Invisible Immigrants*, 118, 125; DeWolfe, "Discoveries of America," 38–9; British Library, Sloane 922, ff. 105–7; Cressy, *Coming Over*, 200. In fact, the copy of Cole's letter is undated, so we can't be certain that it is an answer to Wallington's. It might have been received first – unlikely, since Wallington's bound manuscript of letter copies arranges the items in chronological order, and Cole's follows Wallington's there. Or the letters might have crossed, and Cole's arrived after Wallington's was dispatched to New England – also unlikely, since after a break of seven years, their correspondence is unlikely to have been resumed simultaneously without prompting from one of them.

28 Alexander Allison, Logan Co., Illinois, to Alexander Wark, Bathgate, West Lothian, Aug. 4, 1843, Emigrants' Letters, File 74, p. 6, British Library of Political and Economic Science (BLPES); Richard Mighell, Zanesville, [Ohio], to Father and Mother, [Brighton, Sussex], April 26, 1831, Mighell Papers, AMS 5575, ESRO; Erickson, *Invisible Immigrants*, 219; Cobbett, *The Emigrant's Guide*, 56.

29 John Burgess to William Kensitt, East Grinstead, Sussex, *NCC*, 112; Cobbett, *The Emigrant's Guide*, 65; Erickson, *Invisible Immigrants*, 372.

30 Erickson, *Invisible Immigrants*, 201, 416–17.

31 Knight, *The Emigrant's Best Instructor*, 5; Erickson, *Invisible Immigrants*, 36; Smith, *Complete Works*, **1**, 348; Altham, *Three Visitors to Early Plymouth*, 38.

32 Arthur Miller, *Timebends: A Life*, paperback edn. (London: Methuen, 1988), 113–14.

33 Joyce Appleby, "The Radical Double-Entendre in the Right to Self-Government," in Margaret and James Jacob, *The Origins of Anglo-American Radicalism* (London: Allen & Unwin, 1984), 275–83.

34 Sacvan Bercovitch, *The Puritan Origins of the American Self* (New Haven: Yale University Press, 1975), *passim*.

35 That is to say, not just that they were popular, but that they conformed to Frank Luther Mott's quantitative criterion of selling in numbers amounting to one percent of the American population in the decade in which they were published. See F.L. Mott, *Golden Multitudes* (New York: Macmillan, 1947).

36 Smith, *Complete Works*, **1**, 195, **2**, 30–1.

37 "Pumpions" are pumpkins; "putchamins," parsimmins; "humorists" is

used in the sense of people of mercurial disposition, subject to fantasies and to changing their minds frequently; "Tuftaffety" is tufted taffeta, hence: luxuriously dressed.

38 Henry Adams, "Captaine John Smith," in *The Henry Adams Reader*, ed. Elizabeth Stevenson (New York: Anchor Books, 1959), 32, 40, 43–44, 47, 50.

39 See Fender, *Plotting the Golden West*, *passim*, but especially 85–103.

40 See above, pp. 43–4.

41 This case has been put most fully by Robert Edson Lee in *From West to East: Studies in the Literature of the American West* (Urbana: University of Illinois Press, 1966); see my discussion of the issue in *Plotting the Golden West*, 162–200.

42 Mason Wade, ed., *The Journals of Francis Parkman*, 2 vols. (London: Eyre & Spottiswood, [1947]), **2**, 386, 387; subsequent references to this edition will be given in the text, by date of entry. Text for my discussion of the book version is the 1849 edition, as edited by David Levin (New York: Penguin Books, 1982).

43 Herman Melville's review of *The Oregon Trail* appeared in *The Literary Review* for March 31, 1849; see also *The Oregon Trail*, ed. David Levin, 18–21; Francis Jennings, "Francis Parkman: A Brahmin Among the Untouchables," *William and Mary Quarterly*, 3rd Series, **42** (1985), 305–28.

44 Wade, ed., *The Journals of Francis Parkman*, **2**, 385–6; Levin, ed., *The Oregon Trail*, 9–10, 24.

45 Lee, *From West to East*, 80.

46 Frances Trollope, *Domestic Manners of the Americans*, ed. Donald Smalley (New York: Vintage Books, 1960), 395–6.

47 Francis Parkman, *The Oregon Trail*, ed. E.N. Feltskog (Madison: University of Wisconsin Press, 1969), 625.

Falling away

1 Francis Higginson, "New England's Plantation," *CHMS*, **1** (1792, rpt. 1806), 120; "Anne Higginson to John Winthrop" [*ca.* April, 1631], *Winthrop Papers*, **3**, 22–3.

2 Cobbett, *A Year's Residence*, paras. 18, 339, emphases are Cobbett's; Birkbeck, *Notes*, 103, 102, 149.

3 John Burgess to Thomas Hallett, Mount Pleasant, New York, Oct. 29, 1794; *ibid.* to his son John, Sept. 18, 1794; Erickson, *Invisible Immigrants*, 418, 217.

4 Erickson, *Invisible Immigrants*, 276–96, *passim*.

5 Janet Johnston to Jane Johnston in Stirling, from Beverly, Upper Canada, April 27, 1846 and Jan. 30, 1847, Emigrants' Letters, File 75, p. 26, British Library of Political and Economic Sciences (BLPES), London School of Economics; Erickson, *Invisible Immigrants*, 175–8. Rebecca Butterworth's "bilious fever" could have been black water fever, induced by malaria. Calomel, or mercurous chloride, was given as a laxative. In certain circumstances it converts to mercuric chloride, which is corrosive and could have attacked the mucous membrane if held in the mouth for any time.

6 Emerson, *Letters from New England*, 63, 214; Thomas Hutchinson, *The History of the Colony and Province of Massachusetts Bay*, ed. Lawrence Shaw Mayo, 3 vols. (Cambridge, MA: Harvard University Press, 1936), **1**, 405; Pond's letter is in *Letters from New England*, 64–66, but I have copied from the text in *The Winthrop Papers*, **3**, 17–19; Emerson, 214.

7 Wilbur Shepperson, *Emigration and Disenchantment: Portraits of Englishmen Repatriated from the United States* (Norman: University of Oklahoma Press, 1965), 4, 5–6; types, causes and the general literature of back-migration, especially as regards the twentieth century, are surveyed by George Gmelch, "Return Migration," *Annual Review of Anthropology*, **9** (1980), 135–59.

8 Jonathan Boucher, St. Mary's, Caroline [*sic*], to Rev. and Mrs. John James, St. Bees, near Whitehaven, Cumberland, July 25, 1769, July 4, 1767; from Annapolis Maryland, April 4, 1771; from Port Royal, Virginia, Sept. 14, 1759, June 18, 1766; from St. Mary's, March 9, 1767, June 22, 1767, Nov. 28, 1767, Boucher Papers, 1738–1804, BOU/A/1/3–23, ESRO.

9 John Fisher to [?], [New York], Nov. 30, 1834, Rawlinson Papers, Regional History Collection (RHC no. 122), Lewis Historical Library, Vincennes University, Vincennes, Indiana. This is, of course, a different John Fisher from the one who settled apparently so happily in Michigan in 1831, dying there some time after 1840. Robert Owen, the progressive mill-owner of New Lanark, Scotland, had led a party of settlers to New Harmony, on the Wabash River in Indiana in 1825; after three years the experiment had failed and the colony was dissolved.

10 "[Letter from Thomas Lechford to Hugh Peters]," Boston, Nov. 3, 1638, "Note-Book Kept by Thomas Lechford...," ed. Edward Everett Hale, *Archaeologica Americana: Transactions and Collections of the American Antiquarian Society*, **7** (1885), 47; Thomas Lechford, *Plain Dealing: or, Newes from New-England*, (London: 1642), rpt. *CMHS*, 3rd Series, **3**

(1833), 101–2, 125; Jonathan Boucher, St. Mary's, Caroline [*sic*], June 22, 1767, to Rev. and Mrs. John James, St. Bees, near Whitehaven, Cumberland, ESRO.

11 Henry Bradshaw Fearon, *Sketches of America: a Narrative of a Journey of Five Thousand Miles through the Eastern and Western States of America...*, 3rd edn (London: Strahan and Spottiswood, 1819), 175, 262–3, 440; William Savage, *Observations on Emigration to the United States of America, Illustrated by Original Facts* (London: Sherwood, Neely and Jones, 1819), 6, 8, 15, 23, 37; *A Clear and Concise Statement of New-York...Containing a Faithful Account of many of those Base Impositions...Practised upon British Immigrants...*(Belper: 1819), [1], 5, 6, 10, 9, 7–8, 13, 14.

12 Boucher, BOU/A/1/3, ESRO; Fearon, *Sketches of America*, 11, 35, 39, 283–4, 172, 58, 247, 311, 192–3.

13 Holditch, *Observations on Emigration*, 58; Savage, *Observations on Emigration*, 9–10, 59, 56, 57; Frances Trollope, *Domestic Manners of the Americans*, ed. Donald Smalley (New York: Vintage Books, 1960), 316–17.

14 Shepperson, *Emigration and Disenchantment*, 66–8, 69–70; John Fisher to [?], [New York], Feb. 8, 1835, Rawlinson Papers, Lewis Historical Library.

15 Lechford, *Plain Dealing*, 121, 123; Boucher to James, Nov. 16, 1773, Jan. 7, 1776, BOU/1/25, BOU/1/28. ESRO. Boucher's reaction to the student's commencement address prompts the question: in what sense could Boucher himself be said to have been educated? Able to use words like "peregrination," to be ordained in the Anglican ministry and to manage a school attended by George Washington's stepson, he nevertheless responded with incredulity to a thesis which, however diversely it had been applied by the political right and left (by Hobbes and Tom Paine, say) was already a hoary commonplace of political theory by the time Boucher heard it parroted at Princeton. In the eighteenth century the intellectual divide between those educated in the classics and in the more "dismal" sciences of economics and politics was as wide as the arts–science split in the 1950s – and more portentous for the course of history.

16 Lechford, *Plain Dealing*, 78–9.

17 [Sidney Smith], Review of Adam Seybert, *Statistical Annals of the United States*, *Edinburgh Review*, **33** (1820), 79; Review of Morris Birkbeck, *Notes on a Journey in America...*, *Quarterly Review*, **19** (1818), 70; Review of W. Faux, *Memorable Days in America*, *Quarterly Review*, **29** (1823), 363, 359, 369, 365. (The *Quarterly* reviewer quotes large extracts

from Faux's book, indicated here in the usual way, with single quotes inside double. Ordinary double quotes are the words of the reviewer.)

18 Trollope, *Domestic Manners*, 174, 167; Savage, *Observations on Emigration*, 11–12; Charles Dickens, *American Notes for General Circulation*, ed. John Whitley and Arnold Goldman (Harmondsworth: Penguin Books, 1972, rpt. 1985), 180, 205, 198, 205.

19 Alexis de Tocqueville, *Democracy in America*, **2**, Part 1, Chapter 8, trans. George Lawrence, ed. J.P. Mayer (New York: Doubleday Anchor books, 1969), 485; Thomas Cole, "Essay on American Scenery," *The American Monthly Magazine*, **1** (1836), in John Conron, ed., *The American Landscape: A Critical Anthology of Prose and Poetry* (New York: Oxford University Press, 1974), 577–8; Birkbeck, *Notes on a Journey in America*, 39; Review of *Notes*, *Quarterly Review* **19** (1818), 62; see my fuller discussion of this issue in "American Landscape and the Figure of Anticipation: Paradox and Recourse," in *Views of American Landscapes*, ed. Mick Gidley and Robert Lawson-Peebles (Cambridge: Cambridge University Press, 1989), 51–63.

20 Trollope, *Domestic Manners*, 4–5, 33, 60, 62, 89, 95–6.

21 Savage, *Observations on Emigration*, 31–2; Trollope, *Domestic Manners*, 49–50.

22 Lechford, *Plain Dealing*, 79n.

23 Dickens, *American Notes*, 54–5, 63, 66, 69, 70–1, 262–3, 265–6.

24 Lucy Downing to Margaret Winthrop, John Winthrop, 1636–7, *The Winthrop Papers*, **3**, 278, 367, 279, 368, 279, 280, 420.

25 John Bailey to Increase Mather, Limerick, Ireland, May 27, 1682, June 6, 1683, June 12, 1683, "The Mather Papers," *CHMS*, 4th Series, **8** (1868), 487, 490, 491, 490, 493.

26 Kenneth W. Shipps, ed., "The Puritan Emigration to New England: A New Source on Motivation," *NEHGS*, **135** (1981), 90, 92.

27 John Retsolloh to Thomas Dyer, Bristol, March 10, 1663, J. Davis Papers, Massachusetts Historical Society (MHS), Boston.

28 Edward Howes to John Winthrop, Jr., London, 1631–6, *Winthrop Papers*, **3**, 55, 66, 94, 114, 133, 138, 291, 54, 76, 94, 113, 76n, 54, 76, 94, 111, 73, 75, 77, 134, 164–5.

29 Cressy, *Coming Over*, 201.

30 Stephen Winthrop to John Winthrop, Jr., July 14, 1650; Robert Child to John Winthrop, Jr., Gravesend, Aug. 26, 1650, Winthrop Papers, MHS. In his *The Winthrop Family in America* (Boston: Massachusetts Historical Society, 1948, 65) Lawrence Shaw Mayo, being much imbued with the dominant discourse, tries his best to recuperate Stephen Winthrop's

defection from New England: "In the autumn of 1645 or the winter of 1646 he returned to England... This was Stephen's sixth transatlantic voyage, and it turned out to be his last. After a troublous year in England he was more than ready to come home, but his creditors would not allow him to leave the realm."

31 The standard view is set out most completely in Bercovitch, *The Puritan Origins of the American Self*, *passim*; see also Patricia Caldwell, *The Puritan Conversion Narrative: The Beginnings of American Expression* (Cambridge: Cambridge University Press, 1983), *passim*, but especially 133–4; Andrew Delbanco, "The Puritan Errand Re-Viewed," *Journal of American Studies*, **18** (1984), 343–60; *The Puritan Ordeal*, (Cambridge, MA: Harvard University Press, 1989).

32 George Selement and Bruce C. Wolley, eds., *Thomas Shepard's Confessions*, Publications of the Colonial Society of Massachusetts, Collections (PCSMC), **58** (Boston: Colonial Society of Massachusetts, 1981), 33, 123, 121, 87, 2.

33 Robert G. Pope, ed., *The Notebook of the Reverend John Fiske, 1644–1675*, PCSMC, **47** (Boston: Colonial Society of Massachusetts, 1974), 147, 7, 30.

34 *A Volume Relating to the Early History of Boston, Containing the Aspinwall Notarial Records from 1644 to 1651* (Boston: Municipal Printing Office, 1903), 5.

35 Bercovitch, *Puritan Origins*, 118.

36 Thomas Shepard, "The Autobiography," in *God's Plot: The Paradoxes of Puritan Piety: being the Autobiography & Journal of Thomas Shepard*, ed. Michael McGiffert (Amherst: University of Massachusetts Press, 1972), 40–2, 51–2, 63–5, 58–60.

37 "John Dane's Narrative, 1682," *New England Historical and Genealogical Register*, **8** (1854), 147, 149. 150, 151, 154–5.

38 *Shepard's Confessions*, 48, 51–2, 69, 90.

39 John Dane, Verse Narrative of his Life, New England Historic Genealogical Society Library, MSS Cb. 1014, p. 12. Judging from his use of it elsewhere in the manuscript, "eth" seems to be Dane's contraction for "in the," rather than (as might be guessed from the context here) "either."

40 John Cotton to John Dodd, *Letters from New England*, 217.

41 "Cushman's Discourse," *Chronicles of the Pilgrim Fathers*, 264–5.

42 James Sherley, William Collier, Thomas Fletcher and Robert Holland to William Bradford, Isaac Allerton and William Brewster, Dec. 18, 1624 [in

Robert Chushman's hand and attributed to him], *CMHS*, **3** (1794, rpt. 1810), 31.

43 "Verses by Governor Bradford," *PMHS*, **11** (1869–70), 478, 473.

44 *Winthrop's Journal*, **1**, 201–2.

45 *Ibid.*, **1**, 165; "Pratt's Apology," *CMHS*, 2nd Series, **7** (1818), 127, 128.

46 Thomas Dudley to John Woodbridge, Ro[x]bury, July 8, 1648, H.H. Edes Papers, MHS.

47 John Bailey to Henry Bailey, Watertown, NE, Sept. 26, 1688, Thomas Jollie Papers, Dr. Williams's Library, London.

48 "Cushman's Discourse," 265.

49 Turner, *The Ritual Process*, 107.

50 [Rebecca Burlend], *A True Picture of Emigration*, ed. Milo Milton Quaife (Chicago: Lakeside Press, 1936, 21, 22–4; further page references will be bracketed in text).

51 Dickens, *American Notes*, 206.

"Ruins so Soon!"

1 Sarah Kemble Knight, private journal of a journey from Boston to New York in October, 1704, in *The Puritans: A Sourcebook of their Writings*, ed. Perry Miller and Thomas Johnson, 2 vols. (New York: Harper & Row, 1963), **2**, 429–30; Miss Cooper [*sic*] "A Dissolving View," in *The Home Book of the Picturesque: or American Scenery, Art, and Literature* (1852), rpt. ed. Motley F. Deakin (Gainsville: Scholars' Facsimiles & Reprints, 1967), 81, 91–4.

2 Review of *A Journal of the Voyages and Travels of a Corps of Discovery, under the Command of Captains Lewis and Clark...*, by Patrick Gass, *Quarterly Review*, **1** (1809), 301; review of *Travels in America...*, by Thomas Ashe, *Edinburgh Review*, **15** (1809–10), 448–9.

3 N. P. Willis, *American Scenery*, 2 vols. (London: George Virtue, 1840), **1**, 2; Thomas Cole, "Essay on American Scenery," *The American Monthly Magazine*, **1** (1836), in John Conron, ed., *The American Landscape: A Critical Anthology of Prose and Poetry*, (New York: Oxford University Press, 1974), 577–8; Henry Wadsworth Longfellow, "Our Native Writers" (Graduation Oration at Bowdoin College, 1825), in Robert E. Spiller, ed., *The American Literary Revolution, 1783–1837* (New York: Doubleday Anchor Books, 1967, rpt. New York University Press, 1969), 390; Cole, 571; Edward Tyrrell Channing, "On Models in Literature," *North American Review*, **3** (1816), 202–9, in Spiller, 155.

4 Cole, 578, 571; for further discussions on this topic, see Stephen Fender, "American Landscape and the Figure of Anticipation," Robert Clark, "The Absent Landscape of America's Eighteenth Century," and Allen J. Koppenhaver, "The Dark View of Things: The Isolated Figure in the American Landscapes of Cole and Bryant," all in Mick Gidley and Robert Lawson-Peebles, eds., *Views of American Landscapes* (Cambridge: Cambridge University Press, 1989); also Tony Tanner, *Scenes of Nature, Signs of Man* (Cambridge: Cambridge University Press, 1987), especially 1–45.

5 Whitman's praise of the prairies comes in *Specimen Days* (1882), in the text he reproduces of a speech he *would* have given at a large popular meeting in Topeka, Kansas, had he not "had such a good time and rest, and talk and dinner, with the U[niversity] boys, that I didn't drive over to the meeting and speak my piece."

6 Benjamin Franklin to Peter Collinson, May 9, 1753, *The Papers of Benjamin Franklin*, ed. L.W. Labaree, *et al.* (New Haven: Yale University Press, 1961), **4**, 479–80, 485.

7 Franklin's "Observations Concerning the Increase of Mankind," published in London in 1755, though probably written in 1751, bases its predictions of population increase on the attractiveness of America to English migrants; his long letter, sent to *The Publick Advertiser* in 1773 to protest against a proposed government act to prevent emigration to America, was not published, because Parliament decided to postpone discussion of the law until more data could be gathered on how many British subjects were actually leaving the realm.

8 Winthrop, *Journal*, **1**, 58.

9 A similar example, similarly moralized, is that of James Collins, the "Irishman who worked on the Fitchburg Railway," who sells Thoreau his shanty for lumber to build the hut on Walden Pond. Shiftless and rootless, the Collins family are lighting out (it doesn't say why), leaving only their debts and a dead cat behind them. If only they could be more like him, Thoreau implies, and be content with simple things, instead of wasting their money on "a silk parasol, gilt-framed looking glass, and a patent new coffee mill," they might not have been forced to sell up. What he doesn't say is that now that the Fitchburg Railway is finished, Collins has been laid off, and has to go elsewhere to find work – in other words, that the subversive, alternative "economy" which Thoreau boasts of having demonstrated has been subsidized by the material and human waste of the very commercial system he claims to have transcended.

10 John Pory to the Earl of Southampton, Plymouth, Jan. 13, 1623, in *Three*

Visitors to Early Plymouth, ed. Sydney V. James, Jr. (Plymouth: Plimoth Plantation: 1963), 6; *Mourt's Relation*, 21.

11 Alexis de Tocqueville, *Democracy in America*, **1**, Second Part, chapter 9, ed. Mayer, 284.

12 That is her actual age. Figuratively, she is as old as her family, an "immemorial lady – two hundred years old on this side of the water, and thrice as many, on the other."

13 For a perceptive discussion of window views and other panoramic vistas in *Madame Bovary*, see Jean Rousset, *Forme et Signification: essais sur les structures littéraires de Corneille à Claudel* (Paris: Librarie José Corti, 1962), 109–33; Paul de Man translated this chapter as "*Madame Bovary*: Flaubert's Anti-Novel," and included it in his Norton Critical Edition of *Madame Bovary* (New York: Norton, 1965), 439–57.

14 I have kept to the Doubleday text of 1900 here, since it is what Dreiser published and what "American Literature" has known as *Sister Carrie*, until the resurrection of the suppressed manuscript published in the Pennsylvania Edition of 1981.

15 Richard Slotkin, *Regeneration Through Violence: The Myth of the American Frontier, 1600–1860* (Middletown, Conn: Wesleyan University Press, 1973), 107–8.

Conclusion: lighting out

1 Rupert Wilkinson, *The Pursuit of American Character* (New York: Harper & Row, 1988), 71–112, *passim.*

2 Erickson, 177; Susanna Moodie, *Life in the Clearings versus the Bush* (1853), (Toronto: McClelland & Stewart: New Canadian Library, 1989), 12; *ibid.*, *Roughing it in the Bush* (1852), (Toronto: McClelland & Stewart: New Canadian Library, 1989), 475–76.

3 Semour Martin Lipsett, "Three Decades of the Radical Right: Coughlinites, McCarthyites, and Birchers," in Daniel Bell, ed., *The Radical Right* (New York: Doubleday Anchor Books, 1962), 320–1.

4 de Tocqueville, *Democracy in America*, **2**, First Part, chapter 17, ed. Mayer, 487.

Index

Index

Index